Monika Markgraf for the Bauhaus Dessau Foundation

Archaeology of Modernism. Conservation of the Bauhaus Dessau

jovis

Preface

In the semi-basement of the Bauhaus Building, two narrative threads are employed to introduce the modern monument. A series of photographs dating from 1926 to 2003 depict the history of the building. They document its construction in 1926, which attracted widespread attention, its political vilification by chanting national socialists in 1935, and a photo from 1945 captured the destruction of the workshop wing with the shattered curtain wall. They shed light on how the structural shell was repaired with masonry infill walls that replaced the transparent cube, but allowed the use of the building in those times of need. The next photograph depicts the façade remodelled with ribbon windows following a reassessment of its worth in East Germany and its listing in 1964. Likewise recorded is the foundation of the 'Bauhaus Dessau. Zentrum für Gestaltung' in 1986 subsequent to the renovation of 1976. The series ends with a photo from 2003 that references the general renovation of 1996 to 2006, which coincides with the Bauhaus's inclusion on the list of UNESCO World Heritage sites. In the exhibition 'Archaeology of Modernism' in the next room, material fragments from various periods are presented as a contrast to the building's representation via diverse media. Remnants of plaster, pipes, concrete blocks, windows, light switches, flooring materials, etc. possess the character of archaeological finds; some are displayed as artifacts, others as assemblages of materials. This cabinet of materiality not only complements our perception of the Bauhaus Building, which is shaped by the images disseminated in the media, but also leads us to traces that somewhat complicate the building's unambiguous, iconic character. Fragments of Triolin flooring, for instance, not only testify to the Bauhaus's love of experimentation, but also provide insights into the economic and geopolitical contexts of the time. The production of linoleum, for example, relied on imports of raw materials and ended when the industry collapsed during the First World War. Here, a different historiography comes to light, in which the lucent images of a timeless modernity give way to a gradual shift in the world of materials, which is shaped by coexistences rather than discontinuities. Further, the corroded pipework and porous bricks bring to life the environmental influences and weathering which are inscribed in the materials. Both approaches—the visual, pictorial one and the material-based one—form an indispensable foundation for the conservation of the almost one-hundred-year-old historic monument, the Bauhaus Dessau. They serve as a prelude of sorts to a tour of a building which through its use over the years bears the stamp of the turbulent twentieth century and the approach to which reveals the varied attributes of the Bauhaus heritage. The fact that our visitors are greeted by these twin narratives encapsulate what makes our heritage

conservation work at the Bauhaus Dessau so unique. It is clear that if we wish to achieve greater public acceptance, this work must also extend to cultural education. This book, too, is informed by this stance: It not only documents the extensive heritage conservation efforts to carefully safeguard and preserve the Bauhaus Dessau, their guiding principles, objectives, and methodological instruments, but also forms an essential basis for further interdisciplinary research into how to deal with our modern heritage.
Over recent years, the Bauhaus Dessau Foundation has established a specific, internationally recognised expertise in building research and heritage conservation in the field of modern architecture.
In the course of these activities, the Bauhaus Building has become a learning project for all the participating individuals, institutions, networks, and organisations, which is meanwhile held up as an example of best practice for the restoration of other modern buildings. This is due above all to heritage conservationist Monika Markgraf and her assiduous, critical commitment to the conservation of a unique architectural monument of international standing, the eventful history of which must be preserved for future generations.
We are also grateful to those who have consistently supported our conservation work over many years through funding, research, expert opinions, planning and implementation, or other means.

Prof. Dr. Regina Bittner, director ad interim of the Bauhaus Dessau Foundation

Introduction

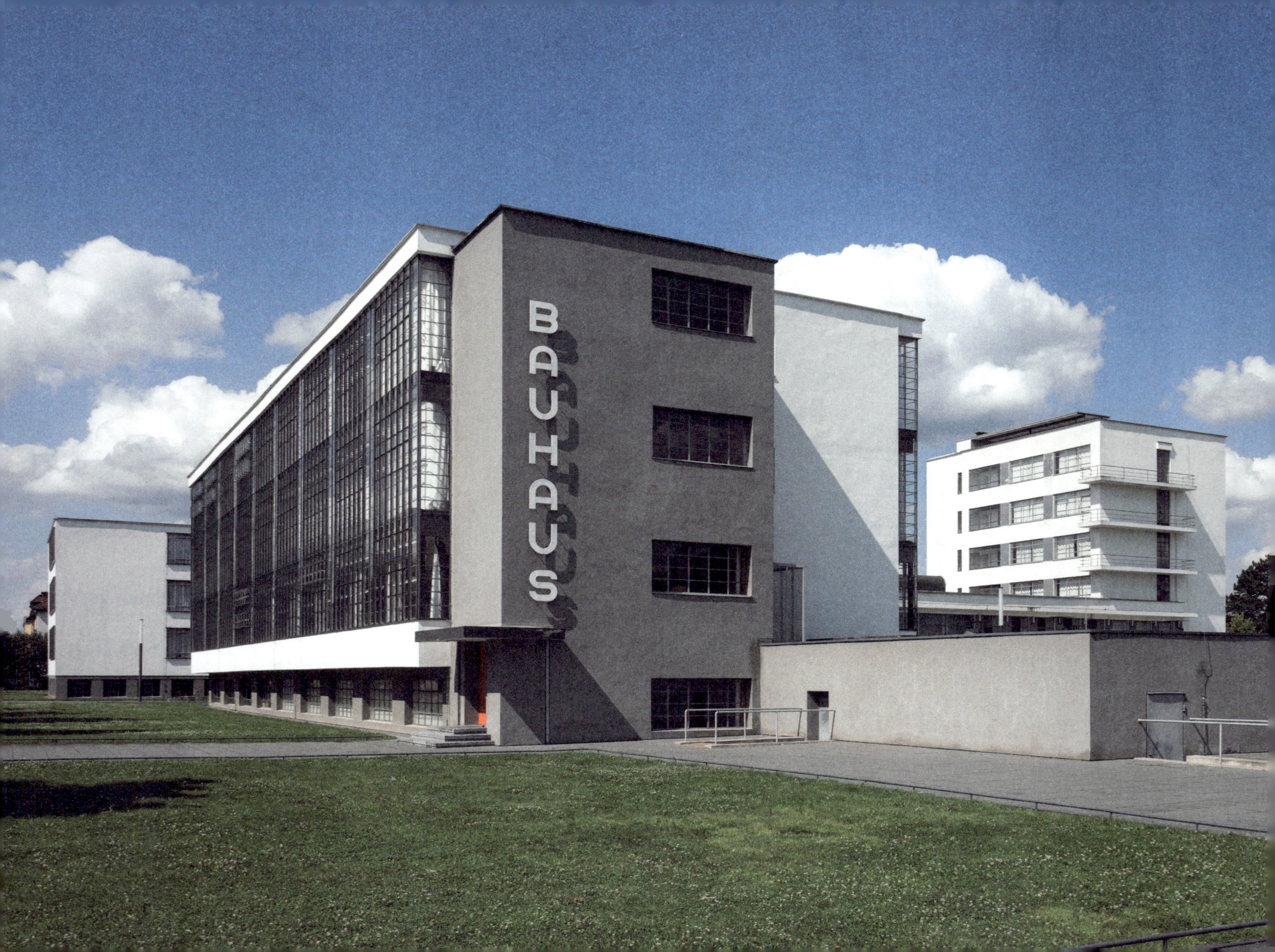
BAUHAUS

Twenty-five years ago, a modern monument was included on the list of World Heritage sites in Germany for the first time. In 1996, five outstanding architectural monuments of the Bauhaus movement were inscribed on the UNESCO list. Known as 'The Bauhaus and its Sites in Weimar and Dessau', these were the School of Arts and Crafts (Henry van de Velde, 1904–11) and the Haus Am Horn (Georg Muche, 1923) in Weimar, Thuringia, and the new Bauhaus school, studio building, and Masters' Houses in Dessau, Saxony-Anhalt (Walter Gropius, 1926).

This achievement would pave the way for a wave of World Heritage applications for modern buildings in Germany that is impressive even by international standards. The most notable new additions to the list included the Zeche Zollverein in Essen, built in the style of *Neue Sachlichkeit* (New Objectivity) (2001), the Berlin Modernism housing estates (2008), Gropius's Fagus Factory in Alfeld, Lower Saxony (2011), the Chilehaus with the Speicherstadt and the Kontorhaus District in Hamburg (2015), and two houses on the Weissenhof Estate in Stuttgart, Baden-Wuerttemberg, designed by Le Corbusier (2016). Last, but by no means least, is the 2017 expansion of the existing portfolio of Bauhaus World Heritage sites to include the five Houses with Balcony Access in Dessau and the Trade Union School of the ADGB in Bernau, Brandenburg, designed by Hannes Meyer.

Evidently, the inclusion of the Bauhaus sites on the World Heritage list following German reunification opened doors for the modern heritage of the twentieth century in both eastern and western federal states. Bauhaus sites have served as an encouraging example, and the Bauhaus institutions involved have provided support or sought-after counsel as centres of competence in matters of architectural history for World Heritage initiatives in Germany and elsewhere in Europe. The Bauhaus's inscription represented a milestone en route to the Modern Heritage programme set out jointly in 2001 by the UNESCO World Heritage Centre, ICOMOS (International Council on Monuments and Sites), and DOCOMOMO (Working Party for the Documentation and Conservation of Buildings, Sites and Neighbourhoods of the Modern Movement). Since the Bauhaus's inscription, the so-called tentative lists of properties considered for nomination have been increasingly filled with internationally renowned modern buildings and architectural ensembles. The national list of nominees includes a large number of twentieth-century candidates while others are found on the nominee lists of the sixteen federal states, which aim to make their initial selection for future application processes in 2021/2022.

The German National Committee of ICOMOS has always had a particularly strong bond with the Bauhaus Dessau World Heritage site. This is of course due to the core task which UNESCO entrusted to ICOMOS at the World Heritage Convention of 1972 as well as the continuously updated 'Operational Guidelines for the Implementation of the World Heritage Convention'. Together with the International Union for Conservation of Nature (ICUN) and the International Centre for the Study of the Preservation and Restoration of Cultural Property (ICCROM), ICOMOS is one of three

1)
View from the southwest, 2019

bodies which advise UNESCO in its deliberations on matters of World Heritage. It assesses and optimises World Heritage applications, oversees the World Heritage nominations process, and monitors and provides evaluations of inscribed cultural properties, especially as regards the prevention of damaging developments and, where necessary, of dangers and risks to sites. With this in mind, in 1997, ICOMOS Germany became probably the first national committee globally to establish an own expert group to continually monitor and advise World Heritage properties. This meanwhile fifty-strong interdisciplinary team of experienced architects, art historians, archaeologists, restorers, engineers, and even experts in heritage conservation law focuses on the preventive monitoring of World Heritage sites in Germany. Naturally, this step was not motivated by any possible threats to the Bauhaus sites first inscribed on the UNESCO list in 1996; rather, it was occasioned by the inscription of Cologne Cathedral (1994–96) and that of the Dresden Elbe Valley (2006–09) on the Red List of endangered World Heritage sites. However, the newly-established monitoring group was expected to provide professional monitoring and expert advice for the new World Heritage sites in Weimar and Dessau virtually from the start. For all those involved, to one degree or another this cooperation represented a step into uncharted territory. Not only was the conservation of pre- and post-war modern monuments in its infancy, but the conservation and restoration of more recent historical layers and modern materials presented in the general sense a task for which there was far less expertise available than for the restoration of traditional historical buildings or the use of tried and tested methods to fix pre-modern building techniques in need of repair. The Bauhaus sites—the Bauhaus Universität Weimar and the Bauhaus Dessau Foundation alike—offered in some measure a common learning environment for the development and trial of suitable protection and maintenance concepts and long-term strategies for more modern historical monuments. In this respect, the main complex in Dessau—the Bauhaus Building designed by Walter Gropius in 1925/26 and used as a school until its closure in 1932—proved fortuitous. Firstly, the building chronicles the history of the Bauhaus's closure, war-time destruction, and restoration. Secondly, its heritage conservation status had been the subject of frequent debate in the post-war GDR era, too. As such, to a certain extent it served as a repository for the changing reception and rehabilitation history of classical modernism, from the early evaluations of the nineteen-sixties and the renovations for the Bauhaus's fiftieth anniversary in 1976 to the building's formal inscription on the central monument register of East Germany and its subsequent restoration leading to World Heritage status in 1996.

It was and remains especially fortunate that the building's owner and occupier, the Bauhaus Dessau Foundation which was founded in 1994, is duty-bound to preserve it not only from a point of heritage conservation law or in line with the World Heritage Convention but also because its mission is to preserve and pass on 'the ideas and themes of the historic Bauhaus' and to make them available to the public. In detail, this includes the collection, conservation, research into and display of testimonies to the history and impact of the historic Bauhaus. The preservation and interpretation of cultural assets, thus the pursuit of the objectives of heritage conservation, is at the heart of the foundation's work. Rarely has a historical monument or a World Heritage site, let alone a seminal work of modernism, presented itself in situ in such depth, revealing its history, conservation, modifications, and the findings and materials of building archaeology. The exhibition 'Archaeology of Modernism—Building Research Bauhaus Buildings Dessau' opened on the occasion of the Bauhaus Centenary 2019 revealed insights derived from historic building research; the foundation's Building Archive is merely the most recent example of this. Over the past twenty-five years, since its inclusion on the UNESCO list, the Bauhaus Building has made history as a World Heritage site in a remarkable way. The freestanding orthogonal geometric composition of the many parts of the complex with its characteristic steel and glass façades, the connecting bridge over the road, and the emphatically vertical studio building comes to the fore and assumes an exemplary character. The interiors of the building parts as regards the historic room sequences and interconnecting views are also cleared and clarified. And in the details of the surface treatments and colours, the building engineering, or the constructive formation, we see the consistent endeavour to prioritise the conserved, exposed or where necessary reconstructed historic appearance, even when more technically or aesthetically pleasing solutions would have been possible but would have entailed a loss of historic authenticity.

It is probably not always the most immediately eye-catching results that show the successful further development of the heritage conservation strategy for the iconic building. Some successes are to some degree achieved by refraining from interventions. Among them is a sophisticated utility concept which responds not only to functional needs but also to energy requirements. It thus reduces the pressure on spaces and constructions that react sensitively to climatic conditions and dispenses with unsuitable energy-related upgrades. The untrammelled view of the Bauhaus Building from all sides is another case in point; this is the outcome of the Bauhaus Dessau Foundation's endeavours to ensure that the new Bauhaus Museum Dessau, which opened in time for the Bauhaus Centenary 2019, is located outside the World Heritage site. The striking impact of the Bauhaus complex in the urban setting is enabled not by the much-vaunted further development of the old through modifications, extensions, or superstructures, but by the pertinent authorities' calculated rejection of additional construction on the heritage site.

Last but not least, a quarter of a century of World Heritage status has also brought a shift, or a noticeable broadening, of perspective regarding the conservation of the Bauhaus Building. The major challenges and investments remain, among them climate change, energy savings, or the implementation of a contemporary tourism infrastructure, as do the associated discourses and controversies in the world of conservation about interventions which are both appropriate and effective. But the development of a long-term strategy for the continuous care and maintenance of the Bauhaus Building—a lasting conservation concept as an alternative to the cyclical, recurring general renovation—has gained a new status. The development of a conservation management plan for the building in the scope of the programme 'Keeping It Modern' sponsored by the Getty Foundation and the connection between this digital record and the building's facility management database has not only created an enormously instructive and complex information system but also opened up options for a systematic maintenance plan and ensured that inspections are made at regular intervals. The Bauhaus will remain a modern icon and an inspiring learning environment for future generations.

Prof. Dr. Jörg Haspel
President of the German National Committee of ICOMOS

The Building

2)

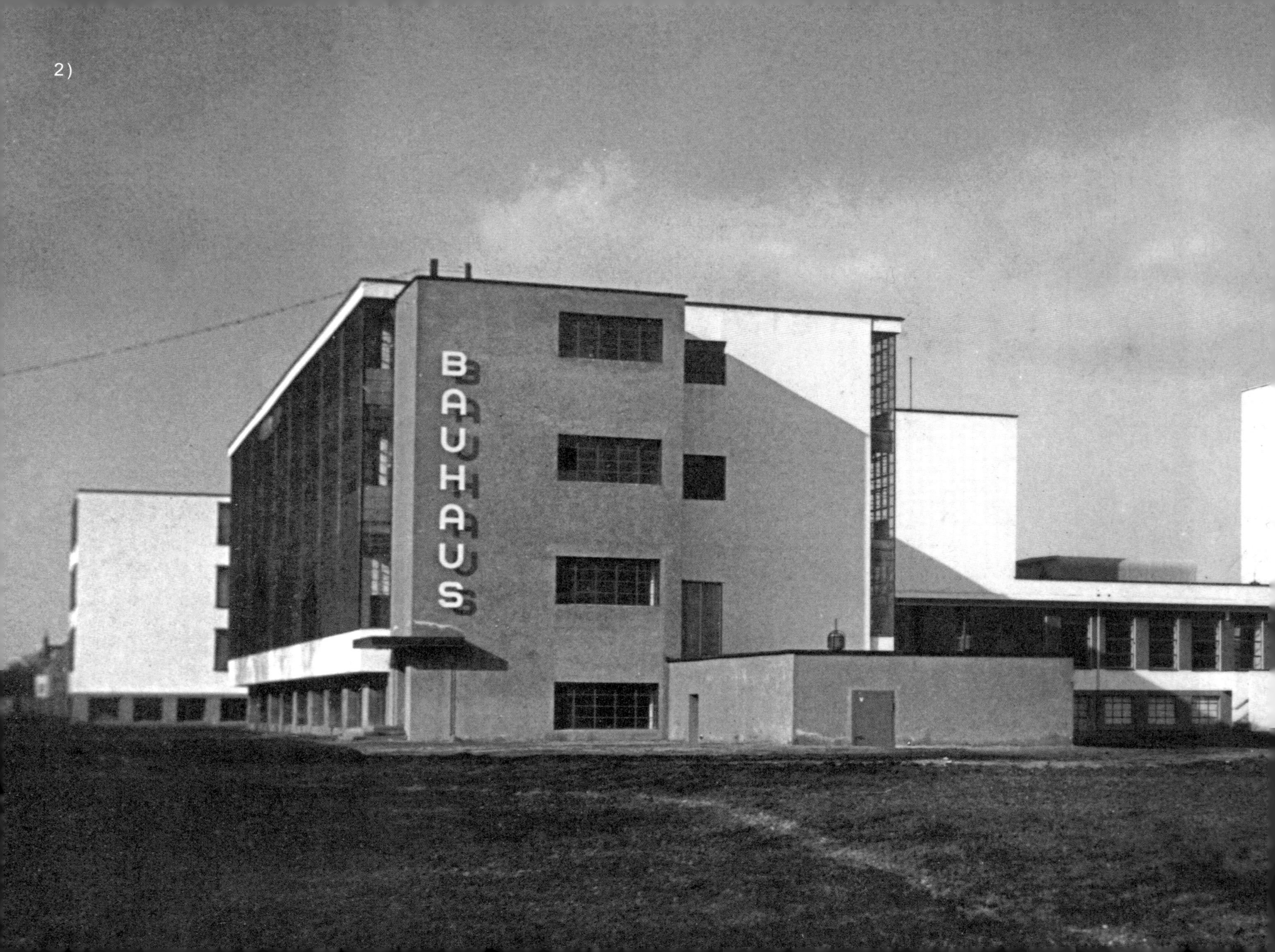

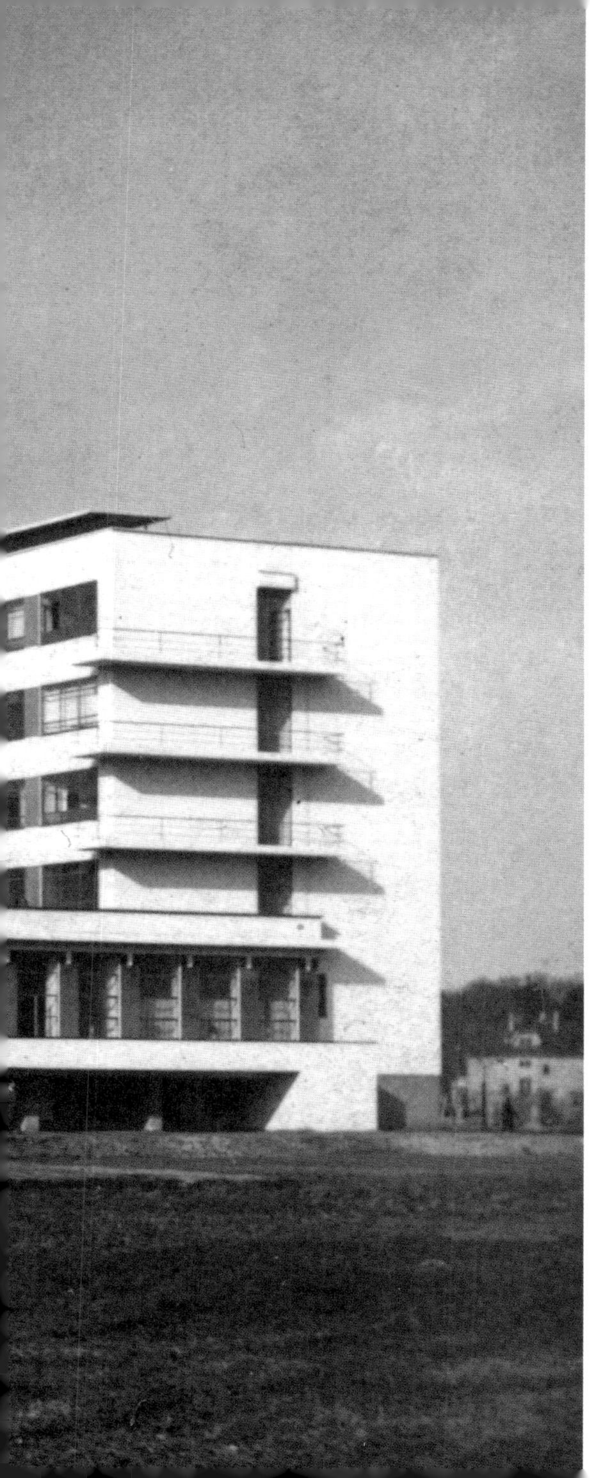

The Building
1926–1932

'the basic aim of the Bauhaus was to synthesize all artistic creation into a unified whole, to unite all artistic and technical disciplines into a new art of architecture as their indissoluble components, an art of architecture at the service of a vibrant life.'[1]

This is how in 1923 Walter Gropius formulated the principles which would guide work at the Bauhaus and which eventually resulted in the maxim 'Art and technology—a new unity'. When the Bauhaus relocated from Weimar to Dessau, the Bauhaus Building and other buildings erected in Dessau embodied and testified to the Bauhaus's architectonic concepts.[2]
The inauguration of the Bauhaus Building, the construction of which was commissioned by the municipality of Dessau, was celebrated to great public acclaim on 4 December 1926.

The building was designed by Gropius's architecture office, the bauatelier gropius. This was directed by Gropius and counted Carl Fieger, Richard Paulick, Ernst Neufert, and several junior masters and students among its associates. The Bauhaus workshops were actively involved in planning the interiors: the wall painting workshop took charge of the colour design, the metal workshop designed the lighting, the carpentry workshop the built-in features and furniture, the weaving workshop the upholstery and curtain fabrics, and the printing workshop the lettering.[3]

The unusually articulated building was erected on both sides of a public road according to the specifications of an urban development plan. Gropius had to incorporate two schools in the building: He placed the Bauhaus Dessau School of Design on the south side of the road and the municipal technical school, later a vocational school, on the north side. Connected by a two-storey bridge, both schools had steps leading to separate entrances on what is now the Bauhausstrasse. These building parts are not simply juxtaposed but both spatially and architectonically interconnected. The design strove to unify functionality and aesthetics in keeping with the declared goals of the Bauhaus Manifesto. Accordingly, the diverse functions of the building parts find their correlations in the complex design of the cubic buildings, the volumes, façade designs, spatial organisation, surfaces, colour schemes, and lighting of which vary.

The workshop wing is regarded as the 'laboratory of ideas' in which the Bauhaus products were conceived. Its visible concrete skeleton construction and renowned curtain wall made from glass and finely wrought steel profiles are defining elements of the architecture of the Bauhaus, which continue to fascinate us today. They showcase the institution's aspirations towards reform in architecture too.

The five-storey studio building provided accommodation for the Bauhaus students and junior masters. The occupants of the twenty-eight rooms also had access to shared amenities including a kitchenette with balcony and one WC per floor, a roof terrace, and showers and washing facilities in the basement. The building expresses the Bauhaus's notion of modern living and its design incorporating a separate entrance, small individual balconies on the east façade, and a punctuated façade indicates that Gropius envisaged it as a sanctuary of sorts. Nestled between the studio building and the workshop wing is the single-storey festive area comprising entrance hall, auditorium, stage, and canteen. This multifunctional sequence of rooms was used for intramural and public events such as stage productions, lectures, and festivities. With their representational character, these central rooms provide particularly strong evidence of the Bauhaus's design ideas in that they utilised, e.g., technical elements of industrial architecture and modern materials. The lower floor of the bridge was taken up by the administrative offices of the municipal school and the Bauhaus as well as the director's office, for which Gropius designed a unique interior. The upper floor was initially occupied by the bauatelier gropius and subsequently by the Bauhaus's architecture workshop. The façades of the bridge are characterised by long horizontal ribbon windows which underpin its connecting function above and beyond the public road.

In the three-storey north wing, which is rendered white, the classrooms for the municipal school were accessed from a central corridor. Here, built-in cupboards accessible from both sides replace partition walls. Light enters the internal corridor through transom windows situated above the cupboards and glass doors. The architecture is characterised by concrete, steel, and glass, then modern materials which Gropius felt enthusiastic about. From a structural standpoint, it comprises a load-bearing reinforced concrete skeleton with brickwork infill, although load-bearing masonry pillars and walls also feature. The use of concrete constructions enables large openings to be spanned using less material than otherwise required, as may be observed in the workshop wing, as well as projecting elements such as the studio building's seemingly free-floating balconies. The construction is visible in the building's interior; its spaces are shaped by its columns and joists. In especially significant areas such as the entrance hall of the workshop wing or the director's office, certain structural elements are hidden from view in line with the artistic intention. With the exception of the workshop wing, the concrete skeleton is finished with a layer of fine plaster, which is painted according to a colour concept designed by the wall painting workshop. This accentuates the architectural arrangement of load-bearing and infill elements, aids orientation in the building, and works with diverse surface finishes. The ceilings are constructed from reinforced concrete; one exception is the ceiling above the semi-basement floor in the workshop wing, which is a mushroom slab construction.

The façades are finished with a rough plaster imbued with grey colour on the semi-basement level and a smooth plaster painted white on other surfaces. Under the bridge, the surfaces of the structural supports and joists have a striking finish applied using the traditional techniques of a stonemason, and the exterior ceiling areas are painted. The windows are made from steel. The then modern materials steel and glass were used to construct the elegant, extensive glass façades, the transparency and reflections of which have an essential effect on the building's impact. They establish a close connection between interior and exterior and between the different parts of the building. The rejection of decorative elements or ornaments allows the aspects of the variously finished

2)
View from the south, 1926

3)
Isometric view from the southwest, 1926

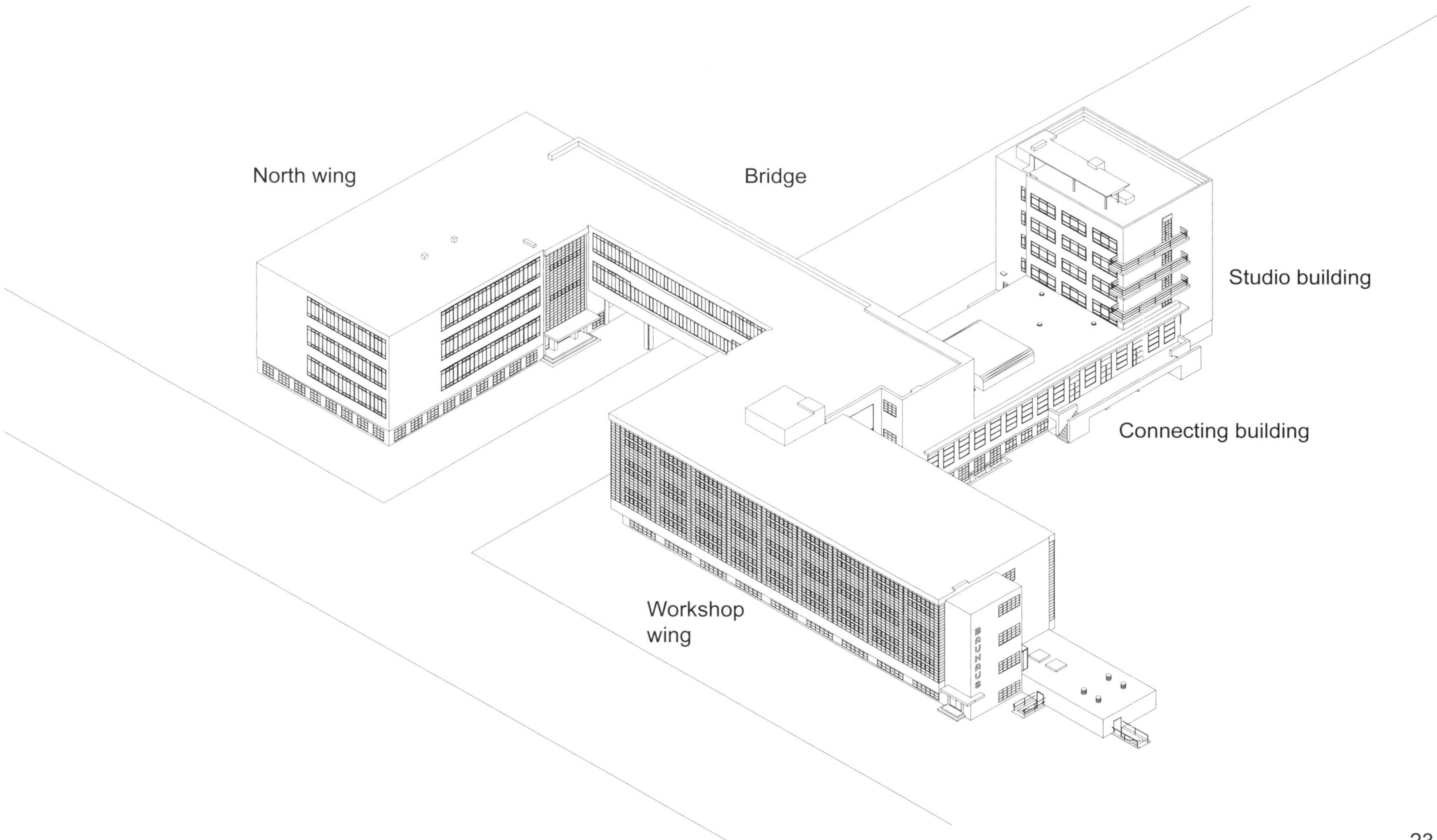

4)
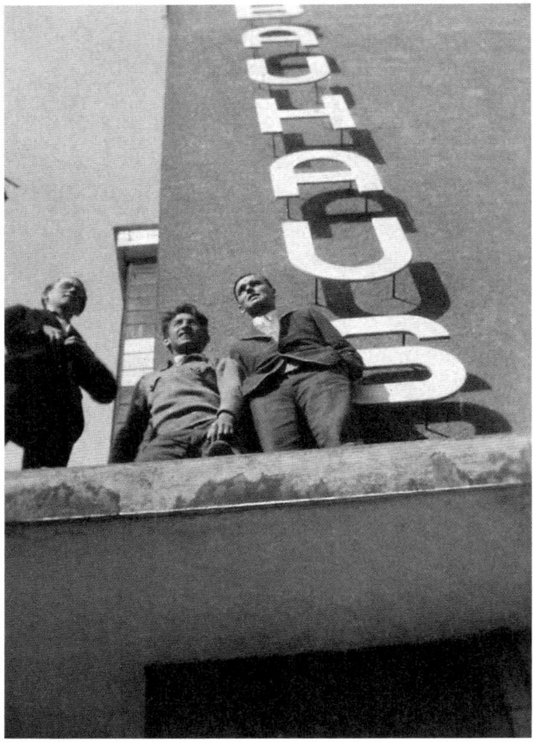

surfaces, colours, and play of light and shadows on the surfaces to unfold to full effect.

Outside the building, the asphalt strip of Bauhausstrasse forms a vital axis that provides access to the many and varied parts of the building via the two entrances for the original two schools. Lawns and trees planted in rows effectively embed the complex in its surroundings. During the Bauhaus era, the outdoor facilities included playing fields for the Bauhaus and a yard for the municipal school. Inside the building, the Bauhaus mainly used the workshops, classrooms, administrative rooms, the studios with communal facilities, and the festive area, while the municipal school used classrooms and workshops in the north wing and offices for administration purposes on the bridge.

Changes were already made in and around the building during its first few years in existence. The outdoor facilities, for instance, were only completed in 1929, the initially white walls of the stage were painted black, and rooms in the studio building were combined in 1930 because more large seminar rooms for classes were needed.

Following Walter Gropius's departure from the Bauhaus in 1928, the Swiss architect Hannes Meyer succeeded him as director. In 1930, Dessau's municipal authorities succumbed to political pressure and dismissed Meyer. Ludwig Mies van der Rohe was then appointed as third director of the Bauhaus. Following the closure of the Bauhaus Dessau in 1932, he continued to direct the school in Berlin until 1933.

4)
Three Bauhauslers in front of the Bauhaus sign, n.d.

5)
Aerial photograph, 1926

6)
Alcar Rudelt teaches students from the building department in front of the Bauhaus, 1932

1
Gropius 2021, p. 7

2
The houses for the Bauhaus masters and the first buildings of the Dessau-Törten Housing Estate, built to plans by Walter Gropius, were also inaugurated in Dessau in 1926. Other buildings erected shortly thereafter based on plans by individuals active at, or closely associated with, the Bauhaus include: Steel House (Muche/Paulick, 1927), Fieger House (Fieger, 1927), Konsum Building (Gropius, 1928), Pump Station (Gropius, 1928), individual Paulick Houses (Paulick, 1928), Employment Office (Gropius, 1929), Kornhaus (Fieger, 1930), Houses with Balcony Access (Meyer and the building department, 1930), Fischer Twin Houses, Großring (Fischer, 1930), Paulick Row Buildings (Paulick, 1931), Engemann Houses (Engemann, 1930–33)

3
Gropius 2021, p. 12

5)

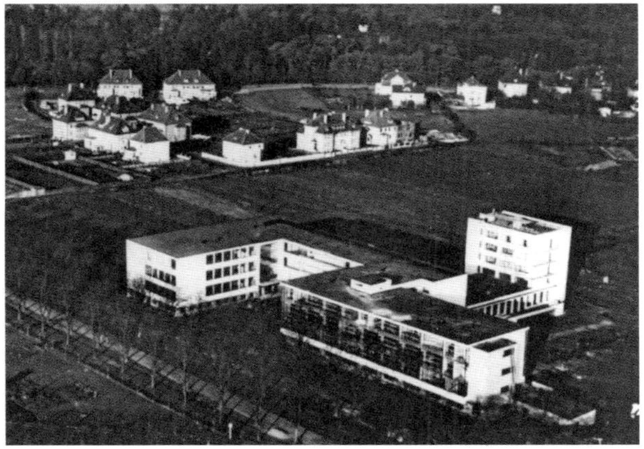

6)

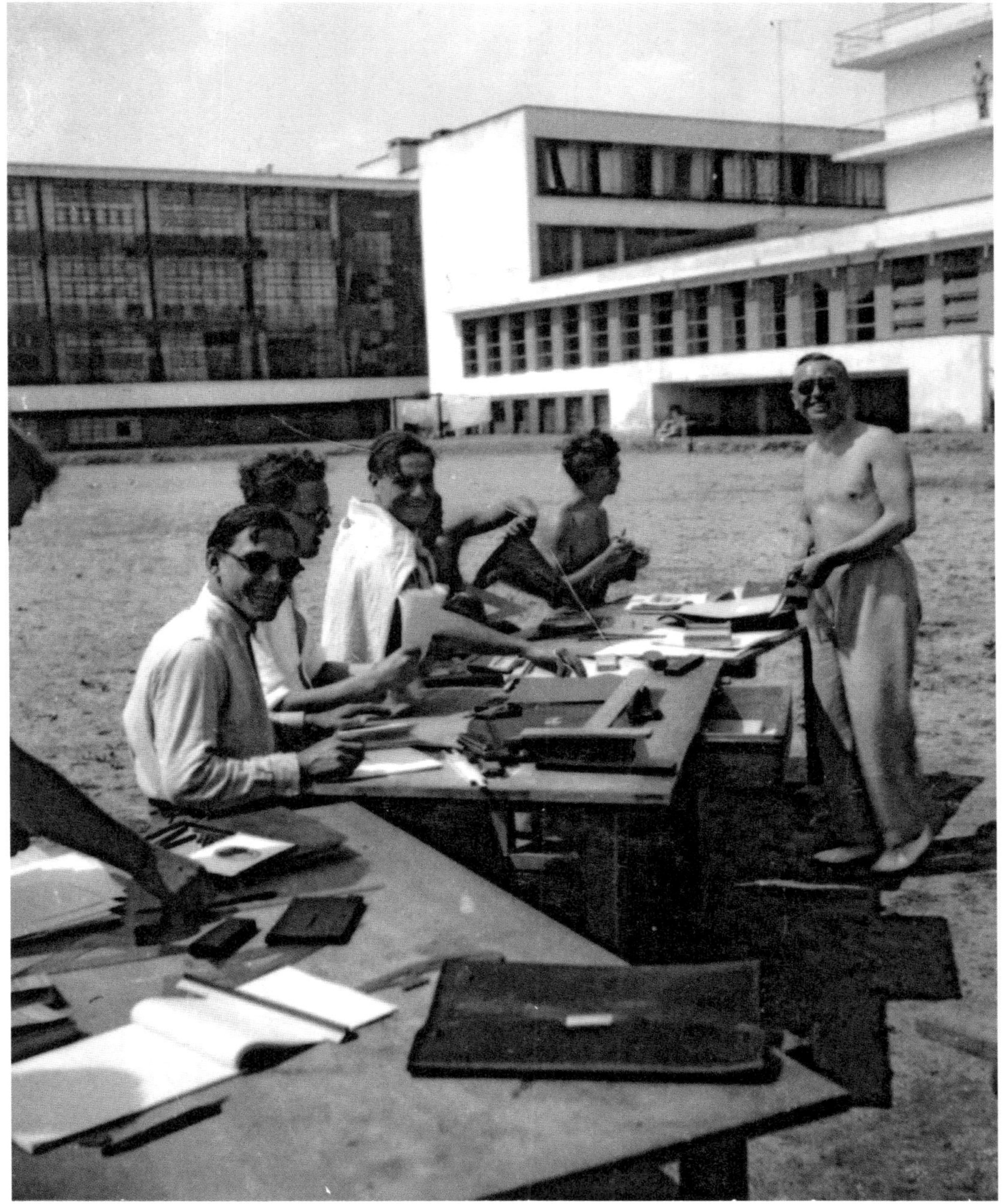

7)

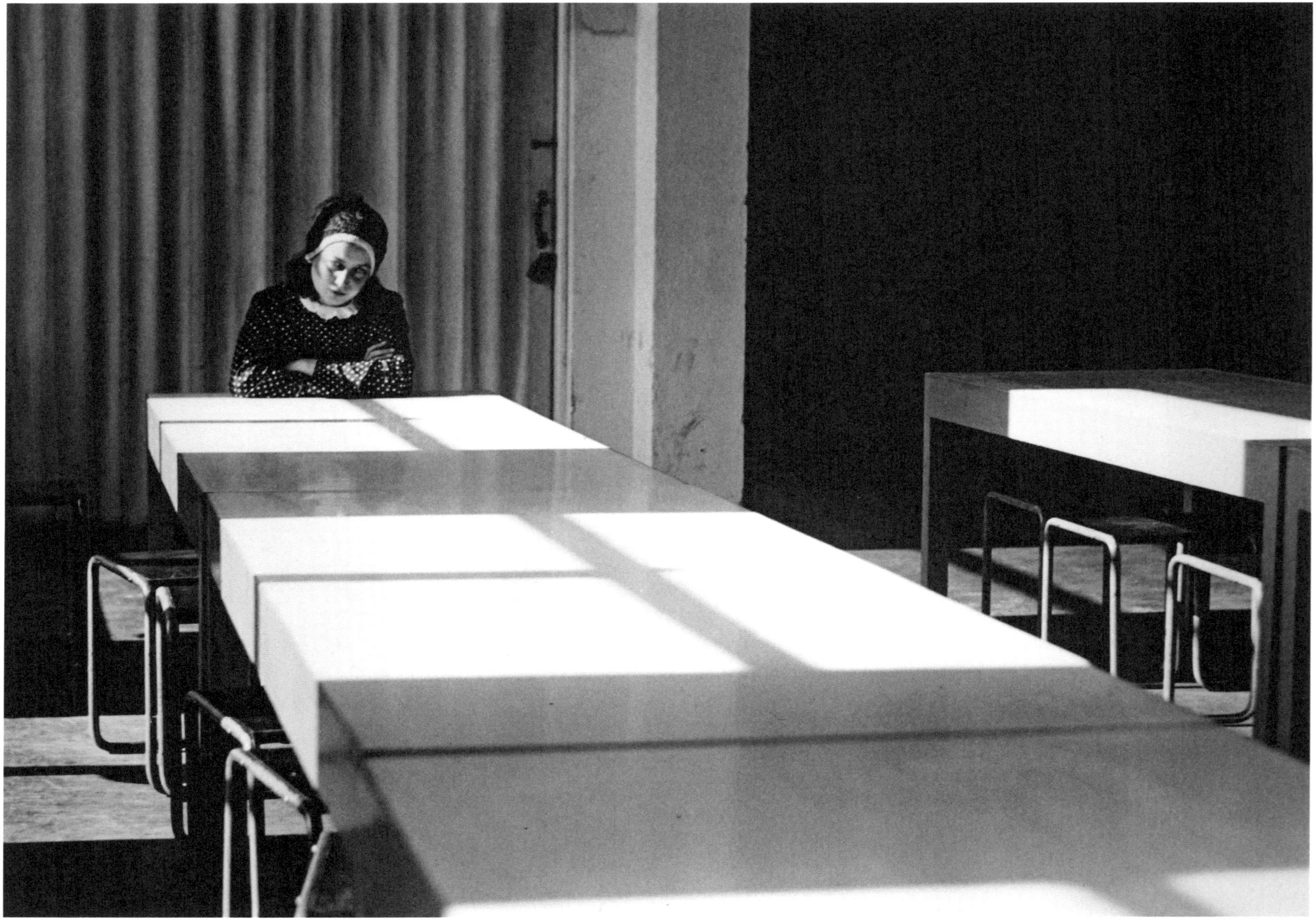

The Building 1932–2021

8)

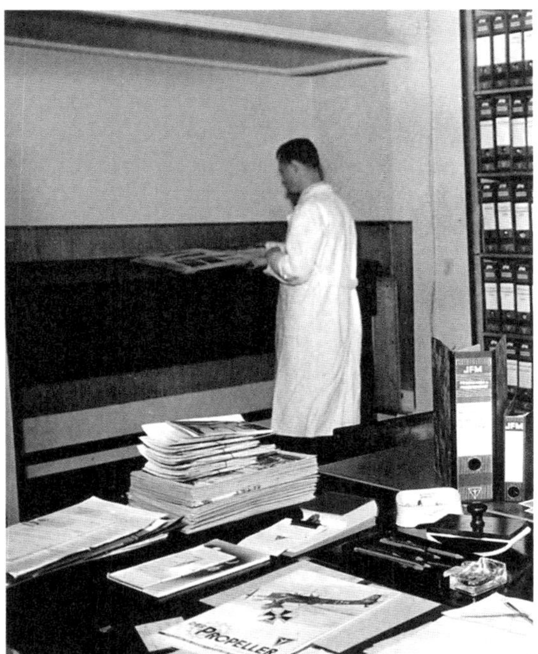

1932–45 Disfigurement and Destruction

The Bauhaus Dessau School of Design was closed on 30 September 1932 on the instigation of the National Socialist German Workers' Party (NSDAP) following a vote by the town council. Because repeated calls for the building's demolition were unenforceable, the Bauhaus Building was utilised for teaching and other purposes even under National Socialist rule. Its users included a school for party functionaries of the district Magdeburg-Anhalt, a *Landesfrauenarbeitsschule* (state vocational school for women), and the party's Chief Office of Construction headed by architect Albert Speer. From 1938, the Junkers works nationalised two years previously began to use more and more of the building for administrative purposes (eighty per cent in 1942). The studio building, for example, was occupied by the propaganda and press department of Junkers Flugzeug und Motorenwerke A.G. (Junkers Aircraft and Motor Works).[1]

During this period, a gently sloping single-pitch roof built over the studio building sealed the roof terrace through which water had frequently penetrated the building. Newspaper articles verify that this measure also provided a welcome opportunity for renewed polemic against the architecture of the Bauhaus.[2] Additional steps such as the installation of an external drainage system with visible gutters and downpipes altered the design of the building even more. Various changes were made inside the building and to the outdoor facilities to meet the needs of the respective users, with little regard to the original structure and aesthetics. During the Second World War, in addition to other air-raid protection measures, the Bauhaus received a dark coat of paint.

During an air raid on 7 March 1945, large parts of the city of Dessau were destroyed. The Bauhaus Building too, was extensively damaged. In addition to the roofs and upper floors of the workshop wing and north wing, most of the damage was to the curtain wall, which was largely destroyed apart from a fragment on the east façade. However, the load-bearing structure of the Bauhaus remained intact enabling emergency repairs to be made to the building in the immediate postwar period (1945). These involved the closure of the façade of the workshop wing with a brick masonry wall punctuated by windows and various structural changes designed to accommodate its use by diverse schools.

7)
Otti Berger in the Bauhaus canteen on the day of the Bauhaus's closure, 1932

8)
Propaganda and press department of Junkers Flugzeug- und Motorenwerke AG in the studio building, ca. 1941

9)

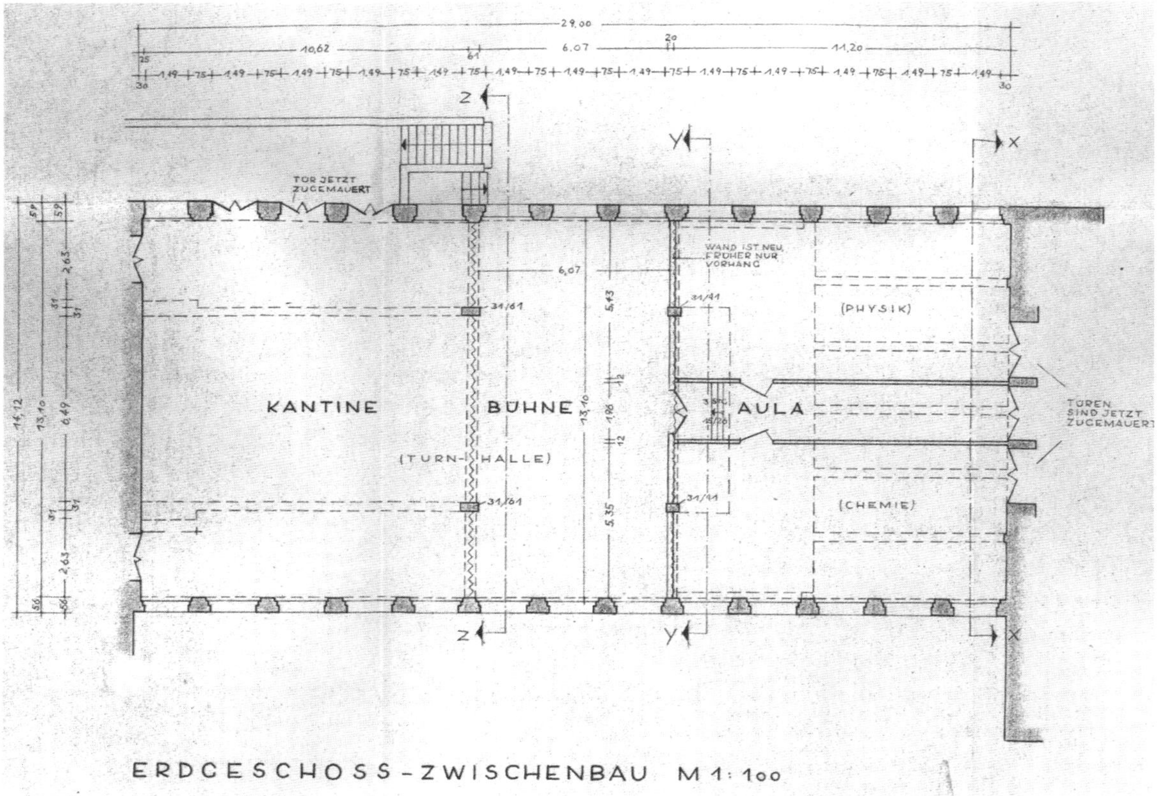

10)

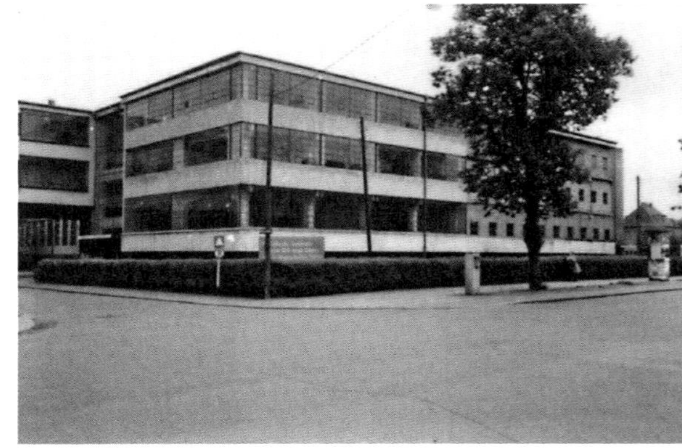

9)
Retrofitted furniture in the connecting building (auditorium, stage, canteen), part of the building inventory documentation compiled by HAB Weimar under the direction of Konrad Püschel, 1964

10)
Modification of the façade of the workshop wing: remnant of masonry wall punctuated by small windows in the background, horizontal steel ribbon windows already installed at the front, ca. 1970

Historic Building

From 1945 onwards, several former Bauhauslers endeavoured to re-establish the Bauhaus Dessau as a school of design.[3] However, these efforts were undermined by the political complexities and disparate priorities of the postwar years. During this period, first attempts were also made to have a preservation order put on the Bauhaus Building just twenty years after it was built. Hinnerk Scheper stated in summer 1945: 'You will be pleased to hear that the Bauhaus Dessau has been placed on the list of modern monuments which are to be protected and preserved. Arrangements are being made for its restoration, financed by the Office for Historical Monuments in Halle; I hope that one day the Bauhaus will once again have its brilliant white aspect.'[4] However, the Bauhaus was not included on the list published in 1962 of the historically important buildings of the GDR,[5] which featured just 32 sites. It was first added to that list *(Liste 1 denkmalwerter Bauwerke der DDR)* in 1964.[6] In April 1974, the city of Dessau ratified the regional list of historical monuments, which included the Bauhaus Building and other buildings by Bauhaus architects, thus formally cementing their status as monuments. A recommendation was simultaneously made for the inclusion of the Bauhaus Building and the Masters' Houses on the list of monuments of special national and international significance *(Zentrale Denkmalliste)*, based on the historic preservation law of 1975. This list of 400 sites, published in 1979, includes the Bauhaus Building as an individual monument, but omits the Masters' Houses.

While the art-historical significance of modern architecture was beyond dispute into the 1970s, the implementation of complex heritage conservation concepts initially remained an exception. Appearing modern to this day, these buildings were instead an integral part of everyday life and rarely acknowledged as historic and artistic landmarks requiring research and protection. Their relatively recent construction also contributed to the fact that the significance of individual buildings was only gradually recognised. Structural modifications and additions also obscured the original qualities of the buildings. This posed a particular risk for this innovative architecture of its time, which represented, and still represents, social, spatial, aesthetic, and technological change.

In 1964, the renowned Italian architectural historian Leonardo Benevolo spoke about the maintenance problems, limited intrinsic value, and brief lifespan of the Bauhaus architecture: 'Now that all former life has vanished, and the opus is just a sorry heap of rubble, strictly speaking, the Bauhaus no longer exists; it is not a ruin, a remnant such as those of the buildings of antiquity, and we are no longer charmed by its appearance; it resembles an empty chrysalis from which the butterfly has flown. The emotion that this spectacle inspires in us is historically reflective, like what we would feel for an object that once belonged to someone famous.'[7]

Although the European Architectural Heritage Year 1975 raised public awareness of heritage conservation, it certainly did not stop the deterioration of modern buildings through neglect or unsuitable building measures, since heritage conservation usually dealt in the first instance with older buildings.

Due to its historical, cultural, artistic, urbanistic, and scientific significance, the Bauhaus Building is now a designated cultural monument.[8] Its protected status and the associated preparation and implementation of renovation measures of 1976, called *Rekonstuktion 1976,* are thus all the more significant because they mark a critical step in the discovery of modernism as a subject of heritage conservation and thus a milestone not only in the history of the Bauhaus Building but also in the history of modern heritage conservation.

11)

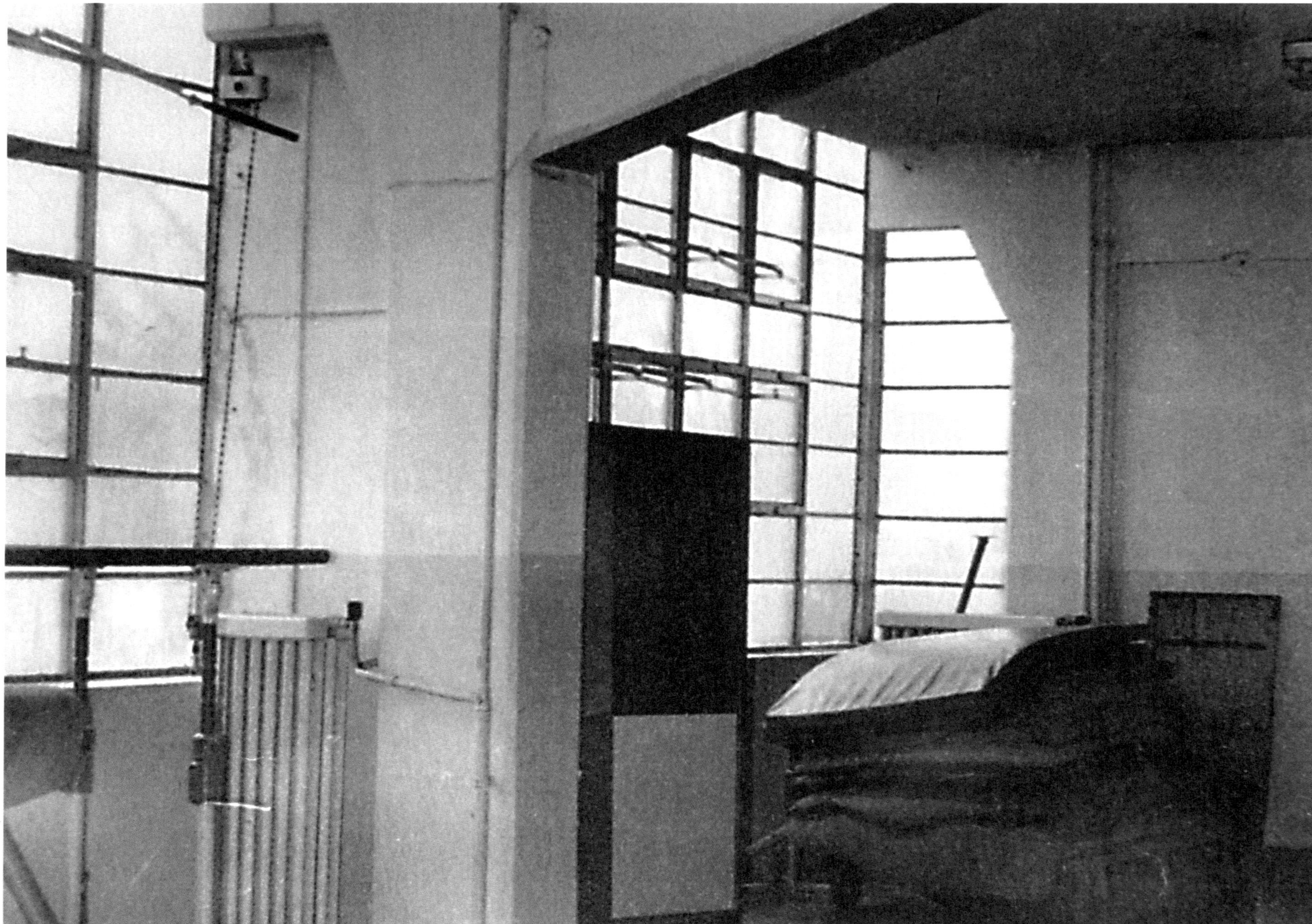

12)

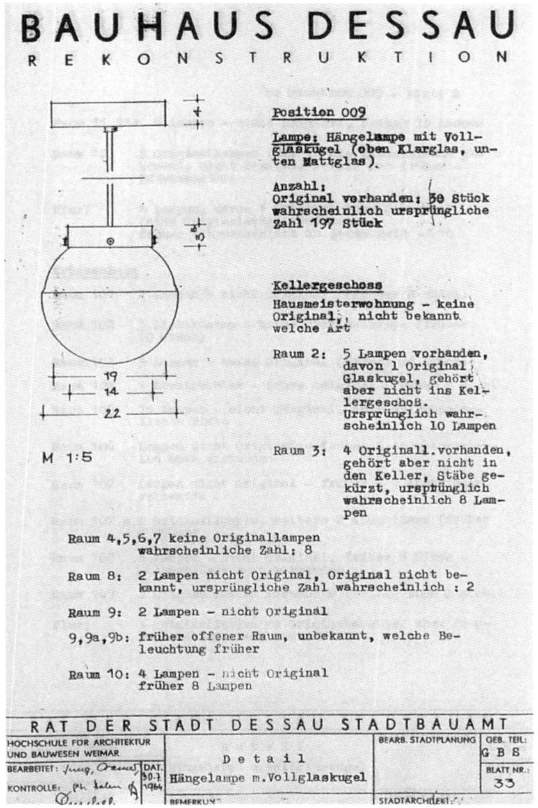

11)
Workshop wing in use as a sports hall, 1975

12)
Glass pendant lamp based on a design by Marianne Brandt, part of the inventory documentation compiled by HAB Weimar under the direction of Konrad Püschel, 1964

1976 Renovation

Around 1960, work on the Bauhaus Building began to extend beyond repairs and modifications to accommodate specific usage requirements and strove for a gradual convergence to the original architectonic quality and appeal. In the workshop wing, the provisional masonry façade punctuated with small windows was thus replaced by a façade comprising horizontal rows of steel windows and breast mouldings.[9] The stairway window openings, which had been closed with brick masonry, were reopened, and large windows were reinstalled although the window divisions and profiles differed from the original. In 1962, the Institute of Urban Development and Architecture at the German Building Academy in East Berlin recommended that the Bauhaus Building be listed and its original condition restored. For this end, a preparatory working group was to be formed.[10]

In 1964, a comprehensive survey of the Bauhaus Building commissioned by the city of Dessau was completed by the Weimar University of Architecture and Civil Engineering (HAB) under Konrad Püschel, a former Bauhausler and professor at the HAB.[11] The survey served as a basis for the renovation of the building and, in addition to complete site measurements inclusive of detailed drawings, runs to a summary of the original building components and interior elements preserved since 1926 and proposals for the reconstruction of missing parts of the buildings, its furniture, and its fittings. The survey was assisted by former Bauhauslers, among them Peter Keler, Bernhard Sturtzkopf, and Marianne Brandt, architectural theoretician Christian Schädlich, and a former administrative assistant at the Bauhaus known as Fräulein Beitz. At this point in time, the building was being used by a trade, a commercial, and a plant's vocational school and a medical technical college.

The detailed planning for the renovation however first went ahead in 1975 following the foundation of a working group concerned with preparations for the fiftieth anniversary of the Bauhaus Dessau. This included representatives of the city of Dessau, the Office for the Preservation of Historical Monuments, and the municipal archive of Dessau. The city of Dessau commissioned the publicly owned company Industrieprojektierung (VEB IPRO) directed by Wilhelm Schulze to assemble the documentation for the measures. The work on the Bauhaus Building was complete within a year. The building was officially reopened on 4 December 1976, the fiftieth anniversary of its inauguration.

Critical components of the renovation of 1976[12] comprise the reconstruction of the curtain wall based on the historical model and the restoration of the original spatial configuration of the festive area. Furthermore, improvements were made to the interiors, and deficiencies in hygiene and structural faults were remedied. In addition to works on the roof terrace of the studio building, the extensive replacement of rendered surfaces inside and outside the building, the windows on the bridge, north wing, and studio building were replaced over the following years. In 1976, part of the building was repurposed in a way that tied in with the historic significance of the Bauhaus with the foundation of the Wissenschaftlich-Kulturelles Zentrum Bauhaus (WKZ, Scientific and Cultural Centre Bauhaus), holder of a collection and archive on the history of the Bauhaus. In 1987, the institution Bauhaus Dessau – Zentrum für Gestaltung der DDR (Centre for Design of the GDR) opened in the Bauhaus Building.

The renovation of 1976 centred on the restoration of the original appearance of the building. 'It (the task of conservation) entails the step-by-step reconstruction of the entire complex with the aim of restoring the original artistic impression. … This is what comprised the principal value of the Bauhaus complex: the interpenetration of interior and exterior spaces, the mutual interaction of design and function. … The colour design will be reproduced as far as possible; it does not claim to be a reconstruction but assumes that with the adoption of the fundamental conception it will come closer to the original than if it were abandoned and completely redesigned.'[13]

Above and beyond the restoration of the historic tableau and the unique interaction of functional and design aspects, less attention was paid to the materiality and fabric of the building, the surface structures, and the colour design. Certain aspects of the renovation, such as the loss of many original windows and rendered surfaces, complied with the practices of the time,[14] but were later viewed with a more critical eye. The image of the Bauhaus created at the time also shaped the way it was subsequently seen. The windows, for instance, were painted black inside and out, rather than white or grey, creating sharp contrasts which reinforced the notion of a black and white modernism.

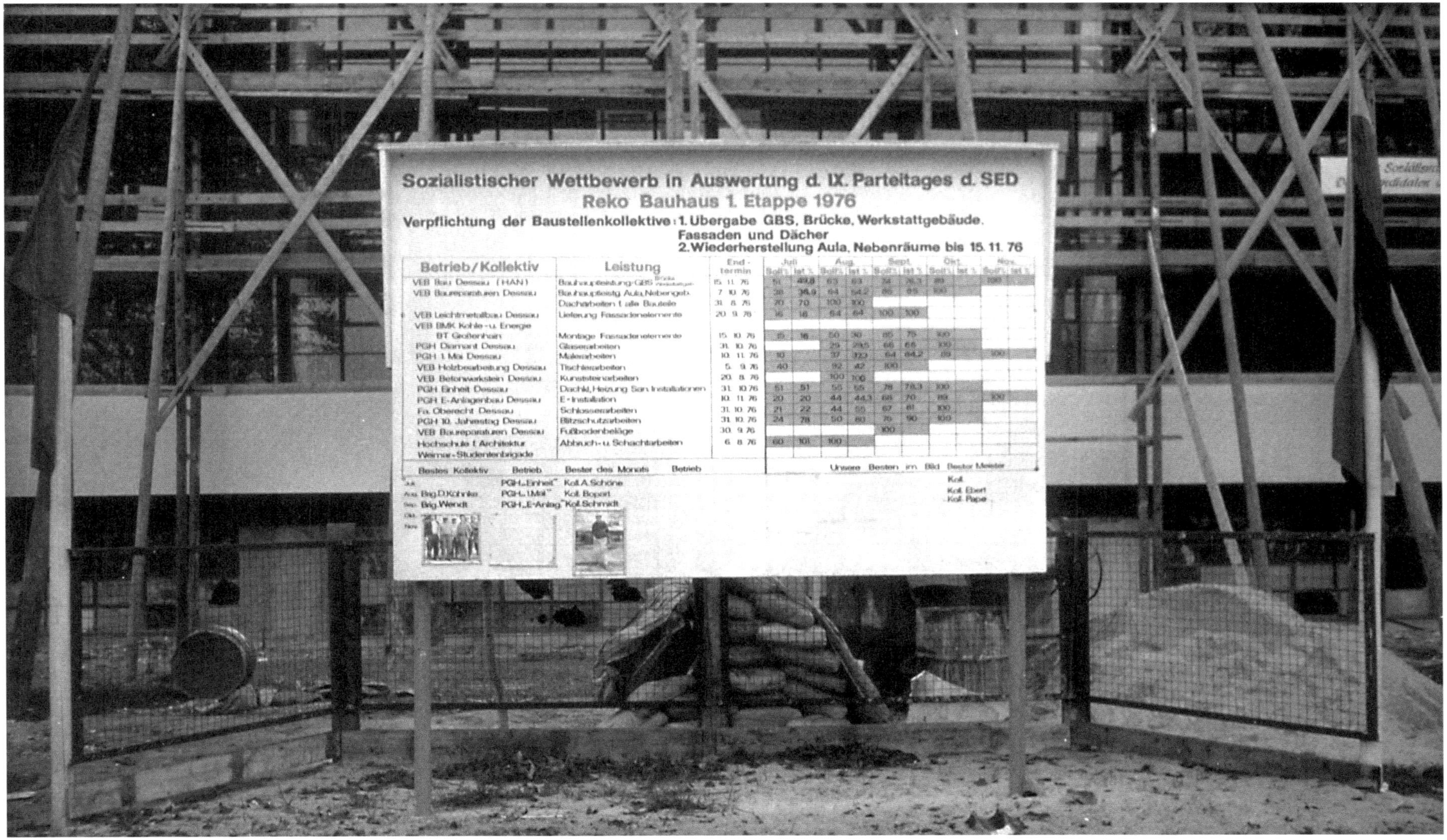

13)
Renovation of 1976

14)

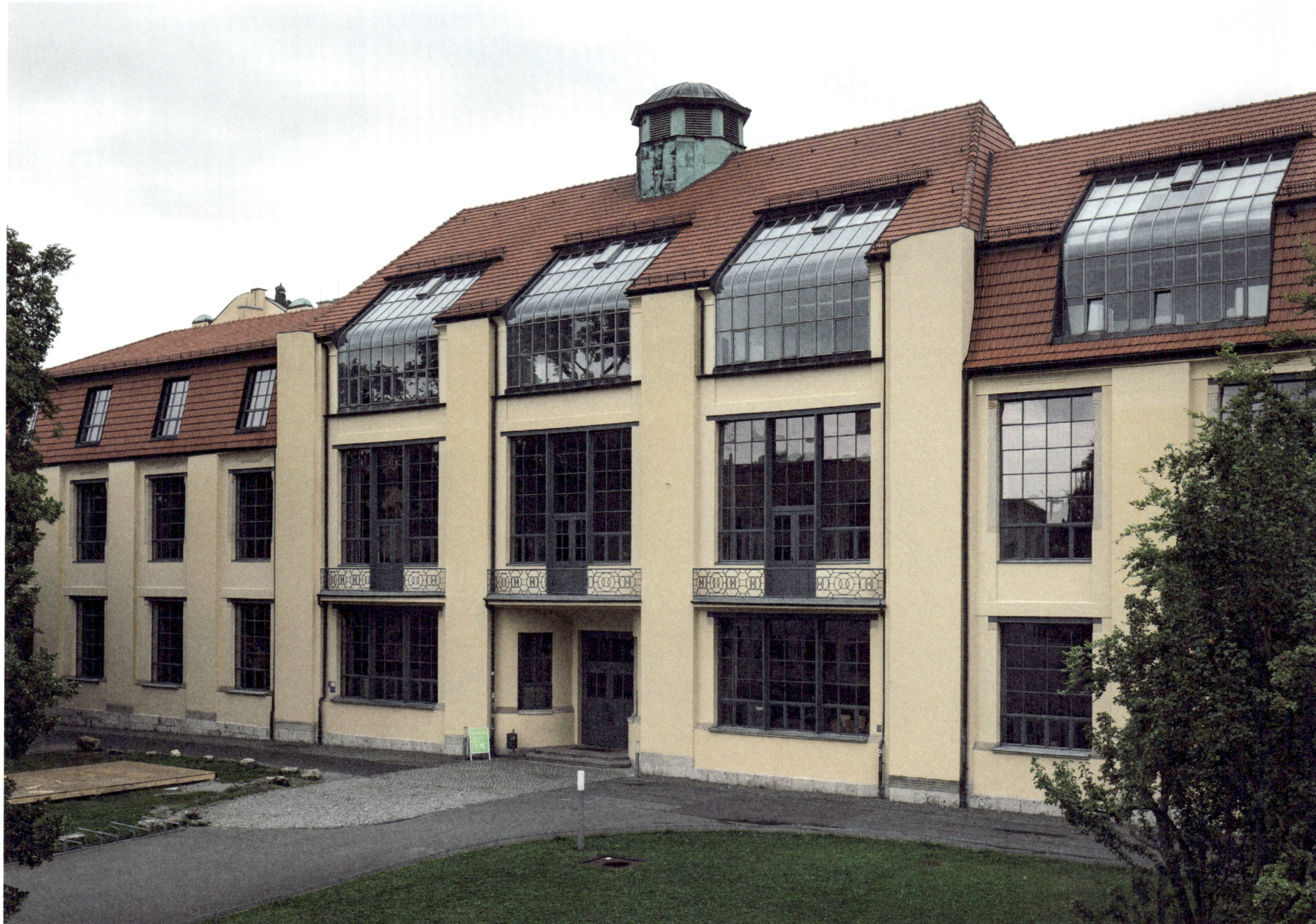

5)

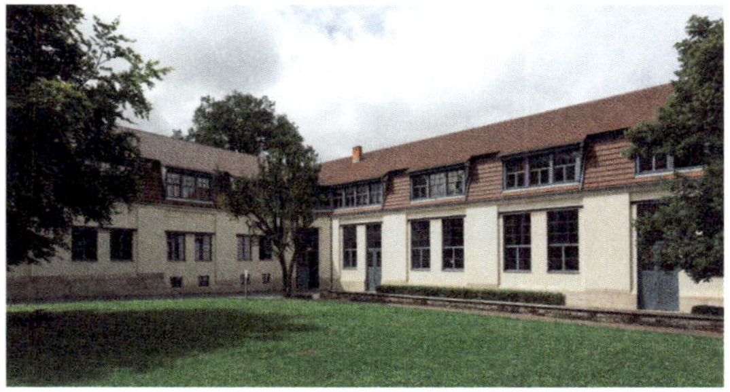

6)

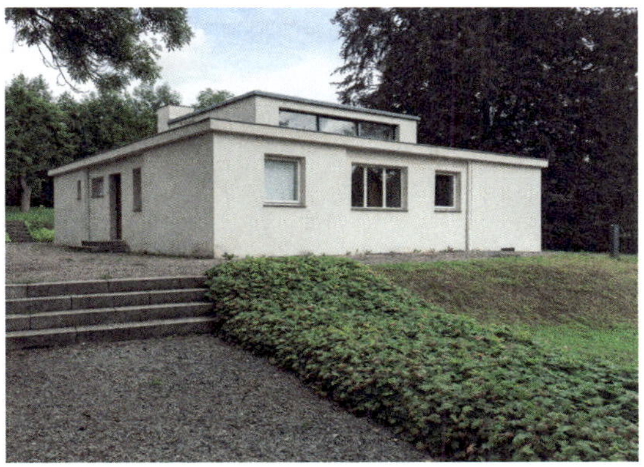

14)
Former Grand-Ducal Saxon Academy of Fine Arts, Weimar (architect: Henry van de Velde, 1905/1911)

15)
Grand Ducal-Saxon School of Arts and Crafts, Weimar (architect: Henry van de Velde, 1906)

16)
Haus Am Horn, Weimar (architects: Georg Muche, Richard Paulick, 1923)

World Cultural Heritage

The Bauhaus Building and the Masters' Houses in Dessau, together with the former Academy of Art, the former School of Arts and Crafts, and the Haus Am Horn in Weimar, the birthplace of the Bauhaus, were inscribed on the UNESCO list of World Heritage sites as 'The Bauhaus and its Sites in Weimar and Dessau' in 1996.[15] In 2017, UNESCO approved its expansion to include the Houses with Balcony Access in Dessau and the Trade Union School of the ADGB in Bernau.[16]

With its inscription on the list of World Heritage sites, the Bauhaus Building is acknowledged as a seminal work of European cultural history, which reflects the creative principles of functionalism and exemplifies the school model developed at the Bauhaus. It testifies to an architectonic renewal wrought by the use of new materials, the rejection of traditional forms of representation, and the development of new spatial interconnections.

The application for inclusion in the list of World Heritage sites describes a specific quality of the Bauhaus architecture: 'Their consistent artistic grandeur is a reminder of the still uncompleted project for "modernity with a human face", which has sought to use the technical and intellectual resources at its disposition not in a destructive way but to create a living environment worthy of human aspirations.
For this reason, they are important monuments not only for art and culture, but also for the historic ideas of the 20th century. Even though the Bauhaus philosophy of social reform turned out to be little more than wishful thinking, its utopia became reality through the form of its architecture. Its direct accessibility still has the power to fascinate and belongs to the people of all nations as their cultural heritage.'[17]

The 'outstanding universal value', the authenticity, and the integrity of the World Heritage site is to be preserved for the benefit of the human race worldwide. UNESCO is thus involved through the World Heritage Committee and the International Council on Monuments and Sites (ICOMOS) in the preservation of these values of the cultural heritage.

17)

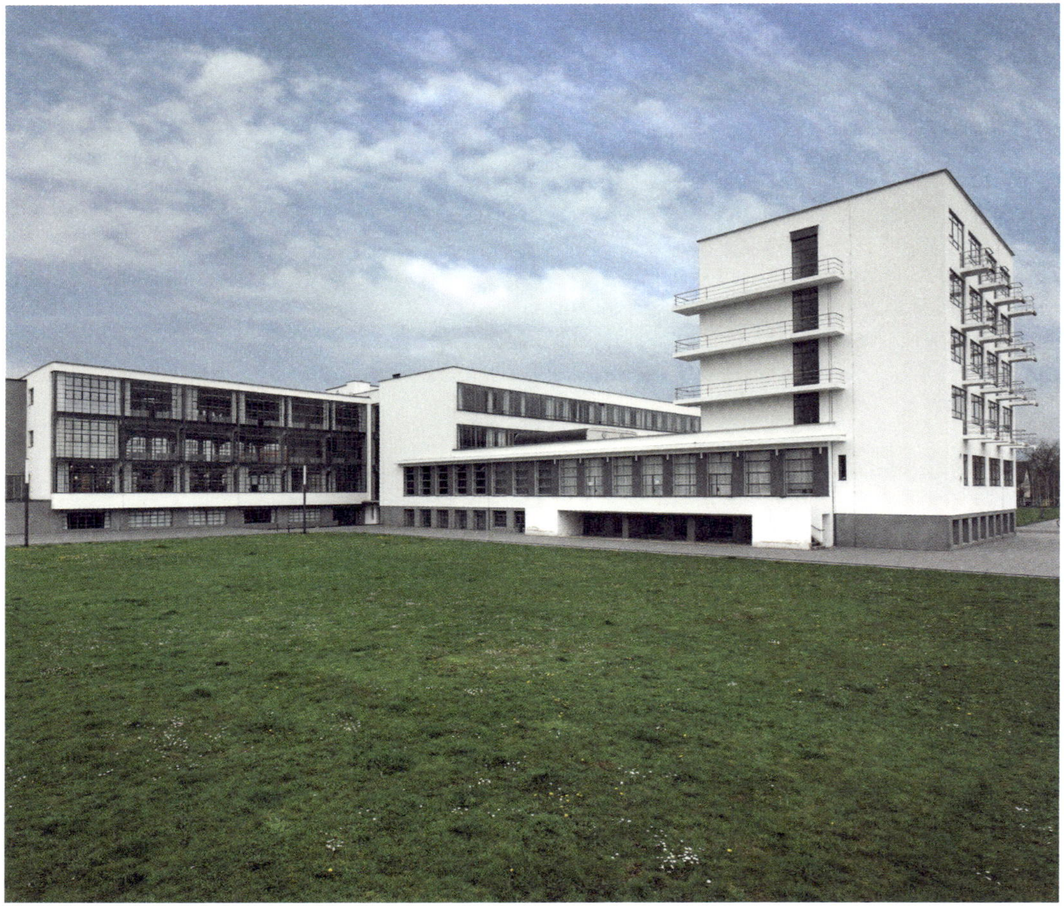

18)

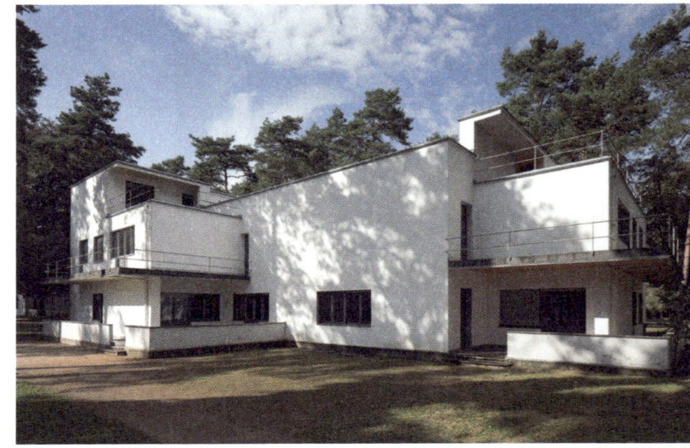

19)

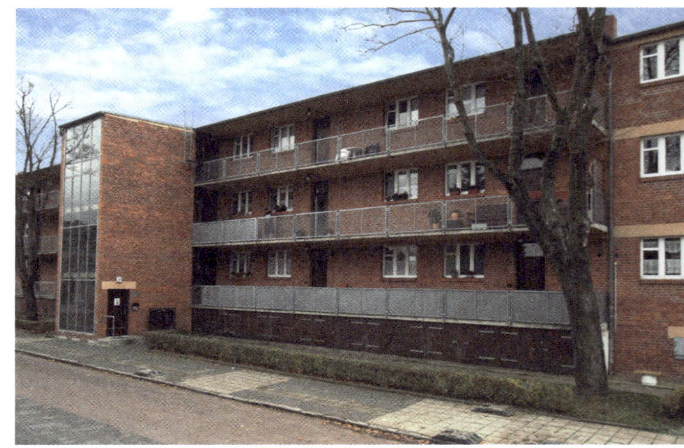

20)

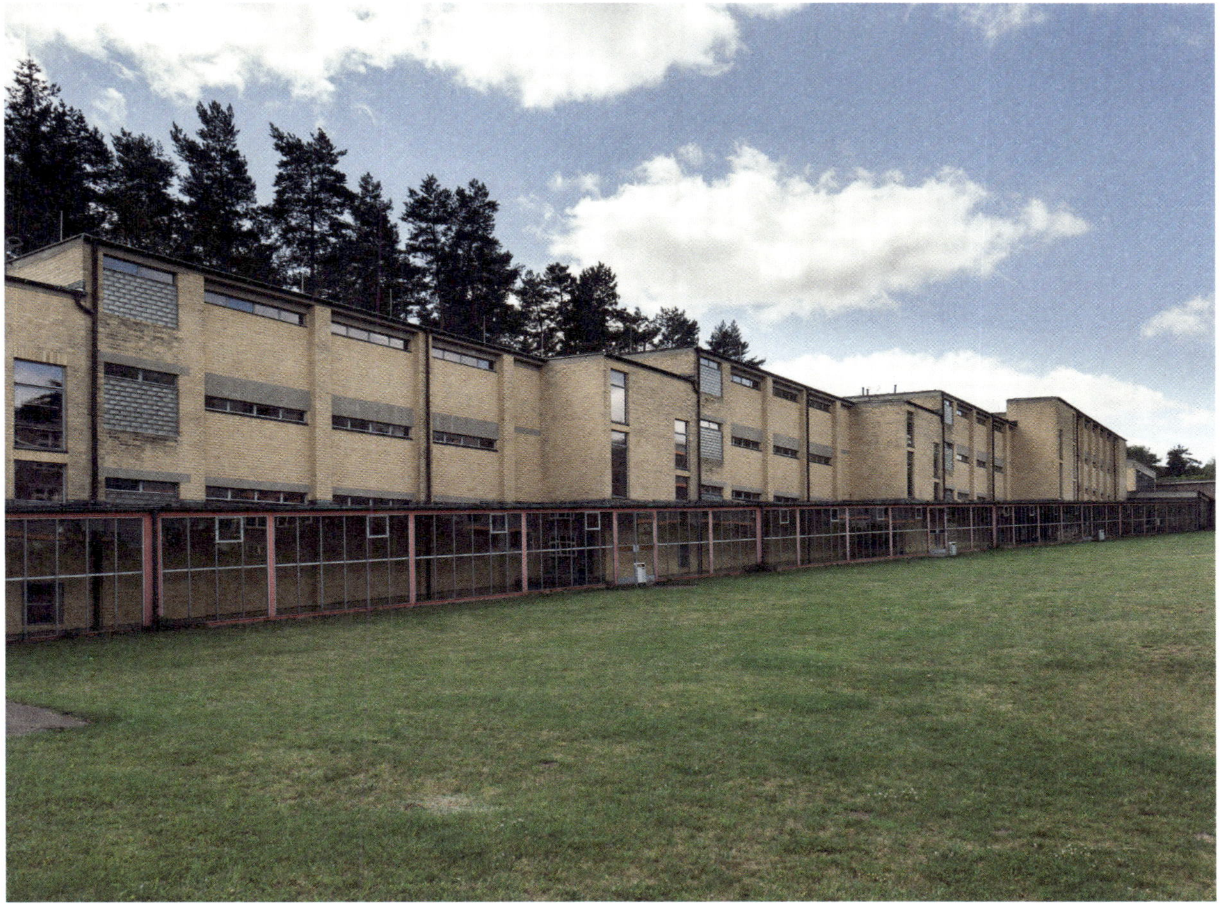

17)
Bauhaus Building, Dessau (architect: Walter Gropius, 1926)

18)
Masters' Houses, Dessau (architect: Walter Gropius, 1926)

19)
Houses with Balcony Access, Dessau (architect: Hannes Meyer and the Bauhaus building department, 1930)

20)
Former Trade Union School of the ADGB, Bernau near Berlin (architect: Hannes Meyer and the Bauhaus building department, 1930)

21)

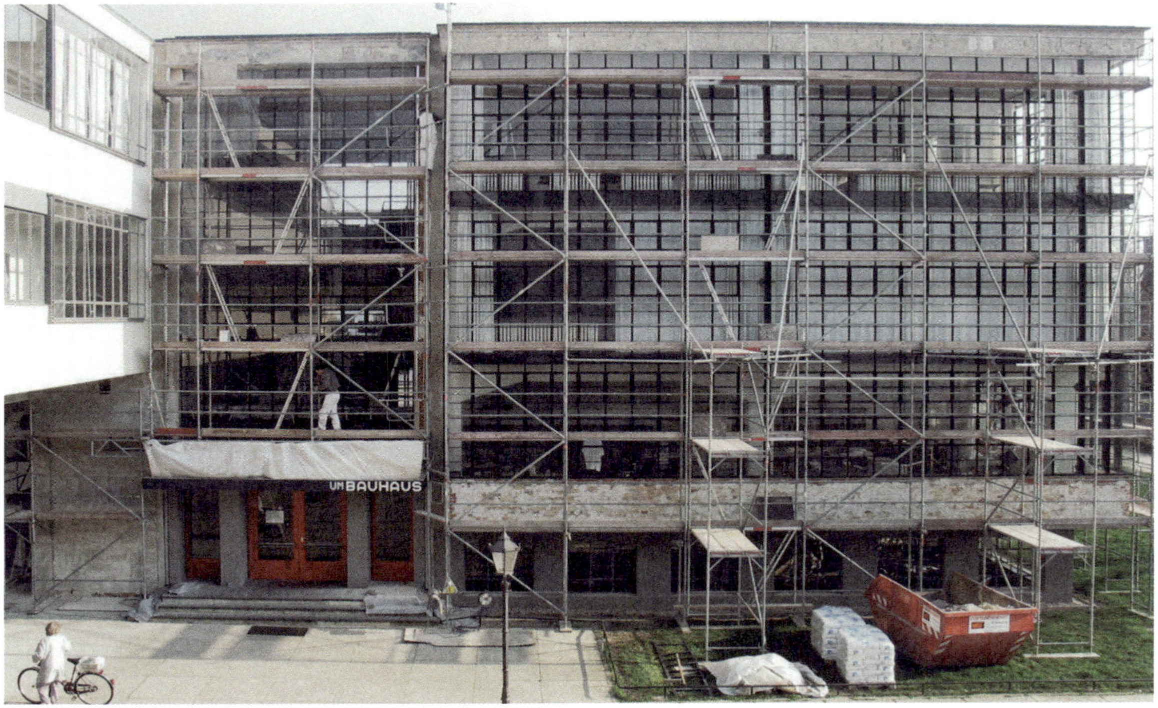

22)

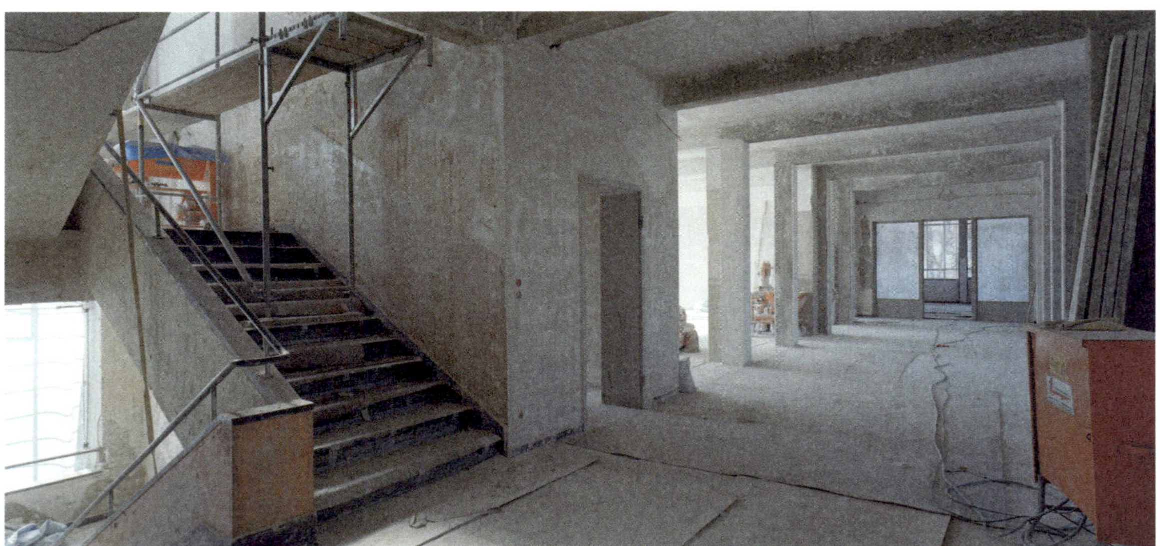

21)
General renovation
1996–2009: maintenance
work on the façade,
workshop wing, 2004

22)
General Renovation
1996–2009: building works,
north wing, 2006

1996–2009
General Renovation

Twenty years on from the renovation of 1976, the Bauhaus Building was once again showing significant signs of deterioration and damage. The planning and implementation of measures to deal with these were set out in the framework of an overarching concept. In 1996, the year of the Bauhaus's inclusion on the UNESCO World Heritage list, a so-called general renovation of the building was agreed. The works were completed on the building in 2006 and on the external facilities in 2009.

The work began with extensive research, reports, and surveys in order to create an inventory and to ascertain the renovation objectives. Because much of the documentation dating from the building period or from later measures is incomplete, most of the information about the material substance of the building was gathered on site and supplemented by the findings of archive research. Architectural and art-historical analyses, an evaluation of historic photographs, files and other archived documents on the one hand, and site measurements, a room book, and damage mapping, materials technology and structural assessments on the other provided a basis for planning. During the general renovation from 1996 to 2009, the materiality of the fabric of the building as well as the history of the building increasingly came to be seen as undeniable and crucial constituents of the monument, as had long been the norm for older buildings.

Based on the extensive studies, a general concept for dealing with the building was developed, the findings of which were presented in the conservation objectives[18] of 1999. These set out guidelines for all phases of the general renovation, which will also serve as a basis for the development of plans for future building measures. The conservation objectives were coordinated with technical planners, restorers, and experts regarding specific aspects, and with the historic monuments protection authority of the city of Dessau, the State Office for the Preservation of Historical Monuments Saxony-Anhalt, and commissaries of ICOMOS.

In addition to the established legislation, regulations, and guidelines for the renovation of listed buildings in Germany, national and internationally relevant conventions such as the principles of heritage conservation adopted by ICOMOS,[19] the Venice Charter,[20] or the Burra Charter[21] provide orientation for the planning.

Areas have been identified in the building in which the focus is on restoration and reconstruction, on maintenance and repair, or on upkeep and possible replacement. The main focus is on those areas which essentially define the value of the building as a cultural monument and World Heritage site. Here, the aim is to reproduce as faithfully as possible the original context of 1926. Changes made to the Bauhaus Building should remain easy to read; that said, the individual time layers are evaluated differently. The condition of 1926 is awarded the highest priority provided it is backed by the relevant findings, since the work completed in 1926 by Walter Gropius in collaboration with the Bauhaus workshops is regarded as the original condition and therefore as having the greatest artistic value. Changes made while the building was still in use by the Bauhaus, e.g., under Ludwig Mies van der Rohe, are also reinstated if they may be scientifically substantiated. All areas are depicted in a binding plan (historic allocation concept) in the conservation objectives.

The festive area for instance, a sequence of rooms of central significance, is defined as an area scheduled for restoration and reconstruction. The studio building, currently utilised as a guest house by the Bauhaus Dessau Foundation, is among the areas earmarked for maintenance and repair, in which the outcomes shaped by the renovation of 1976 are to be preserved. In parts of the workshop wing, the room layout may be changed because while the sense of space is shaped by the visible concrete skeleton and glass façades, the room layout was already being practically modified to suit the needs of the users in 1926. During all the measures, the original fabric and overall structure of the building are to be treated with utmost care.

The main outcomes of the general renovation from 1996 to 2009 include: the conservation of the load-bearing structure of the building envelope, the recreation of relevant original sequences of rooms, the discovery and recreation of the original colour design and surface finishes including those of floors, the replication of the original lighting elements, and the reorganisation of the outdoor facilities. The conservation objectives also inspired ideas pertaining to the long-term development of the building, specifically as regards the preservation of the original materiality and time layers and the efforts towards a long-term maintenance concept.[22]

23)
Overview of planned measures to reduce energy consumption in the Bauhaus Building, 2011

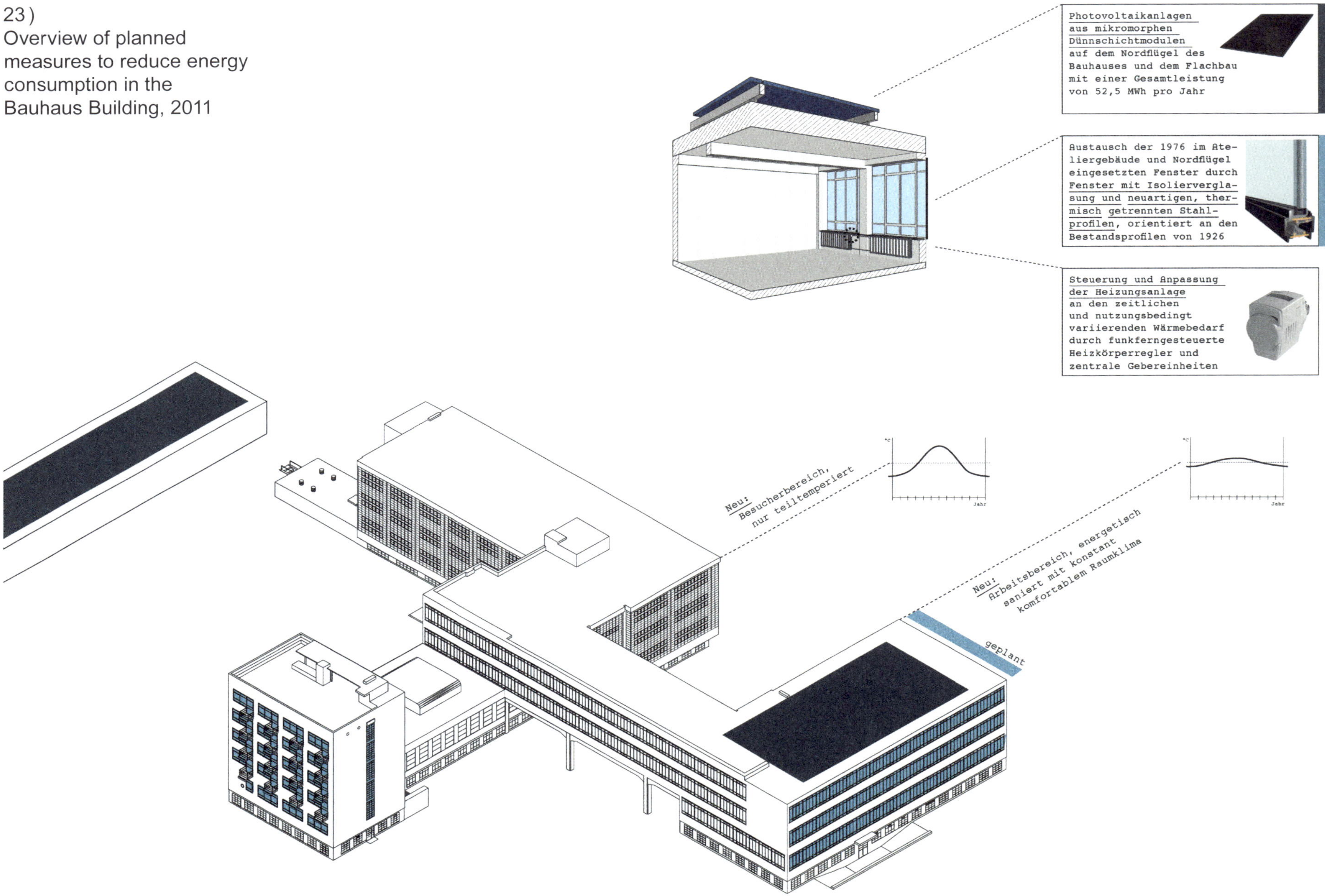

2009–2015 Thermal Upgrading

The question of the energy consumption in the Bauhaus Building was increasingly prioritised from 2009. The Bauhaus Dessau Foundation thus planned and implemented measures designed to reduce both energy consumption and operating costs, improve user comfort, and contribute to climate protection by reducing the carbon footprint. At the same time, the aim was to come up with innovative and high-quality solutions that might eventually also inspire energy efficiency improvements in other buildings. The project involved the development of an overall concept[23] in which the measures were analysed and assessed in light of their complexity, their effect on each other and on the cultural value of the building, and the implementation of isolated measures. Here, the protection and preservation of the original fabric and the cultural value of the building were prioritised. In an intensive process involving architects, specialist engineers such as stress analysts, construction physicists, or heating specialists, and users and proxies of the monument protection authorities, it was possible to regularly review all steps and decisions.

One measure entailed the technical optimisation of the heating system by way of radio-controlled thermostats; in most of the rooms, neither the regulators nor the radiators dated back to the original construction period, and the new thermostats fit unobtrusively into the overall picture. The installation of a photovoltaic system on the roof of a neighbouring building and on the roof of the north wing of the Bauhaus Building was realised following in-depth deliberations, albeit with a time limit. As a 'fifth façade', the roof is of particular significance to the architecture; however, this change in this area entails only minimal interventions in the fabric of the building and is reversible.

A focal point of the overall concept for energy efficiency involved exploring options to reduce energy losses by changing the way in which the building is used. Here measures included relocating the art collection and the library, uncoupling a storage building from the heating system, and relocating workplaces in the building. The concentration of offices in one part of the building removes the need to continuously maintain high temperatures in another part of the building.

The thermal upgrading measures also entailed the development of a window construction comprising thermally broken steel profiles and double glazing. Due to the particular relevance of the glass façades as regards the 'outstanding universal value' of the Bauhaus Building, this plan was only feasible as part of an overall concept, as ICOMOS emphasised in a statement: 'We therefore propose this step is reconsidered with a view to whether it adequately balances the concerns of both energy and heritage conservation. Only such an overall concept … can deliver a well-founded rationale and weighing of interests and simultaneously ensure that the widely recognised quality of the general renovation 1996–2006 can be maintained with the current measures. Given the exceptional symbolic effect and importance of the Bauhaus Building, the current energy-related operating costs and user comfort as well as the cultural and environmental overall balance must be examined from a long-term perspective.'

The overall concept included decisions on selected façades for which windows with thermally broken profiles and double glazing were designed with extremely high-quality detailing and execution.[25]

24)

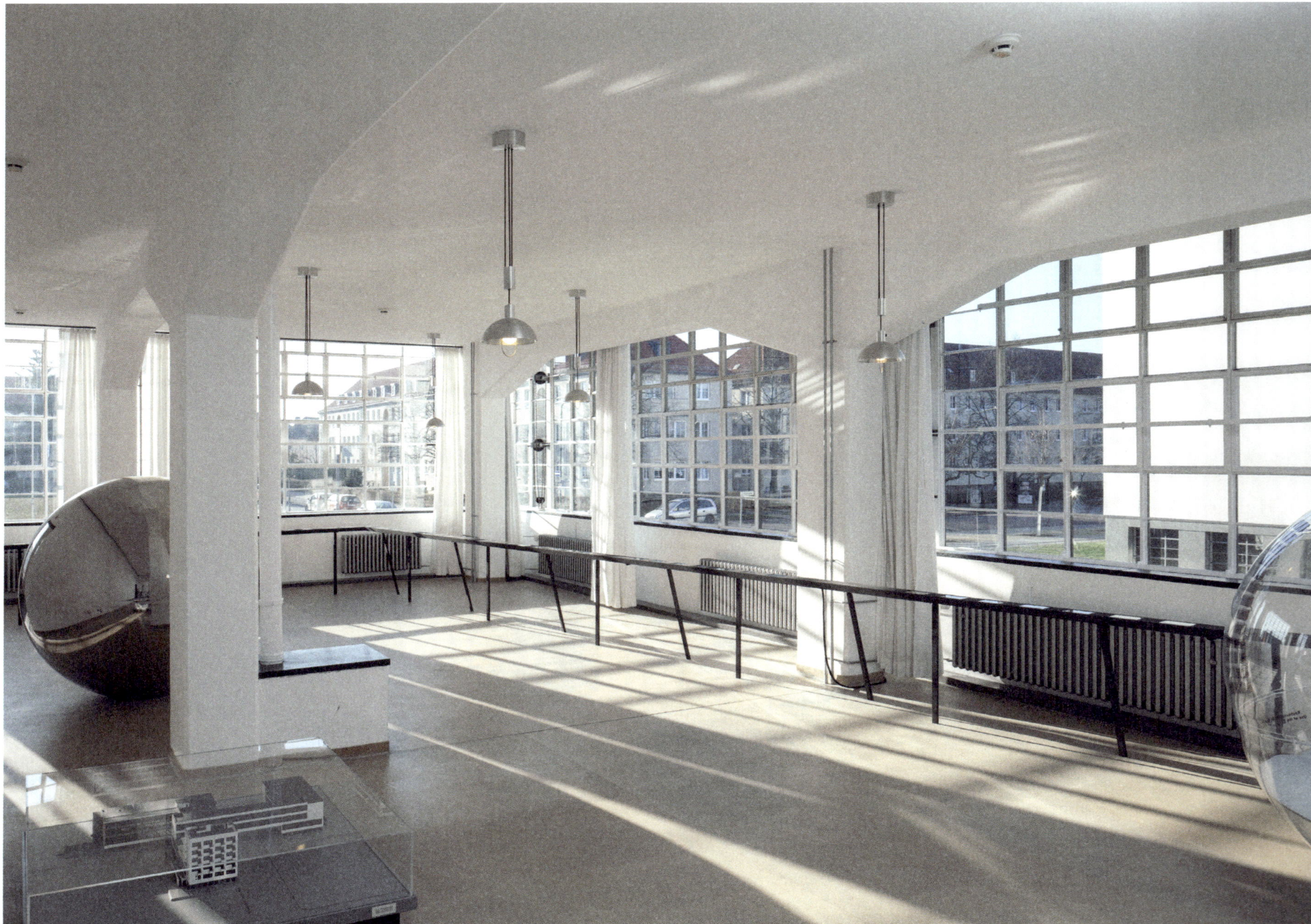

25)

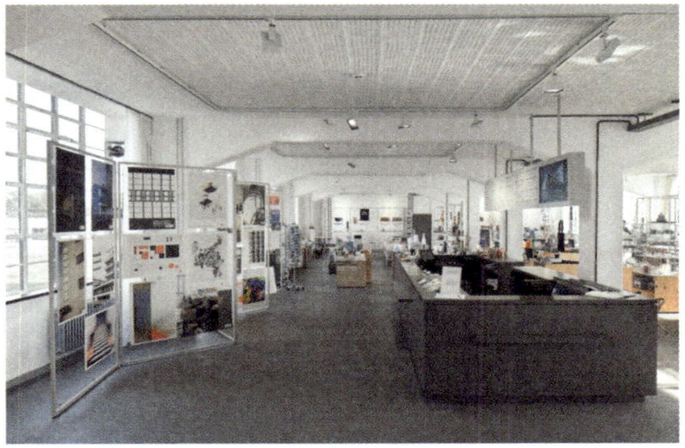

26)

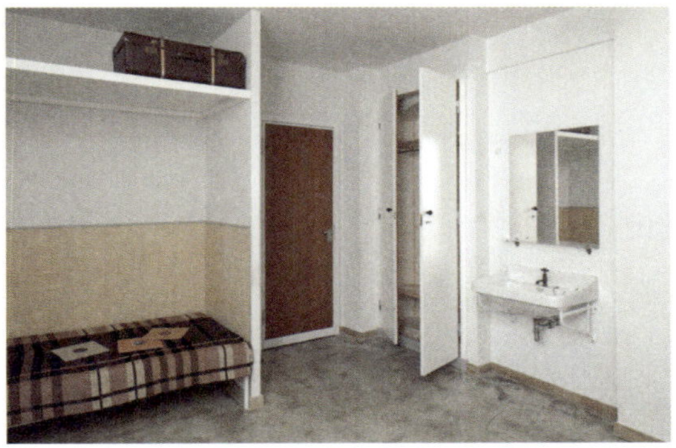

24)
Visitor information,
workshop wing, 2014

25)
Visitor information
and shop,
workshop wing, 2014

26)
Recreated room,
studio building, 2014

2009–2015
Tourism Development

With the intensified public interest in the Bauhaus and the Bauhaus buildings, the improvement of tourism provisions and the mediation of the UNESCO World Heritage sites of the Bauhaus became a priority. In the Bauhaus Building, an overall concept developed from 2009 encompassed the development of a visitor information centre, the reorganisation of guided tours, infrastructural improvements, and the presentation of historic spaces to communicate their historic uses. The visitor information centre on the ground floor not only provides quick and clear access to information but also, due to its location in the workshop wing with its distinctive atmosphere behind the curtain wall, offers a first impression of the remarkable architecture.

Based on extensive research, the layout of the director's office was recreated as faithfully as possible. Work on the studio building focused on improving the visitor experience of its historic, programmatic structure as a collective residence. This included the recreation of Marianne Brandt's well-documented studio, a further review of the possibility of opening the roof terrace to visitors, acoustic improvements in the seminar rooms in the north wing, and the development of spaces for museum educational services.

The range of provisions for visitors and guests was further improved by a garage with bicycle parking spaces, a cloakroom and toilets on the basement floor, and the installation of shower cubicles in the studio building.[26]

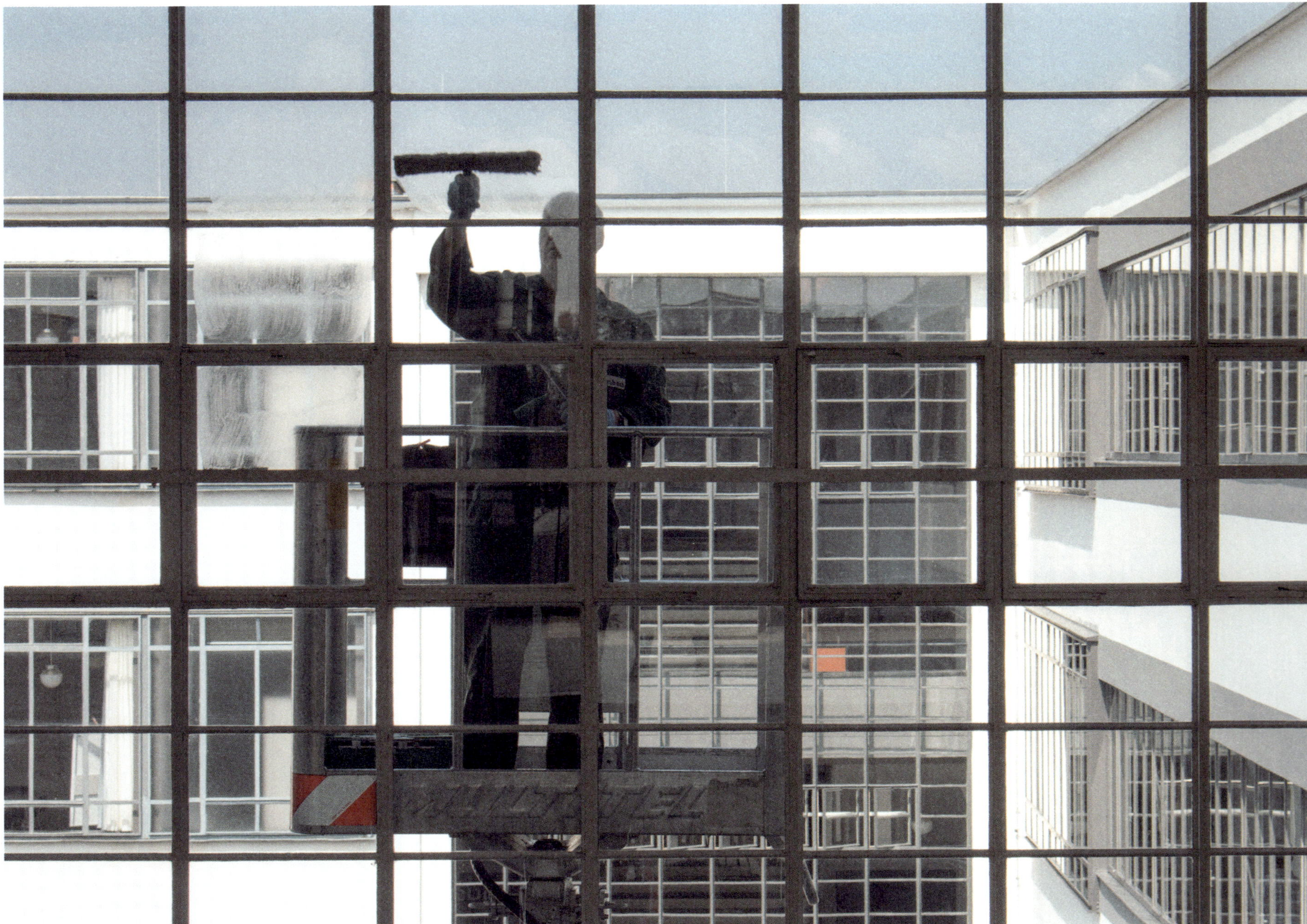

27)
Cleaning the glass façades, 2015

Long-term Conservation

Today, the long-term conservation of the Bauhaus Building by means of continuous maintenance increasingly forms the focus of planning, the aim being to ensure the long-term survival of the building, its materiality, and its architectonic impact. This includes the planning and implementation of building measures, work on updating the conservation objectives, and the development of a conservation management plan inclusive of database. The conservation objectives for the Bauhaus Building also set out the goals for the future long-term and scientific approach to the World Heritage and act as a guideline for the planning of maintenance measures, modifications, and changes of use. Based on new knowledge and requirements, the objectives published in 1999 were updated in 2014.[27]

Structural measures focus less on changes than on preservation by means of, e.g., proactive maintenance, conservative modifications, or repairs. Here, examples include the renovation of the studio building façade, the restoration of the textile components of the auditorium seating, or changes in the outdoor area.[28] Currently, there are indications that climate change with its extreme heat, unusual storms, and intense precipitation events poses just as much of a threat to the Bauhaus Building as it does to other listed buildings by increasing the movements of different building parts and the formation of cracks, or placing a greater burden on sensitive structures such as the curtain wall. A precise investigation of the causes, effects, and possible preventative actions is underway.

The continuous specialised care and maintenance of the Bauhaus Building, especially in view of its intensive use, is essential in order to preserve the original building fabric, ensure the quality of these works, and avoid complex repairs, restorations, or replacements. UNESCO also monitors the ongoing and systematic maintenance and care of World Heritage sites and requires the presentation of a management plan.

The Bauhaus Dessau Foundation has compiled a conservation management plan for the Bauhaus Building.[29] One critical aspect is the creation of a database to record detailed information for maintenance purposes. Historical information for every building component and each surface, including construction date, alterations, or colour, is listed alongside relevant data regarding care and maintenance, e.g., information on materials or techniques. The database complements a pre-existing facility management database used by the Bauhaus Dessau Foundation, the applications of which enable the planning of heritage-relevant measures such as appointments for maintenance and inspection or the creation and monitoring of new contracts.[30]

1
Werner 2014/I

2
The headline in the *Anhaltische Abendzeitung* states: 'Roof of the Bauhaus—sins of omission righted', in: *Anhaltische Abendzeitung,* 10 January 1934.

3
Cf. Manzke/Thöner 1996; Oswalt 2014

4
Letter from Hinnerk Scheper, 7 July 1945, Houghton Library 46/282 et seqq.

5
German Ministry of Culture, 1963

6
Dessau municipal archive, SB 68, fol. 17: file memo, 10 May 1964

7
Benevolo 1964, p. 58

8
Classification criteria as per the register of monuments of the city of Dessau, status 2003, based on the heritage protection law of the federal state of Saxony-Anhalt, 21 October 1991, version of 22 December 2004

9
Schlesier/Püschel 1964, introduction

10
Korrek/Wolf 2016

11
Schlesier/Püschel 1964, p. 24 et seqq.

12
In the GDR, the term *Rekonstruktion* described a substantial measure comprising not only partial reconstructions, but also restoration, maintenance, and new editions. As such, it differs from the contemporary definition, which is based inter alia on the Burra Charter (2013) and is described in detail in Chapter 10 (Long-term Conservation).

13
Berger 1976/II, p. 558–59

14
The Weissenhof Estate in Stuttgart was renovated in a very similar way in the early 1980s. Cf. Staatliche Hochbauverwaltung Baden-Württemberg 1987.

16
The declaration: 'Justification for Inscription: The Committee decided to inscribe the nominated property on the basis of cultural criteria (ii), (iv) and (vi) considering that the site is of outstanding universal value since these buildings are the seminal works of the Bauhaus architectural school, the foundation of the Modern Movement which was to revolutionize artistic and architectural thinking and practice in the twentieth century. The Committee also noted that this type of inscription testifies a better recognition of the 20th century heritage.'

17
Cf. https://whc.unesco.org/en/list/729 (7 February 2021); Markgraf 2017/I

18
Advisory Body Evaluation (ICOMOS), 1996; https://whc.unesco.org/en/list/729/documents

19
Arge Bauhaus 1999; Pro Denkmal 2014

20
Petzet 1992

21
The International Charter for the Conservation and Restoration of Monuments and Sites (1964) was adopted by the second International Congress of Architects and Technicians of Historic Monuments.

22
The Charter of Burra, which defines the procedures to be followed in the conservation of culturally significant objects, was adopted by Australia ICOMOS and last updated in 2013.

24
The general renovation was planned and implemented under the aegis of the Staatshochbauamt Saxony-Anhalt (now Landesbetrieb Bau- und Liegenschaftsmanagement Sachsen-Anhalt) with architects Brambach und Ebert Architekten, Halle/Saale; Pfister Schiess Tropeano, Zurich; Johannes Bausch (Bauhaus Dessau Foundation), Dessau and Berlin; and Mann Landschaftsarchitekten, Kassel.

23
ZUB 2010; Brenne 2011; Transsolar 2011

24
ICOMOS Preventive Monitoring 2010

25
The overall concept was planned by Brenne Architekten, Berlin; Transsolar, Stuttgart; Zentrum für Umweltbewusstes Bauen e.V., Kassel.

26
The structural measures were planned by Brenne Architekten, Berlin.

27
The conservation objectives were updated by ProDenkmal, Bamberg and Berlin.

28
The building measures were planned by AADe-Atelier für Architektur und Denkmalpflege, Dessau/Köthen/Leipzig.

29
The Bauhaus Dessau Foundation sought funding to finance a concept for the long-term and continuous maintenance of the Bauhaus Building from 2004. From 2017 to 2021, it compiled a conservation management plan with funding from the Getty Foundation and the federal state of Saxony-Anhalt.

30
The conservation management plan was planned by ProDenkmal, Bamberg/Berlin, and the Bauhaus Dessau Foundation. The database system was developed by Byron Informatik AG, Basel.

28)
Restoration of Triolin flooring, 2004

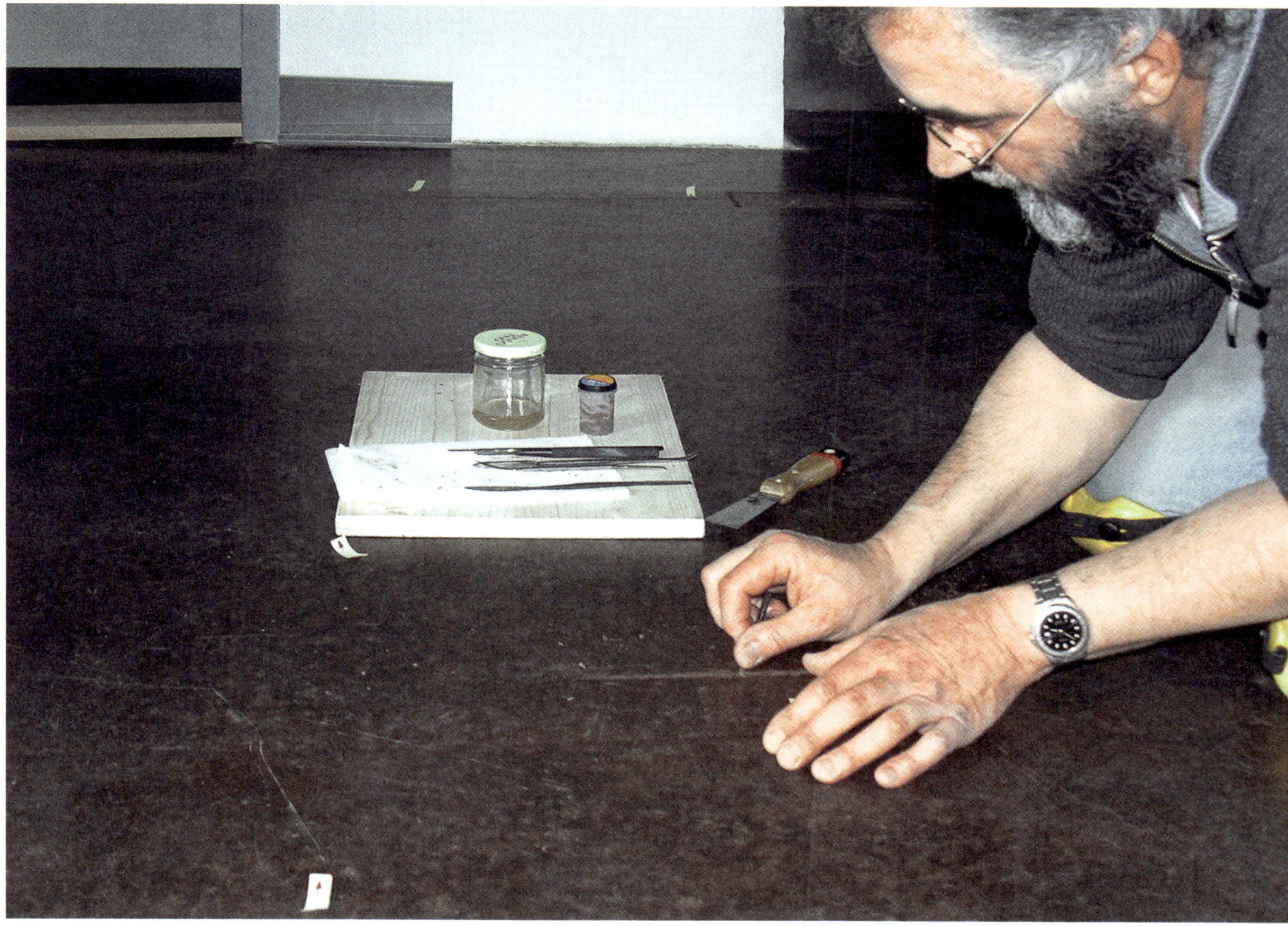

View from southwest

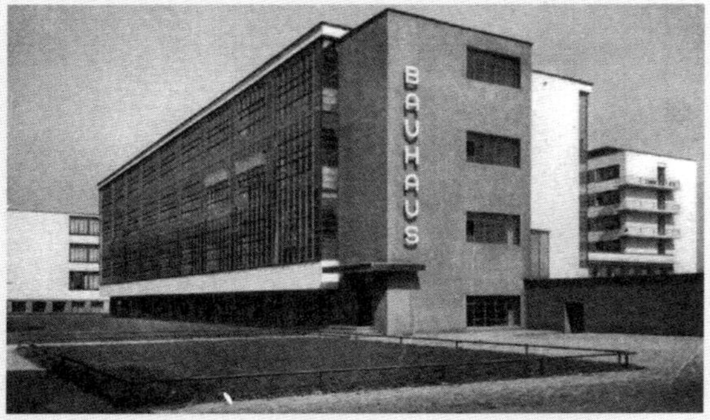

29)
1926

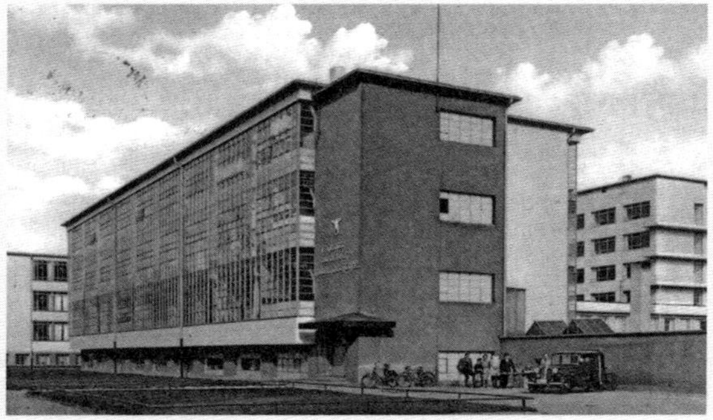

30)
1938

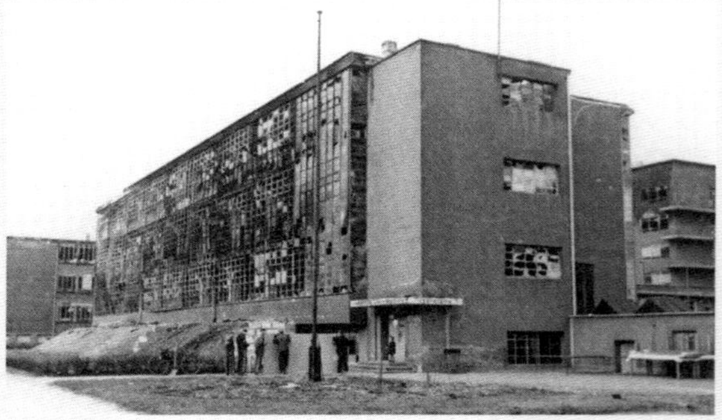

31)
1945

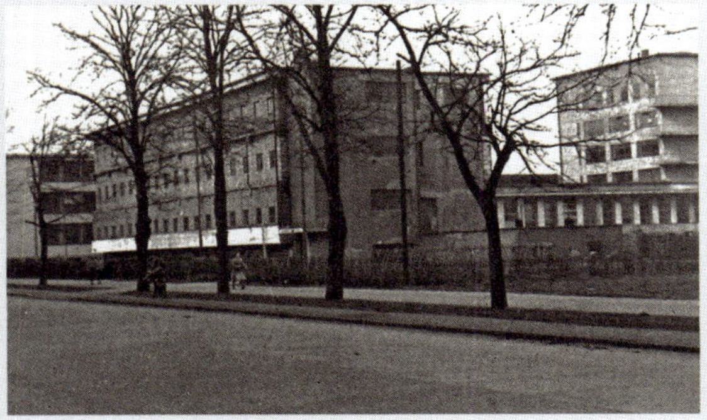

32)
1958

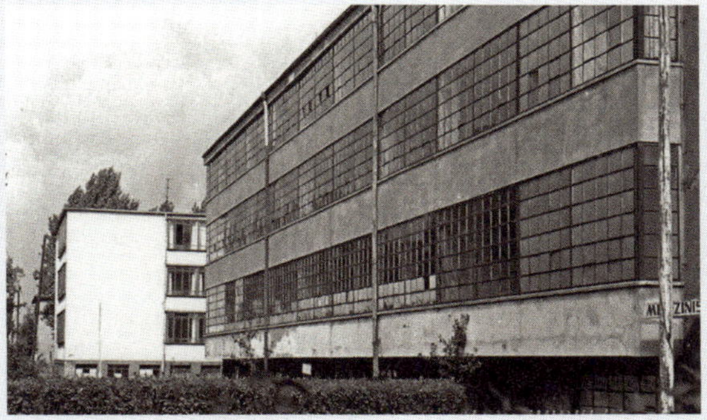

33)
1972

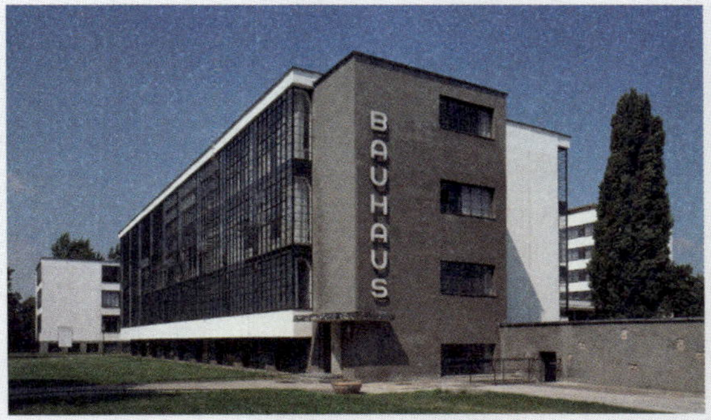

34)
1996

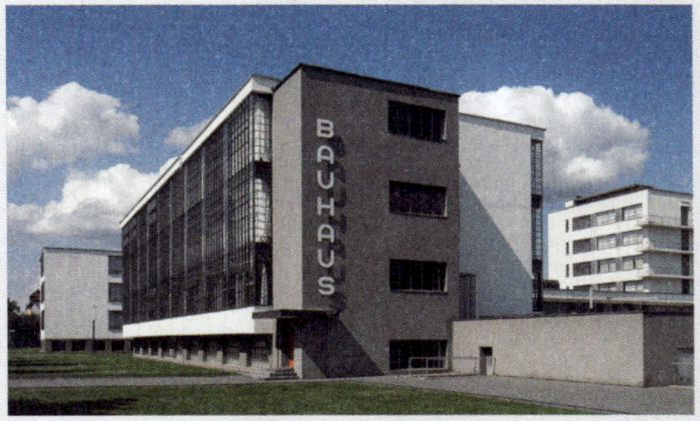

35)
2017

Key
Semi-basement

1 Vestibule
2 Classroom / Lessons
3 Office / Masters / Heads
4 Equipment storage room / Storage / Teaching materials / Files
5 Studio / Guest room
6 Kitchen
7 WC / Shower / Bathroom
8 Changing room / Washroom
9 Cleaning supplies room
10 Exhibition space
11 Building services
12 Janitor
13 Basement
14 Printing workshop
15 Dyeworks
16 Drying room
17 Wood store / Storage
18 Sculpture workshop
19 Packing room
20 Wood chips
21 Coal bunker
22 Heating cellar / Boiler room / Boiler
23 Workshop / Heating outer office
24 Stage workshop
25 Fitness room
26 Utility room
27 Storeroom
28 Bicycles
29 Transformer room / Canteen air conditioning
30 Caretaker's flat
31 Model-making workshop
32 Photo laboratory
33 Teaching materials
34 Carpentry workshop
35 Lounge / E-distribution
36 Accumulator room
37 Stage room
38 Staff
39 Boiler room
40 Canteen
41 Book shop
42 Klub im Bauhaus
43 Multi-purpose room
44 Props

Semi-basement
1926

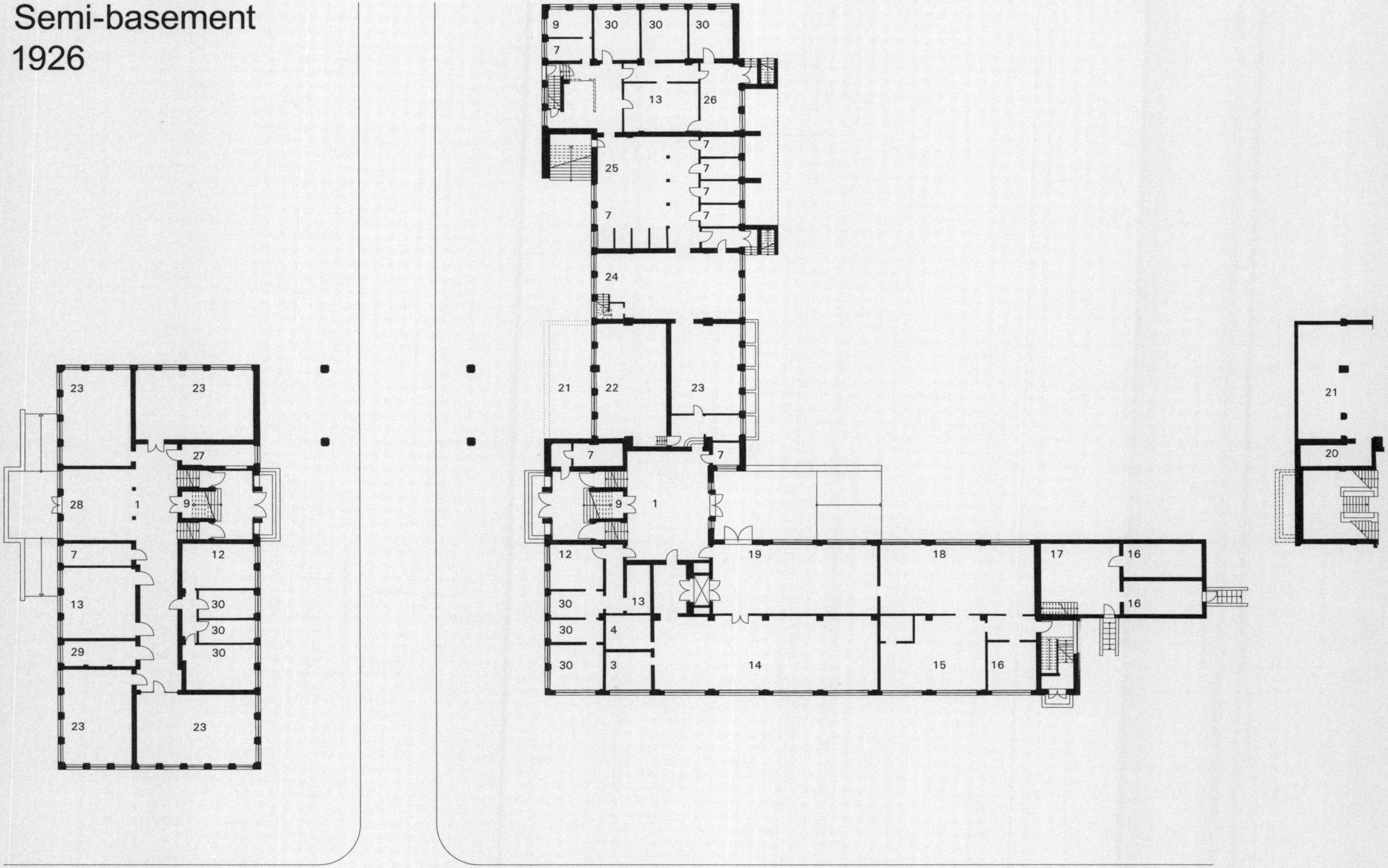

Semi-basement
1964

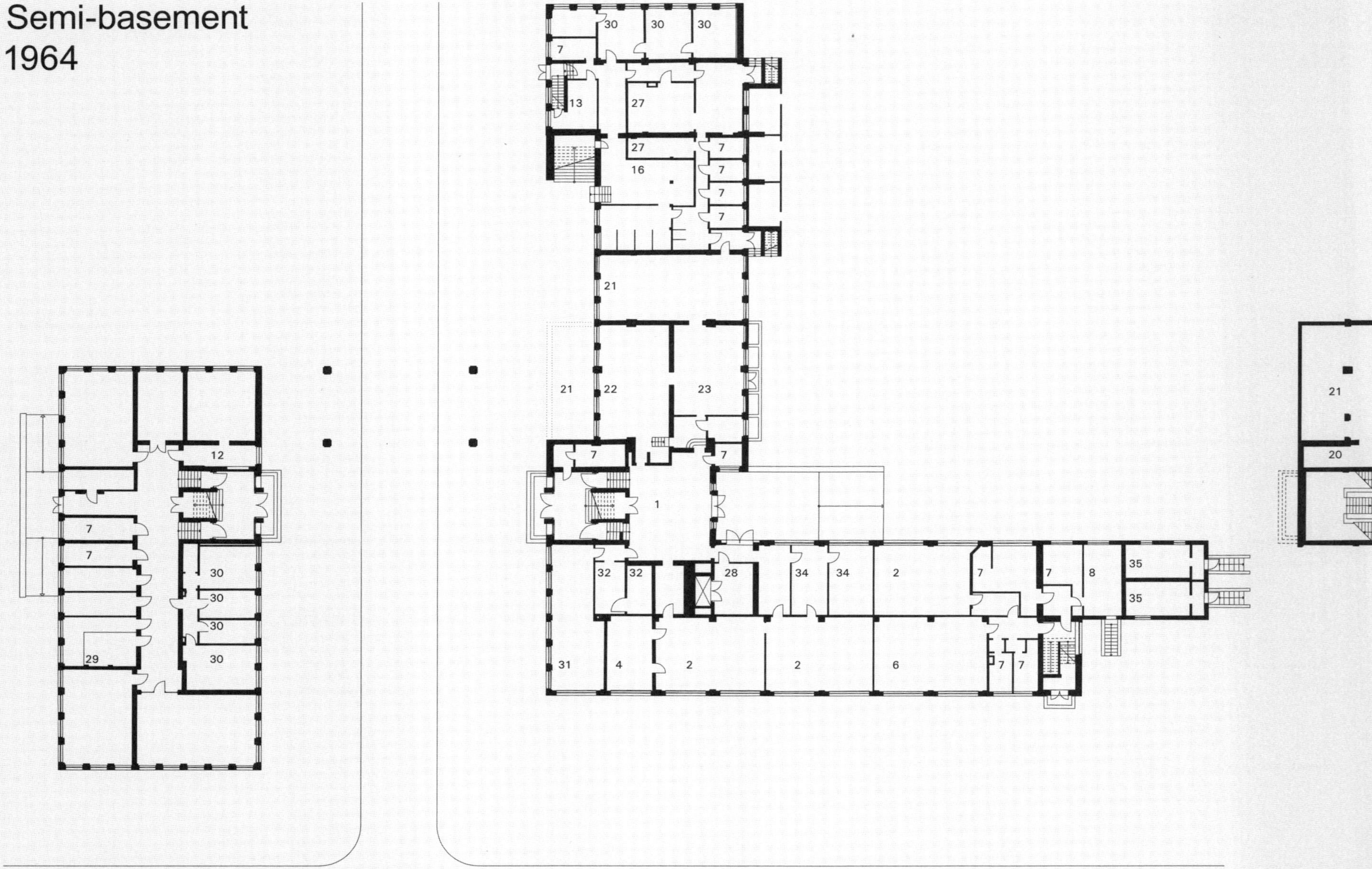

37)

Semi-basement
1976

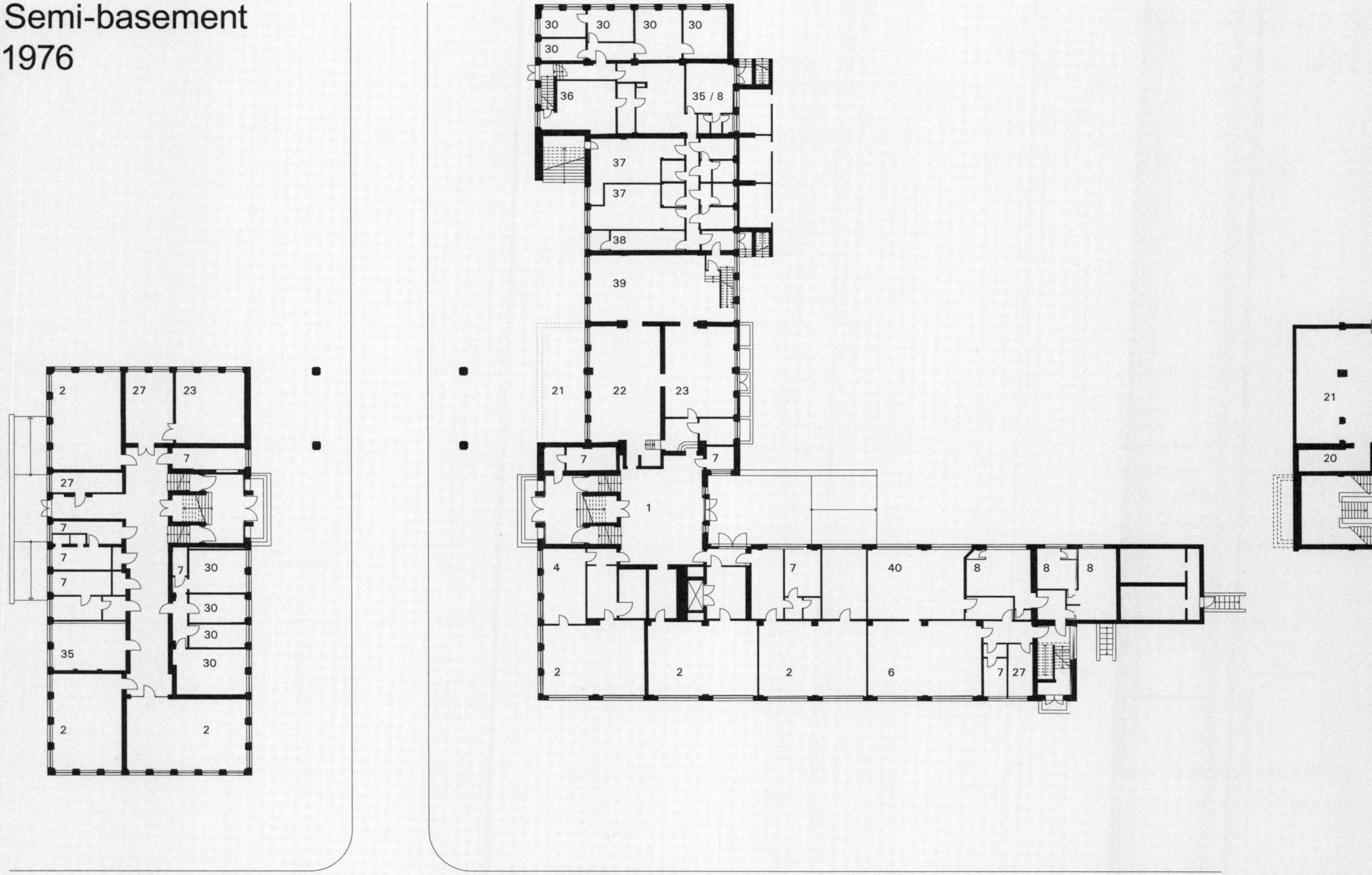

Semi-basement
1996

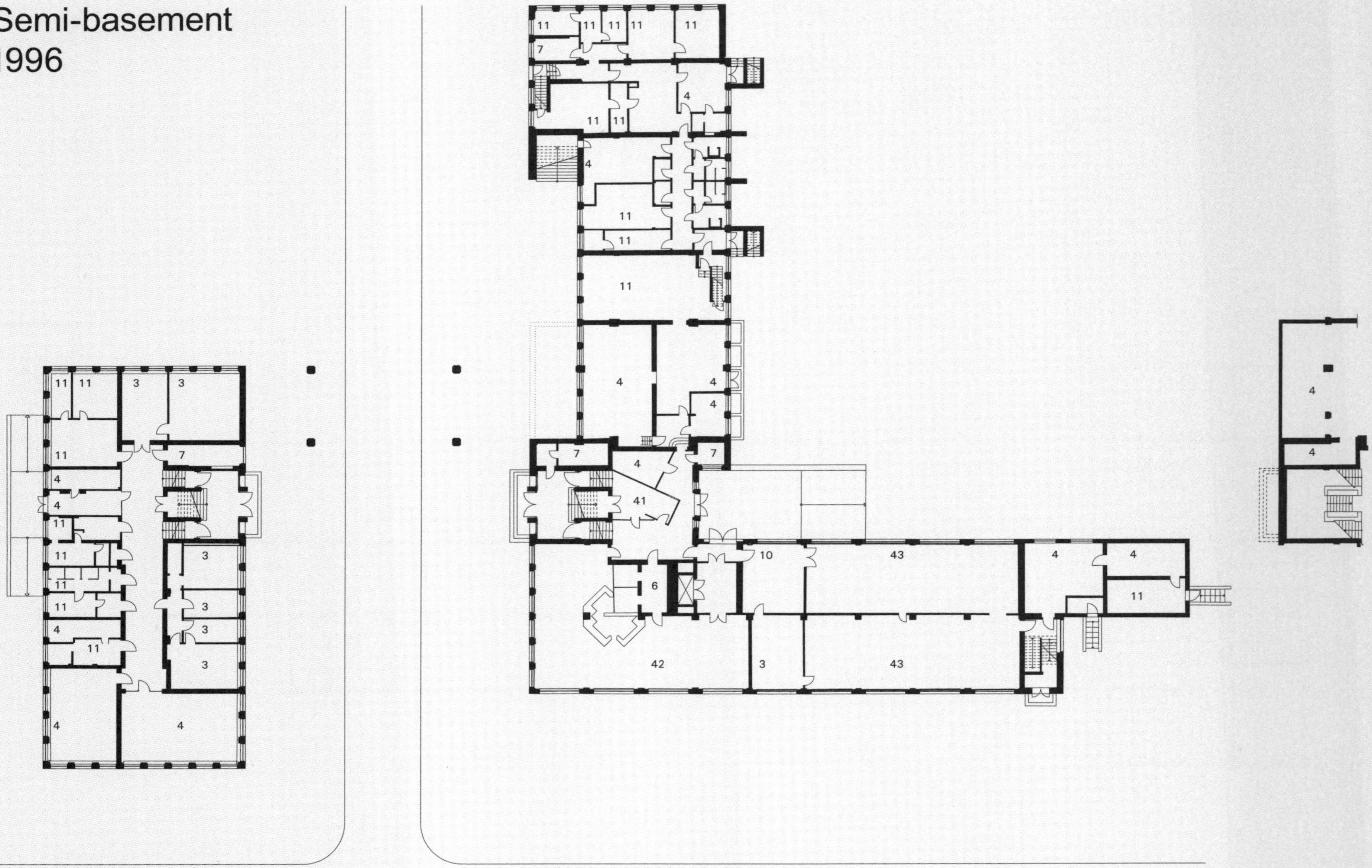

39)

Semi-basement
2021

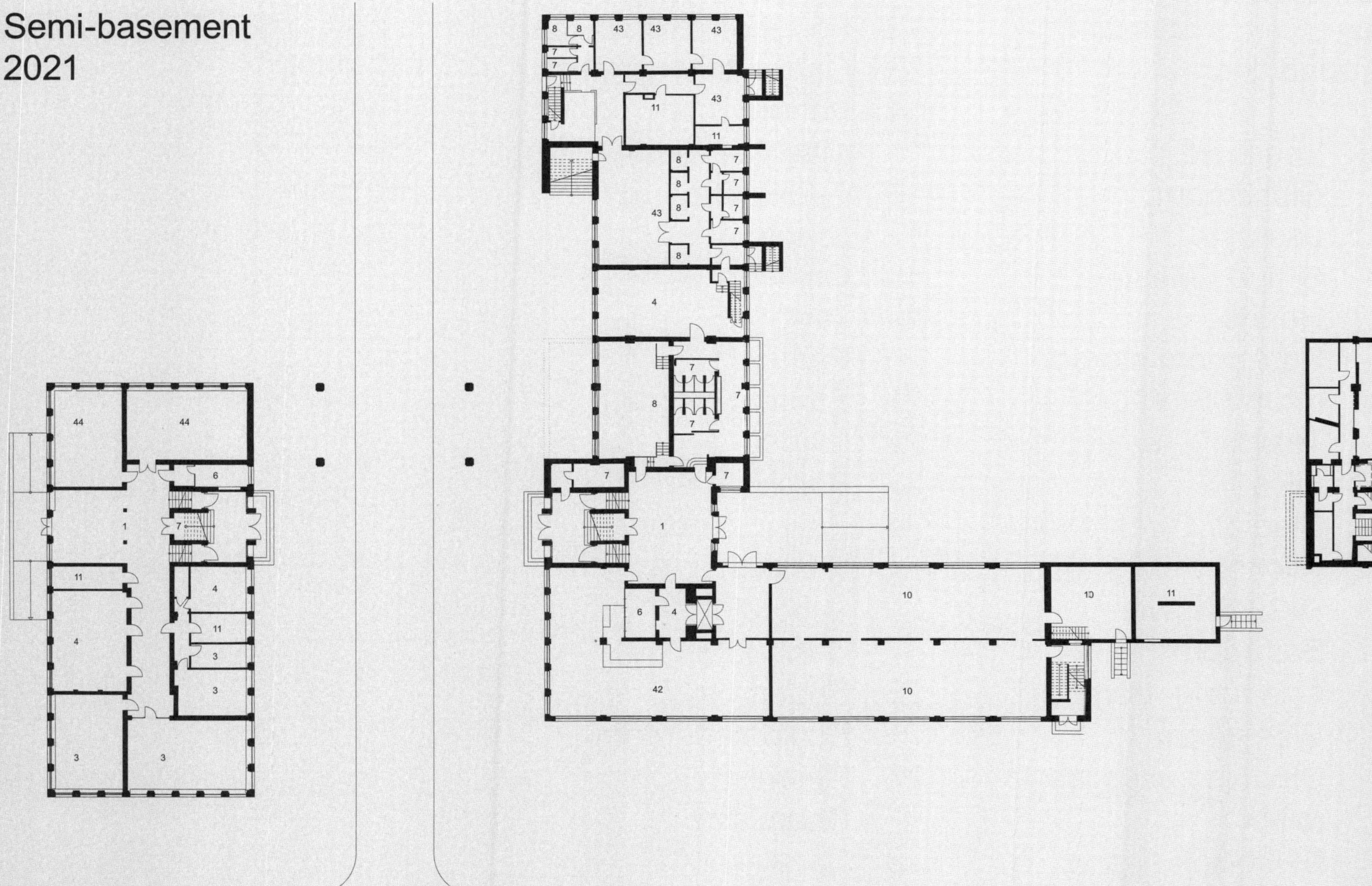

Key
Ground floor

1 Vestibule
2 Classroom / Lessons
3 Office / Masters / Heads
4 Equipment storage room / Storage / Teaching materials / Files
5 Studio / Guest room
6 Kitchen
7 WC / Shower / Bathroom
8 Changing room / Washroom
9 Cleaning supplies room
10 Exhibition space
11 Building services
12 Foreman's room
13 Carpentry workshop
14 Veneer room
15 Machine room
16 Auditorium
17 Stage
18 Canteen
19 Terrace
20 Pantry
21 Student rooms
22 Larder
23 Porch
24 Physics room / Physics
25 Laboratory / Darkroom
26 Sports hall / Equipment room
27 Chemistry room / Chemistry
28 Caretaker

Ground floor
1926

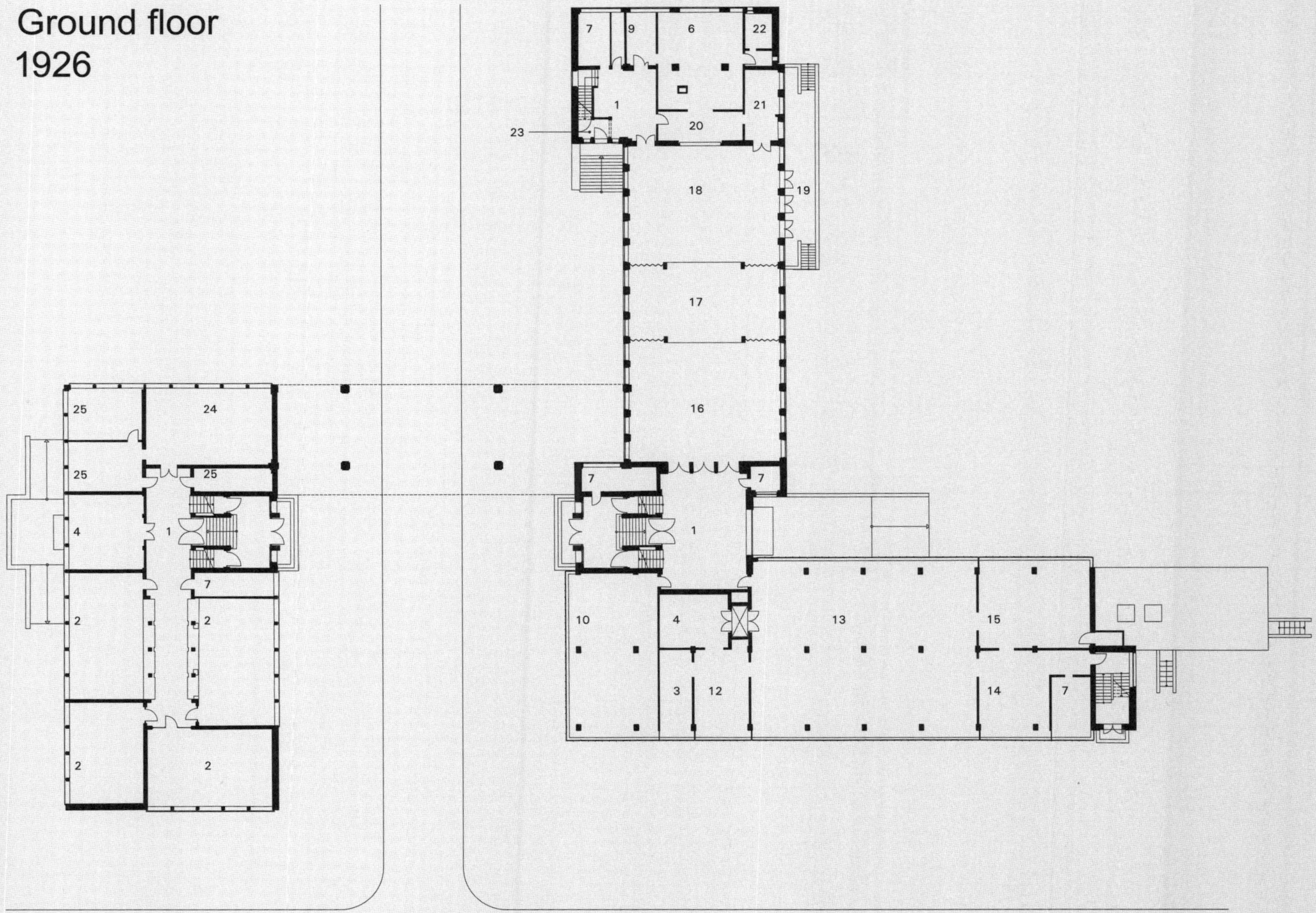

Ground floor
1964

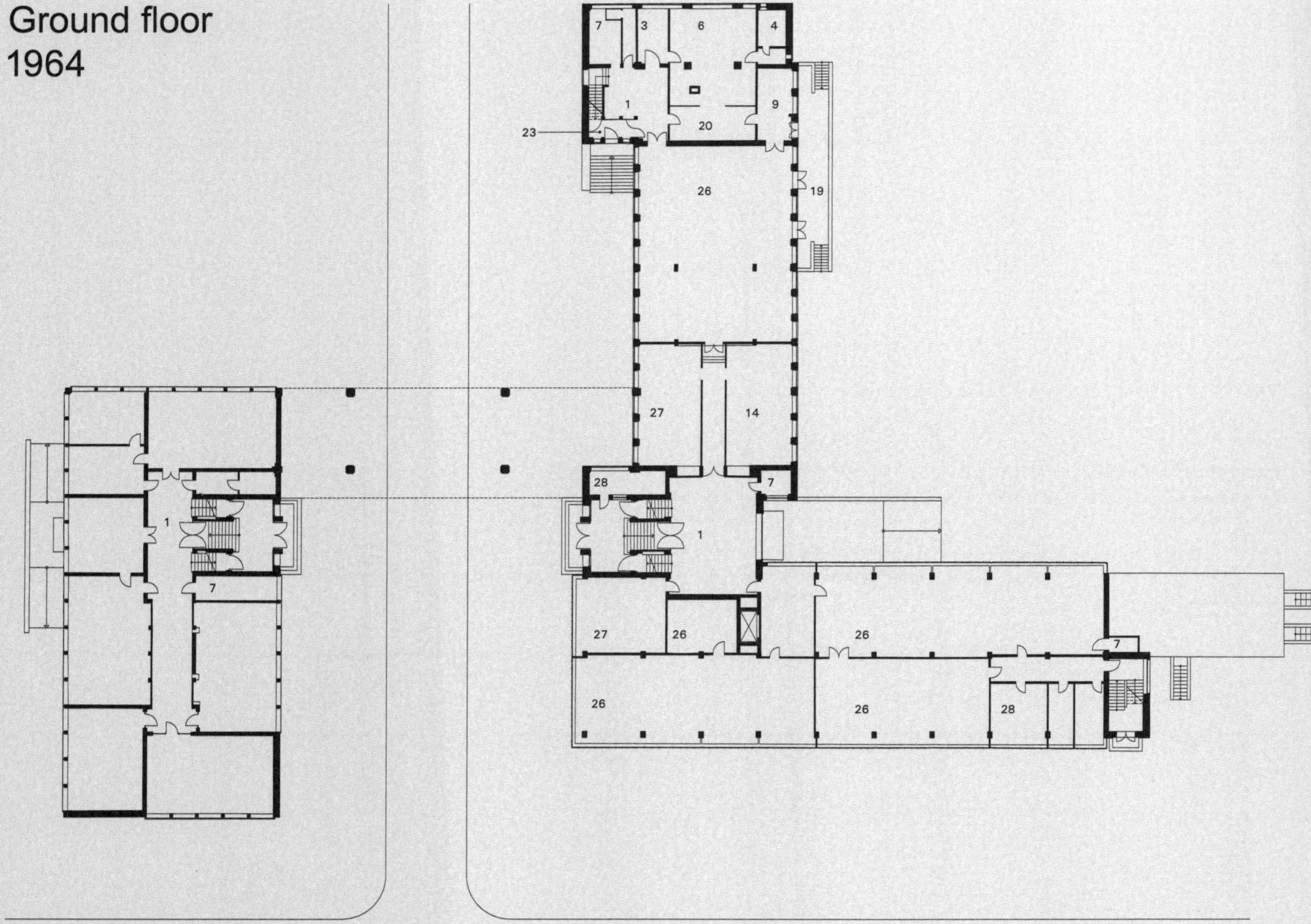

42)

Ground floor 1976

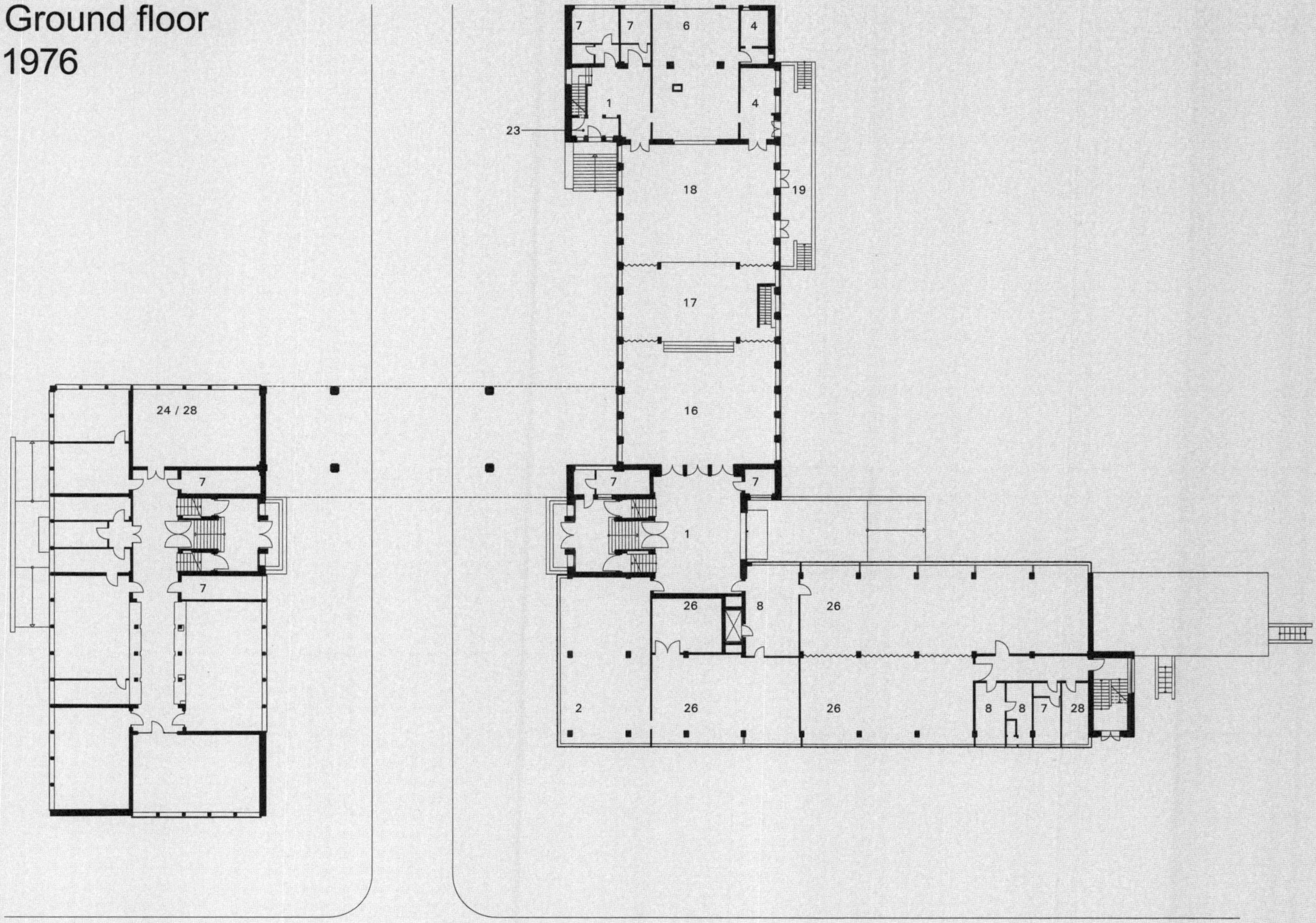

43)

Ground floor
1996

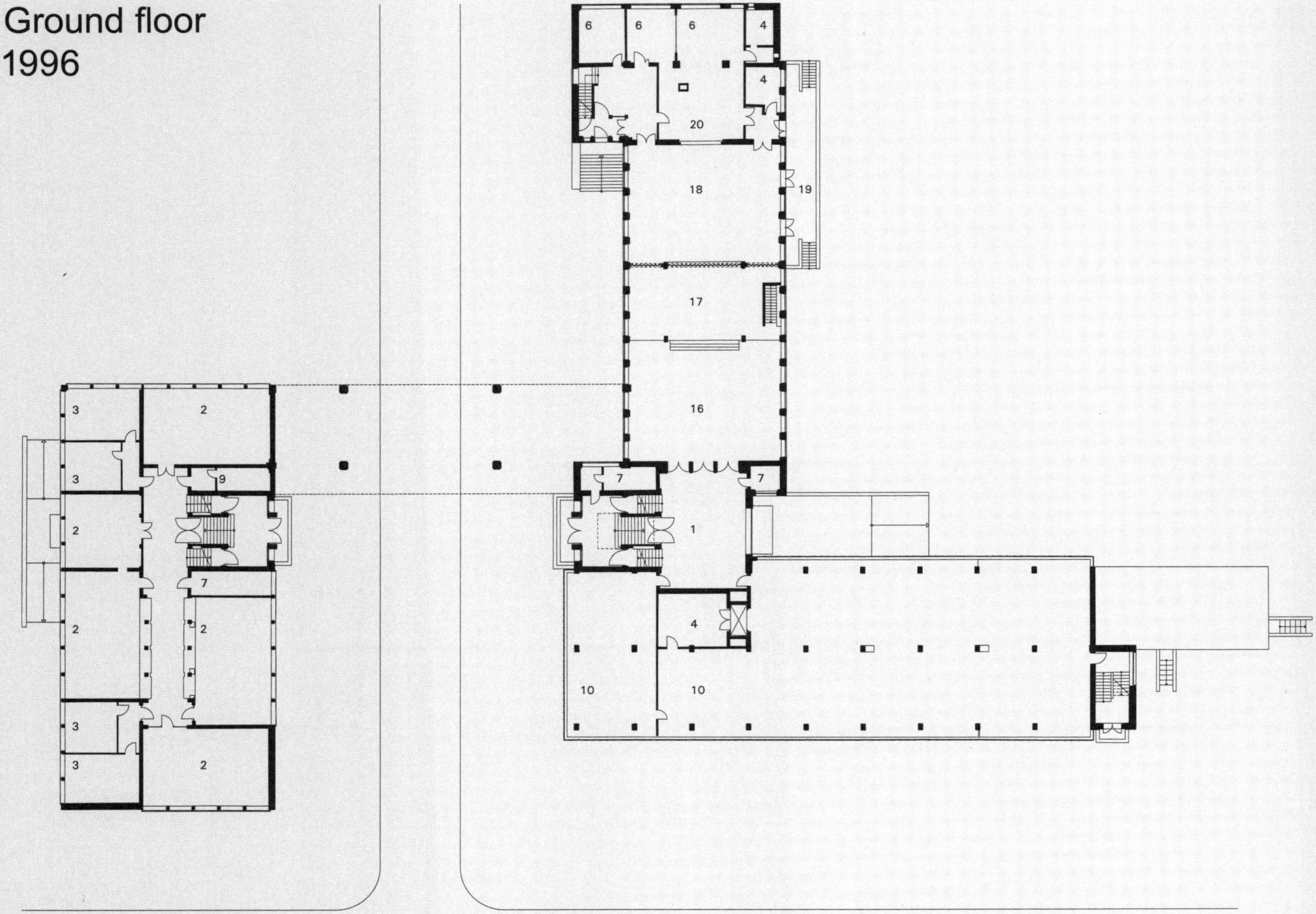

44)

Ground floor 2021

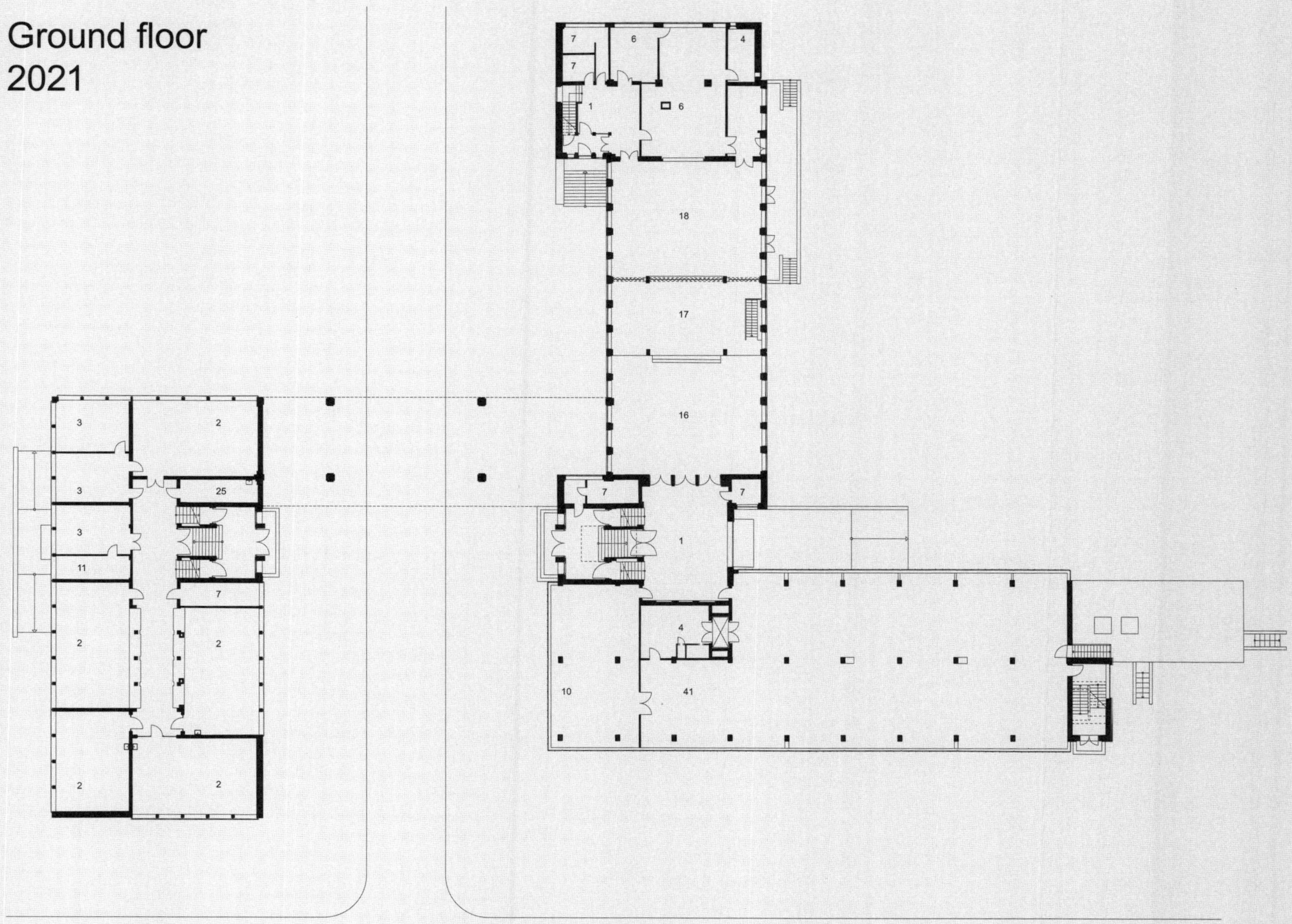

Key
First floor

1 Vestibule
2 Classroom / Lessons
3 Office / Masters / Heads
4 Equipment storage room / Storage / Teaching materials / Files
5 Studio / Guest room
6 Kitchen
7 WC / Shower / Bathroom
8 Changing room / Washroom
9 Cleaning supplies room
10 Exhibition space
11 Building services
12 Preliminary course
13 Weaving workshop
14 Classroom
15 Typing room
16 Waiting room
17 Bookkeeping
18 Bauhaus administration
19 Director's offices
20 Meeting room
21 Administration office
22 Library
23 Teachers' room
24 Storage
25 Director's room

First floor
1926

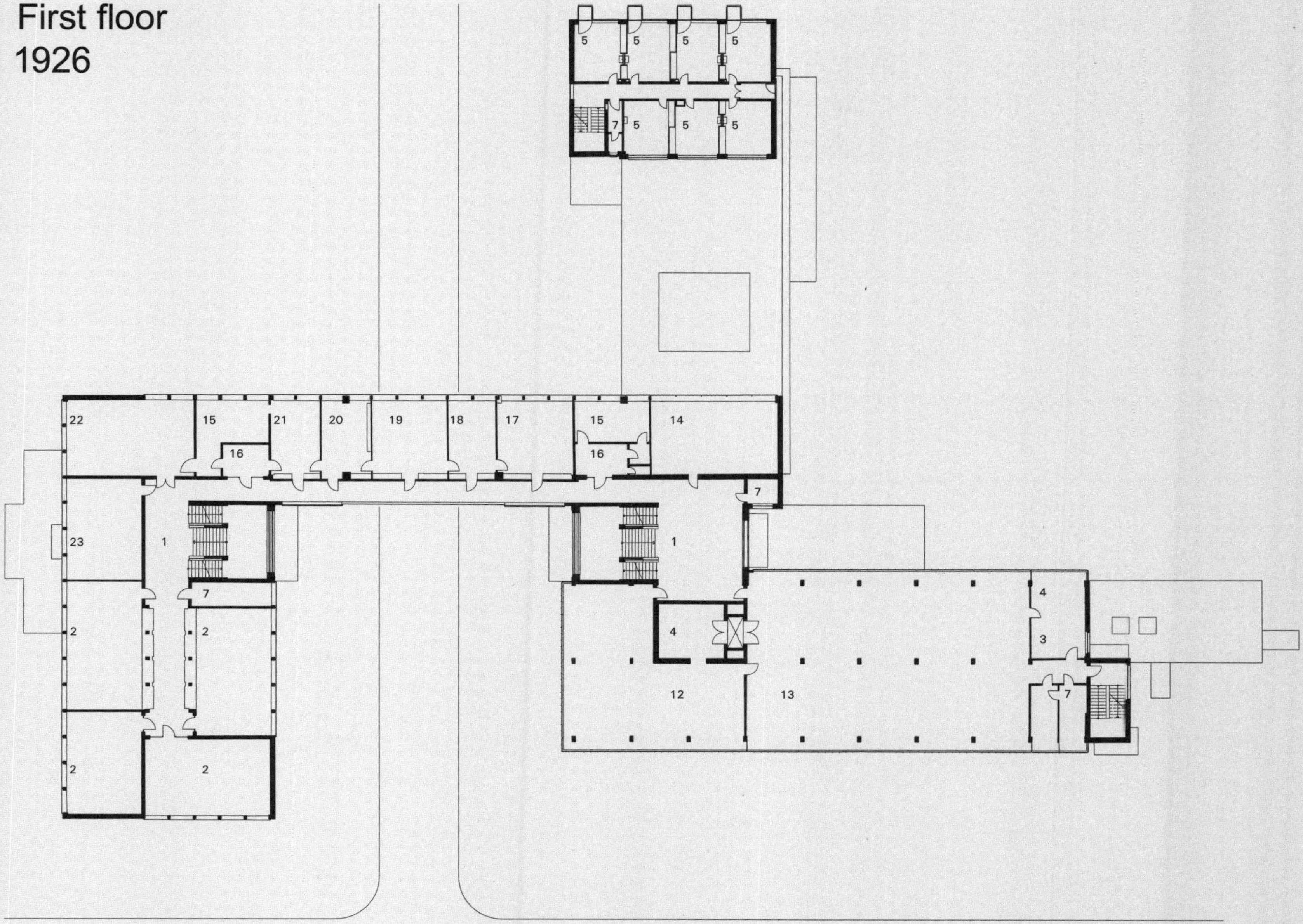

First floor
1964

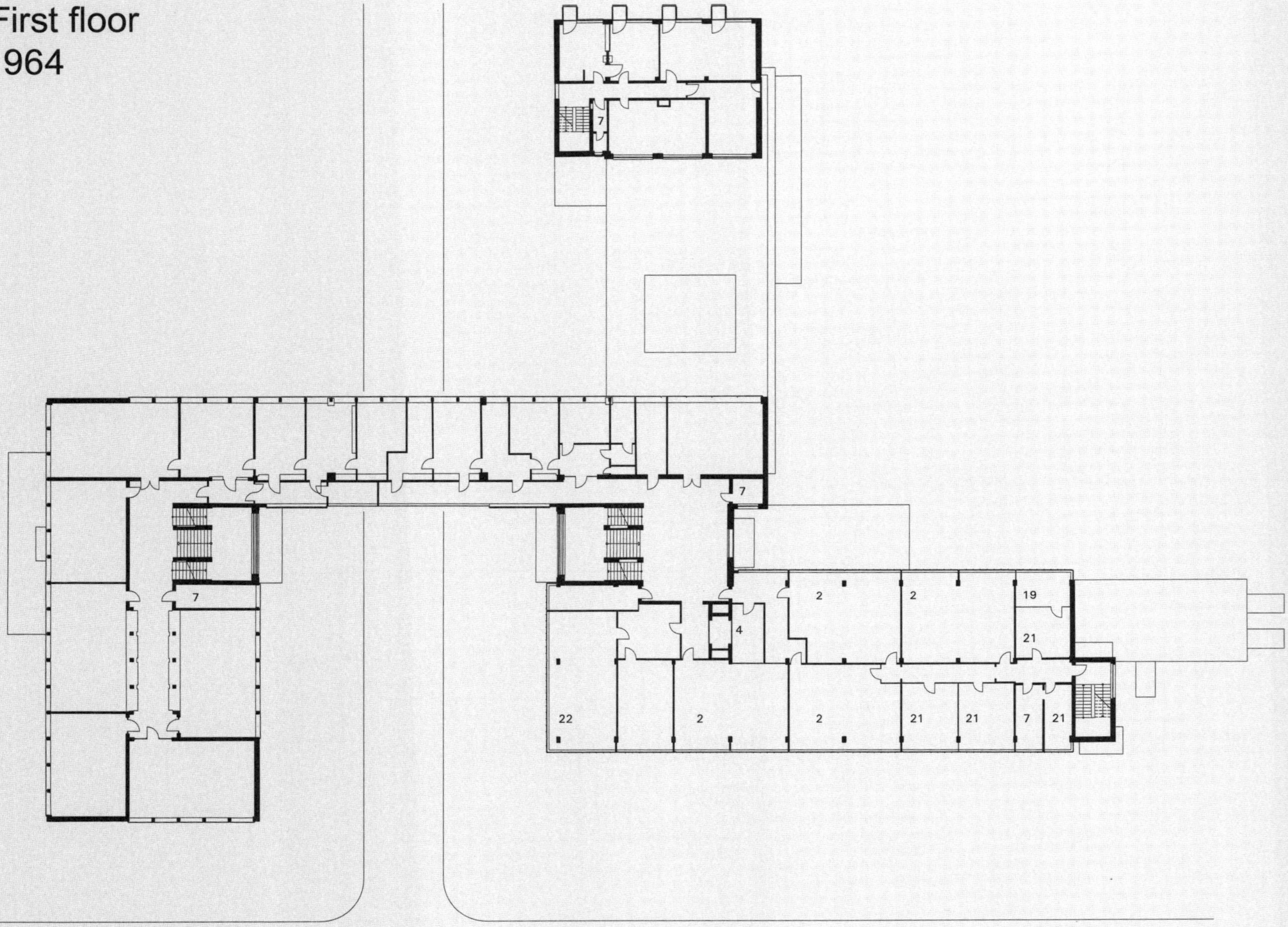

47)

First floor
1976

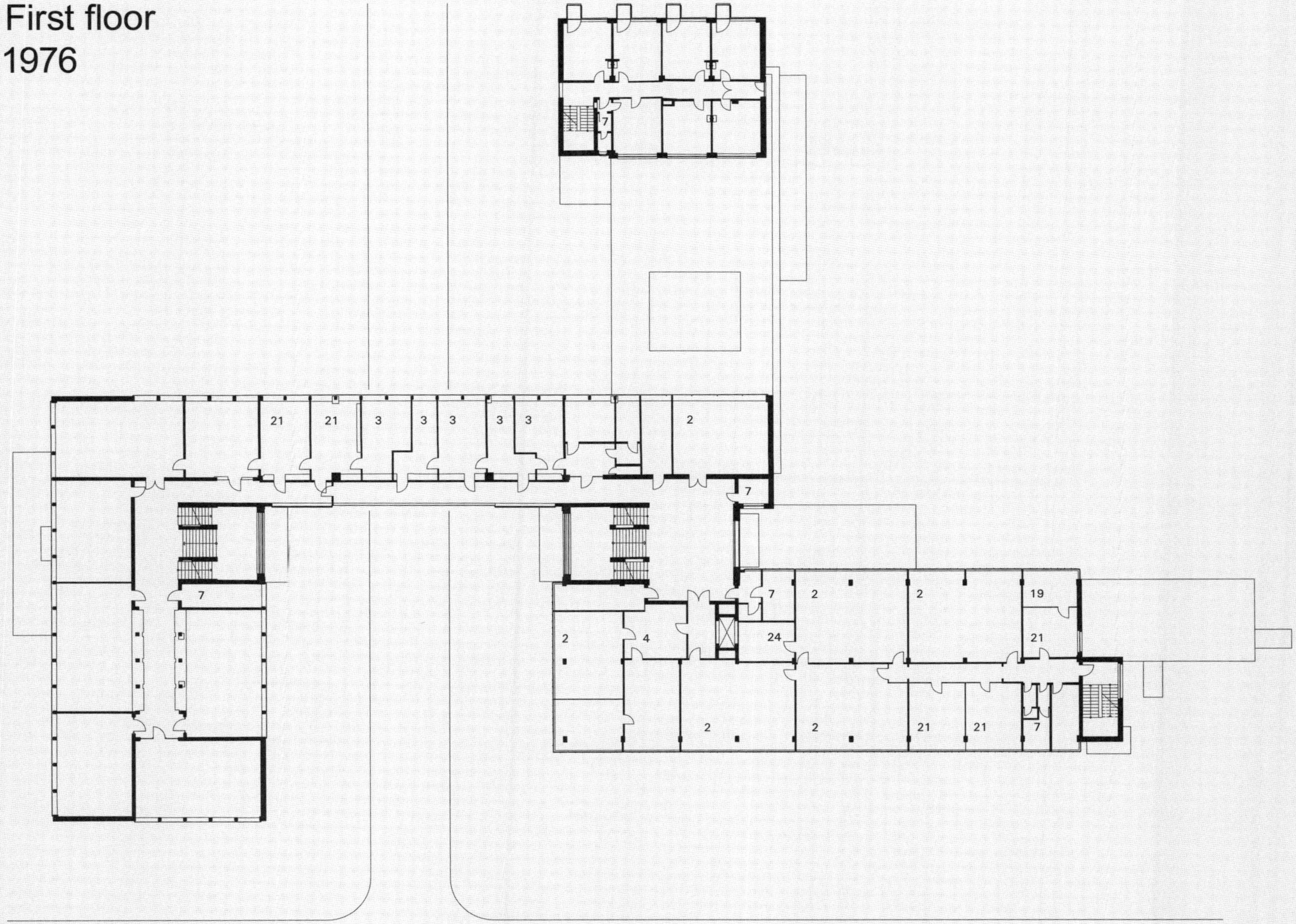

First floor
1996

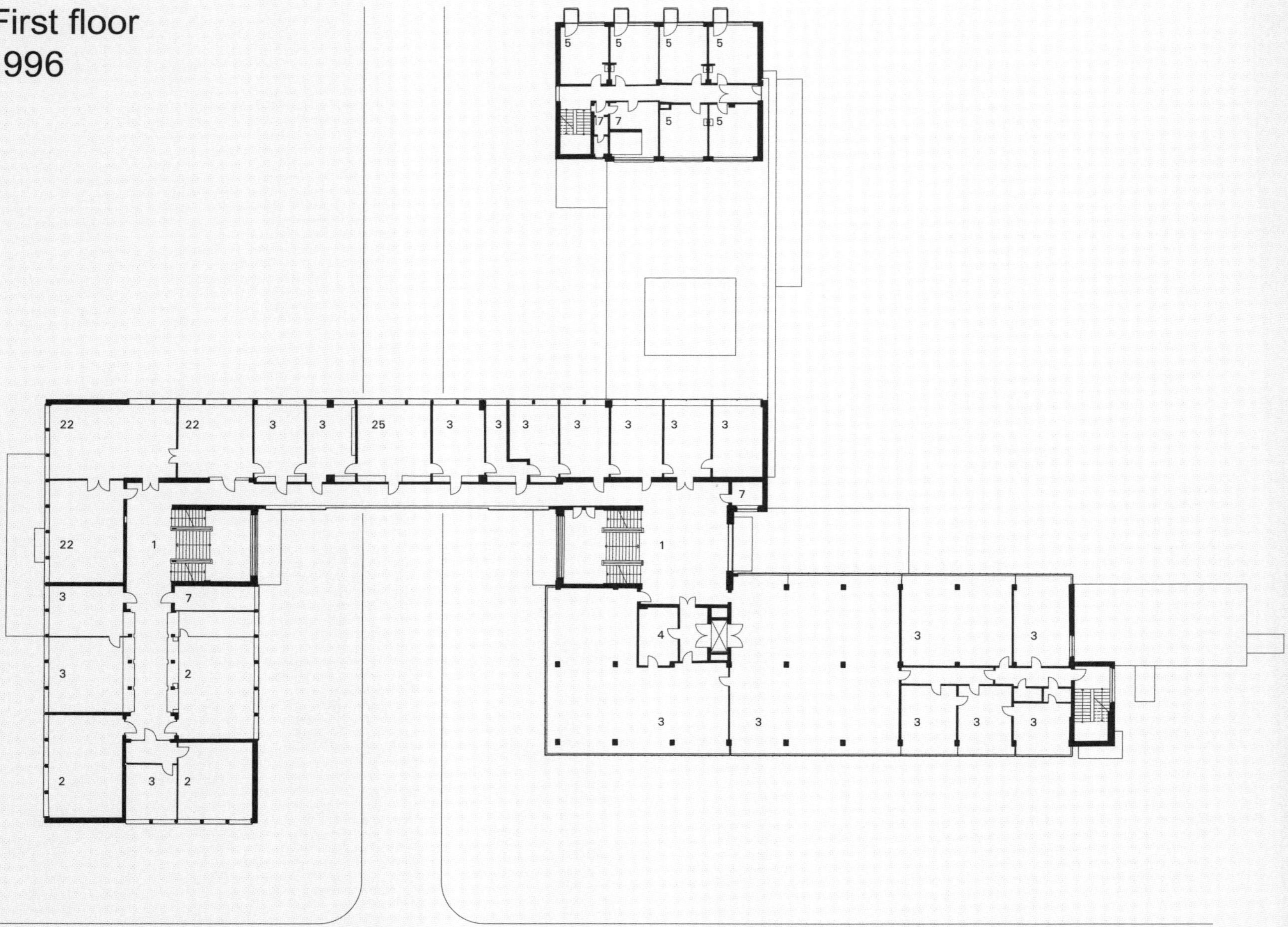

49)

First floor
2021

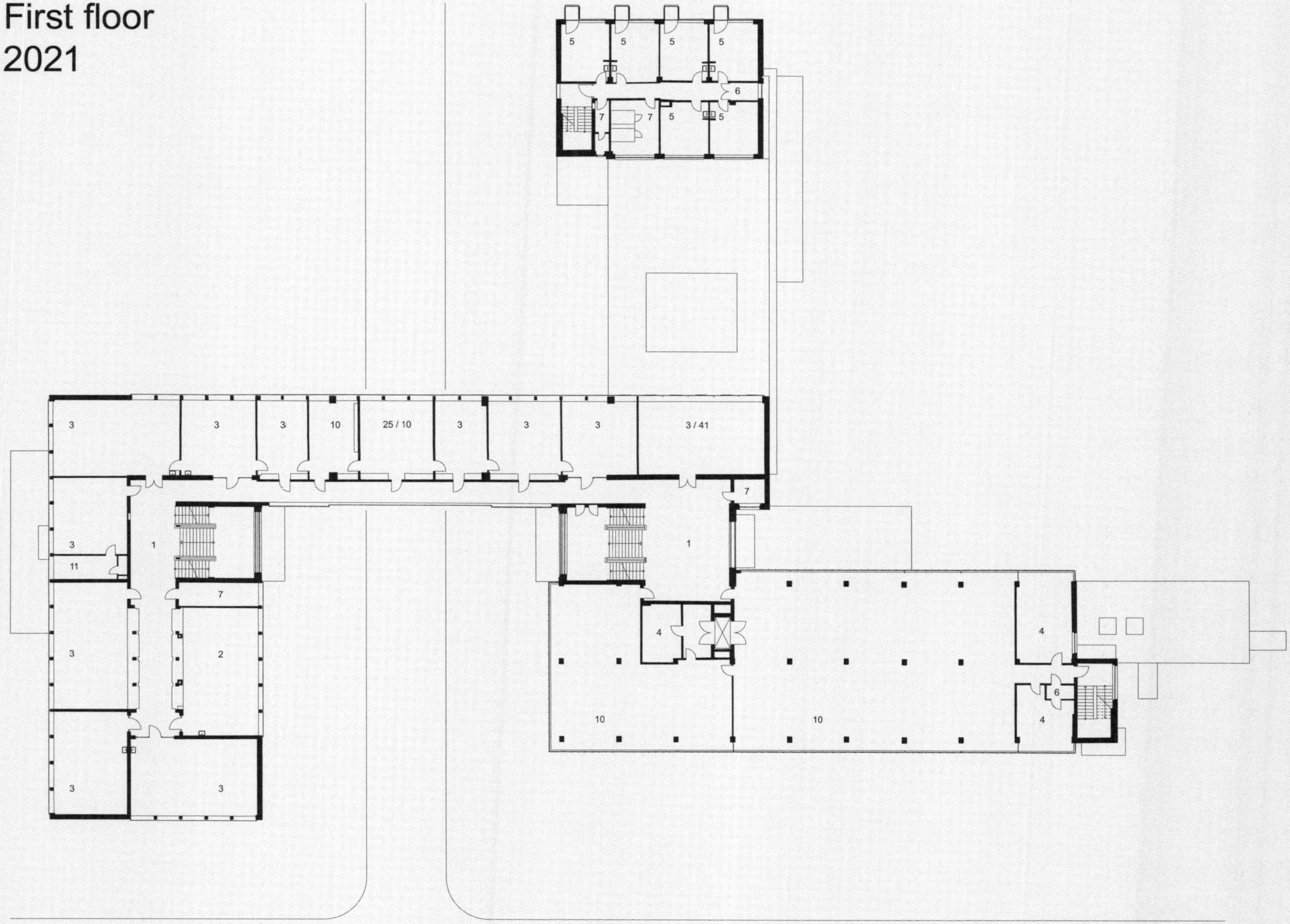

Key
Floors 2–4

1 Vestibule
2 Classroom / Lessons
3 Office / Masters / Heads
4 Equipment storage room / Storage / Teaching materials / Files
5 Studio / Guest room
6 Kitchen
7 WC / Shower / Bathroom
8 Changing room / Washroom
9 Cleaning supplies room
10 Exhibition space
11 Building services
12 Grinding room
13 Electroplating
14 Metal workshop
15 Smithy
16 Machine room
17 Cloakroom
18 Wall painting workshop
19 Paint shop
20 Lecture room
21 Architecture room
22 Storage space

Floors 2–4
1926

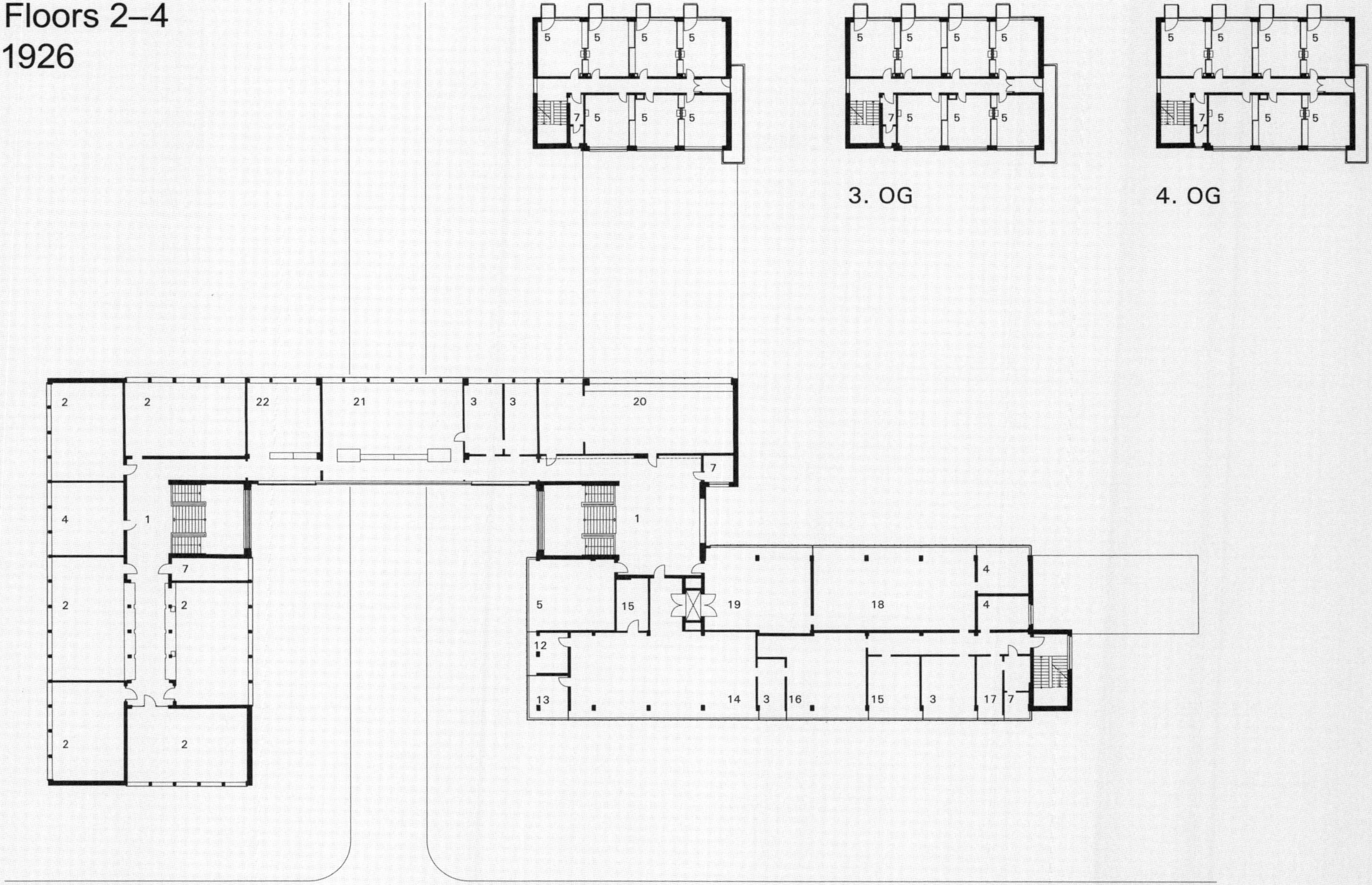

Floors 2–4
1964

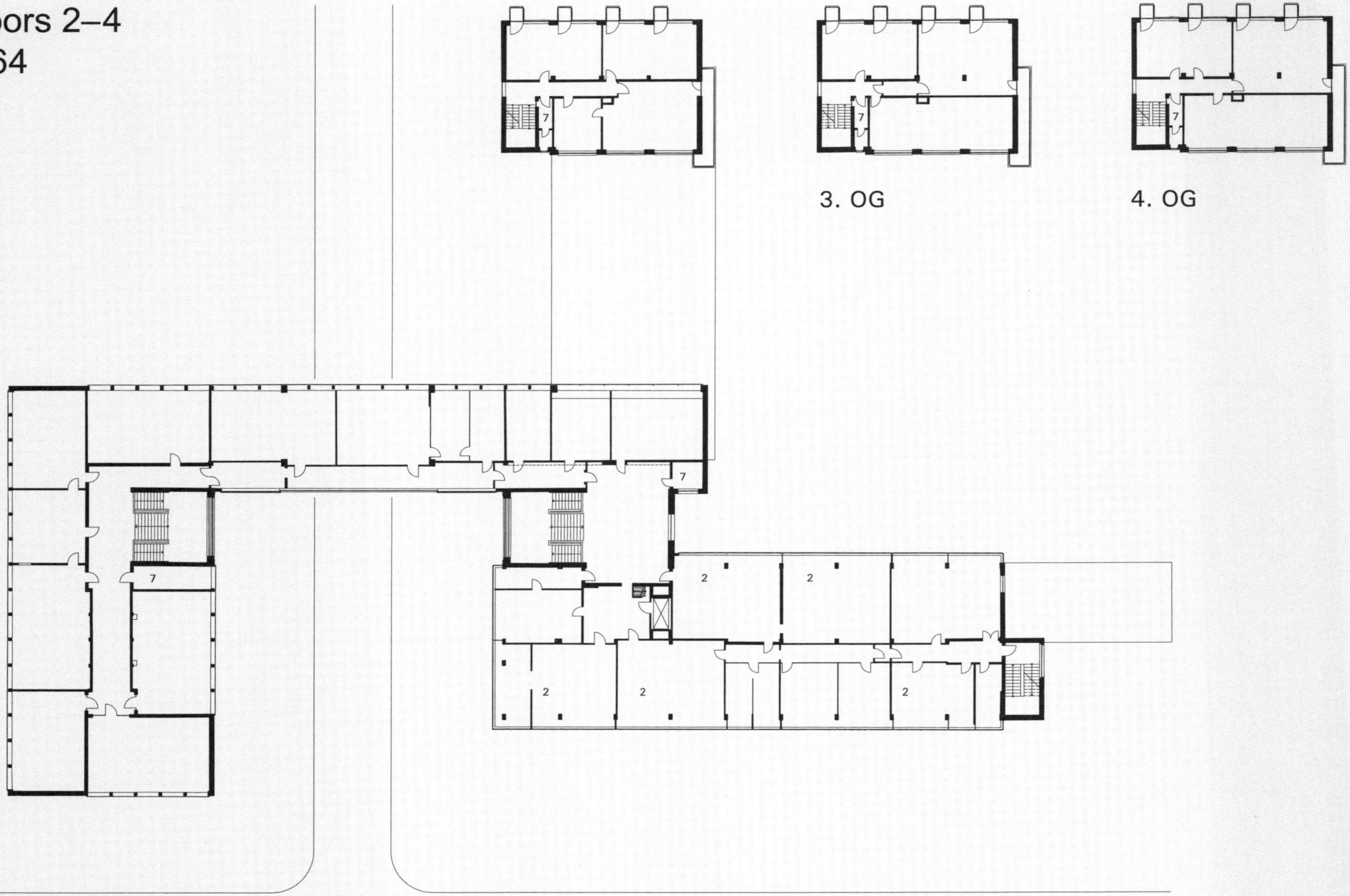

52)

Floors 2–4
1976

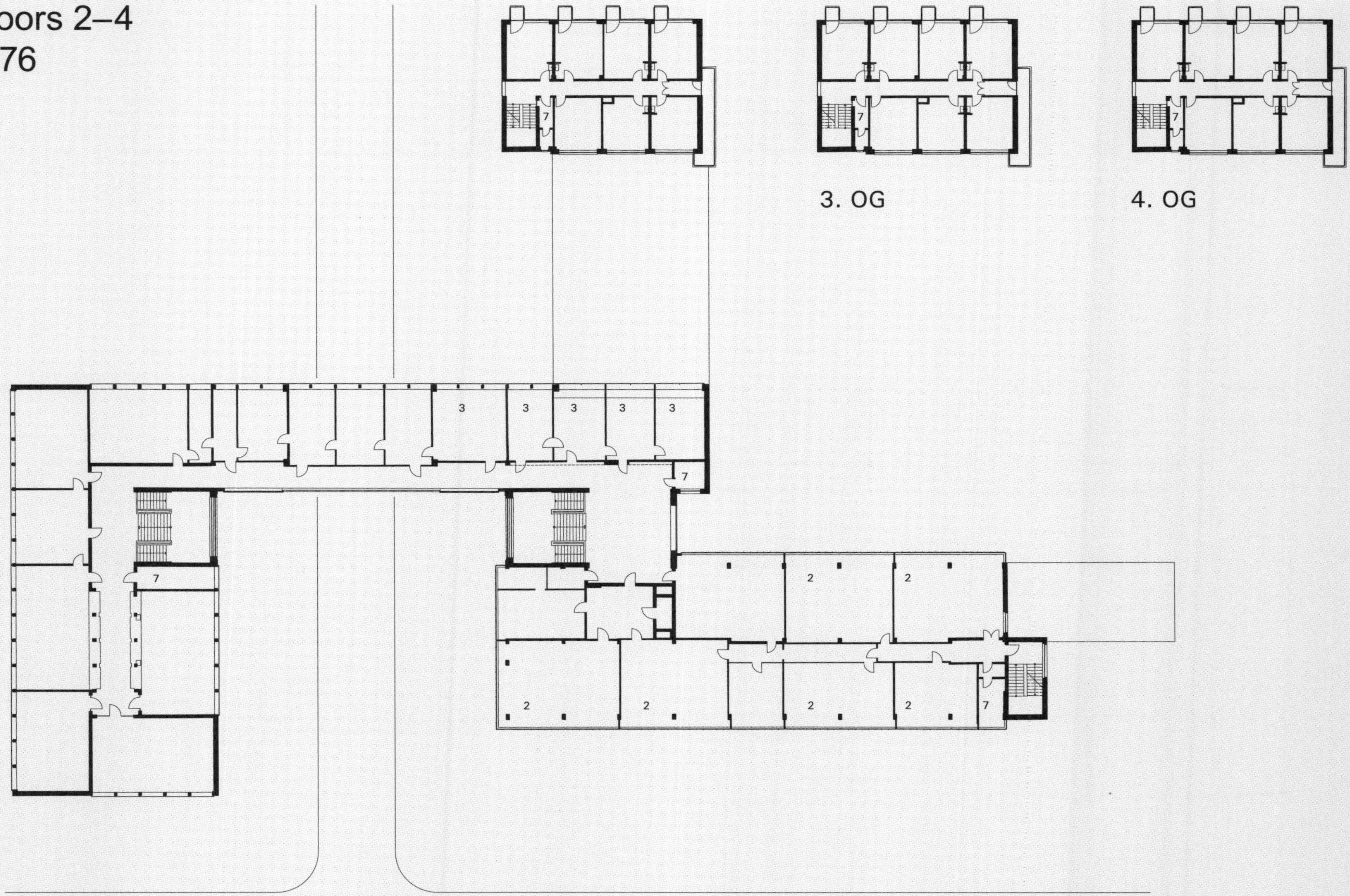

Floors 2–4
1996

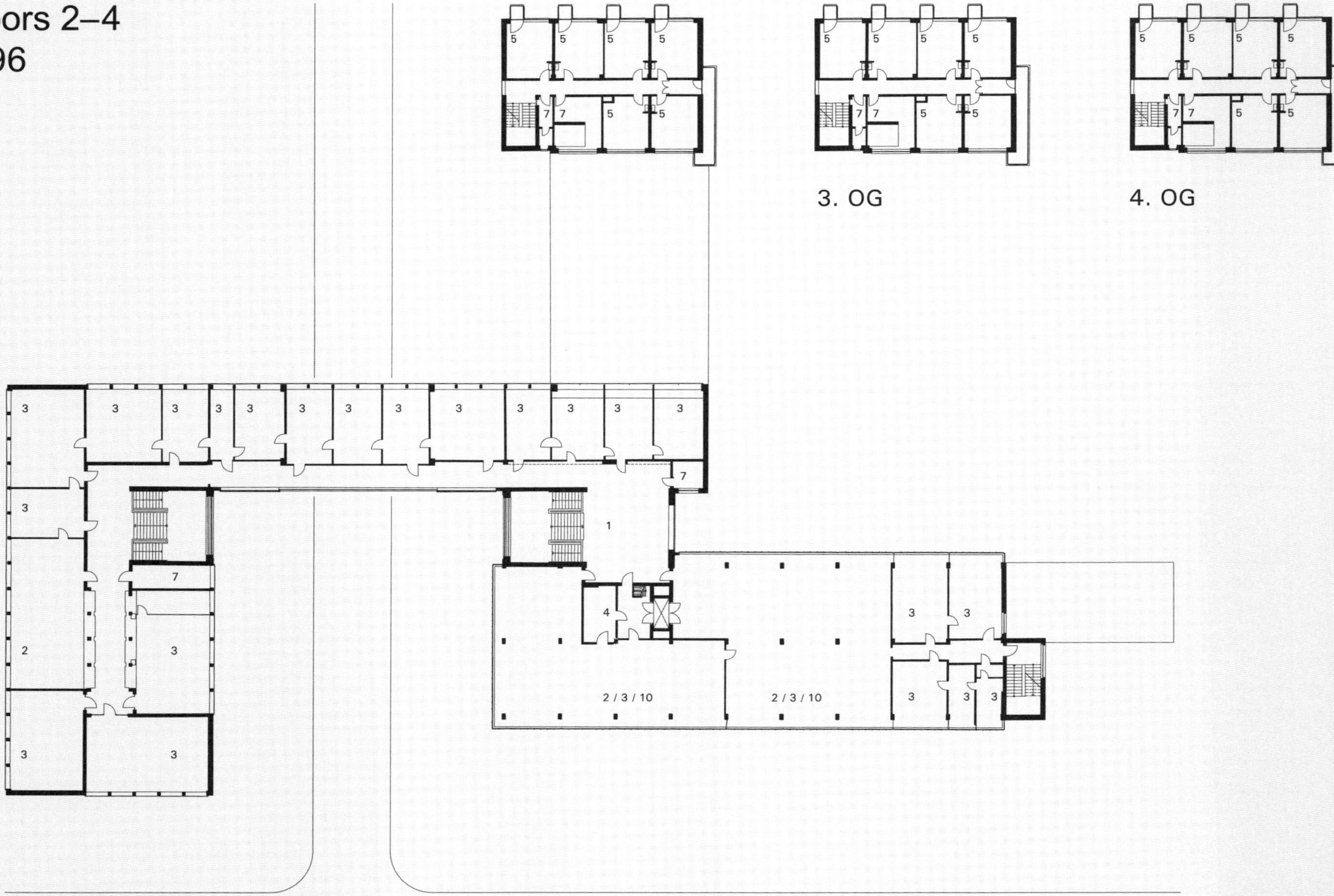

54)

Floors 2–4
2021

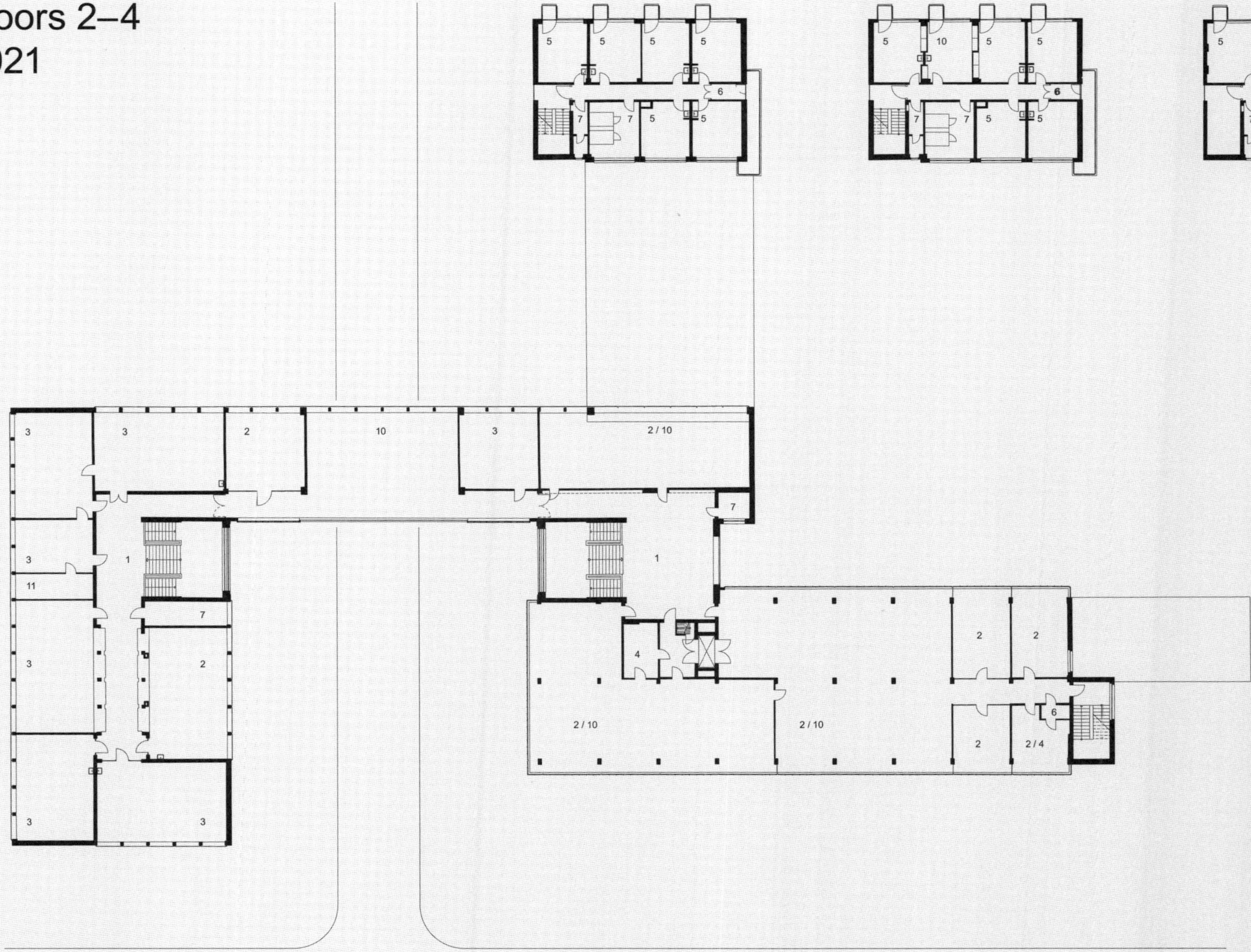

Elevations and sections 2021

56)
West elevation, 2021

57)
West elevation and section of north wing and workshop wing, 2021

58)
West elevation and section of staircases, 2021

59)
West elevation and section of connecting building, 2021

56)

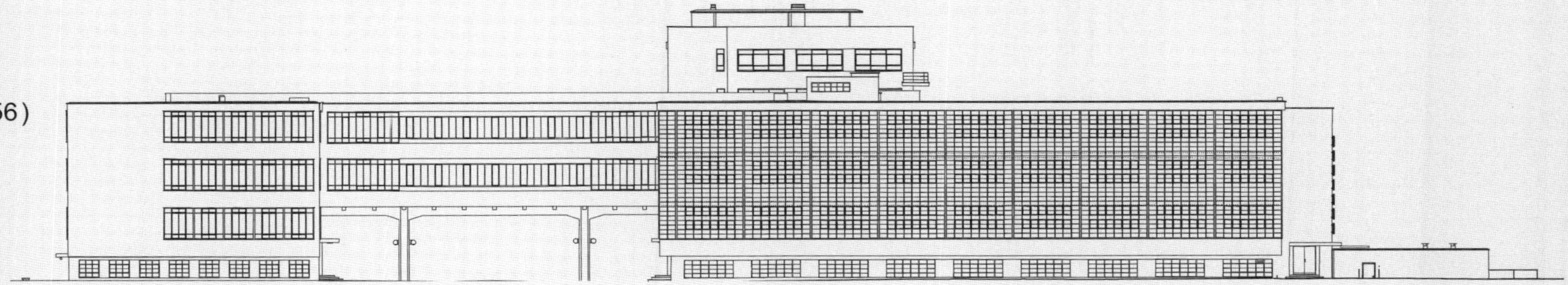

57)

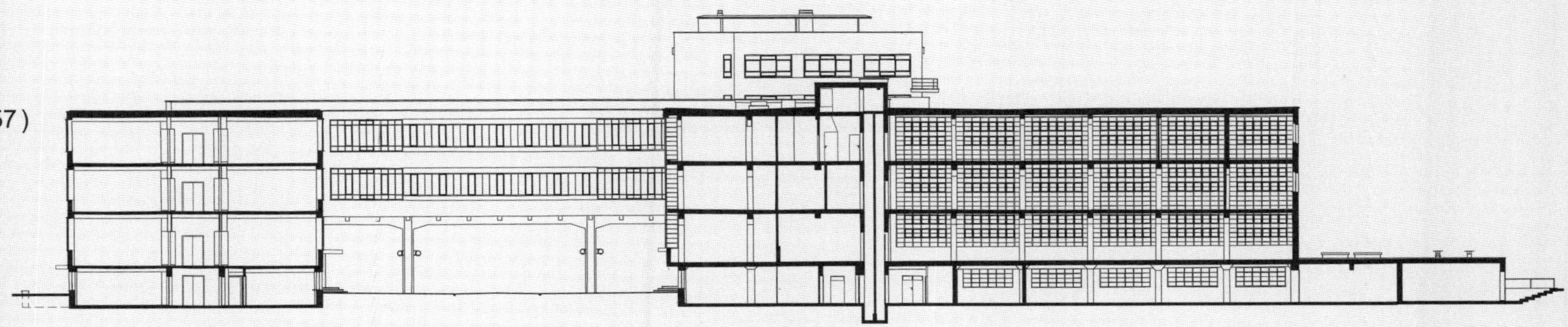

58)

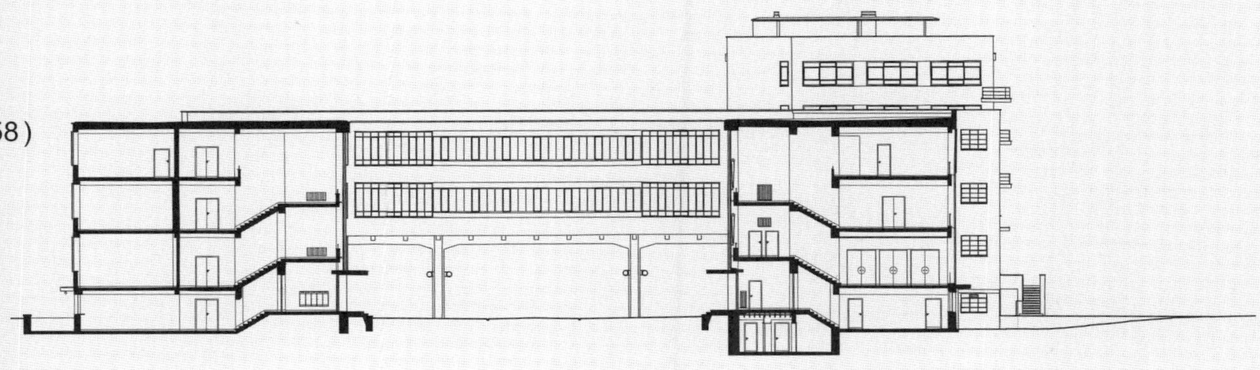

59)

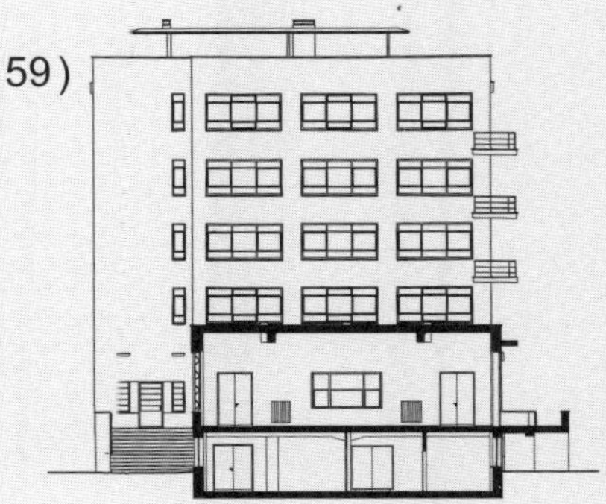

60)

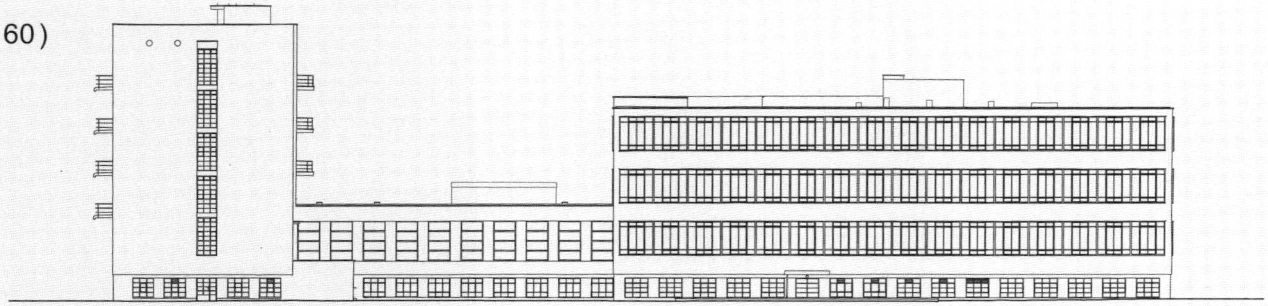

61)

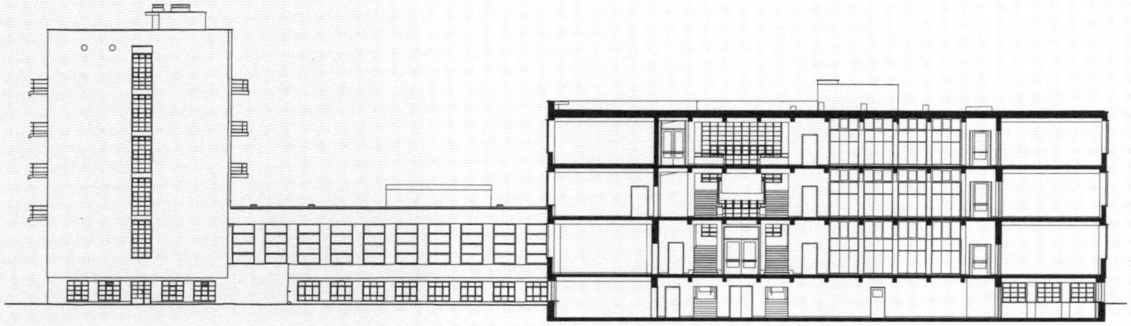

62)

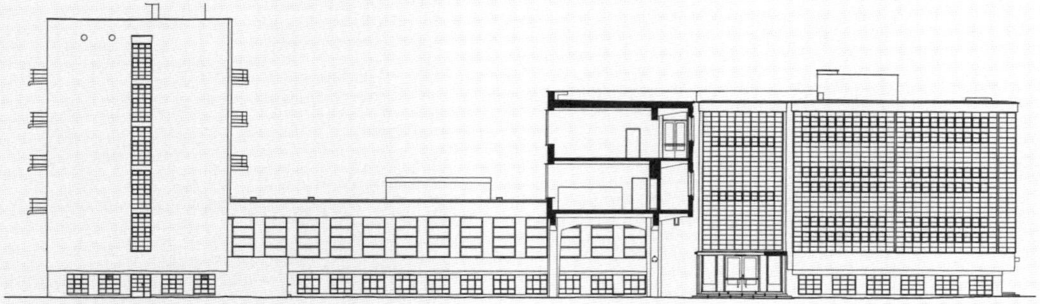

63)

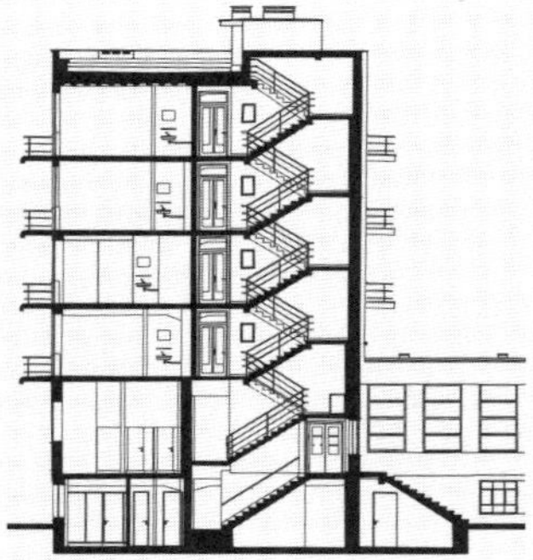

60)
North elevation, 2021

61)
North elevation and section of north wing, 2021

62)
North elevation and section of bridge, 2021

63)
Section of studio building, 2021

64)
East elevation, 2021

65)
East elevation and section of connecting building, 2021

66)
East elevation and section of staircases, 2021

64)

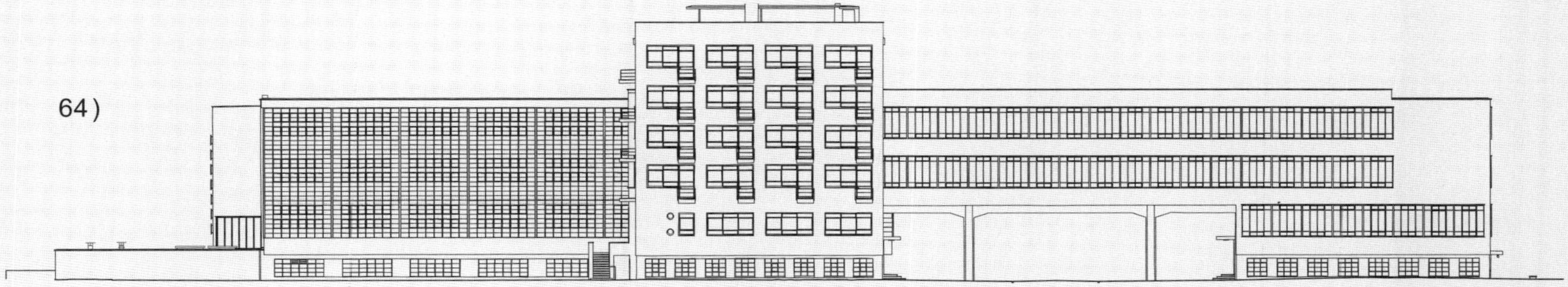

65)

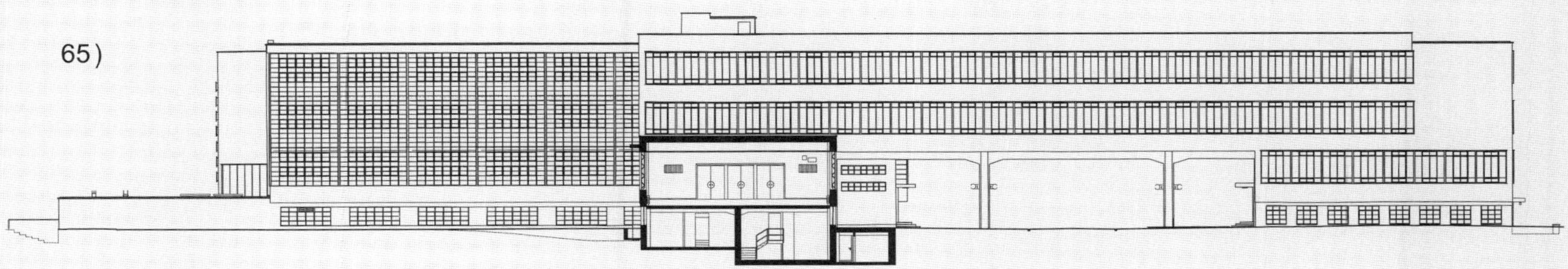

66)

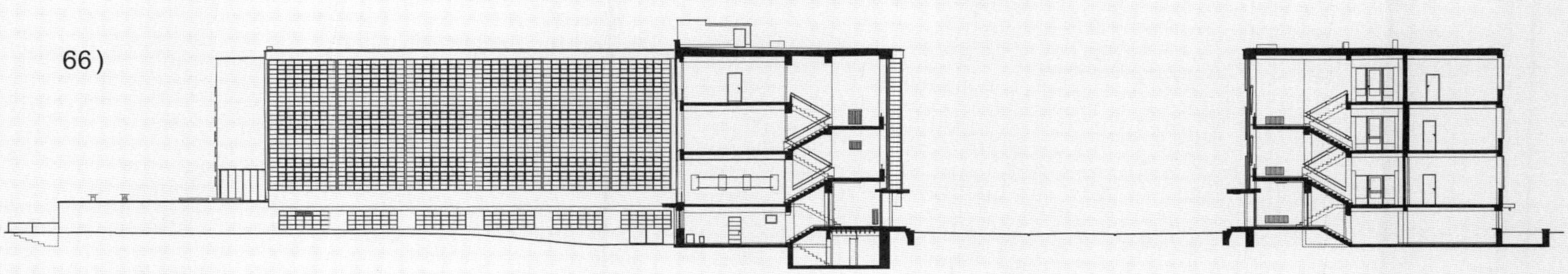

67)

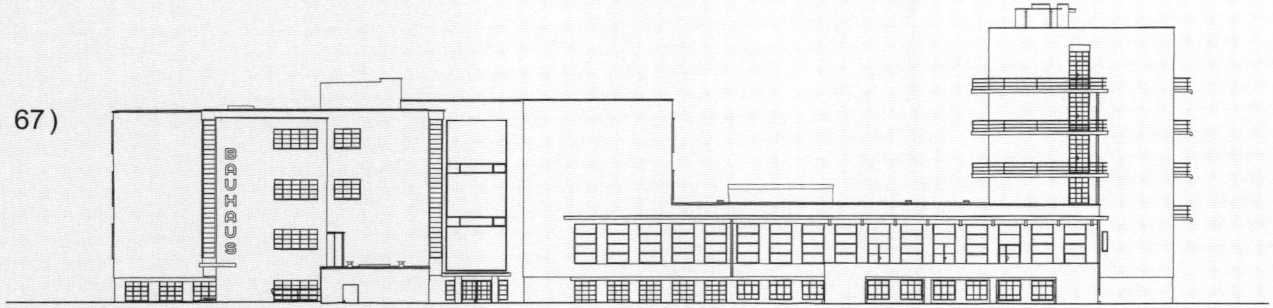

68)

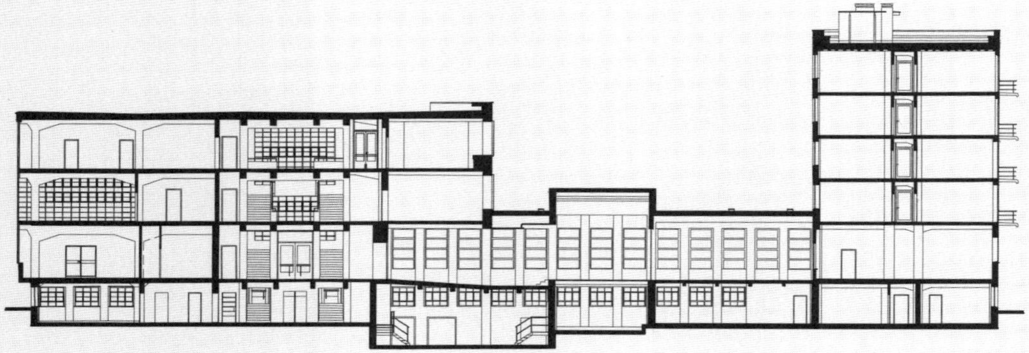

69)

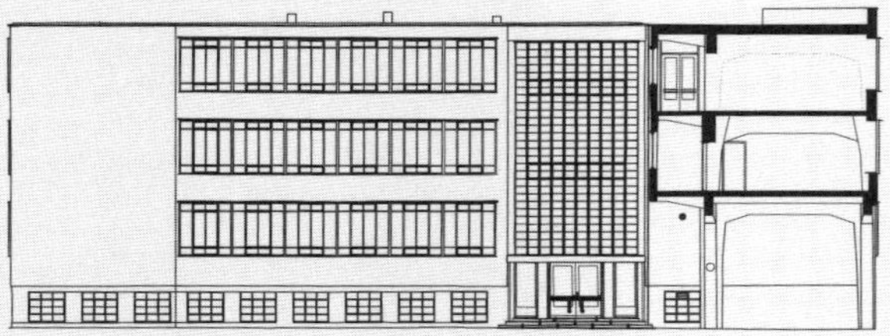

67)
South elevation, 2021

68)
Section of workshop wing, connecting building, and studio building, 2021

69)
South elevation and section of bridge, 2021

Building Shell

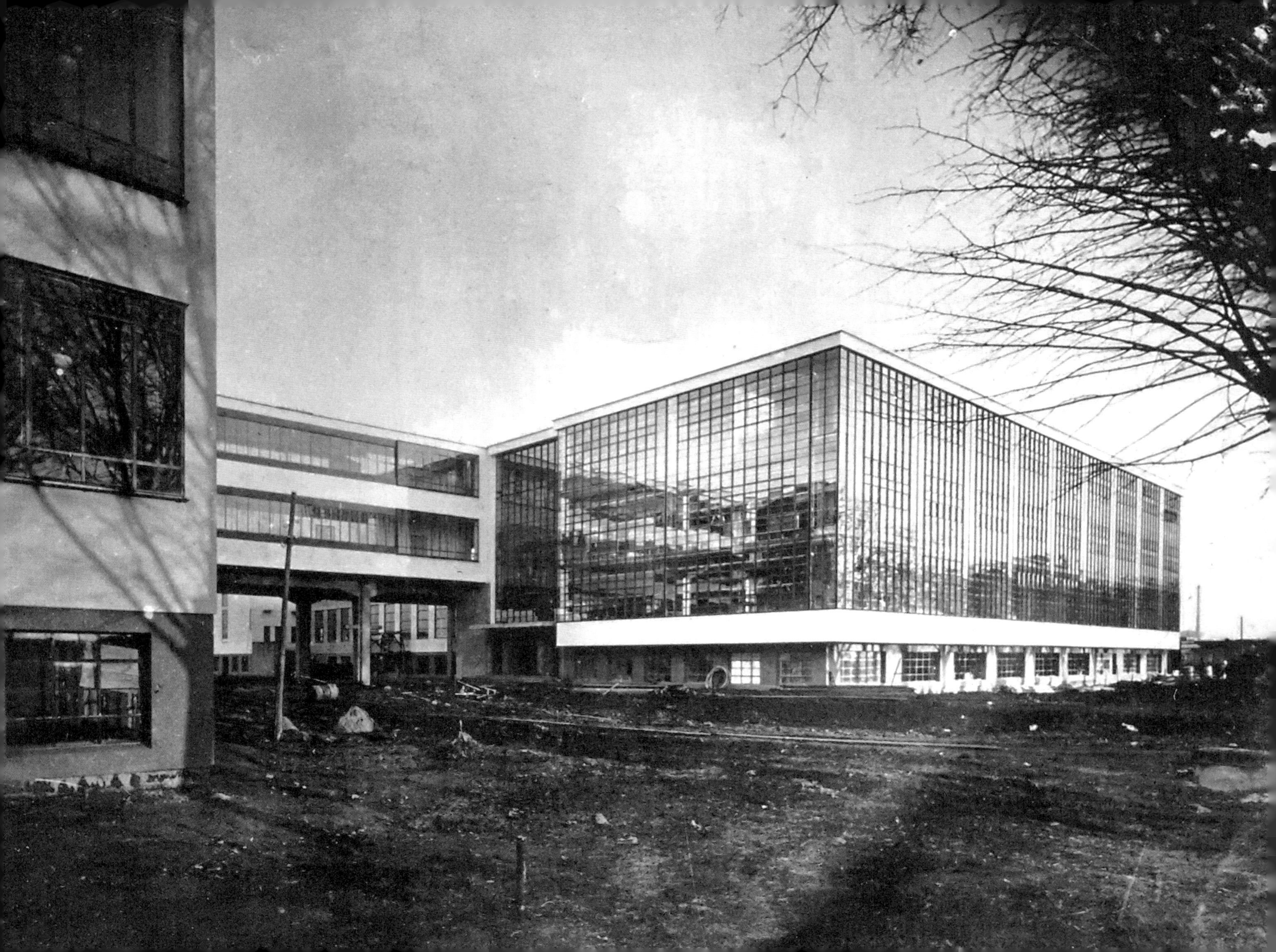

Building Shell
Glass Façades

The glass façades of the Bauhaus Building are fundamentally important to the architecture. They not only fulfil a practical purpose, but also define the character and aesthetics of the building. Not least due to its unique curtain wall, the building had a decisive influence on the evolution of architecture in the twentieth century and remains a source of fascination today.

In association with the configuration of the Bauhaus Building, the glass façades set up multi-layered connections between the building parts and between the interiors and exteriors: views in from the outside, out from the inside, and from one building part to another. In the process, divisions between public, semi-public, and private areas dissolve. The interior-exterior interface is notably shaped by the finely wrought window constructions, which thus gain a vital role in the spatial and aesthetic concept. With the transparency and reflections of the glazed surfaces, these façades contribute to the complexity of the connections between spatial layers and become characteristic components of the architecture. Walter Gropius describes his design and his approach to space as follows: 'an altered sense of space, which reflects the movement, the communication of our time in more supple built structures and spaces, while seeking to maintain the connection between the interior and the surroundings that enclosing walls negate.'[1]

In spatial design terms, the transparency of glass enables us not only to see through it, but also to perceive several spatial layers simultaneously. The reflections of light on the glass surfaces, the mirroring of the building parts and the surroundings add further layers. In addition, the reflected objects are transformed in many and varied ways by the glass panes, especially in the moveable parts of the window construction. The simultaneous views of the façade, of interiors and exteriors, of reflections of areas outside the observer's field of vision, enable diverse spatial realities to interact. Bauhaus master László Moholy-Nagy describes this as follows: 'Fenestrations produced the inward and outward reflections of the windows. It is no longer possible to keep apart the inside and outside. The mass of the wall, at which all the "outside" previously stopped, is now dissolved and lets the surroundings now into the building.'[2] As components fundamental to the architecture, the glass façades are not intended to divide as much as connect interior and exterior, thus help to establish a new sense of space.

The many-faceted play of light and shadows thrown onto the white plaster surfaces or smooth floors through the glass façades further adds to the appeal of this singular building. The constantly fluctuating incident light, the time of day and year, create a flow of fascinating images that also extend outside the building through the light reflections thrown onto the asphalt.

Gropius therefore attached great value to the excellence of the steel construction for the glass façades and to the quality of the glazed surfaces, for which he used polished plate glass. Its particular property is that it provides clear, undistorted views and reflections achieved through a complex manufacturing process, during which the material was ground and polished. Although this type of glass was extremely expensive, Gropius was able to extract favourable terms or even donations of

70)
View from the west, 1926

71)

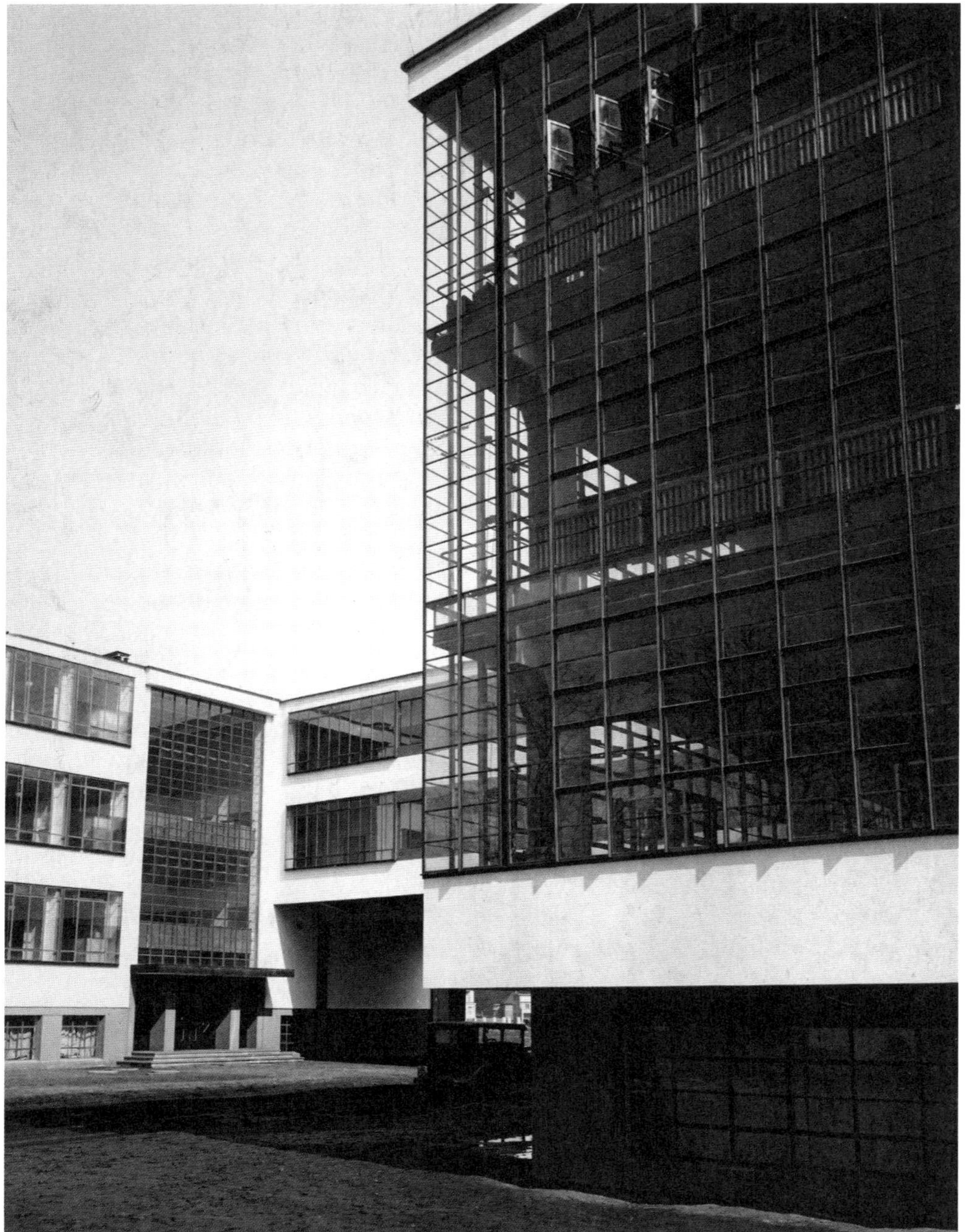

material. As Erich Blunck notes in the *Deutsche Bauzeitung* in 1927, 'the glass was supplied at preferential rates'.[3] Ise Gropius also notes in her diary: 'visit from professor schröter from the plate glass association. very important matter for us. the construction looked good and he even pledged the plate glass not yet donated for the bauhaus part of the new building.'[4] White float glass, which became widespread from the nineteen-sixties, has similar properties and is currently used in the Bauhaus Building.

71)
Glass façades, ca. 1927

72)
Glass façade, transparency and reflections, 2021

73)
Light and shadows in the workshop wing, 2018

72)

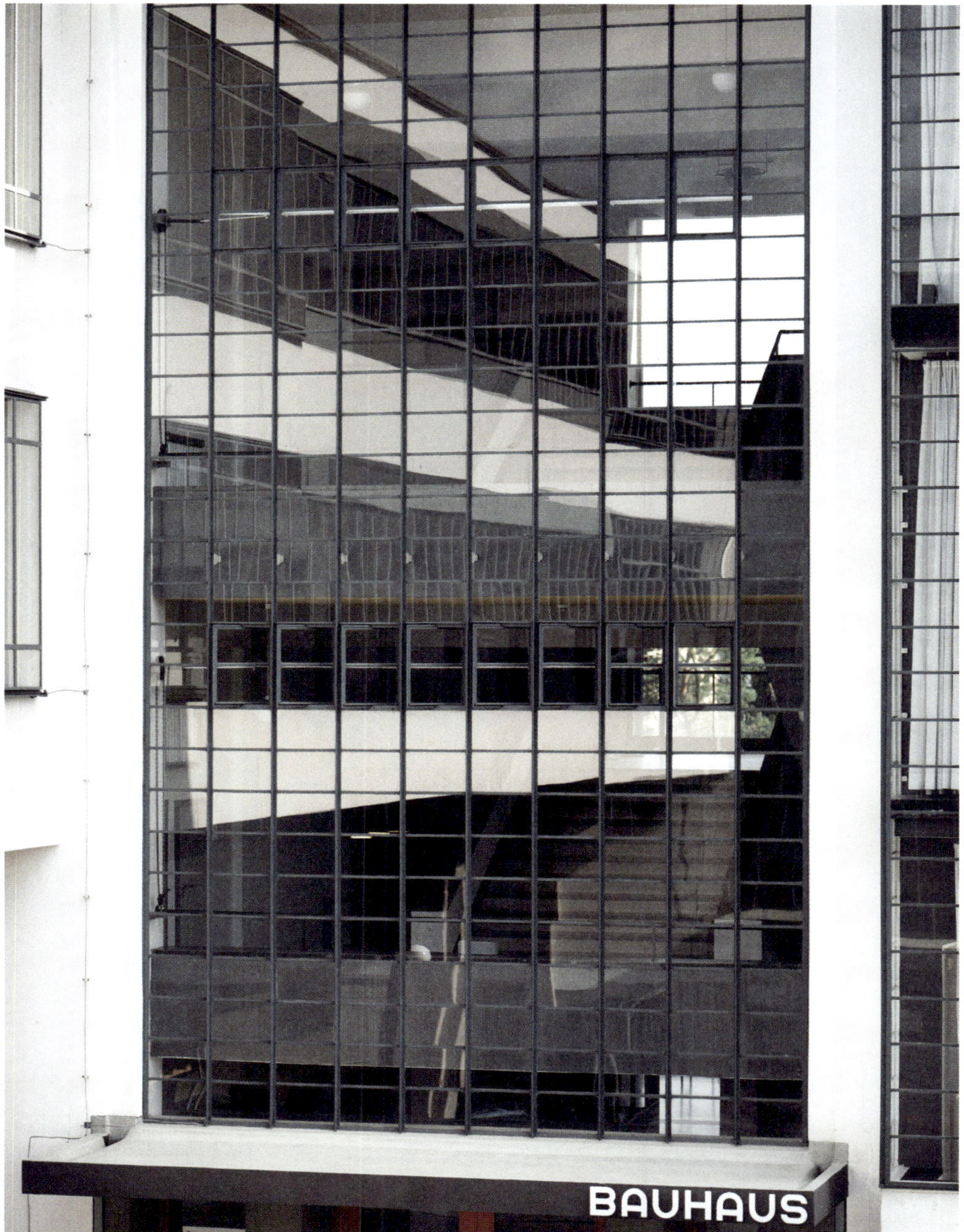

73)

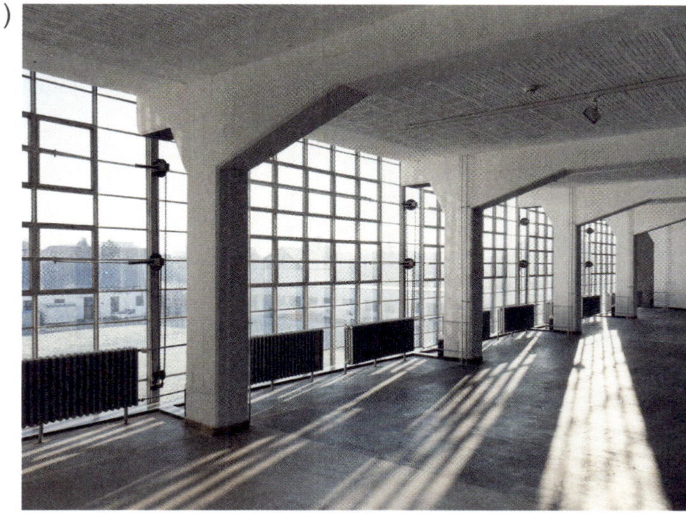

74)

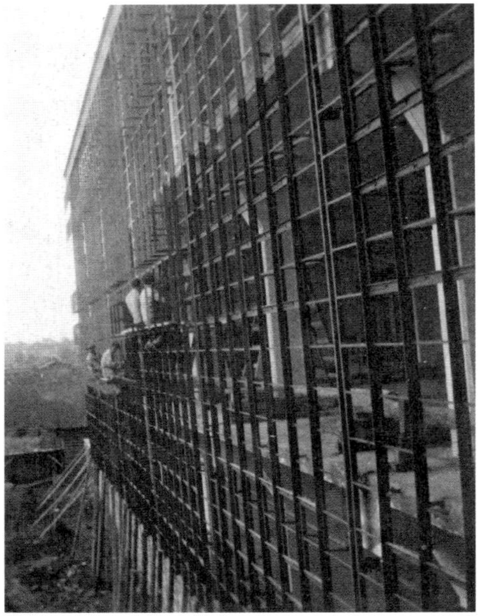

75)

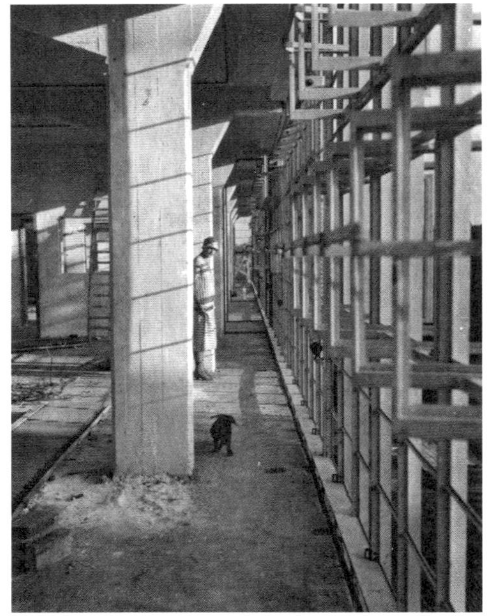

74)
Installation of the curtain wall, 1926

75)
Ise Gropius on the building site standing next to the curtain wall in the workshop wing, 1926

76)
Workshop wing with fragments of the original curtain wall, 1970

76)

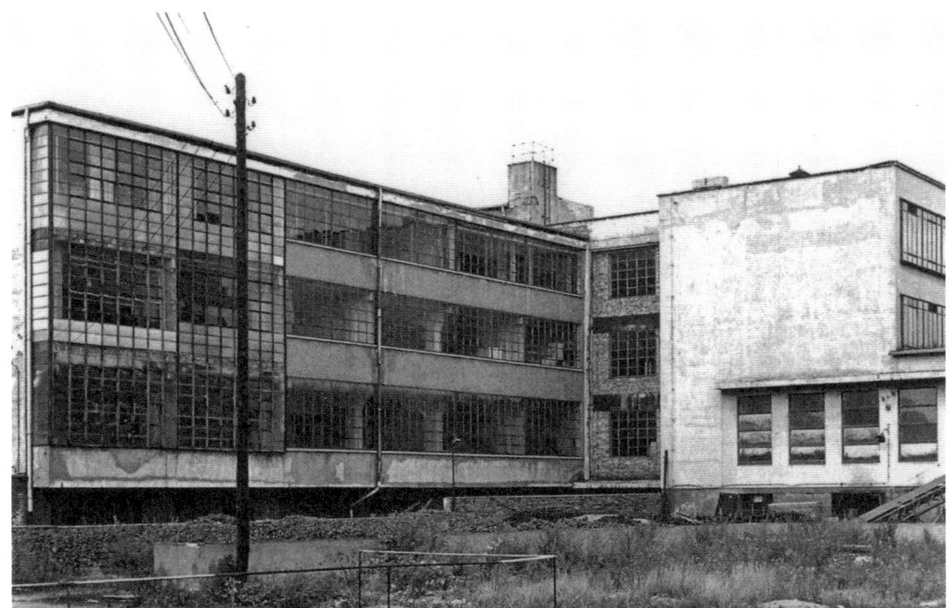

Curtain Wall

The curtain wall of the workshop wing was built in 1926 from steel with vertical supporting beams laid out in a grid. They were anchored to the parapet wall using steel plates and fixed around ten centimetres proud of the floor slabs. In this way, the vertical articulation of the façade was emphasised, and the air circulated over all floors. Casement windows with a pivot opening mechanism installed in the spaces between the supporting beams are grouped in two double rows of six or ten windows per floor and opened using lever locking mechanisms and chain rollers. Highly effective and infinitely variable ventilation is thus enabled with a simple turn of the hand.

For Walter Gropius, it was vital that the steel construction for the curtain wall was executed to a high standard. Although the contracts were supposed to go exclusively to firms based in Dessau, even if companies elsewhere offered lower prices, he insisted the job was awarded to the company Norddraht (Nordische Eisen- und Drahtindustrie) of Rostock. Gropius argued that the smaller companies in Dessau were hardly in the position to fulfil this unusual order. Furthermore, Norddraht had not only produced a meticulously detailed offer, but also submitted models, which were notable for their extremely precise execution. The company also had the necessary profiles in stock and could deliver promptly. The city approved the award of the contract to Norddraht.[5] When it came to the allocation of a separate contract for windows for the Bauhaus Building, Norddraht again submitted the most favourable bid. However, after the Dessau-based company Carl Köckert, which had lost the bid, demanded of the mayor that the contract be given to local firms, in this instance it was commissioned to supply the windows.[6]

The installation of the curtain wall presented a huge challenge. There was no experience of this modern type of construction to draw on, as correspondence between Gropius's architecture office and the company initially commissioned to install it, Robert Richter of Dessau, shows. The company's owner demanded additional remuneration to make the required holes and to cement in place the masonry screws used to attach the steel construction to the reinforced concrete floor slabs.[7] He reasoned that the job did not involve the installation of windows as per usual for a mason but the erection of a steel construction, which was a metal worker's job. Gropius's architecture office refused to pay the costs for the additional services and, after the negotiations had run their course, again commissioned Norddraht with the installation.

The curtain wall, which was to become an outstanding feature of the Bauhaus Building and attain worldwide renown, was assembled from sections on the ground to form large elements, hoisted up, and attached using masonry screws inserted through steel mounting brackets. In 1927, Russian writer Ilya Ehrenburg described a visit to Dessau in the *Frankfurter Zeitung:* 'when i finally caught sight of the "bauhaus", which seems to be all of a piece, like a persistent thought, and its glass walls, forming a transparent angle, flowing into the air and yet separated from it by a precise will—i stood still involuntarily, and this was not amazement at the sight of a sensual invention, no, it was simple admiration.'[8]

77)

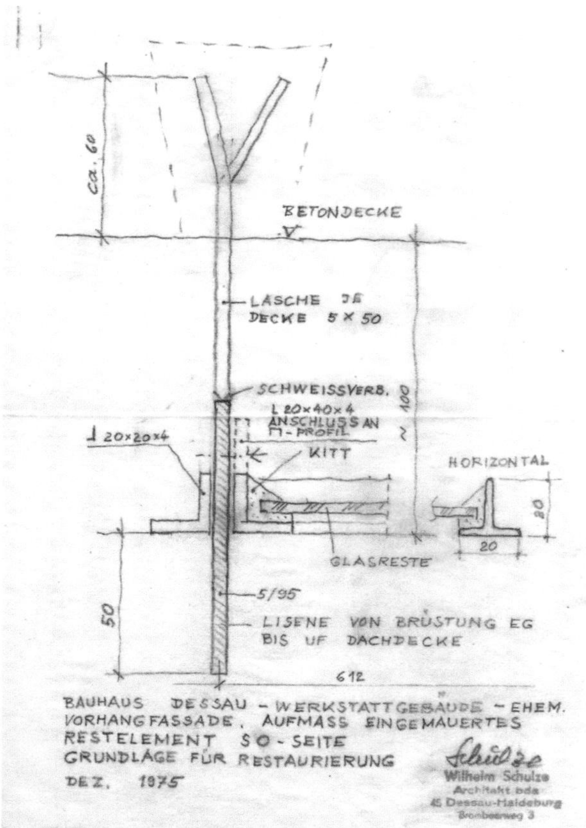

78)

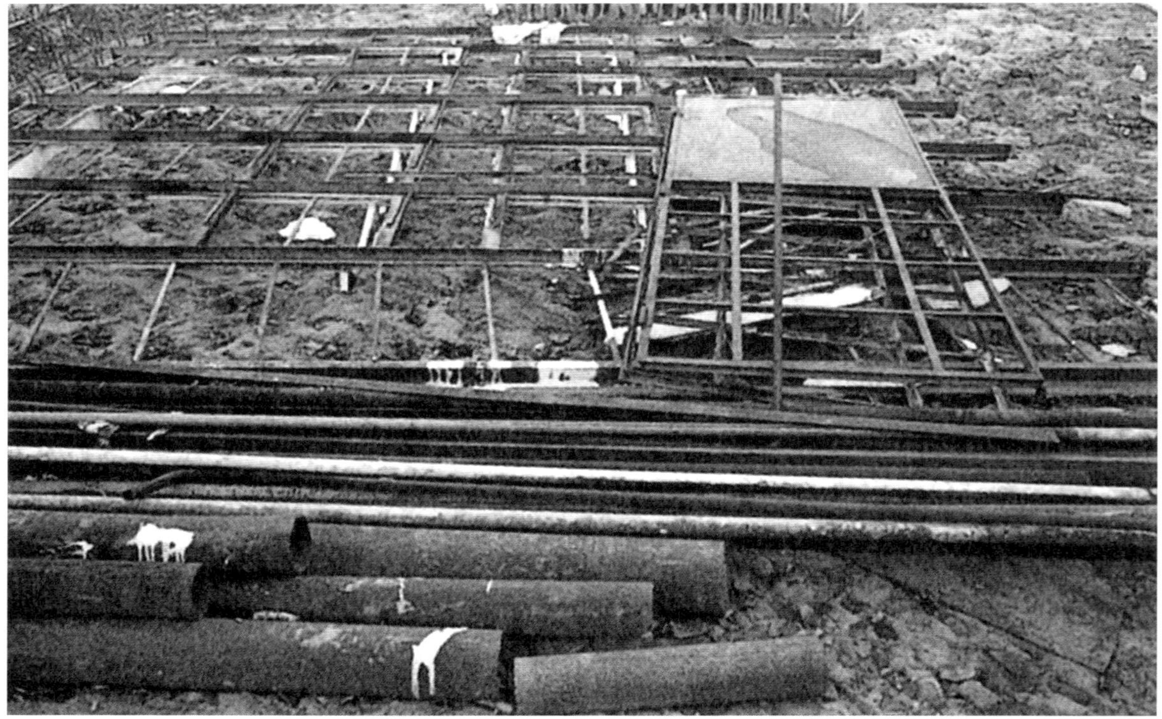

77)
Measured drawing of fragment of the original curtain wall, 1975

78)
Fragments of the curtain wall outside the Bauhaus Building, 1976

The building's current curtain wall is a reconstruction dating from the renovation of 1976 which enables the architectonic and spatial impact of the Bauhaus to be experienced again following its destruction in 1945. On closer scrutiny however, a comparison of the historic documentation and the 1976 façade reveals differences in both materials and colour design: in 1976, the steel was replaced by aluminium, and the profiles were finished with black anodised paint inside and out rather than in grey or white. Further differences include discrepancies in the profile dimensions and changes to the opening mechanisms. Regrettably, the last piece of the original curtain wall was lost during the renovation of 1976. As a result, the only firm evidence of the original construction is found in black and white photographs. Original detail drawings and measurement drawings of the façade elements which still existed in 1976 were likewise lost, with the exception of one detail sketch from 1975.[9]

In 1975, the architect of the project, Wilhelm Schulze,[10] pushed for anthracite-coloured anodised aluminium as a material for the façades rather than the initially envisaged steel, reasoning that it would not require constant maintenance, the construction process would be simplified, and it could be manufactured by a local company[11] at short notice. After a decision had been reached not to use insulated glass for the glazing, which would have been too heavy for the aluminium profiles, this construction was chosen. The authority then responsible for the protection of historical monuments attached little significance to the deviation from the original construction.[12] The gap which originally existed between the floor slabs and the curtain wall was closed in 1976, and as a result, the vertical alignment of the façade now has an additional horizontal aspect.

A survey completed in 1999[13] of the technological condition of the curtain wall confirmed that its quality is such that it permits maintenance and long-term conservation, provided measures to this end are ongoing. With the curtain wall of 1976, valuable evidence of the renovation has thus been preserved. The maintenance continuously required since then includes addressing corrosion on the sheet metal components used to connect the glass façade to the solid structure, the replacement of missing parts on the supporting beams, and the closure of cracked joints. Old putty around the glass planes is replaced with new as required, sealing materials are fitted to moving parts, and the lever locking mechanisms are serviced to ensure full functionality. Should the need to replace glass sheets arise, white float glass is used.

To reinforce the homogeneous appearance of the Bauhaus Building, the metal construction was painted in the colours found on all original windows, which were ascertained by means of restoration research: white on the inside, grey on the outside. Although the closure of the gap between the floor slabs and the curtain wall mars the aesthetic impact, it will remain in place for the time being for fire prevention and sound insulation reasons.

Current observations of the curtain wall indicate the occurrence of more recent changes, possibly caused by the consequences of climate change, such as rising temperatures and more powerful storms. Detailed investigations and analyses have therefore begun anew.

79)

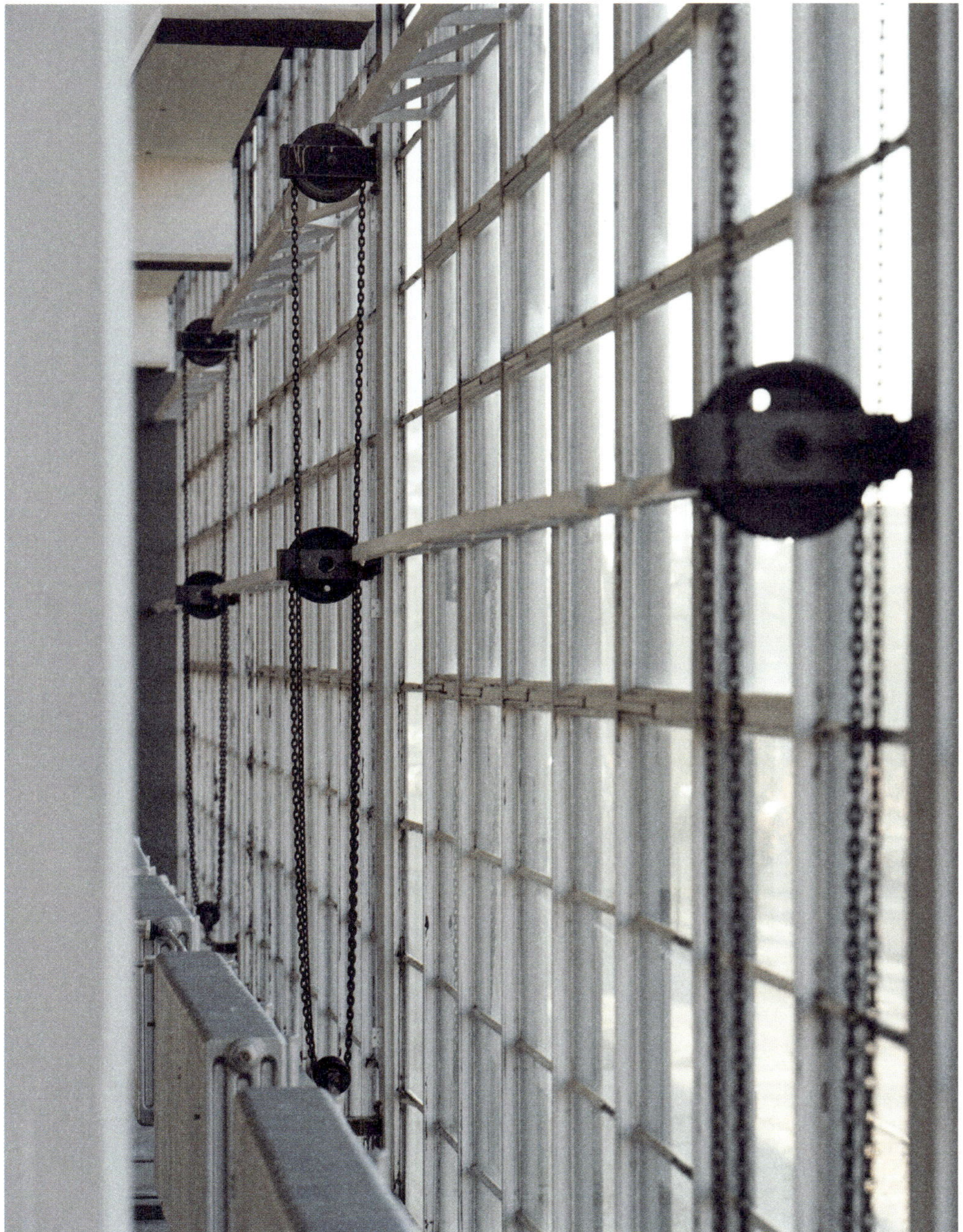

80)

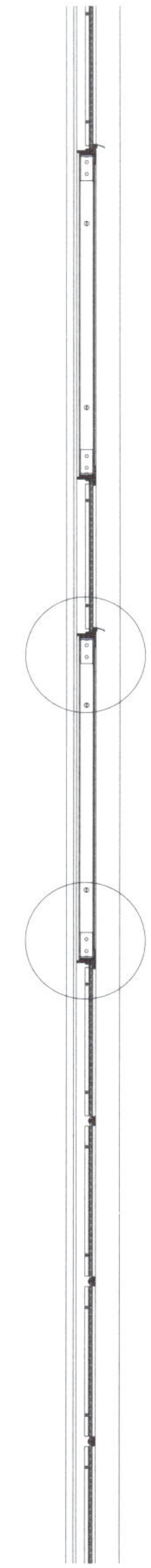

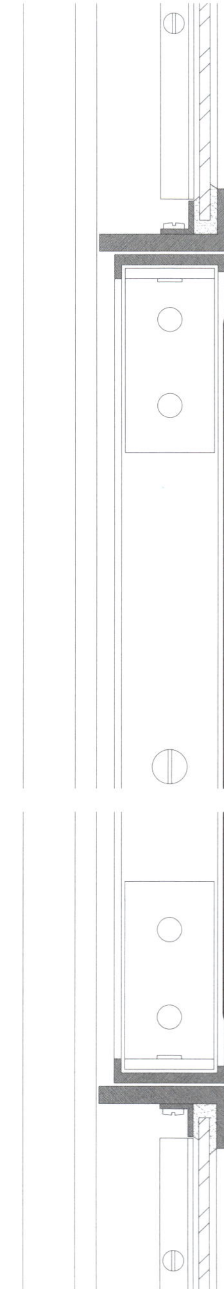

81)

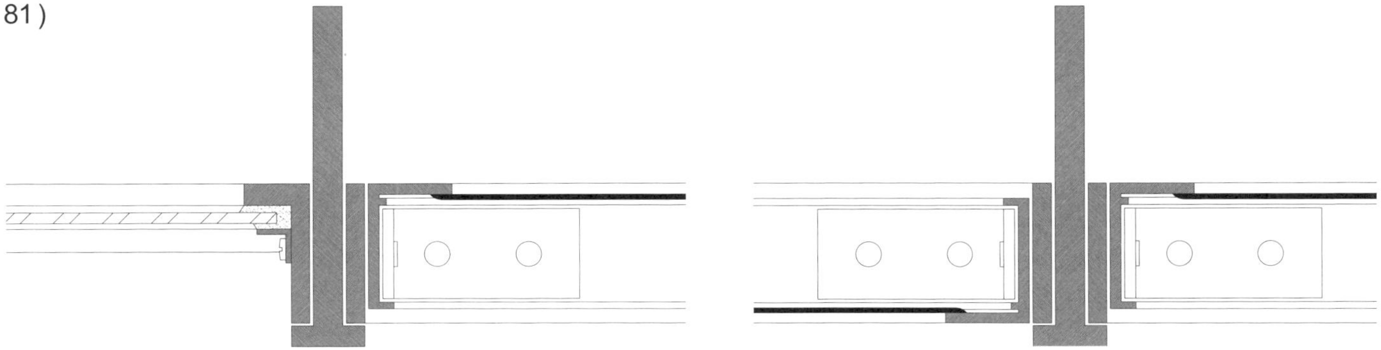

79)
Curtain wall with windows and opening mechanisms, 2021

80)
Curtain wall, vertical projection, 2003

81)
Curtain wall, horizontal projection, 2003

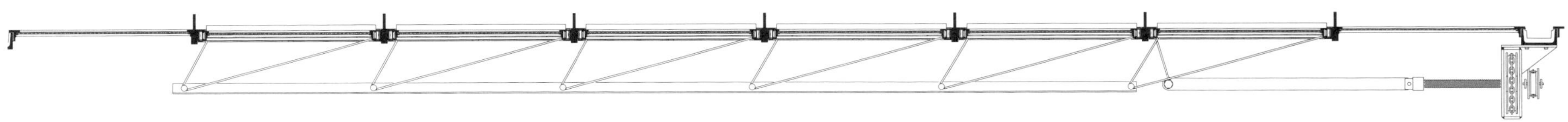

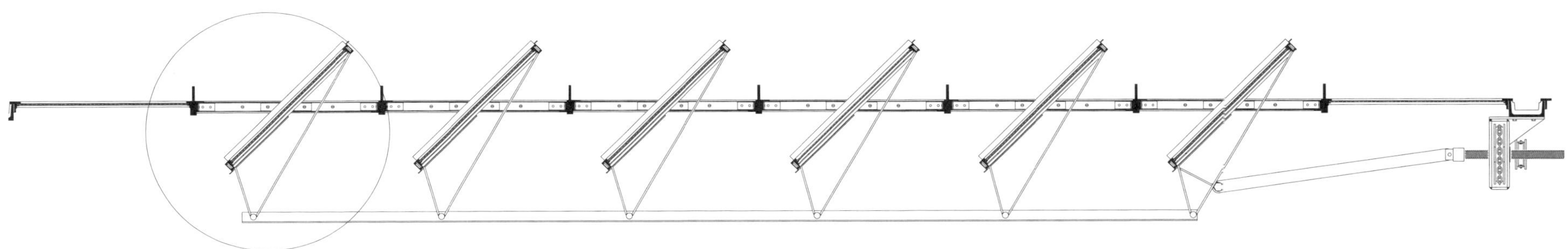

82)

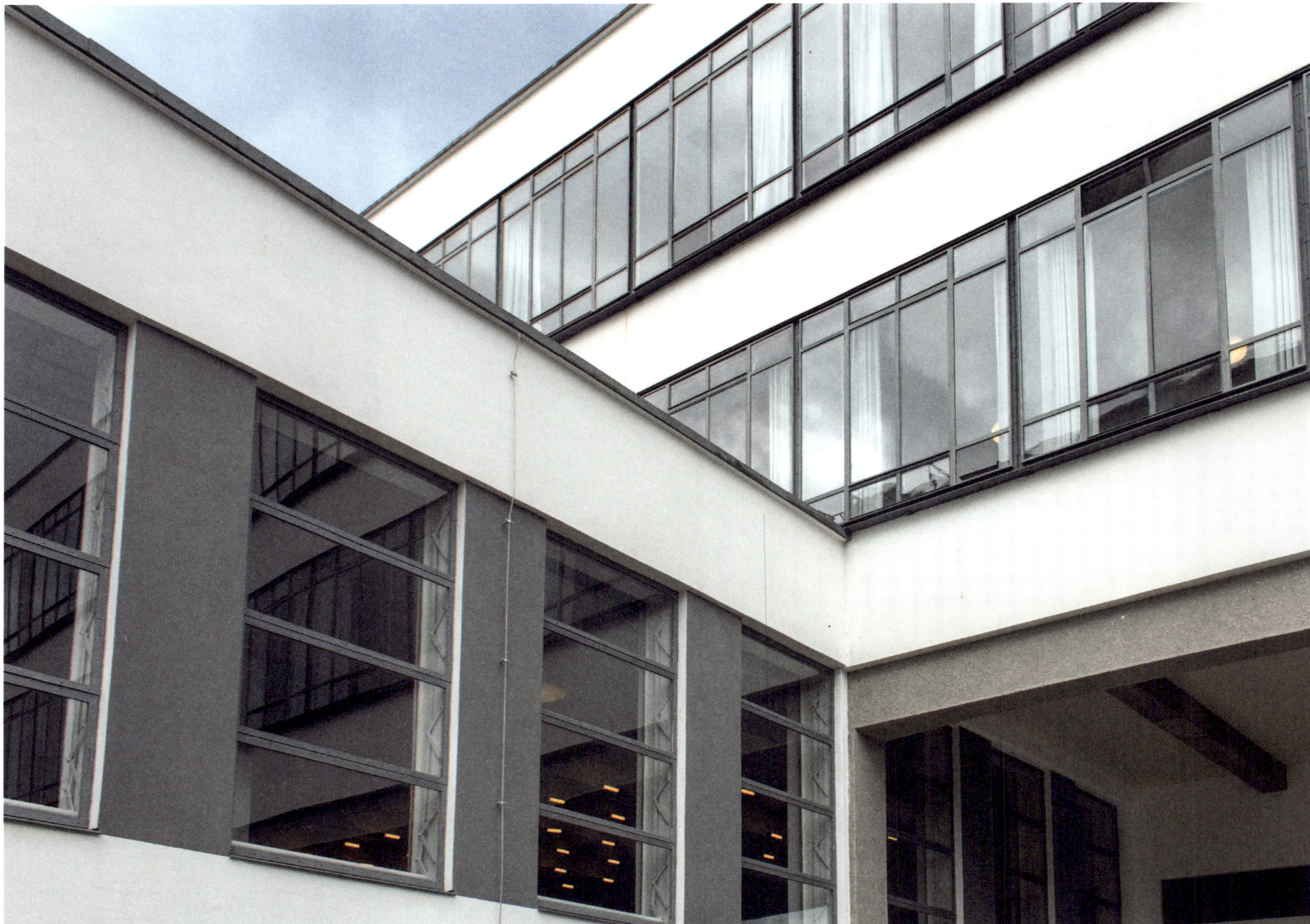

Other Windows

In addition to the curtain wall, Walter Gropius had other windows installed in the Bauhaus Building. These differ in terms of size, placement, opening mechanisms, and the way in which they are installed in the wall. Original windows have been preserved in just a few areas, among them the festive area, the semi-basements of the north wing and workshop wing, and the south stairway.

The large glazed façade on the south side of the stairway in the workshop wing has a particular role to play. It was not, as Walter Gropius still publicly maintained in 1930,[14] fitted with the same detailed arrangement of panes as the workshop façade, but consists of three undivided glass sheets, each measuring more than three by four metres, and two narrow glazed strips at ceiling height. Seen from inside the building, these glass façades are prominently located, directly opposite the main entrance in the vestibule on the ground floor and on the upper floors. As such, they directly confront people entering the building with the architectonic possibilities of the modern materials concrete, glass, and steel. They likewise convey the theme of mutual penetration of interior and exterior, and they frame the view of the workshop wing, the 'laboratory of ideas' with its important building element, the curtain wall. These windows were destroyed in an air raid during the Second World War and reconstructed during the renovation of 1976.

The festive area of the Bauhaus Building is likewise equipped with a distinctive complex of windows, which Adolf Schneck wrote about in 1932.[15] The windows are rectangular in shape and vertically aligned; together they form a horizontal row in the exterior façade, aided by the grey finish on the columns between the windows. The individual windows are each equipped with four mechanically coupled, horizontally pivoted sash windows. The three or four windows (twelve or sixteen casements) are connected by adjusting wheels, drive shafts and lever locking mechanisms and can be put in motion simultaneously. By these means, the process of opening the windows becomes highly effective and infinitely variable. They were made by the company Norddraht, which featured these festive area windows in an advertisement in the *Bauwelt Katalog* of 1929.[17] These original windows dating from 1926 remain in situ in the Bauhaus Building and are being preserved for the future by means of meticulous restoration.

Other windows in the Bauhaus Building which substantially affect the views of it include the ribbon windows in the north wing and the bridge, which stand proud of the façade and are attached to steel profiles. In 1926, these featured large pivot casements, a small bottom-hung casement fitted with bascule locks, and a small top-hung casement with a rod mechanism at the top. The window casements opened inwards; the glass panes were fixed in place with putty seams. The windows on the west façade of the bridge have a similar design. Smaller windows with pivot casements and bascule locks are found in the semi-basements and on the south side of the workshop wing. A variant featuring one large, undivided pivot casement and two smaller top- or bottom-hung casements was installed in the studio building. Special formats were also used. The many different windows correlate with the respective functions or design intentions and are a defining feature of the façade design of the Bauhaus Building.

The overwhelming majority of the original steel windows in the north wing, bridge, and studio building were removed from the building during the 1976 renovation. Therefore, at the same time as the lost curtain wall was being reconstructed, the surviving windows were being removed, discarded, and replaced by simplified steel replicas. At first glance, the view remained the same. But a closer look reveals a different method of construction on the profiles and new functions for the opening mechanisms. The panes of glass are held in place by metal brackets, not putty, and the window fittings are new. There are no pivot-hung casements, which modifies not only the functionality, but also the view: when the windows are closed, the lack of visible profile shows. Furthermore, these windows were not painted white inside and grey outside according to the historical model, but black both inside and out. A clear deviation from the original windows is therefore apparent in the details. This direct and precise comparison is possible because a small number of the original windows have been preserved in the building or in the Building Research Archive. In the semi-basements of the studio building and connecting building, the original windows were replaced by simplified replicas with a modified muntin design.

Despite the aforementioned deviations from the original models, the windows reconstructed in 1976 do not significantly compromise the appearance of the building and are being main-

83)

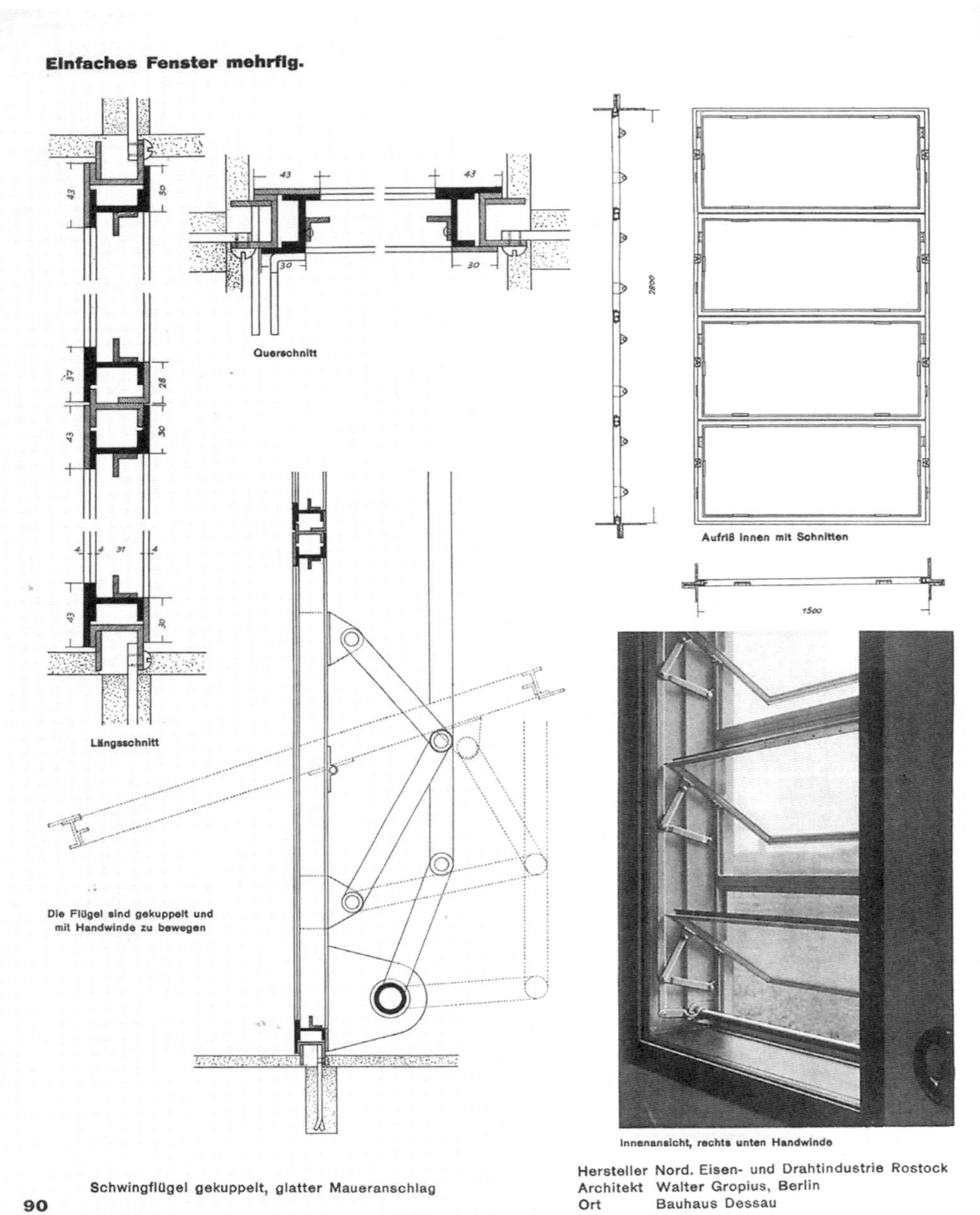

tained, also as testimonies to the renovation of 1976, by treating rust spots and replacing missing parts. To support the overall impression of the Bauhaus Building, they are painted white on the inside and grey on the outside based on the evidence found on original windows.
If any of these windows are so badly damaged that maintenance is no longer possible, they are replaced by reconstructions based on the original model. In 2000 for example, the bottom sections of the 1976 windows in the bridge and studio building which are adjacent to the roof of the connecting building and had been shortened to accommodate an addition to the roof, were now too short. Because it was not possible to add the missing pieces as part of the maintenance process, and due to the fact that the restoration of windows is reserved to those dating from 1926, the damaged windows were removed and replaced by reconstructions of the original windows.

82)
Glass façades of the bridge
and the connecting building,
2021

83)
Window, festive area,
1926

84 a)
Window details,
semi-basement,
north wing, 1926

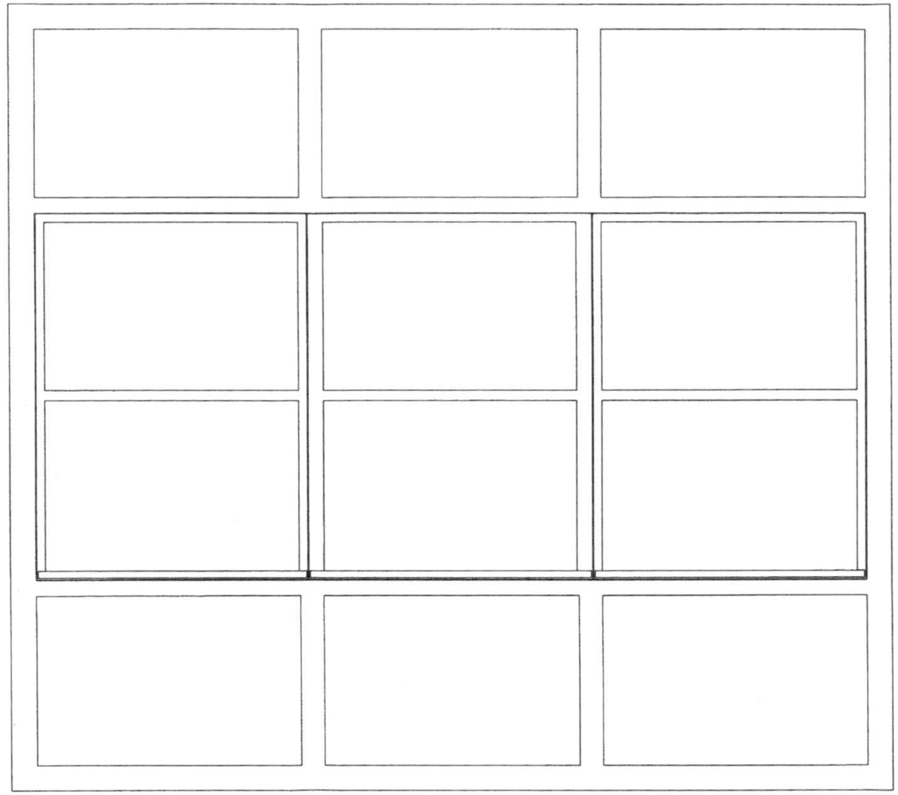

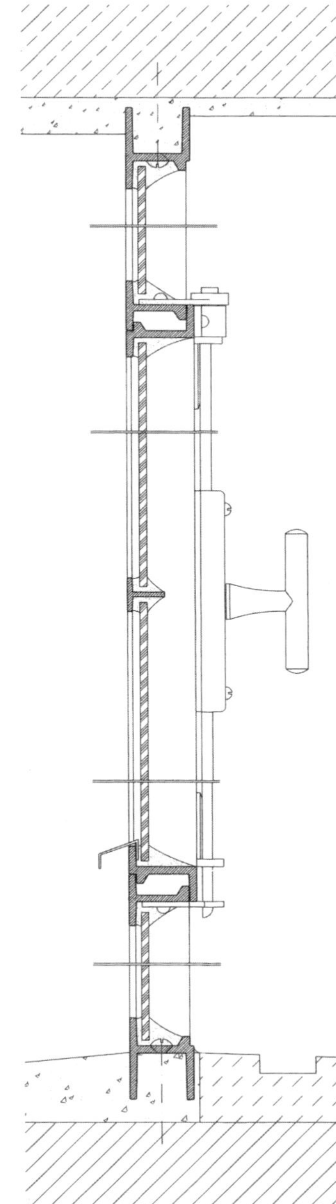

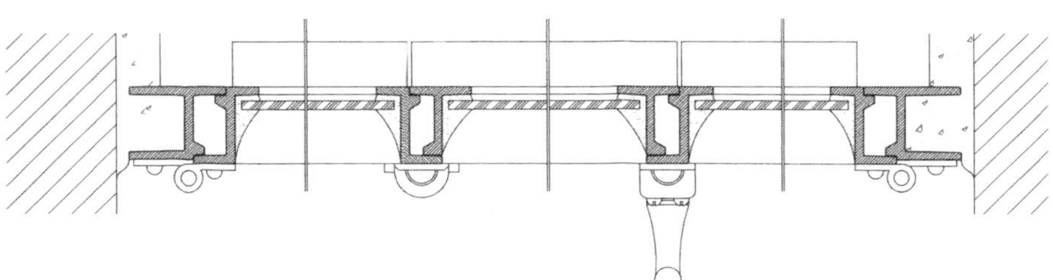

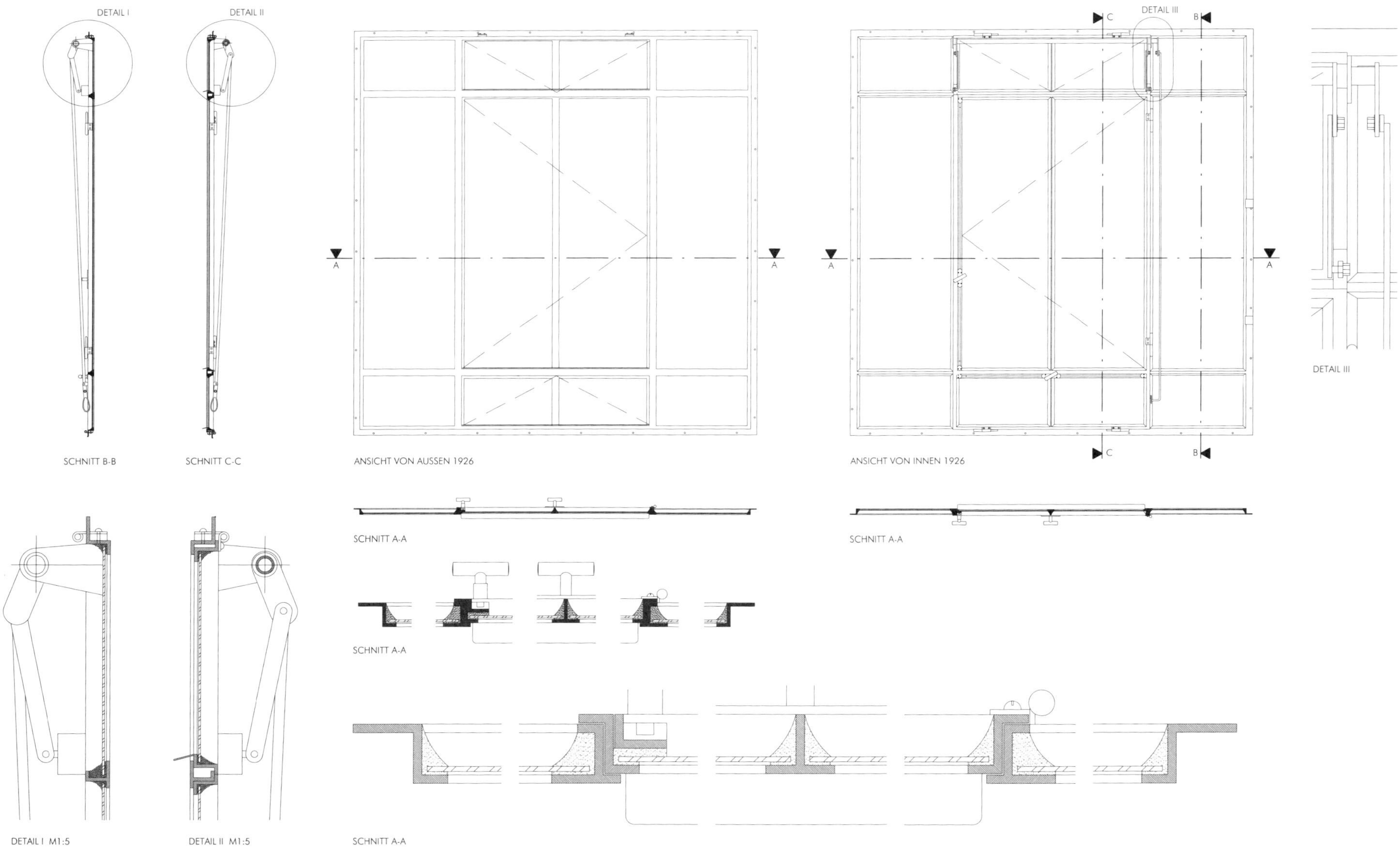

84 b)
Window, bridge,
1926

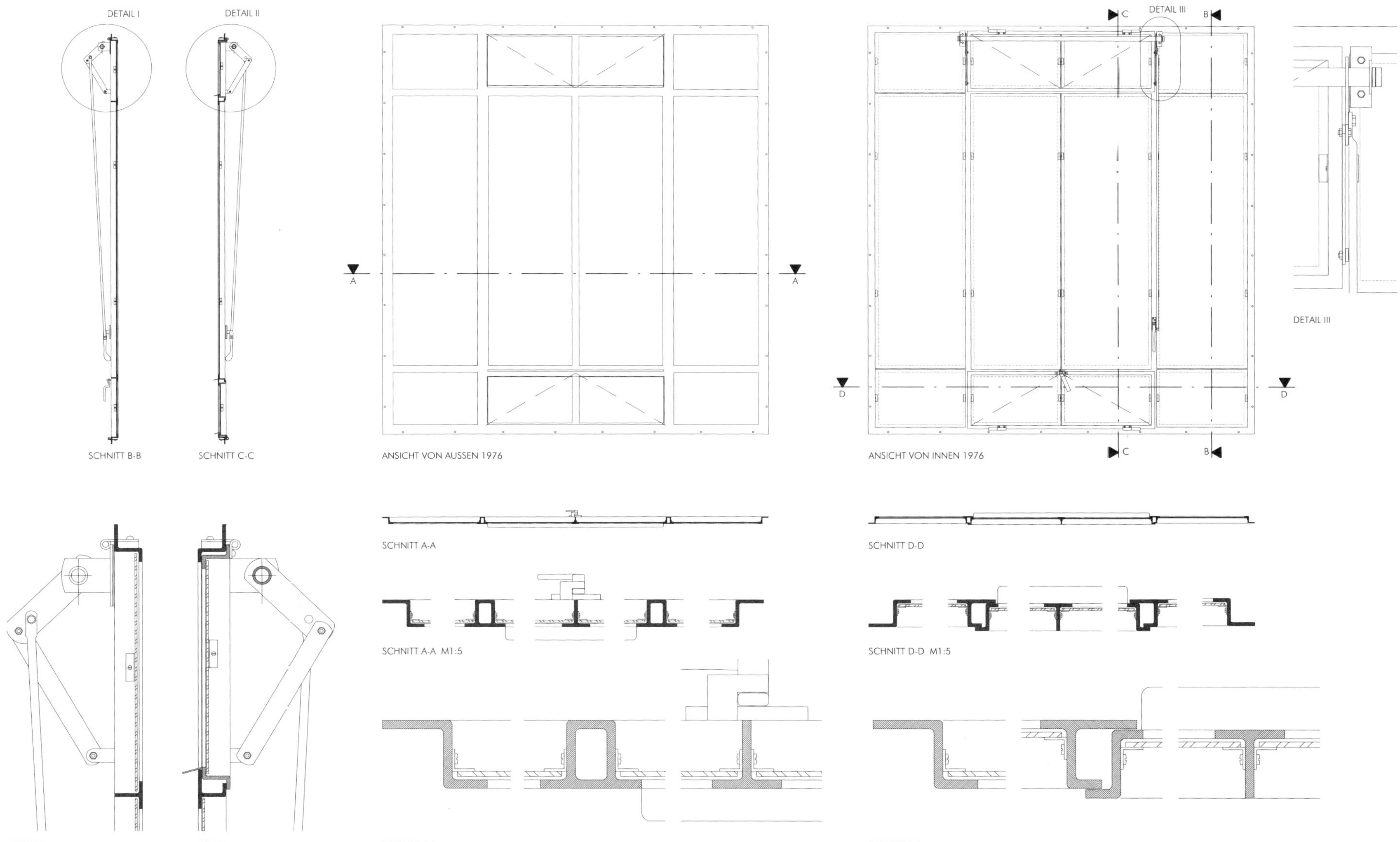

84 c)
Window, bridge,
1976

85)

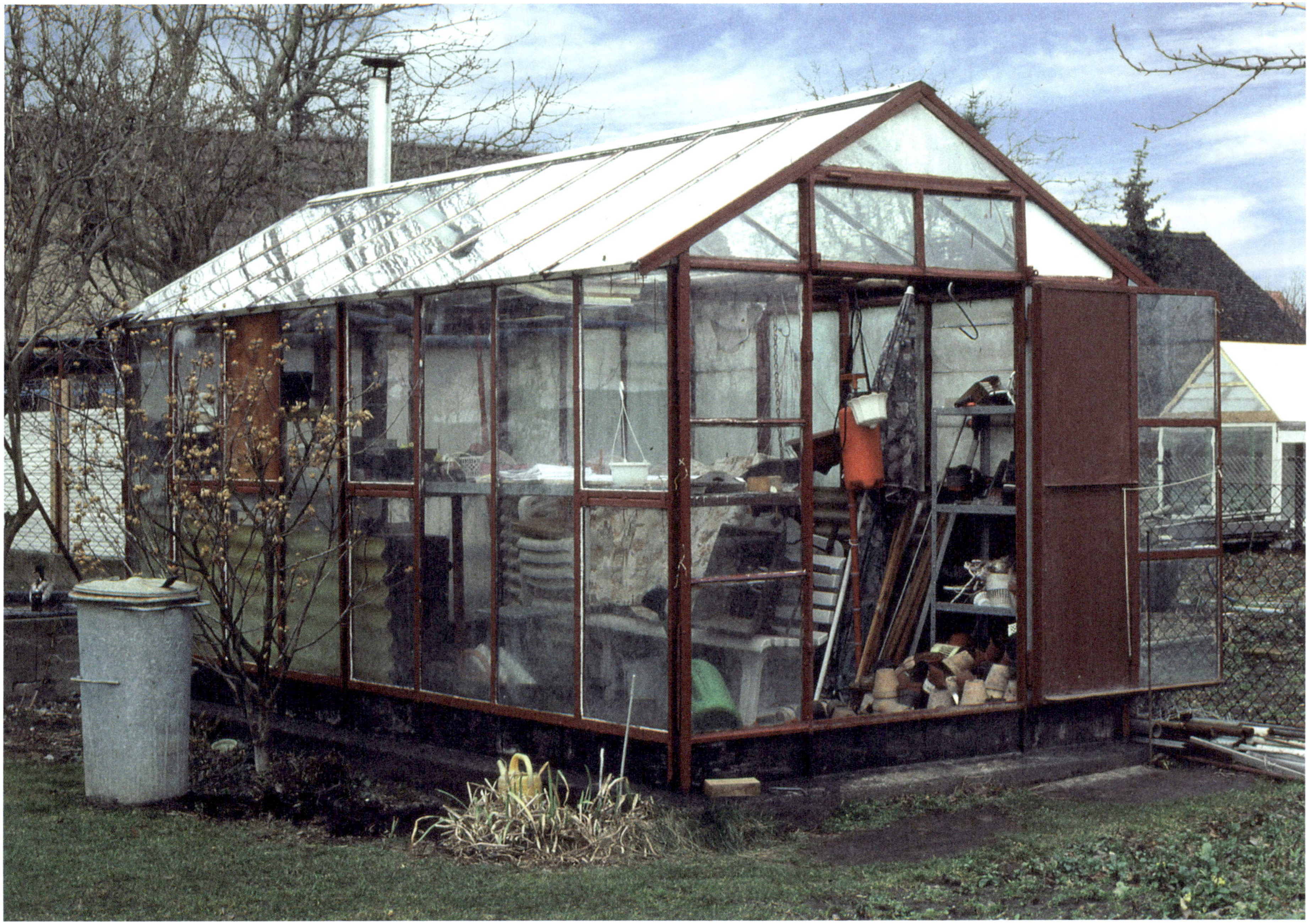

86)

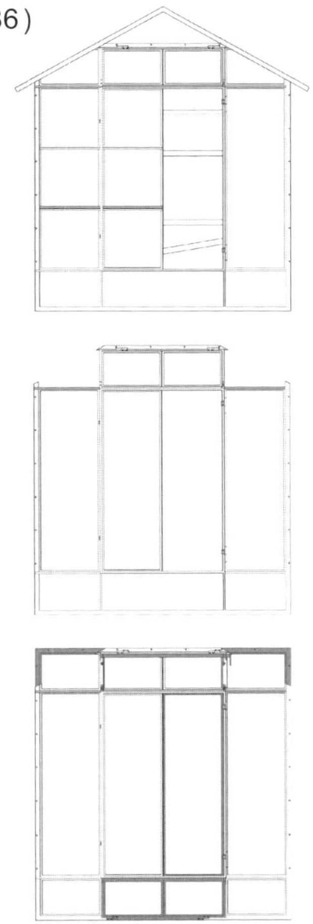

85)
Greenhouse made from original Bauhaus windows, 2001

86)
Restoration of a window from the greenhouse, 2001;
top: view of the gable,
centre: incomplete window,
below: completed window

Rediscovery of Original Windows

Original windows from 1926, which were believed permanently lost, were later rediscovered. These had been removed from the building in 1976 and were installed in greenhouses in the interim. The greenhouses were first catalogued and dismantled; the original windows built into them were then documented in drawings and photographs, painstakingly restored, and reinstalled in the Bauhaus Building. This example illustrates how the approach to building components relies not only on aspects of building technology, but also on the appraisal of the components and their preservation value: while certain windows were not deemed worthy of preservation in 1976 and discarded, the very same windows were meticulously restored in 2001.

Reducing Energy Loss

As a component of the measures implemented from 2009 to 2015 to reduce energy losses in the Bauhaus Building, some the simplified window reconstructions of 1976 were replaced by windows with thermally broken steel profiles and double glazing. The different requirements were first investigated and assessed in an overall report[18] featuring contributions from Brenne Architekten, Transsolar, Zentrum für Umweltbewusstes Bauen, and the Bauhaus Dessau Foundation. Firstly, the glass façades were analysed and evaluated in respect of their cultural, historical, and aesthetic relevance to the building and categorised according to date of origin, historic importance, and importance to the building's appearance. On this basis, decisions were reached on which glass surfaces are to be preserved with the existing profiles and glazing, which glass surfaces may be altered, and what must be considered when alterations are made. Detailed calculations showed how, and in which areas, upgrading the windows with thermally broken steel profiles and double glazing would enable significant reductions in energy consumption. Finally, areas in the building fitted with the simplified reconstructions of 1976 were earmarked for possible modifications. Here, limiting the planned changes to selected areas should contribute to the long-term conservation of the historic glass surfaces in other areas.

For the elected areas on the north and west façade of the north wing and the east façade of the studio building, windows were designed which help cut energy losses and are likewise compatible with the building's cultural significance and aesthetic impact. Seen from the front, these reconstructions have the same profile width as the historic windows, are divided in the same way, have top-hung, bottom-hung and pivot casements that provide the same functions and, with lever locking mechanisms and bascule locks, even have the same fittings. Based on the polished plate glass originally utilised, white float glass was used for the double glazing. The option of adding another energy saving coating to the glass planes was rejected because this would alter the appearance of the building too radically.[19] These windows mainly differ from the originals due to the depth of the thermally broken profiles, the weight of which also modifies their use, and due to the double glazing which under scrutiny reveals a doubled reflection. Also their thickness transforms the sense of space.

The refurbishment of the windows is associated with a depletion of the monument value. This concerns, for instance, differences in profile depths in comparison with the original windows, the different way of handling the heavy casements, the transformed appearance of the building as regards the transparency, reflections, and colour of the glass panes, and in general the loss of the sensory experience provided by the historic context. However, the loss of monument value in certain areas is counterbalanced by gains in others. In addition to reduced energy consumption and the improvement of user comfort, these notably include a greater likeness to the original appearance as regards profiles and opening mechanisms (in comparison with the 1976 windows) and especially the long-term conservation of the building fabric.

Several of the 1976 reproductions which were removed from the building are preserved in the Building Research Archive of the Bauhaus Dessau Foundation. Others have found a new use in the project 'bauhaus reuse'[20] and are installed in temporary pavilions in Berlin.

Particular care and attention must be paid to the conservation of the few surviving original windows in the Bauhaus Building. These are meticulously restored: old putty seams are replaced by new ones, damaged glass panes are replaced by five-millimetre-thick white float glass, flaking paint layers are removed, rust spots are treated, substitutions are made for missing parts, warped vent windows are fixed, and all moving parts are cleaned and oiled. Finally, the windows are painted with an alkyd resin paint on top of anti-corrosion protection. Because the glass façades and windows are such defining elements of the Bauhaus Building, with the exception of the clearly defined areas for windows designed to reduce energy losses, the use of single glazing is specified in order to conserve the steel profiling, mirroring effects, reflections, and intersecting vistas. In this way, the complex impact of the glass façades can develop unhindered to full effect.

The approach to the windows in the Bauhaus Building also exemplifies the ways in which the demands arising from the use of the building and the attitudes towards heritage conservation have changed over recent decades. While original windows were replaced by simplified reproductions in 1976 rather than repaired, today the preservation and conservation of the original fabric of the building is awarded the highest priority. The objective right now is not only to restore the artistic impression but also to safeguard the monuments in terms of its materiality and as a historical testimony. However, the necessity of addressing reductions in energy consumption—not least due to climate change—has also entailed compromises in respect of heritage conservation. Following a thorough and intensive deliberation process in the framework of an overall concept, this resulted in further changes being made to non-original windows.

Today, original windows from 1926, reconstructions made in 1976 and in 2000[21] as well as energy-saving windows[22] dating from 2012 to 2014 are found alongside one another in the Bauhaus Building. The renovation of the windows has as many diverse objectives as the renovation of other areas of the building. These include the restoration and reconstruction of original windows, the maintenance of reconstructions dating from 1976 including the curtain wall, and the construction of new windows with thermally broken steel profiles and double glazing. The homogeneous colour design based on the historic model allows the differences to take a back seat in favour of the overall impression. On closer inspection a piece of the history of the Bauhaus thus remains identifiable and the original light, airy, and elegant appearance of the building can evolve to full effect.

1
Gropius 2021, p. 135

2
Moholy-Nagy 1929 (1947), p. 62

3
Blunck 1927, p. 153

4
Ise Gropius, diary entry of 6. June 1926, unpublished document in the Bauhaus-Archiv / Museum für Gestaltung Berlin; cit. in Rehm 2005, p. 34

5
Stadtarchiv Dessau, SB 1, fol. 37 et seqq.

6
Stadtarchiv Dessau, SB 1, fol. 58 et seqq.

7
Stadtarchiv Dessau, SB 1, fol. 139 et seqq.

8
Ehrenburg 1927, p. 17

9
Wilhelm Schulze, Bauhaus Dessau—workshop wing, curtain wall façade, measurement, remaining element embedded in the wall of the southeastern side. Basis for renovation. December 1976, unpublished document in the Building Research Archive of the Bauhaus Dessau Foundation

10
Wilhelm Schulze was responsible for planning the renovation of 1976 on behalf of the Volkseigener Betrieb Industrieprojektierung Dessau (VEB Ipro).

11
Wilhelm Schulze, letter of 2 December 1975, unpublished document in the Building Research Archive of the Bauhaus Dessau Foundation

12
„Dabei erscheint es von geringerer Bedeutung, daß als Material für die Konstruktion Profile aus Leichtmetall statt aus Eisen verwendet werden.“ (In this context, it seems to be of less importance that the material for the renovation will include profiles of light metal instead of iron.) Berger 1976/I, p. 725

13
MFPA 1999

14
Gropius 2021, p. 36

15
Schneck 1932, p. 90

16
The company Norddraht also supplied windows and entrance doors for the Dessau-Törten Housing Estate, phase Sietö I-1926.

17
Bauwelt Katalog 1929/30, p. 1035

18
Markgraf/Weisbach 2011

19
Brenne/Nickmann/Mathijssen/Weller/Reich 2012, p. 348–63

20
Cf. www.bauhaus-reuse.de (6 May 2021)

21
The restoration and reconstruction of original windows was planned by Brambach und Ebert Architekten, Halle/Saale, and Pfister Schiess Tropeano, Zurich.

22
The planning for the energy-saving windows was executed by Brenne Architekten, Berlin.

87)
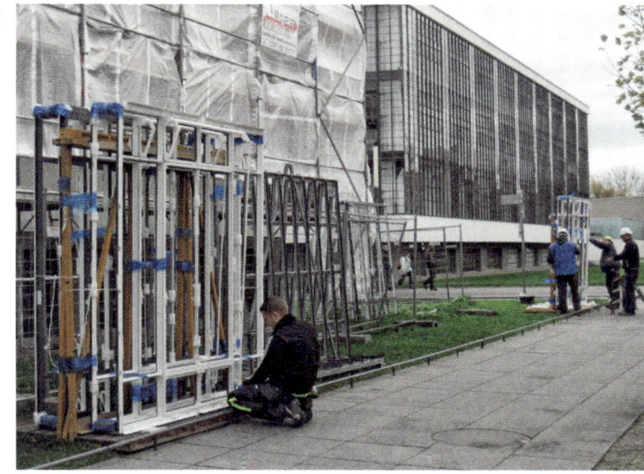

88)
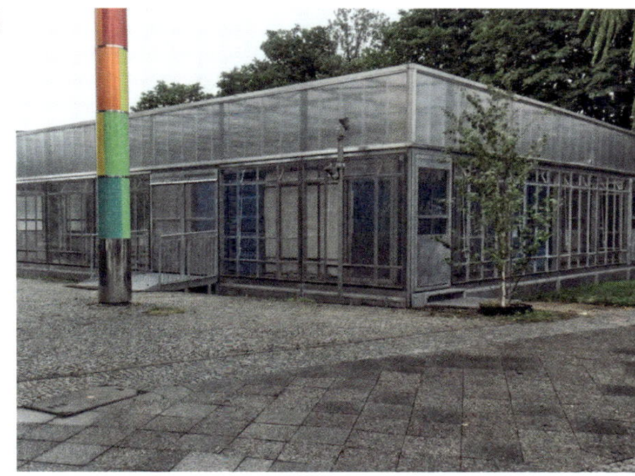

87)
Installation of new windows to reduce energy loss, 2013

88)
Pavilion comprising Bauhaus windows reconstructed in 1976 and removed in 2013 during renovation works, 2015

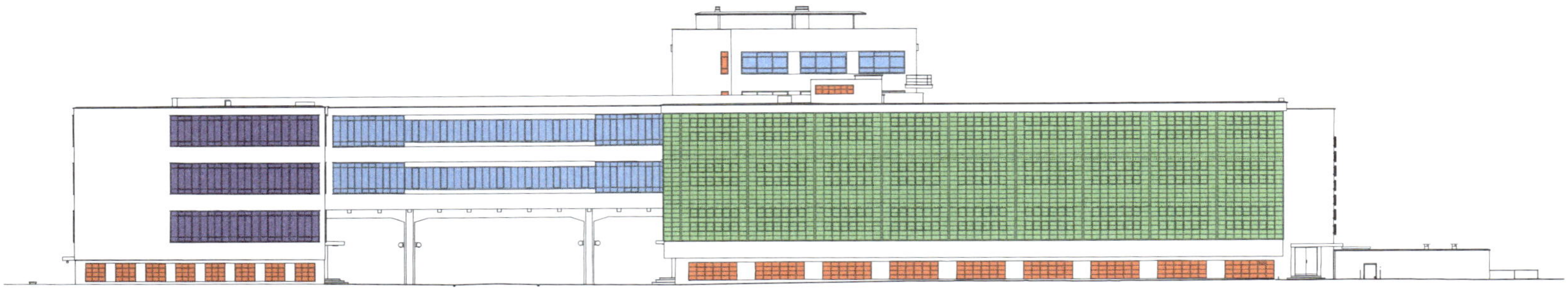

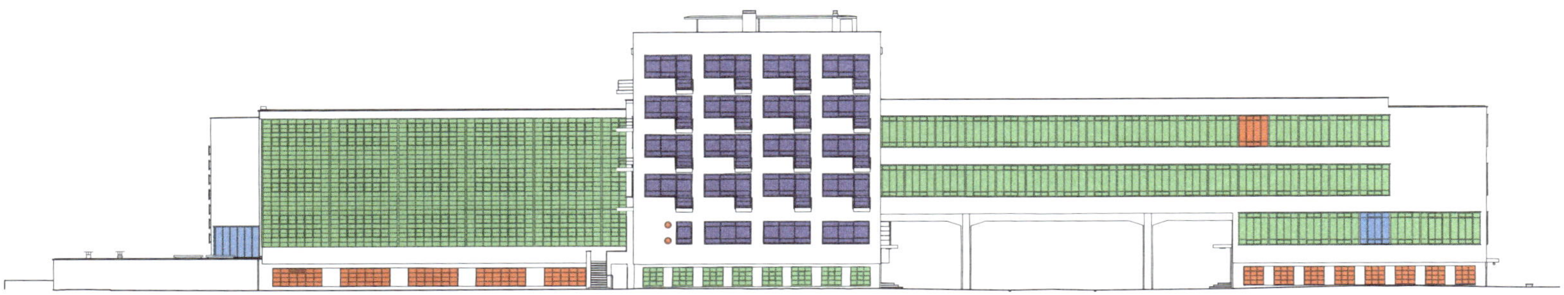

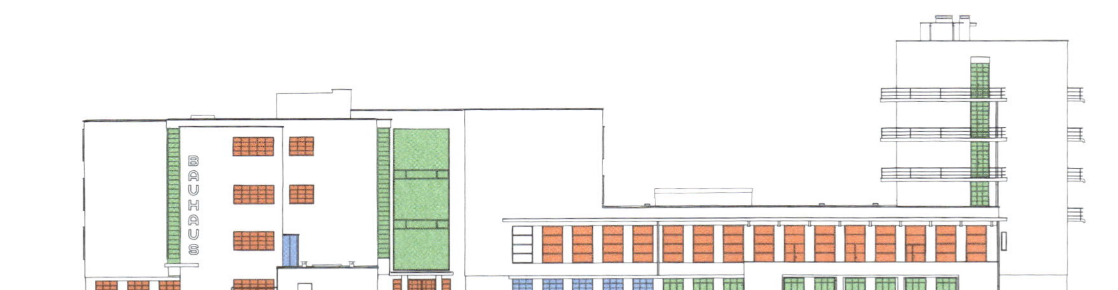
BAUHAUS

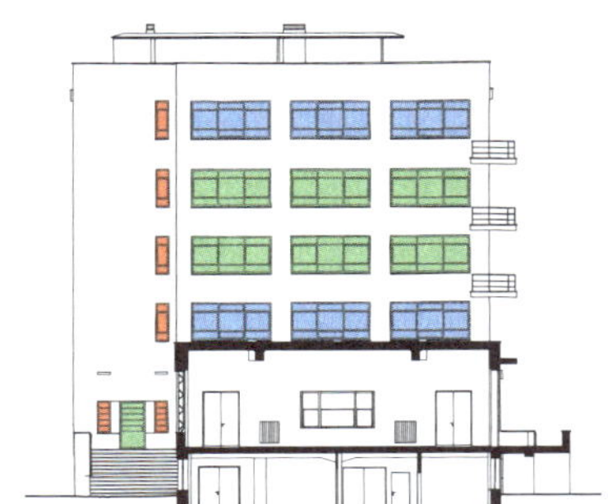

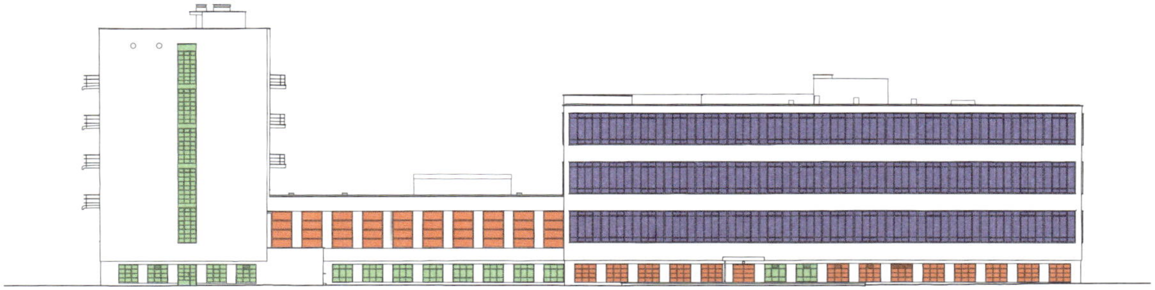

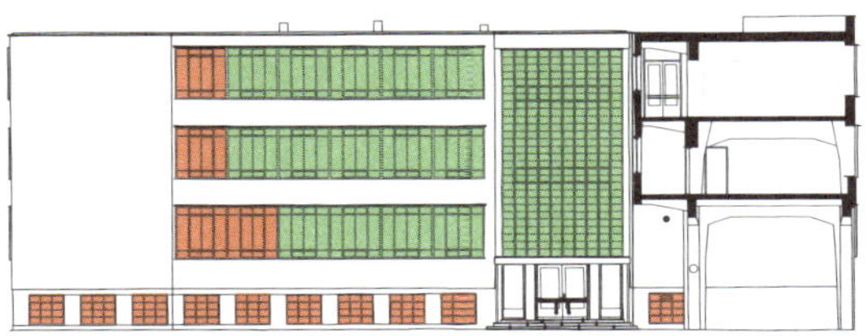

89)
Elevation showing ages of windows, 2021

1926

1976

2001 / 2006

2012 / 2014

90)
Comparison of windows

View from the outside,
details (r.): top 1926,
centre 1976, bottom 2011

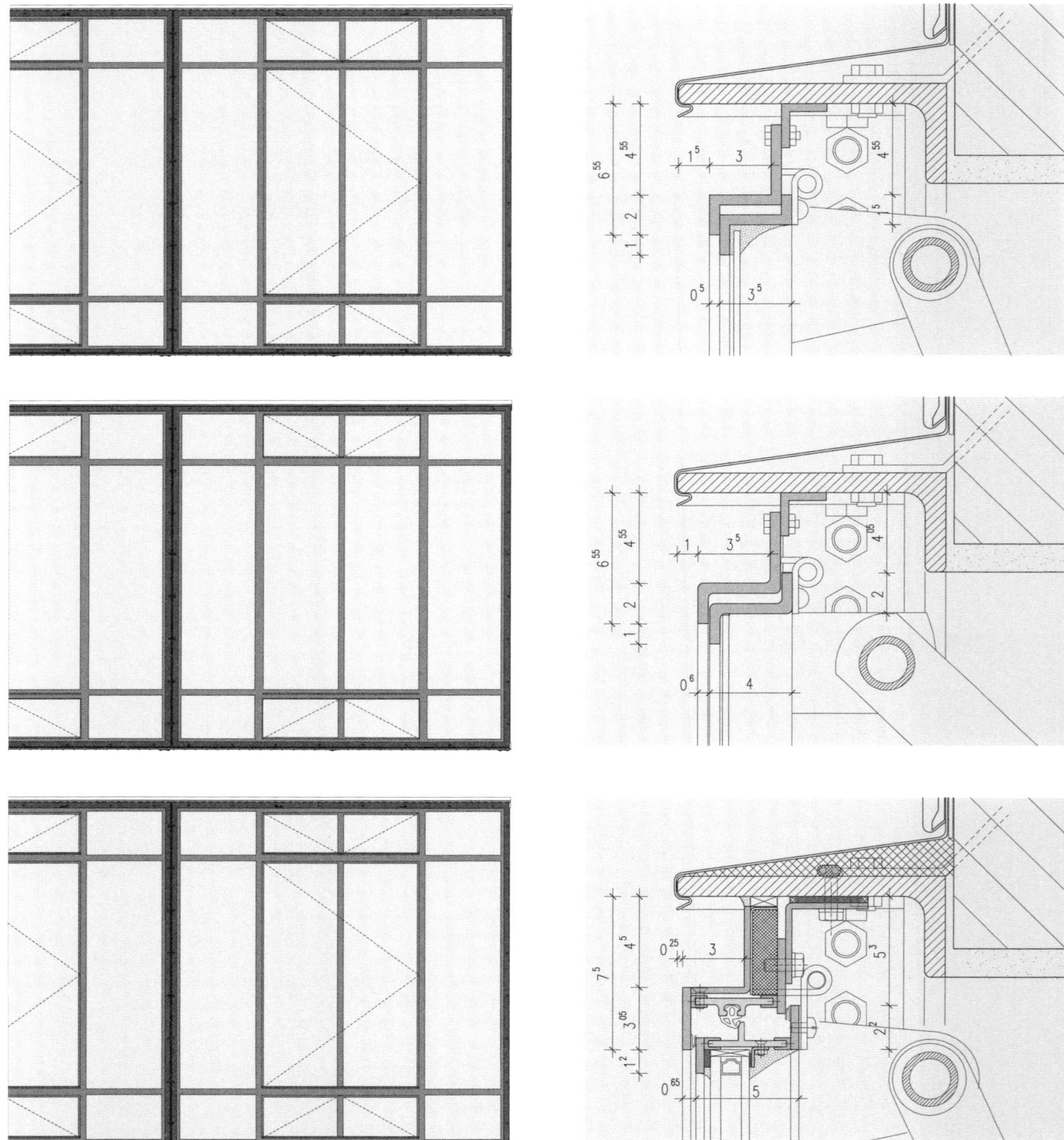

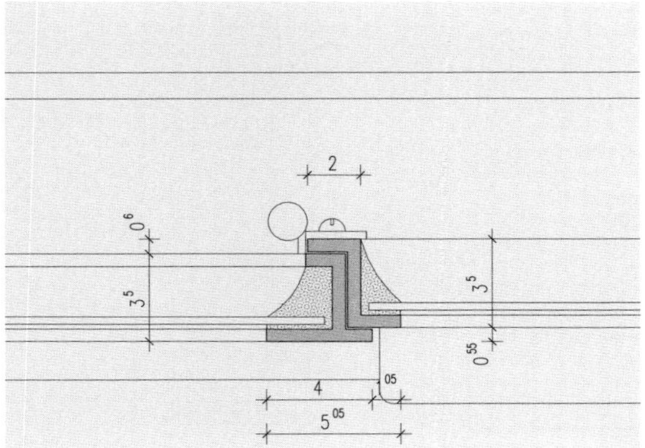
2
0^{6}
3^{5}
3^{5}
0^{55}
4
05
5^{05}

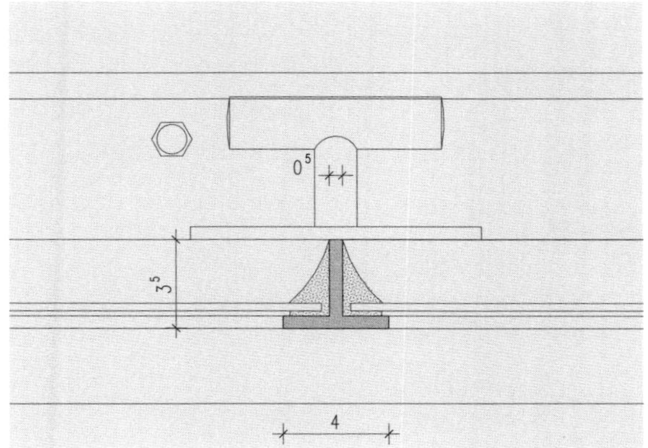
0^{5}
3^{5}
4

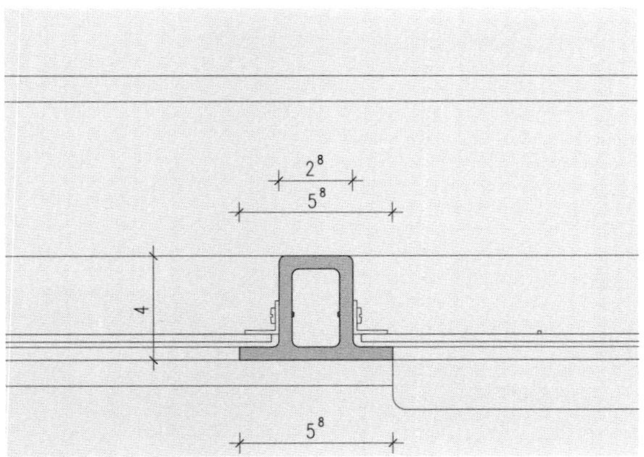
2^{8}
5^{8}
4
5^{8}

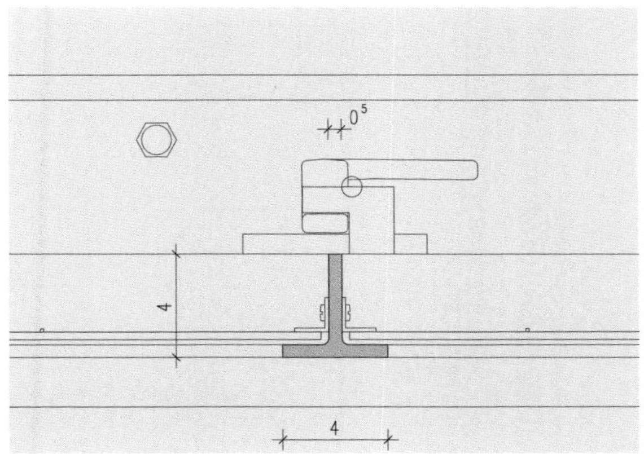
0^{5}
4
4

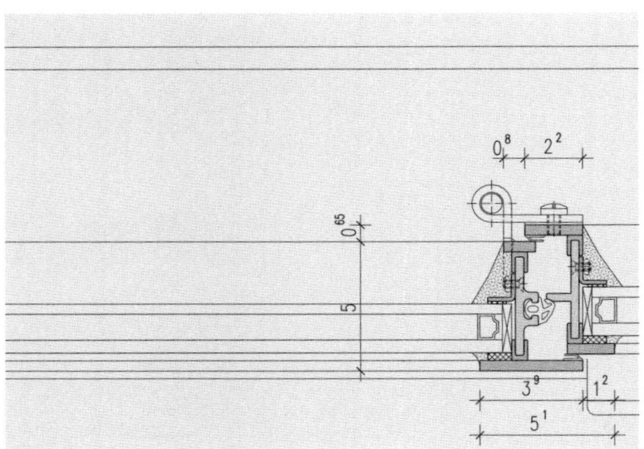
0^{8}
2^{2}
0^{65}
5
3^{9}
1^{2}
5^{1}

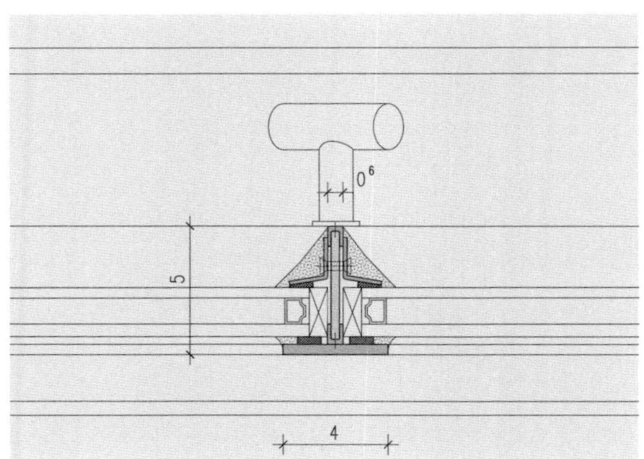
0^{6}
5
4

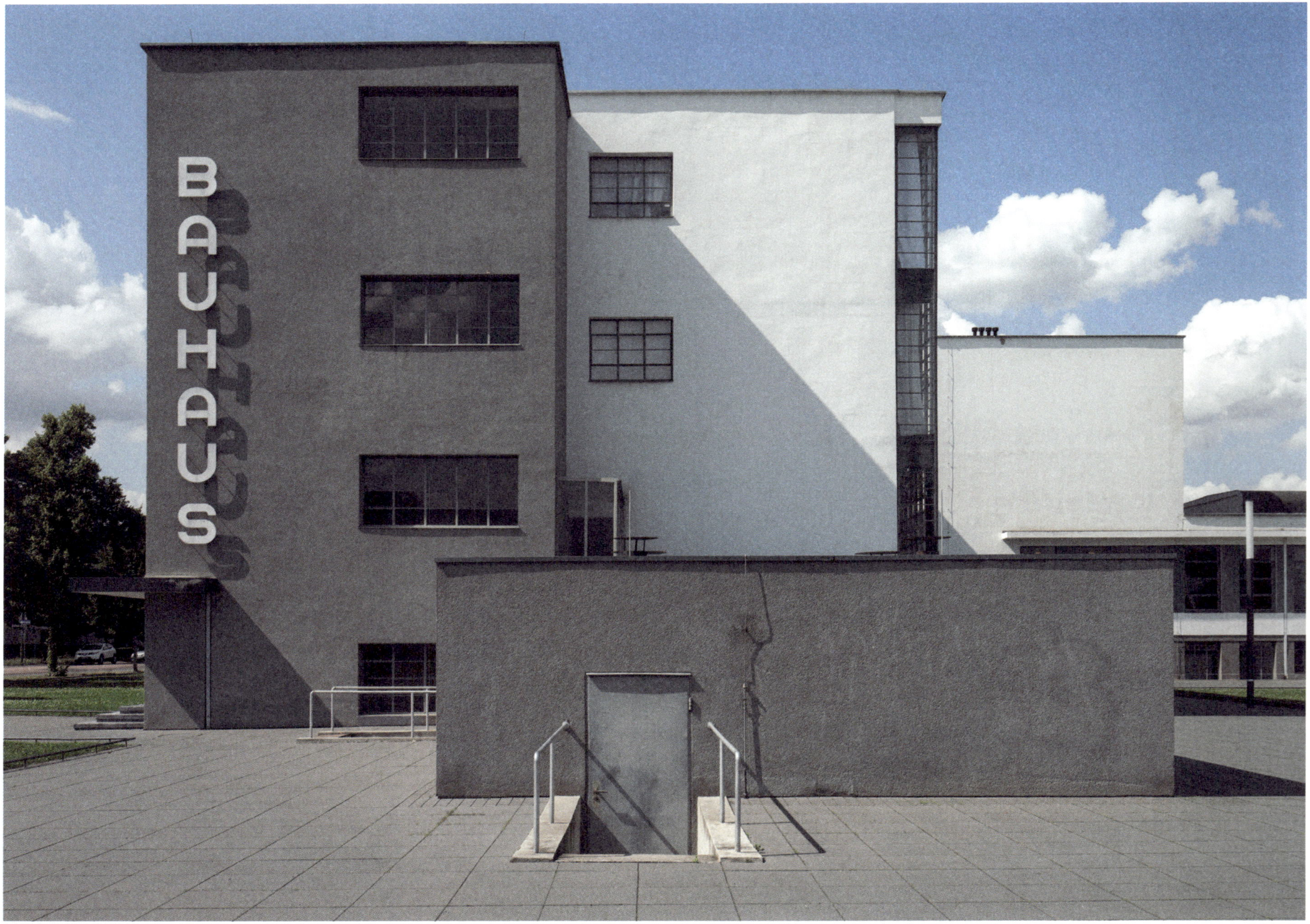
BAUHAUS

Building Shell Rendered Façades and Roofs

91)
Wall surfaces with rough grey render with mica content and smooth white render, 2017

Rendered Façades

The external walls of the Bauhaus Building are constructed as a reinforced concrete skeleton with infill comprising various masonry materials, in part also as all-brick walls. These walls were rendered 'in 1926 with a natural hydraulic lime slaked on the building site and fine, locally sourced, primarily siliceous aggregates with a small percentage of coarse particles. Following a first spray-coat, this is applied with a trowel in the form of a single layer of skim plaster and finished with a wooden float.'[1] Lime paint was then applied wet-on-wet. The semi-basement areas of the building and the south end of the workshop wing feature a rough grey scratched render with a high mica content (Muscovite, particle size three to six millimetres).

During the renovation of 1976 and over the following years, the original lime plaster on the upper floors was extensively replaced by cement plaster coated with diffusion-proof paint. The original plaster is largely preserved in the studio building only. Several layers of paint were found here up to 2001: the original whitewash, oil-based camouflage paint dating from the Second World War, and a diffusion-proof coat containing PVC, most probably dating from 1976. Following a rough mapping of the current situation, the layers on top of the original plaster surfaces were removed with great care, enabling the partial preservation of the original layers. The remaining original plaster was carefully stabilised, and cement infills and badly damaged plaster areas that could not be saved were removed. The missing areas were filled in using a mortar based on the historical material, onto which a layer of chalk paint is applied wet-on-wet. As envisaged, using historical materials and techniques, this created a tableau that embraced certain anomalies as was the case in the 1920s.

The cement plaster areas which replaced the original lime plaster in 1976 combined with the diffusion-proof paint, which it was impossible to remove, to form a thick layer of plaster and paint. Here, hollows had already formed, which presented a risk of long-term damage to the building. This layer was therefore removed as carefully as possible during the renovations of 2001 and replaced by lime mortar and a coat of chalk paint according to the original model. Due to the effects of weathering, the white-painted plaster façades must be regularly repaired and repainted. This was most recently done on the studio building in 2018, seventeen years after it was last painted in 2001.

During the renovation of 1976, the original render on the semi-basement was replaced with a black-pigmented cement render, changing the shape of the structure. A small fragment of the original render found in the studio building in 2001 supplied evidence of the original composition, colour and mica content. This was preserved in the Bauhaus Dessau Foundation's Building Research Archive. The non-original, dark grey semi-basement render was removed and replaced by a lime render with mica content resulting in the original surface structure. The Bauhaus Building's basis which is rendered in this material, is exposed to splash water, snow, and road salt in an extreme way. It is not possible to make isolated repairs to the coloured render; the render reconstructed in 2002 was thus completely replaced from 2019

92)

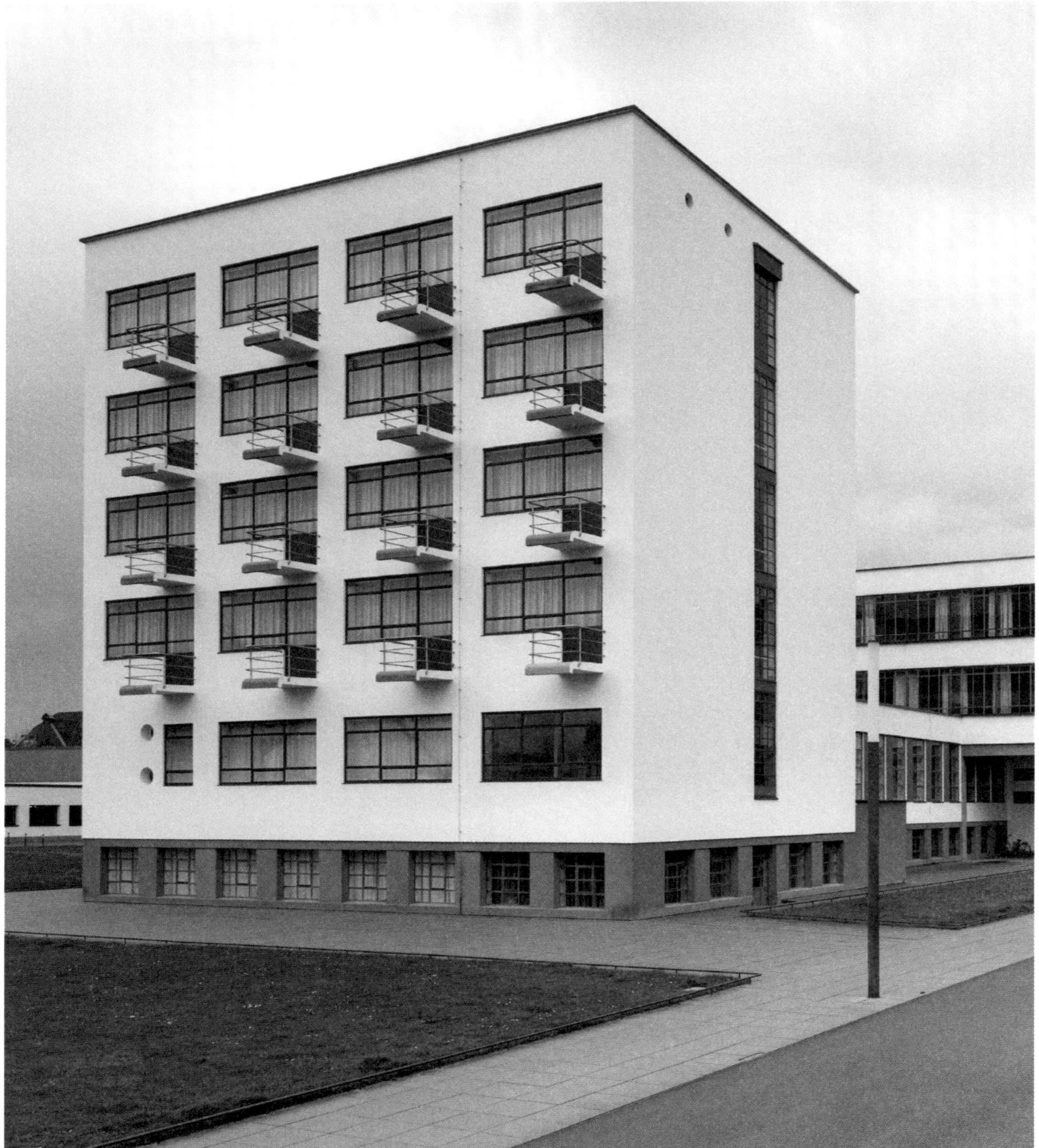

to 2021, again based on the same material composition as the original find.

The rendered outer shell of the Bauhaus Building contains cracks which cannot be fully eradicated because they have structural causes. One example is the roof of the studio building, where two building components—the building slab and the attic or the parapet wall of the roof terrace—meet and move at different rates because they are exposed to different climate conditions. The building elements therefore react to climate fluctuations with different movements, which cause the render to crack. The paint on these cracks flakes off, water penetrates, the render crumbles, and the façade is first visually impaired, later at risk of critical damage. The cracks are therefore closed with banked hemp fibres under a permanently elastic acrylic layer and covered with a sprayed-on mineral layer of fine sand, onto which the façade colour is painted. In this way, the cracks can absorb the movement without damage being done to the building.

Since 2021, the rendered surfaces of the Bauhaus Building have been monitored and assessed, also with regard to the effects of climate change including extreme weather conditions such as excess heat or rain. These changes can place new stresses on the surfaces or lead to greater movements in the structure and thus the formation of cracks. It remains to be seen whether the methods of maintenance and repair used to date will change in future or not, given the conditions of climate change.

92)
Studio building following restoration of the façade, 2021

93)
Stabilisation of indentations in rendered surfaces, 2019

94)
Repair of cracks in render, 2004

Cross section of proposed layer build-up (diagram: P. Schoene, qualified restorer)

a) Crack in concrete
b) Gap filled with organic fibre material
c) Permanently elastic layer
d) Mineral layer

Lime render

Limewash coat

93)

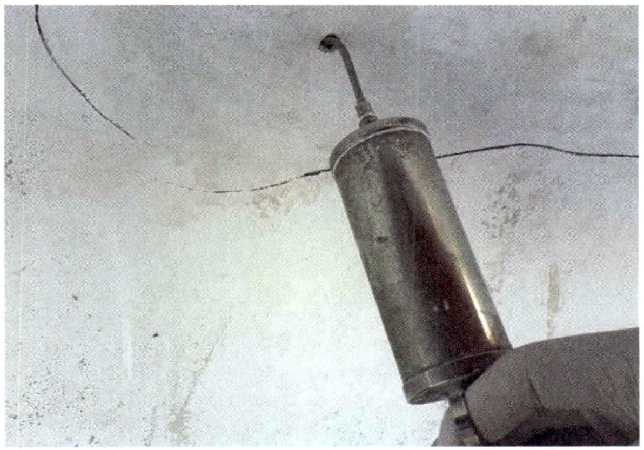

94)

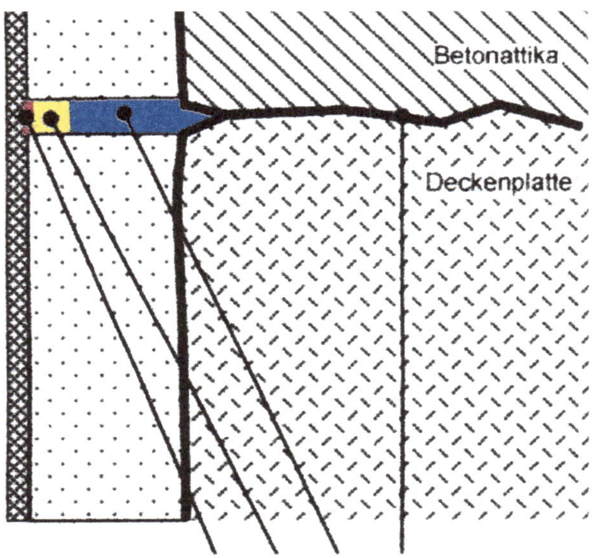

95)

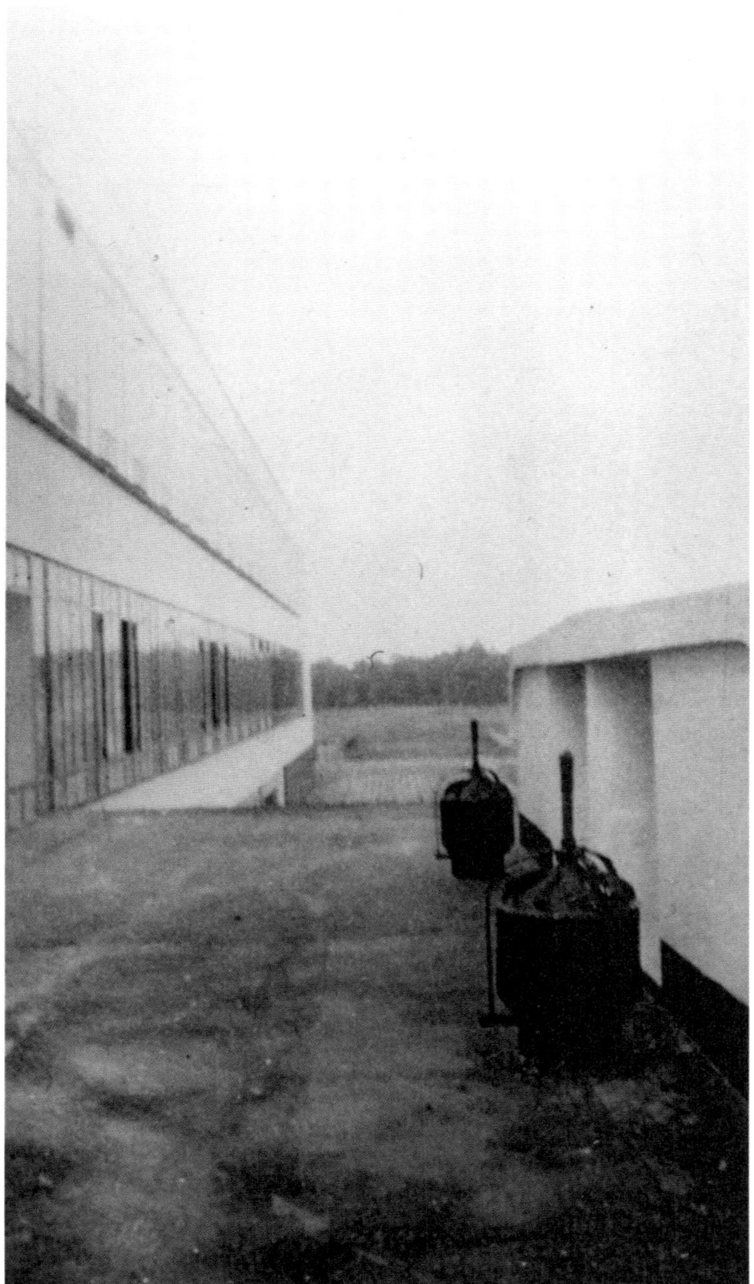

95)
Roof, connecting building, 1926

96)
Layers added retrospectively to the roof of the connecting building, 2000

Roofs

Walter Gropius regarded the roof as one of the façades of the building which required attention: 'With the development of air transport the architect will have to pay as much attention to the bird's-eye perspective of his houses as to their elevations'[2] He advocated the construction of flat roofs, for example by organising a survey on the experiences with flat roofs among internationally renowned architects like Peter Behrens, J.J.P. Oud, or Le Corbusier, which was published in the journal *Bauwelt* in 1926.[3] Among their advantages, he listed the more practical square roof spaces, the utility value of the roof areas, or the better options for extensions.
During essential renovation works not only the repair of damage to the roof cladding or leaks but also the design intention must therefore be considered.

In 1926, the roofs of the Bauhaus Building (except for the roof terrace of the studio building) were inaccessible flat roofs with internal drainpipes. Walter Gropius describes the roof membrane as follows: 'the roof terraces with welded asphalt tiles on a torfoleum insulation layer, the non-accessible flat roofs are covered with lacquered burlap over a torfoleum insulated layer and levelling concrete.'[4]

Following the closure of the Bauhaus Dessau, a flat pitched roof was built over the studio building. In addition, roof overhangs and external gutters and downpipes altered the function and appearance of the roofs.
These modifications were reversed during the renovation of 1976.

96)

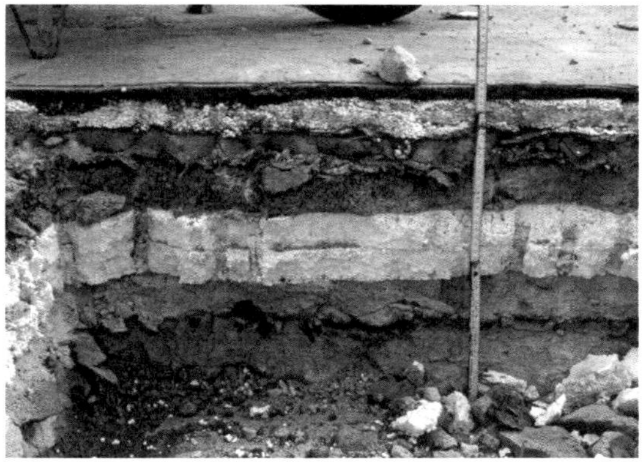

During the early nineteen-nineties, the roofs of the workshop wing, bridge, and north wing were refurbished and upgraded. The roof of the festive area and the roof terrace of the studio building were renovated in 2001. The roof of the studio building required further renovation in 2014.

The roof of the festive area was frequently repaired over the decades, with new layers of sloping screed, insulation, and sealing materials being added to combat penetrating damp. As a result, the roof had 'grown' by around half a metre. This compromised the outer appearance of the building due to the changed proportions and the fact that nearby windows had been partly swallowed up by the roof build-up. Furthermore, due to the pressure of the increased weight, on the inside the ceiling had begun to warp slightly. The removal of this roof build-up in 2001 constituted an intervention in the evolved structure of the monument. While the pressure on the plaster on the inner side of the roof was thus reduced, the plaster failed to adjust to the altered load and was additionally compromised over the course of the building measures by water penetration and vibrations. As a result, it cracked and detached itself in parts from the ceiling. On the one hand, the work on the roof was essential to preserve the historical monument, on the other, losses inside the building caused by this work were unavoidable. This example demonstrates just how interconnected the building components are and how much care must be taken with evolved contexts when dealing with a historical monument.

During the removal of later layers, remnants of the original Torfoleum insulation were discovered. Because the preservation of this historical insulating layer would have prevented the future protection and waterproofing of the roof, the original material was removed and preserved in the Bauhaus Dessau Foundation's Building Research Archive. Following the removal of the roof build-up, modern insulation materials and sealants were installed.

Gropius designed the terrace on the roof of the studio building as a 'roof garden on the studio building (the students' gymnasium)'.[5] Here, in the nineteen-twenties, the students exercised and performed plays, and the Bauhaus masters assembled to have their photograph taken. In 1934, a flat pitched roof was built over the roof terrace to protect the building against penetrating rainwater. But this was also brought forth to make fresh attacks on the architecture of the Bauhaus: 'The Bauhaus Dessau has frequently made an unfavourable impression due to significant structural flaws and material damage. It has already been subject to numerous, extensive maintenance works. Currently, a new roof is being built on one part of the building because the old one was in a derelict state.'[6]

The terrace was restored during the renovation of 1976. However, an expansion tank for the heating system had to be installed, taking over the sunroof, and the flooring comprising large asphalt tiles was replaced by small ceramic tiles. The wraparound bench was backfilled to form a complete parapet.

During the 2000 renovations, as with the roof of the festive area, numerous layers of roof sealant, sloping screed, and heat insulation were removed and replaced by a roof structure comprising modern materials. Because the roof terrace plays such an important role in the design of the Bauhaus Building, the historic sunroof was reconstructed with the aid of original photographs. In the process, the wraparound bench was uncovered and completed based on the historic example. However, it does not comply with the current building laws. While the eighty-centimetre-high parapet built in 1976 did not have the necessary height for a safety barrier, the wraparound bench exacerbates the problem: from the standpoint of building laws, the guard is then effectively only around forty-five-centimetres high. Raising the height of the parapet would change the balanced and finely tuned proportions of the building and was thus not worth considering. Here, the restoration of the original condition according to the heritage conservation objectives and compliance with the building regulations could not be reconciled. In 2014, in association with improvements to the tourism infrastructure of the Bauhaus Building, solutions were sought for unobtrusive or temporary safety barriers to enable public access.
The options considered included barriers made

from glass sheets or moveable wire mesh screens. After weighing the pros and cons, it was again concluded that in respect of installation and use, the necessary safety barriers would lead to far-reaching changes to the building and the way it is perceived, especially on the roof terrace itself, that cannot be reconciled with the building and its impact. Thus, the decision to favour the preservation of the historic bench prioritises the artistic significance of the building over the requirements arising from its use; its unrestricted useability is lost, but the terrace is won as a crucial component of Walter Gropius's building design.

In 2011, in the framework of thermal upgrading measures and following extensive analyses, assessments, and deliberations, a temporary photovoltaic system was installed on the flat roofs of the north wing of the Bauhaus Building and an auxiliary building. It was possible to avoid compromising the views of the building: the system comprises horizontal elements that are visible only from the multi-storey part of the Bauhaus, the studio building, and from the air, not from generally accessible areas of the building or from the surrounding area. At the same time, the system should help lessen the economic pressure on the Bauhaus Dessau Foundation to reduce energy costs and in this way create scope for the development of other, likewise long-term solutions designed to reduce energy consumption. According to the guidelines of heritage conservation, the use of the photovoltaic system is authorised for just fifteen years, after which the system will be dismantled.

To guarantee the long-term conservation of the roofs and the building as a whole, it is vitally important that the roof areas and drainage systems are regularly monitored and cleaned to ensure that damage caused, for example, by blocked drains and penetrating damp does not arise. This is therefore done on a regular basis and following exceptional weather events.

1
Danzl 2002, p. 387

2
Gropius 1965, p. 30

3
Gropius 1926/I

4
Gropius 2021, p. 15

5
Gropius 2021, p. 54

6
e.g. *Anhalter Anzeiger,* no. 34, 9 February 1934

97)

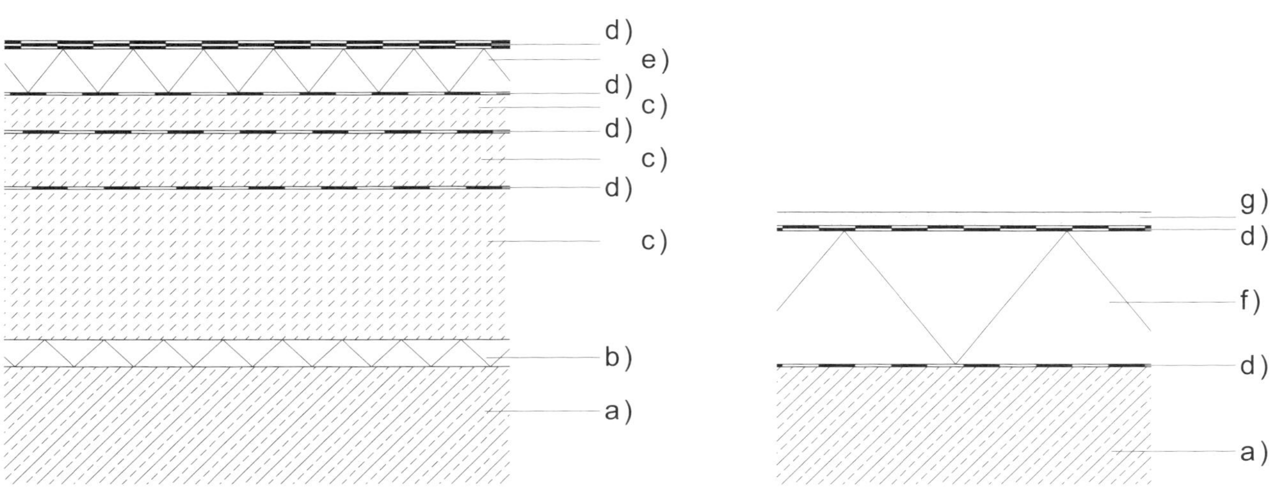

97)
Roof build-up: until 2001 (l.), from 2001 (r.)

a) Reinforced concrete with grout topping
b) Torfoleum insulation, 3 cm
c) Screed 17 cm, 6 cm, 4 cm
d) Bitumen
e) Polystyrene 5 cm
f) Closed cell cellular class in hot bitumen (gradient insulation) 4–15 cm
g) Grey slate cladding

98)
Roof terrace, studio building, 1926

99)
Roof terrace of the studio building following renovation, 1976

100)
Roof terrace, studio building, 2006

98)

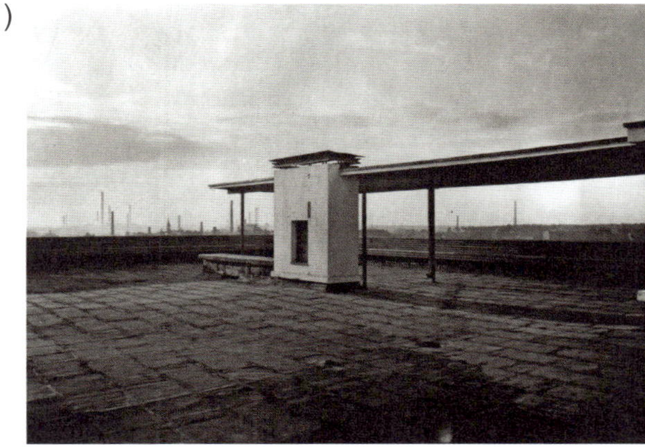

99)

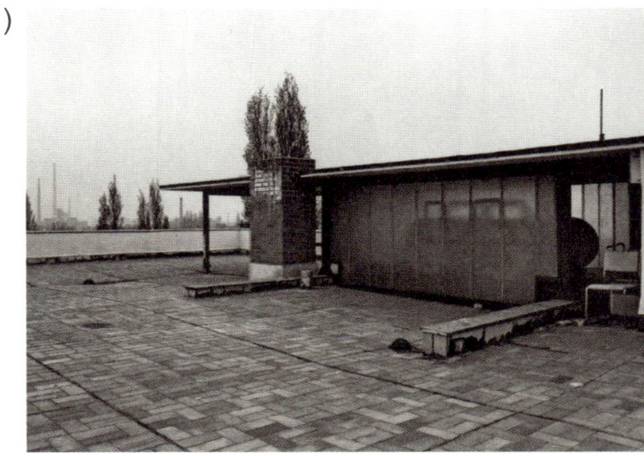

100)

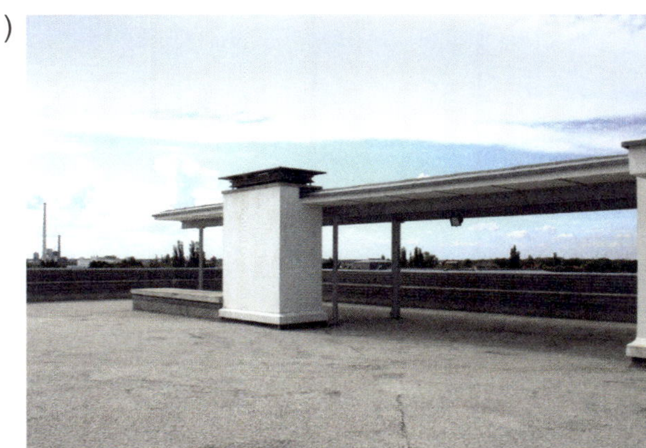

Material and Construction

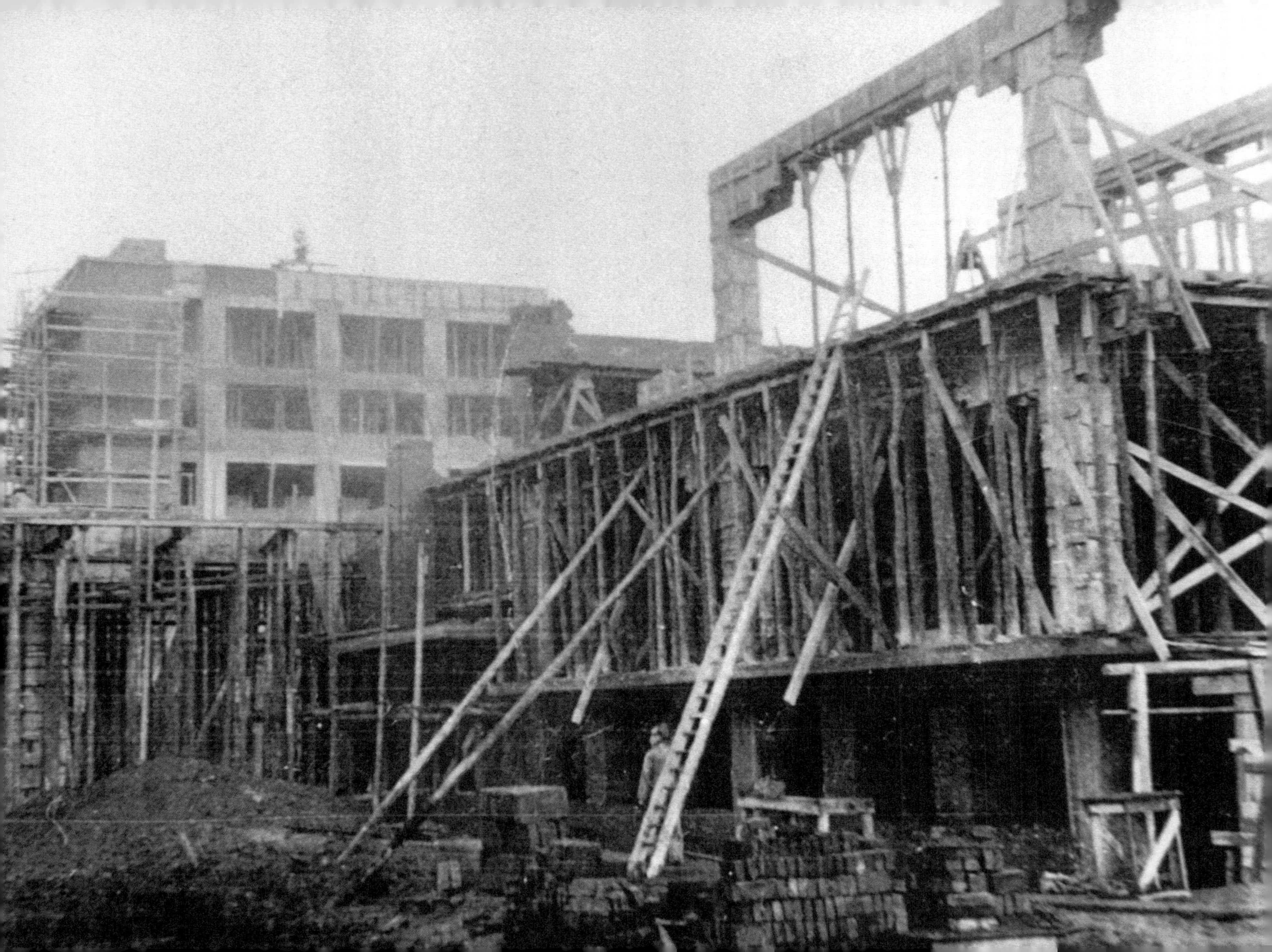

101)
View of workshop wing and studio building under construction, 1926

The extraordinary appeal of the architecture of the Bauhaus Building is also shaped by the creative use of then modern materials. As Walter Gropius writes in 1930: 'New synthetic substances—steel, concrete, glass—are actively superseding the traditional raw materials of construction. Their rigidity and molecular density have made it possible to erect wide-spanned and all but transparent structures for which the skill of previous ages was manifestly inadequate.'[1] Materials inside the building such as Triolin flooring, the nickel-plated surfaces of metallic elements such as fittings, and traditional materials like lime render or terrazzo are likewise crucial components of the architectonic quality which is forged in the interplay of industrial production and the work of artisans and artists.

The availability of the materials shapes the structure and form of the architecture; it promotes the development of new experiences of space and a singular aesthetic. The transformation of social, spatial and design ideas into built reality is also moulded by the potentials and limitations of the materials. The building materials and constructions testify to the architectural technology of the time, are fundamental constituents of the architecture, and carriers of its artistic and historical value. Historic building research provides an understanding of the building through exacting surveys and analyses of its materiality; collaboration with other specialist disciplines such as art history or various natural sciences is likewise essential. Against this backdrop, the Building Research Archive was established by the Bauhaus Dessau Foundation to support research into and the conservation of the Bauhaus buildings.[2]

Due in part to the increasing destruction of the material substance of monuments of New Architecture, the protection and preservation of the remaining building fabric became a necessity. This entailed the consideration of not only the artistic impact of the buildings, but also increasingly their relevance as historical testimonies, including their materiality and the traces of their age. Hartwig Schmidt indicated as much in 1998: 'If we are not prepared to accept aged surfaces, alterations, and a diminished utility value in the buildings of classical modernism, we shall soon have no historical monuments or authentic exponents, just reconstructions that approximate the originals, such as the buildings of the Weissenhof Estate in Stuttgart.'[3]

The Bauhaus buildings still have a modern appeal today and are therefore frequently taken for granted as integral parts of daily life which can be adapted to suit changing needs as required. However, the buildings comply with the standards and norms in force when they were built, which frequently differ from contemporary expectations and requirements. Yet it is precisely these outmoded elements that allow us to appreciate the architecture, its ties to the period, and its historico-cultural significance: in the Bauhaus Building, these include the metallic chains used to open windows with a loud rattle, the Triolin flooring with its specific odour, or the original stonewood screed with its traces of use. The materials, their imperfections, their sometimes old-fashioned characteristics, traces of ageing, and use reveal an aspect of the architecture that enhances our perception of the iconic building's brilliant white exterior.

Extensive knowledge of the architecture and its conservation, also in respect of its materiality, are therefore essential so that all aspects of the Bauhaus Building are understood and the full sensory experience of sounds, smells, or touch are preserved for future generations.[4] The art historian and heritage conservationist Georg Mörsch stressed the relevance of the materials as follows: 'To defend this narrative of the monument is to also defend the monument's material fabric, because it is only through this … that the monument achieves its ever-changing particular effect and its availability for being questioned.'[5]

Because modern architecture is associated with industrial production and new types of in some cases industrially manufactured building products, it is often assumed that worn or broken building components are easily replaced. However, the industrial production of goods in series was frequently stopped after just a short time, and it is thus virtually impossible to find equivalent replacements for building components that can no longer be salvaged or which are lost. The reproduction of historic models in small series is usually unrealistic, and replacing them with similar products often affects the architectonic impression and statement. In some cases, problems with the structural or climatic conditions in the building addition also arise if the new building component's material properties differ from the original. These aspects, too, emphasise the need to study the original building elements and preserve them for the future.

In-depth knowledge of a building material, its composition, ageing behaviour, interaction with other construction materials in terms of building physics and statics, and changes to its material properties caused by historic and current renovation measures are all essential for future conservation concepts. This calls for thorough knowledge not only of the historic building materials, but also of the ageing behaviour of certain substances, the climatic properties, especially in association with other, sometimes modern construction materials, the maintenance requirements, and the materials which may be used to replace missing building parts. During maintenance measures, a lack of information about the material-specific properties of historic building materials frequently results in irreparable damage to the original building fabric. This can detract from the characteristic impact, one consequence of which may be a loss of historical value.

Therefore the building research carried out by the Bauhaus Dessau Foundation contributes to the existing inventory of scientific work on the history of the Bauhaus, in which the historical, structural, and material aspects of the building are studied and documented. Two research projects[6] have begun to scientifically monitor required building measures and to record, document, and preserve building components, construction elements, and materials in a Building Research Archive.[7] Here, the aim is not only to research the original condition in as much depth as possible, but also to focus on changes made to the buildings. In this way, the foundations are laid for further research and for approaches to specific structural problems. The objective is to gain actionable insights into the renovation of the buildings of classical modernism and to develop a firm footing for the classification and evaluation of these buildings in the architectural history of the twentieth century.

102)
Fragments of original concrete (1926) with plaster (1976) on outside edges, 2019

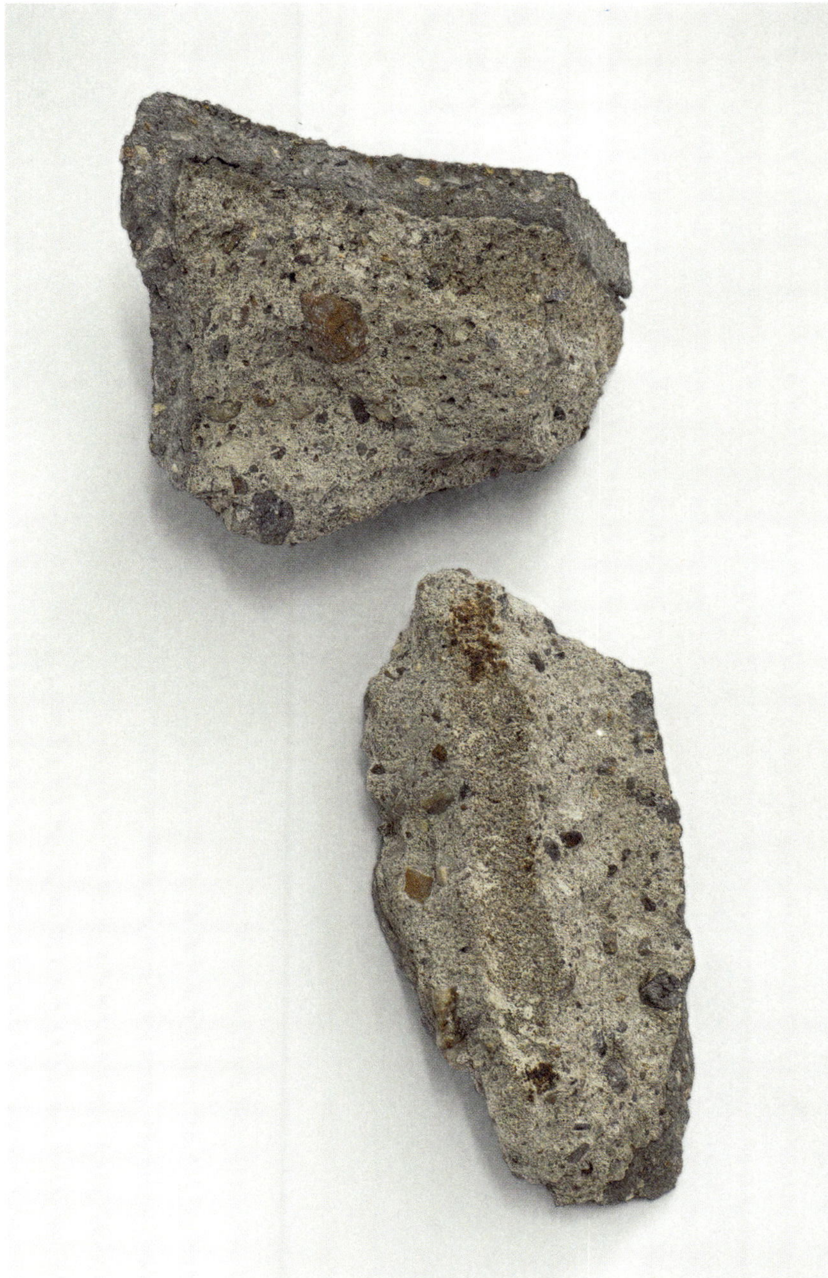

C o n c r e t e

The stabilisation of the load bearing reinforced concrete construction is of central importance to the conservation of the Bauhaus Building. The quality of the concrete varies in different parts of the building. For one thing, the structural work on the building was shared among several firms whose standard of work varied greatly. Then again, the building components are subject to different stresses depending on their location, e.g., penetrating damp. Consequently, in some areas the stabilisation of the concrete only requires cracks to be filled, whereas in others concrete building components must be extensively repaired or largely replaced.

The work on the load bearing construction also entails finding a balance between structural or economic interests and historical and conservation aspects as the radical renovation of the load-bearing construction of pillars and girders under the bridge shows. These were originally executed in exposed concrete, chisel-finished on the surface and nidged on the edges. In this area, the construction is exposed to the weather, and moisture was therefore able to penetrate the concrete over time. This leads to so-called carbonation, a chemical transformation of alkaline components that causes the reinforcement to corrode. The consequences include spalling, further moisture penetration, and extensive damage to the load-bearing reinforced concrete construction. During the thorough renovation of this construction under the bridge in 2003, traces on the concrete indicated that earlier repairs dated back several decades.

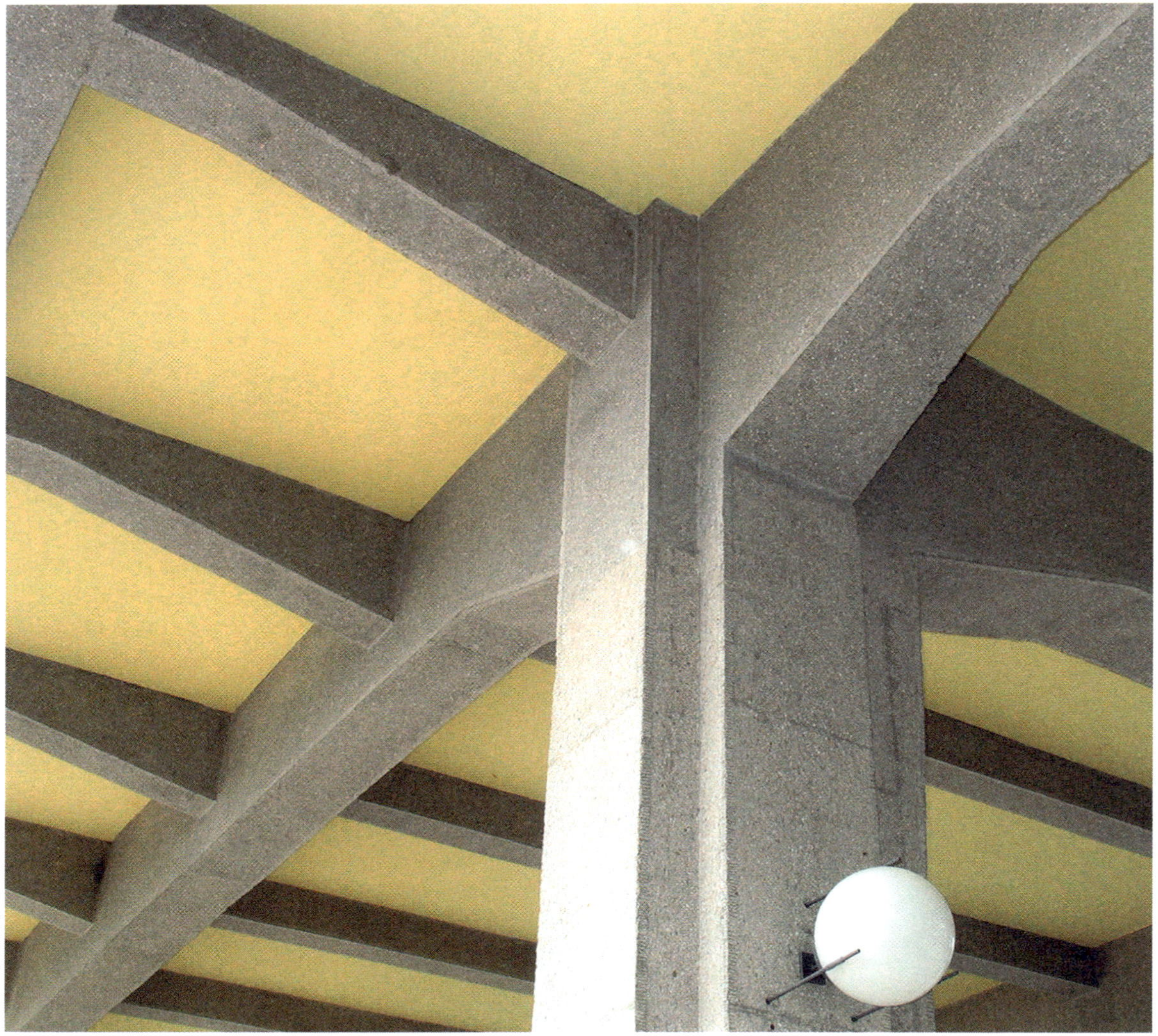

103)
Exposed concrete construction under the bridge, 2004

During the renovation of 1976, efforts were made to resolve the problem by applying plaster to the original surfaces of the pillars and girders, thus fully cladding the construction. 'Because applying the nidged finish to a new concrete cladding caused this to come loose again, a solution was sought and found with the application of a fine-grained pebble plaster. In this way, an approximation of the crystalline look of the original was achieved', explained Wolfgang Paul, who was involved at the time as a representative of Dessau town council.[8] This step preserved the existing original building fabric, albeit with a different surface and in consequence slightly different dimensions. The original chisel-finished surface with nidged edges remained detectable on remnants which were preserved in a few places under the plaster.

Despite the plaster cladding, the concrete and reinforcement continued to deteriorate over the following decades. As a result, although intensive efforts were made to preserve as much of the concrete as possible, in 2003 a thorough renovation of the supports, involving the extensive substitution of materials, became inevitable. The damage to the girders in a more sheltered location was more limited, which meant they could be repaired: damaged areas were removed, the reinforcement was strengthened, and the concrete then replenished.

Alongside structural aspects and matters of technical execution, the focus was on the most faithful possible recreation of the original material composition and surface design of the concrete. Because it is a central public space, the load bearing construction under the bridge plays an important part in the collective impact of the architecture of the Bauhaus Building. The details of the execution must therefore always be considered too.

During the 2003 renovation of the construction under the bridge, the crumbling concrete was replaced where possible, but the original reinforcement was left untouched to minimise interventions in the load bearing structure. But with the preservation of the historic reinforcement and the replacement of the concrete with the necessary cladding, the dimensions of the supports increased to around the size they were prior to the renovation, including plaster. To reinstate the original dimensions with the necessary cladding in place would have meant installing the reinforcement inside the support, thus a more significant intervention in both the load bearing structure and the intact original building fabric. Specialist engineers, authorities for the protection of monuments, the Staatshochbauamt, the state building authority, as well as the architects and the Bauhaus Dessau Foundation were all agreed that the barely perceptible increase in dimensions represents the smallest possible intervention in the historical monument.

The composition of the historic concrete was analysed, and it was recreated with the original colouration, particle size, and details of execution. Following the removal of the crumbling material, the reinforcement was repaired, the new mortar was poured, and the concrete surface still showing the traces of formwork was chisel-finished and nidged on the edges. The horizontal lines show the heights of the formwork sections into which the concrete was poured. This vestige of the casting process cannot be fully avoided and was originally also present.

104)

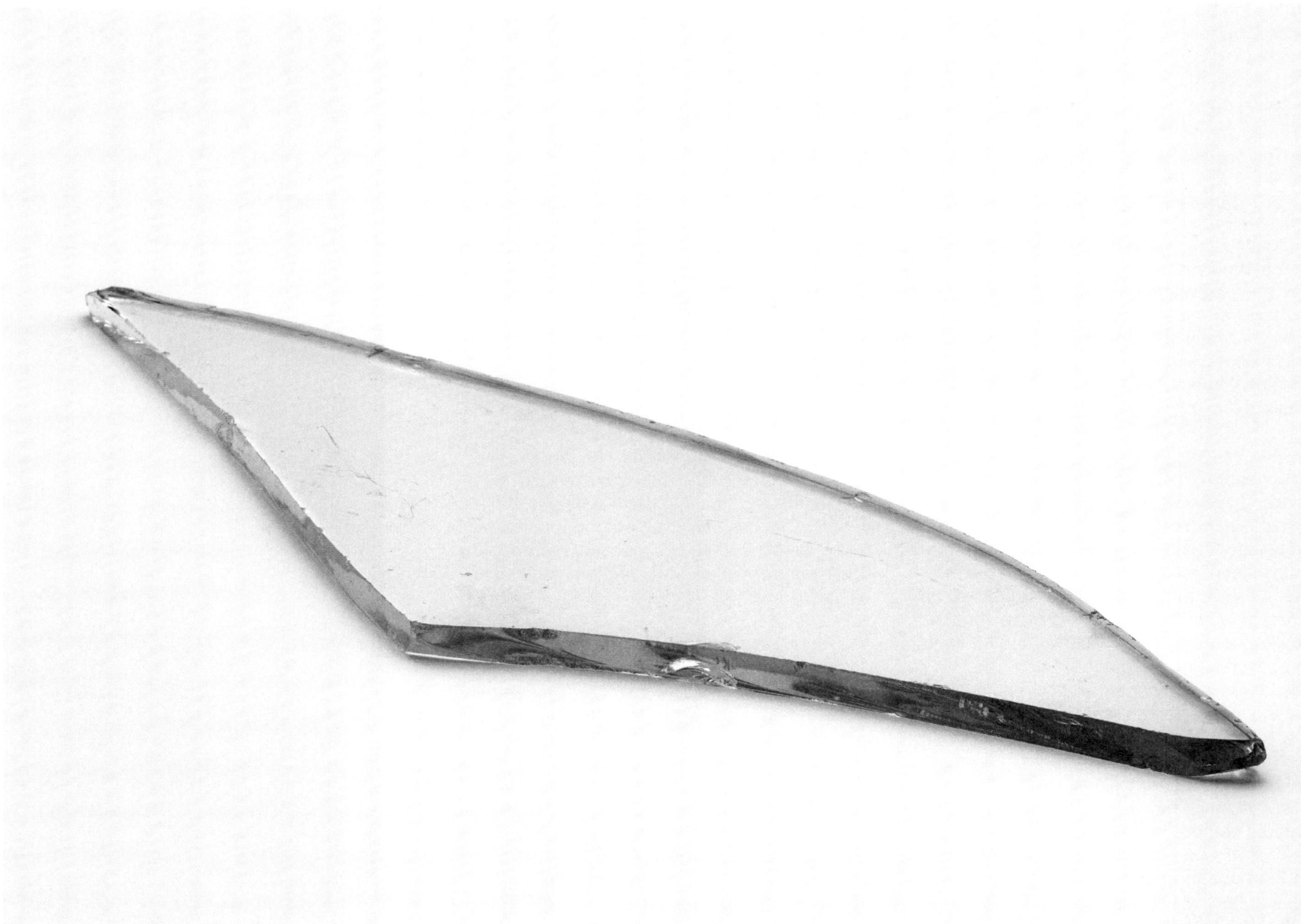

)5)

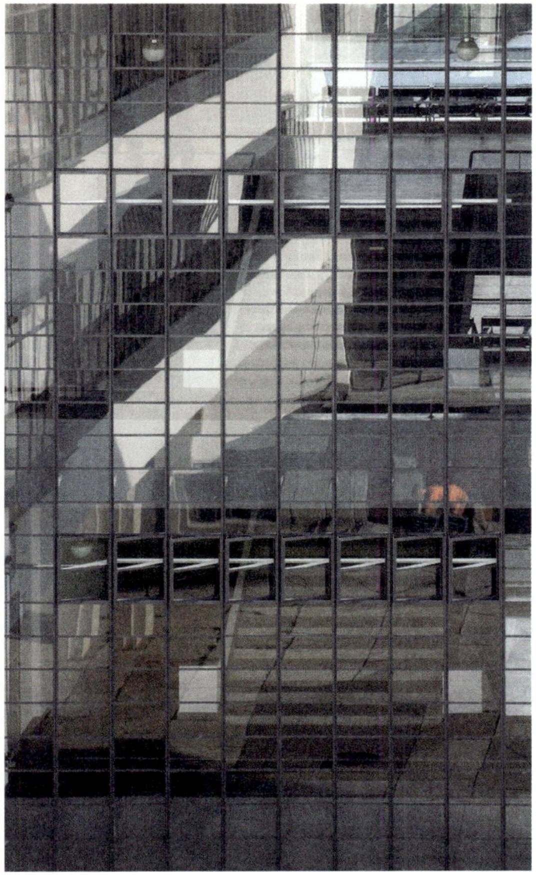

104)
Fragment of float glass from the new building of the School and Museum of Arts and Crafts in Zurich (1933), 2019

105)
Glass façade, transparency and reflections, 2006

Polished Plate Glass

The glass used in the Bauhaus Building in Dessau in 1926 was no ordinary glass, but polished plate glass, as Walter Gropius states in his book *bauhaus buildings dessau:* 'all windows have steel window sashes with double weathering contacts with polished plate glass.'[9] Because the transparency and crystal clear reflections of the extensive glass façades are fundamental to the aesthetic impact of the architecture, Gropius set great store by the use of this material, the benefits of which he praised as follows in an article written in 1926, i.e., when the construction of the Bauhaus Building was underway: 'window glass … transmits blurred light reflexes from outside and a distorting through-vision from inside; it is only the grinding and polishing of a perfectly cut glass pane … that yields perfected exactness and clarity of the noble glass material.'[10] During the manufacturing process, the molten glass is cast onto a flat surface, cooled, ground, and polished with felt disc pads using a fine slurry of water and iron oxide.[11] It was only from 1959 that the manufacture of float glass enabled the production of a cheaper product of comparable quality.

The fascination with glass as a building material is described as follows by the architect Arthur Korn in 1929: 'Thus the peculiar characteristic of glass as compared to all materials hitherto in use becomes apparent: noticeable yet not quite visible. It is the great membrane, full of mystery, delicate yet tough. It can enclose and open up spaces in more than one direction. Its peculiar advantage is in the diversity of the impression it creates.'[12] The properties of the polished plate glass uniquely express this complexity of the material, which continues to fascinate us today. The original glazed surfaces of the Bauhaus Dessau were destroyed and, as far as we currently know, there is no hard evidence that material samples of the original glass have survived. Following the destruction of some in the Second World War, further large areas were mislaid or destroyed during the renovation of 1976. During the reconstruction of the curtain wall the same year, the use of 'thermal glass' and a sun protection layer were also discussed but ultimately dismissed, because such materials would have had an extremely negative impact on the façade. Hans Berger, who supervised the renovation process for the responsible heritage conservation institute in Halle, explained: 'The work on the Bauhaus "monument" is not about what Gropius would do today given a similar situation, but about respecting and documenting the accomplishments of 1926.'[13]

Today, a fragment of the polished plate glass[14] used by Walter Gropius, found in the new building of the School and Museum of Arts and Crafts in Zurich[15] from 1933, serves as a reference piece that enables us to better understand the impact of the Bauhaus Building's glass façades. On this basis, white float glass, which is very similar to polished plate glass, is used in the Bauhaus Building.

106)

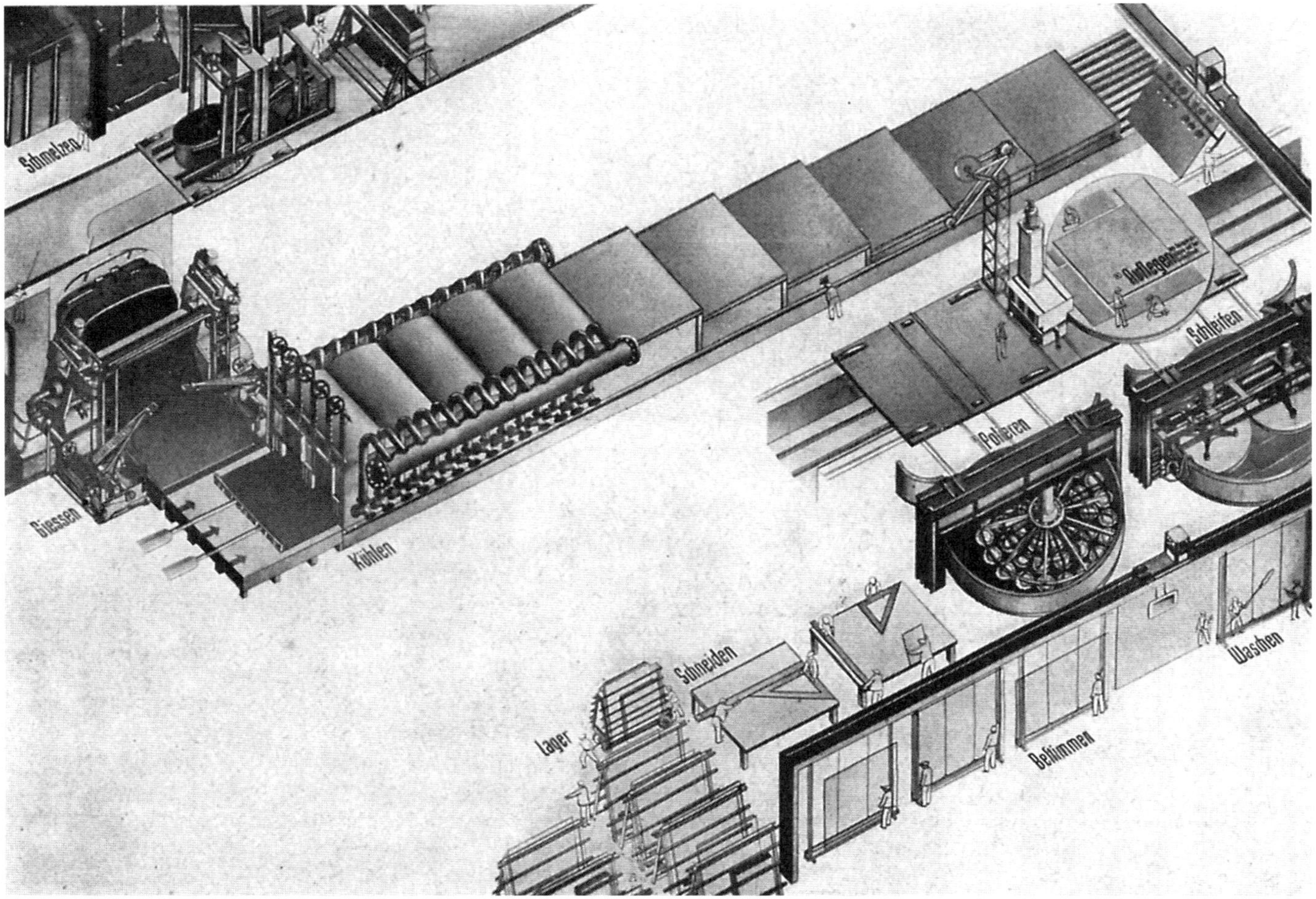

106)
Manufacture of float glass, 1948

107)
Polishing machine in a plate glass factory, 1948

)7)

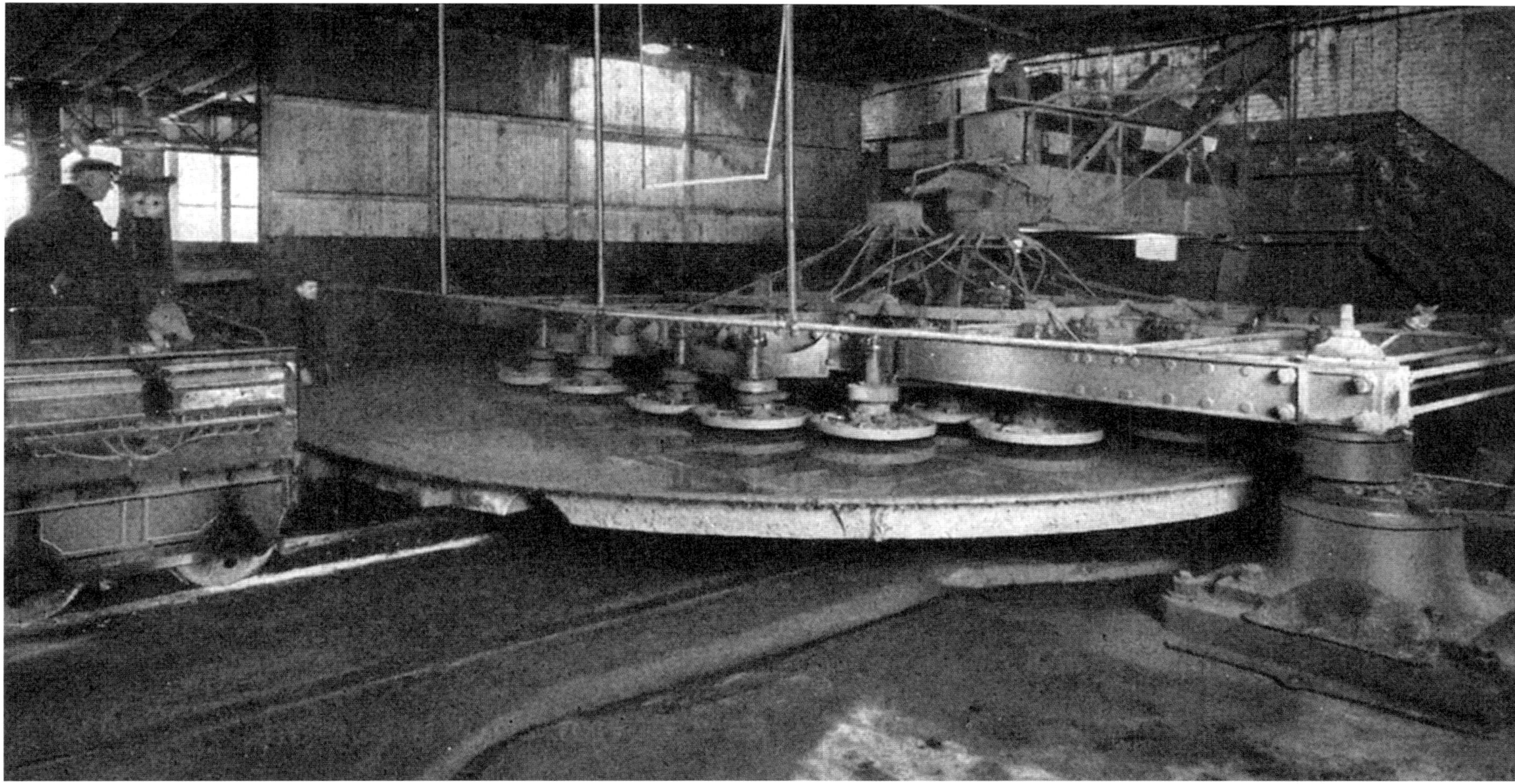

108)

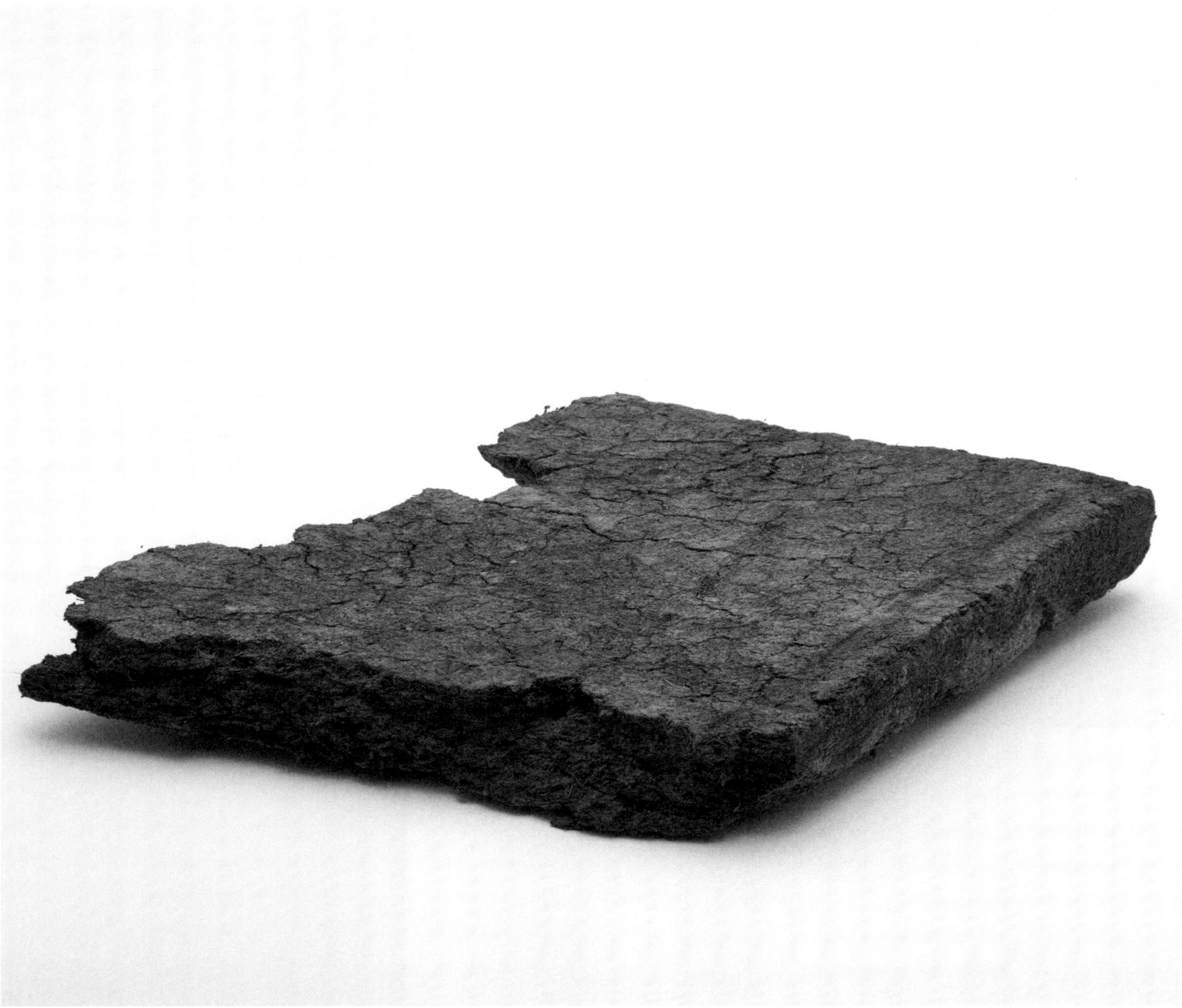

108)
Fragment of Torfoleum insulation slab (1926), 2019

109)
Advertisement for Torfoleum, 1930

110)
Bauhauslers on studio building roof insulated with Torfoleum, 1926

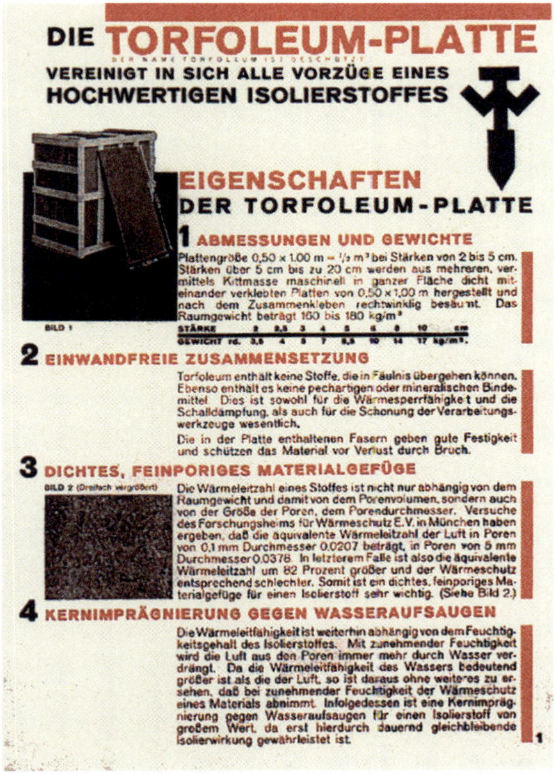

DIE TORFOLEUM-PLATTE

VEREINIGT IN SICH ALLE VORZÜGE EINES HOCHWERTIGEN ISOLIERSTOFFES

EIGENSCHAFTEN DER TORFOLEUM-PLATTE

1 ABMESSUNGEN UND GEWICHTE

Plattengröße 0,50 × 1,00 m = ½ m² bei Stärken von 2 bis 5 cm. Stärken über 5 cm bis zu 20 cm werden aus mehreren, vermittels Kittmasse maschinell in ganzer Fläche dicht miteinander verklebten Platten von 0,50 × 1,00 m hergestellt und nach dem Zusammenkleben rechtwinklig besäumt. Das Raumgewicht beträgt 160 bis 180 kg/m³

BILD 1

STÄRKE	2	2,5	3	4	5	6	8	10	cm
GEWICHT rd.	3,5	4	5	7	8,5	10	14	17	kg/m².

2 EINWANDFREIE ZUSAMMENSETZUNG

Torfoleum enthält keine Stoffe, die in Fäulnis übergehen können. Ebenso enthält es keine pechartigen oder mineralischen Bindemittel. Dies ist sowohl für die Wärmesperrfähigkeit und die Schalldämpfung, als auch für die Schonung der Verarbeitungswerkzeuge wesentlich.

Die in der Platte enthaltenen Fasern geben gute Festigkeit und schützen das Material vor Verlust durch Bruch.

3 DICHTES, FEINPORIGES MATERIALGEFÜGE

BILD 2 (Dreifach vergrößert)

Die Wärmeleitzahl eines Stoffes ist nicht nur abhängig von dem Raumgewicht und damit von dem Porenvolumen, sondern auch von der Größe der Poren, dem Porendurchmesser. Versuche des Forschungsheims für Wärmeschutz E.V. in München haben ergeben, daß die äquivalente Wärmeleitzahl der Luft in Poren von 0,1 mm Durchmesser 0,0207 beträgt, in Poren von 5 mm Durchmesser 0,0378. In letzterem Falle ist also die äquivalente Wärmeleitzahl um 82 Prozent größer und der Wärmeschutz entsprechend schlechter. Somit ist ein dichtes, feinporiges Materialgefüge für einen Isolierstoff sehr wichtig. (Siehe Bild 2.)

4 KERNIMPRÄGNIERUNG GEGEN WASSERAUFSAUGEN

Die Wärmeleitfähigkeit ist weiterhin abhängig von dem Feuchtigkeitsgehalt des Isolierstoffes. Mit zunehmender Feuchtigkeit wird die Luft aus den Poren immer mehr durch Wasser verdrängt. Da die Wärmeleitfähigkeit des Wassers bedeutend größer ist als die der Luft, so ist daraus ohne weiteres zu ersehen, daß bei zunehmender Feuchtigkeit der Wärmeschutz eines Materials abnimmt. Infolgedessen ist eine Kernimprägnierung gegen Wasseraufsaugen für einen Isolierstoff von großem Wert, da erst hierdurch dauernd gleichbleibende Isolierwirkung gewährleistet ist.

1

109)

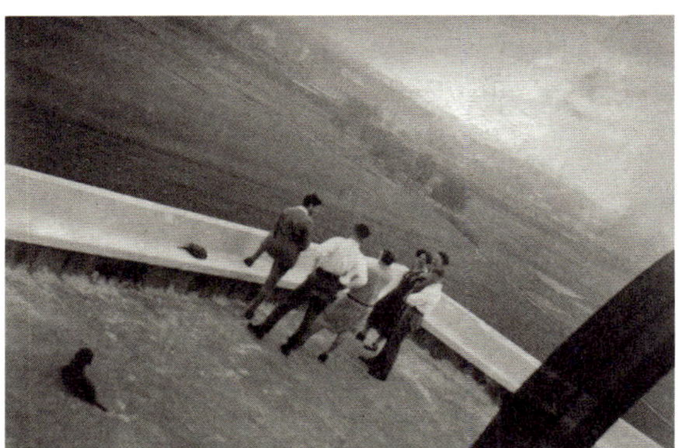

110)

Torfoleum

The Bauhaus Building loses a considerable amount of heat in winter and absorbs a lot of heat in summer through its extensive glazed surfaces, much like other buildings of classical modernism. For this reason, among others, it is important to insulate other parts of the building shell, particularly since the demand for a comfortable ambient temperature has grown since the nineteen-twenties. To improve the insulation in the Bauhaus Building, peat insulation panels were installed as early as 1926 in the flat roofs, the floors of the caretakers' flats in the semi-basements, and the flooring on the lower storey of the bridge. The same material was used to insulate some of the piping.

Torfoleum was not in general use as an insulation material in the nineteen-twenties and presented a challenge for the companies installing it, as the Dessau-based businessman Robert Richter explained in a letter to Walter Gropius: 'The materials you are using in this building are so new that the way they work is far from proven in many respects and as such, you cannot expect a contractor to be fully schooled in the methods of installation.'[16] A representative of Dessau's municipal authorities confirmed the lack of experience of this type of construction during a debate about whether the cracks that appeared in the top layer of concrete following the installation of the panels were caused by the nature of the construction or by flawed workmanship. 'Because we have no experience of the installation, as at the Bauhaus, of Torfoleum panels without fixings on top of the solid ceiling and under the lightweight concrete which serves as an accessible roof, we cannot confidently provide an expert opinion or produce an assessment.'[17]

Torfoleum is a brand name for an insulation material comprising compressed peat, which is impregnated to provide moisture and flame resistance. These peat panels were made by various manufacturers; materials supplied by the Eduard Dyckerhoff Torfoleum works were used in the Bauhaus Building.[18] Dyckerhoff's premises were located on the edge of moorland near Hannover. He had the trade name Torfoleum protected and introduced the material's advantages and instructions for its installation across nine pages of the *Bauwelt Katalog* 1929/30.[19] The lightweight panels are between two and five centimetres thick and measure fifty times eighty centimetres. According to Dyckerhoff, the material has a K-value of 0.04,[20] giving a three-centimetre thick Torfoleum panel the thermal conductivity (or insulation) value of a fifty-six-centimetre-thick masonry wall. In Dessau, the material was used not only in the Bauhaus Building but also in the Masters' Houses, the Dessau-Törten Housing Estate, and the Steel House.

Because the Torfoleum on the roofs and in the floors of the Bauhaus Building was damaged, the panels were carefully removed and replaced by foam glass insulation. Fragments of the historic panels have been preserved in the Building Research Archive.

111)

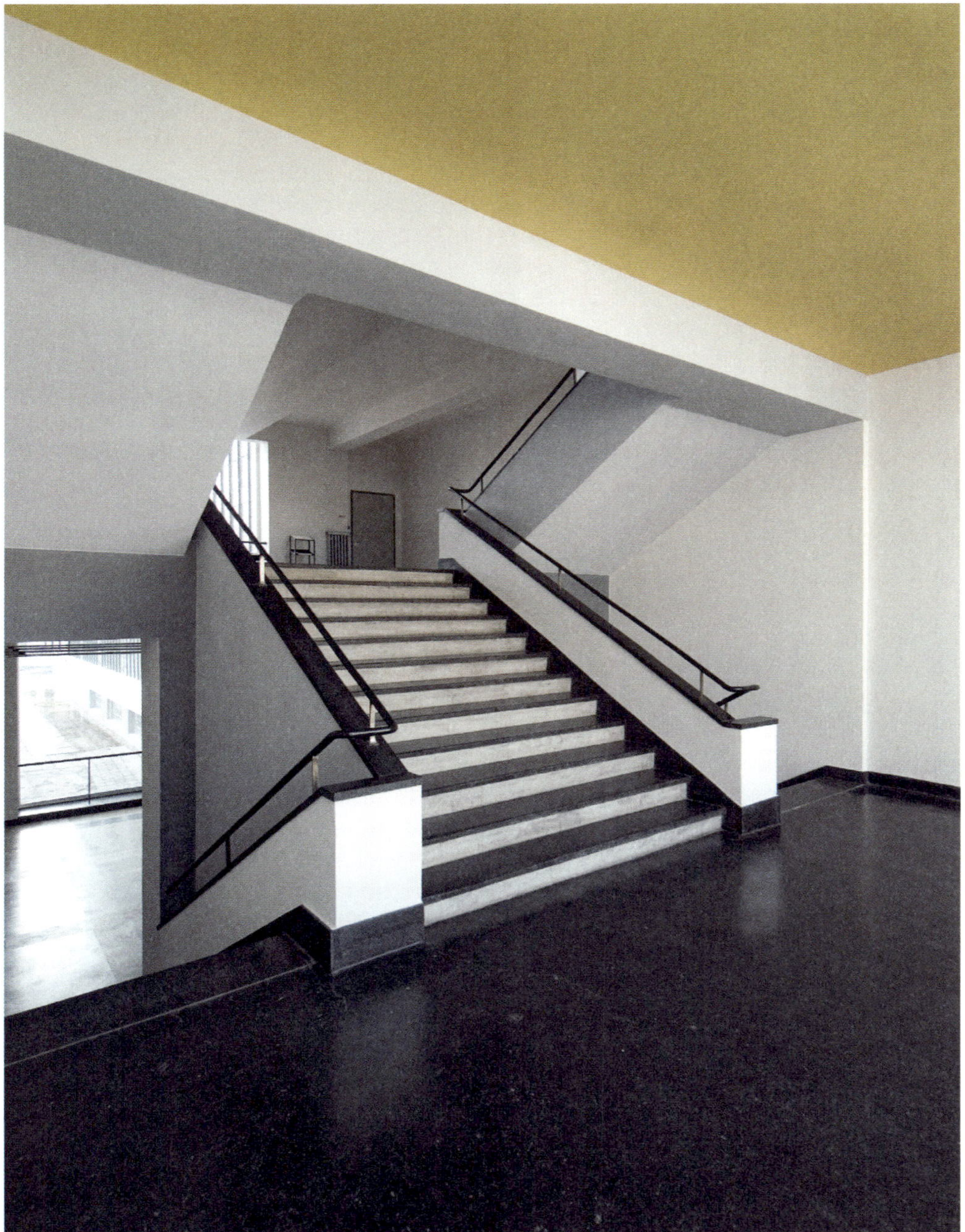

Flooring

The aesthetic appeal of the Bauhaus Building is shaped not only by the colours and surface structures of the ceilings and walls but also by the floors, the materiality and hard and glossy surfaces of which contribute to the overall spatial impression. Gropius used different materials for the floors, chosen according to the functions of the spaces. The entrance areas, stairways, and sanitary facilities feature black terrazzo floors containing Waldheim serpentinite, while screed with a rippled surface effect and unpigmented stonewood floors dominate in the workshop wing. Stonewood screed floors are also found in the classrooms in the north wing, on the bridge, and in the studio building, while the office flooring comprised a seamless, flexible material called Triolin. Asphalt tiles were laid in parts of the semi-basement in the north wing. The company DASAG GmbH continued to produce these in the same colours and dimensions until its closure in ca. 2013.[21]

During the maintenance and renovation of the floors, the original materials are preserved where possible, and improvements are made using identical materials. Visible damage caused by traces of use or alterations is left unchanged, provided it is not too extreme. These traces testify to the age and authenticity of the architecture and therefore enrich the perception of the building not only as a work of art but also as historical site.

Because the floors are significant components of the building's complex design, which are at the same time exposed to considerable wear and tear through frequent use, the Bauhaus Dessau Foundation has methodically complied and evaluated information about the history, composition, production, idiosyncrasies, and care of these materials.

112)

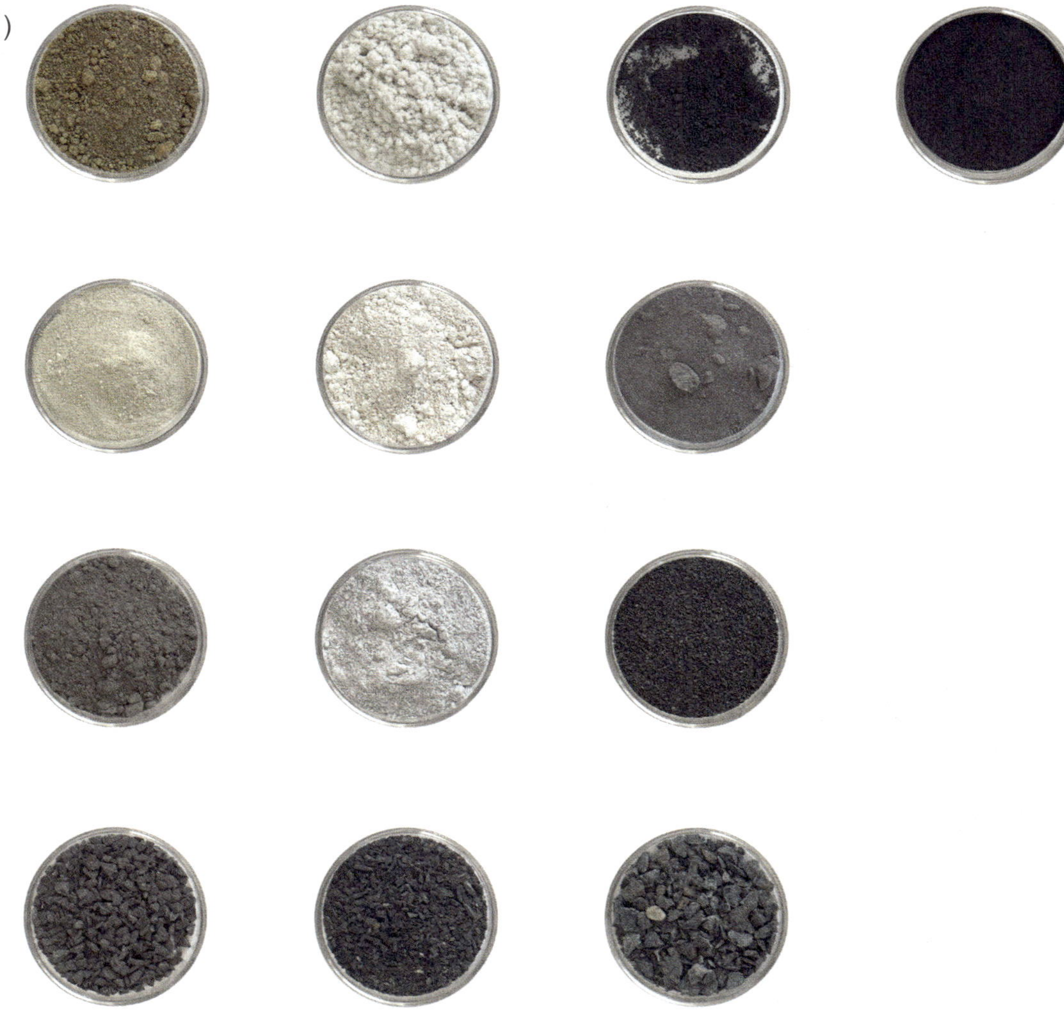

111)
Stairs and landing with terrazzo floor, 2006

112)
Components of terrazzo, 2019

113)

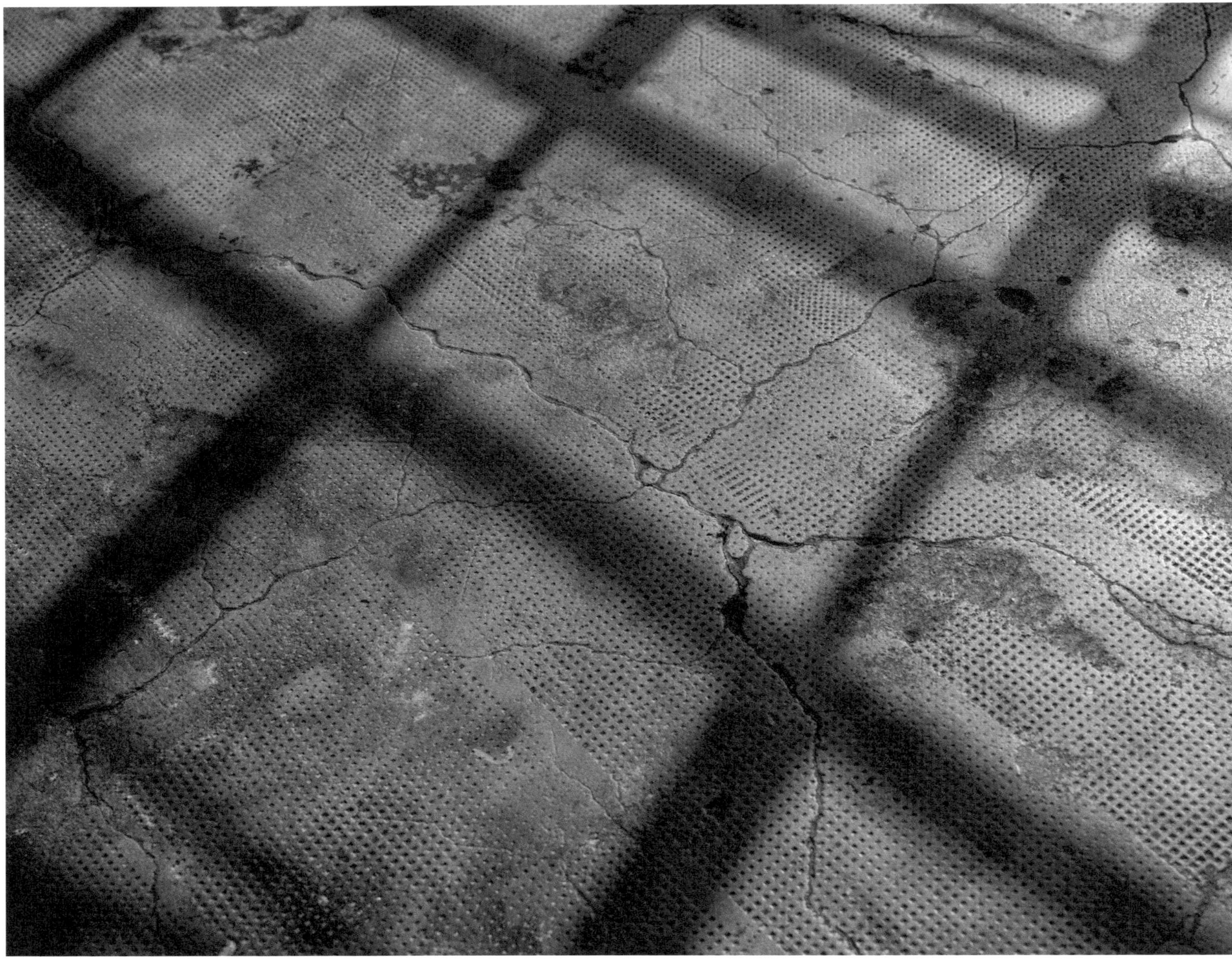

113)
Imprinted screed in the workshop wing, 2021

114)
Roof structure with layers of terrazzo, Triolin and stonewood screed (1926), 2006

114)

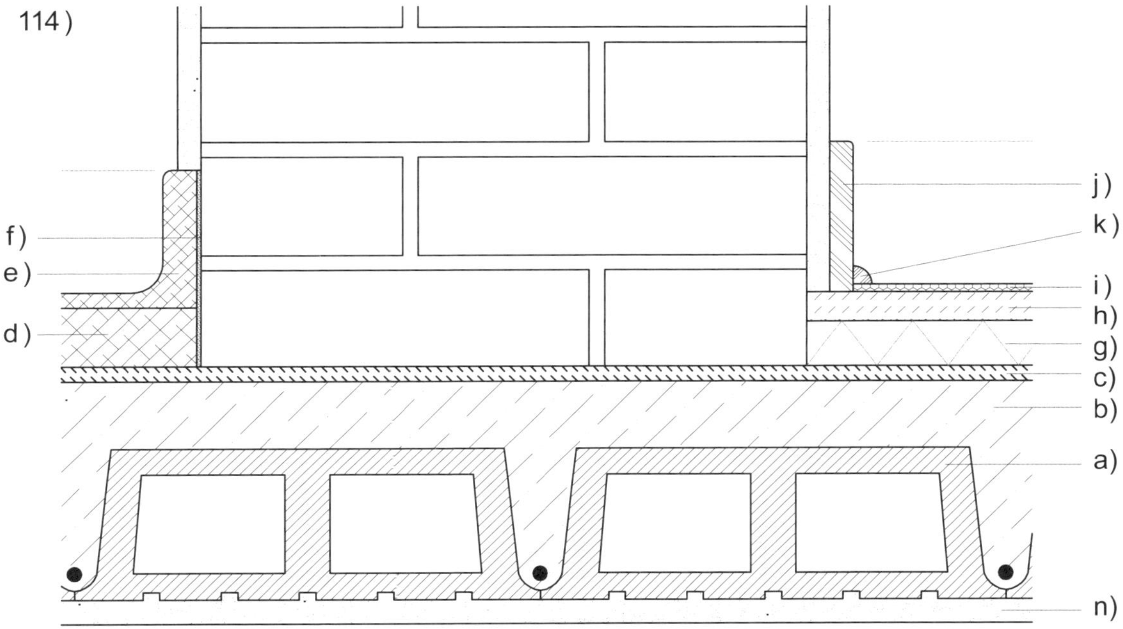

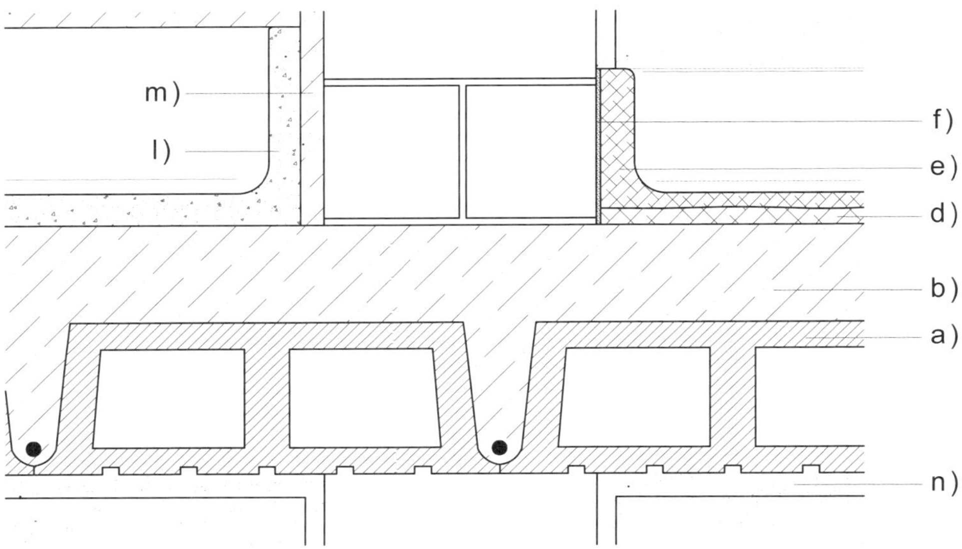

a) Iron-reinforced concrete ceiling, hollow blocks 10 × 30 cm
b) Concrete topping 4–6 cm
c) Levelling layer
d) Stonewood sublayer with a very high proportion of wood (1–4 cm)
e) Stonewood top layer with integrated cove base 1 cm
f) Insulation layer
g) Torfoleum insulation 3 cm
h) Cement screed with wire mesh underlayment 2 cm
i) Triolin flooring
j) Wooden skirting board
k) Quarter round
l) Terrazzo with integrated cove base 2 cm
m) Wall plaster with distemper
n) Ceiling plaster with distemper
o) External render

115)

116)

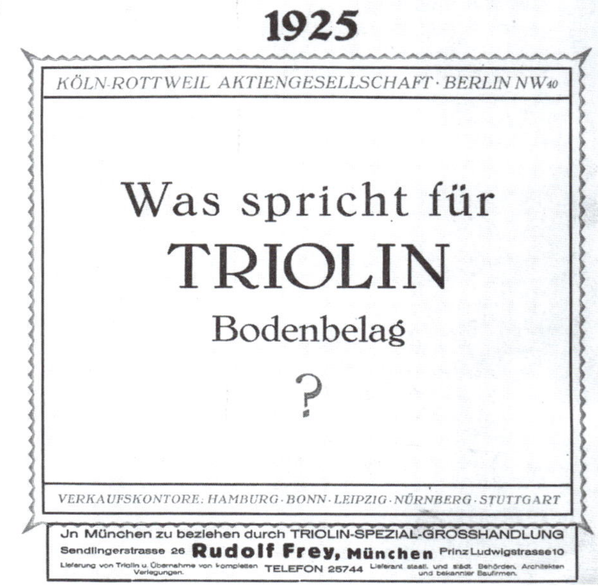

Triolin

In 2002, the findings of research into the materiality of the Bauhaus Building revealed that Walter Gropius had not used linoleum in the Bauhaus Building and the Masters' Houses as previously thought but Triolin,[22] a flooring material previously installed in the Haus Am Horn in Weimar. Triolin, an early, flexible synthetic material made of nitrocellulose, a filling material, and a plasticiser laid on a hemp fibre backing, was produced in a range of colours. The material was developed after the end of the First World War following the collapse of the import-dependent production of linoleum. At the same time, new uses were being sought for the decommissioned production plants for gunpowder and explosives, in which collodion cotton with a high nitrate content was processed. The explosives factory Köln-Rottweil AG developed Triolin utilising this material, received a German Imperial Patent in 1919, and manufactured this affordable flooring. The initially extremely successful product was however unable to assert itself against the competition and as a result, the production of Triolin ended in 1927 and the follow-on product Prisma's production some time after 1930.[23] Today, this means that there is no material available for the necessary repairs to the floors. Used pieces of the historic flooring from the Bauhaus Building and other modern buildings are therefore stored in the Building Research Archive for future repairs and for research purposes.

At first glance, Triolin is barely distinguishable from linoleum. However, the colour palette is different, as is the degree of gloss. It is also generally thinner, and it does not age in the same way as linoleum. The differences become particularly evident when Triolin floors are repaired with linoleum. Just a few square metres of the material have been preserved in situ in the Bauhaus Building. Since 2004, these have been painstakingly conserved, restored, and maintained by a specialist in the restoration of synthetic materials.[24] The restoration of synthetic materials in modern buildings is a relatively recent science, in which there is a considerable need for further research.[25]

117)

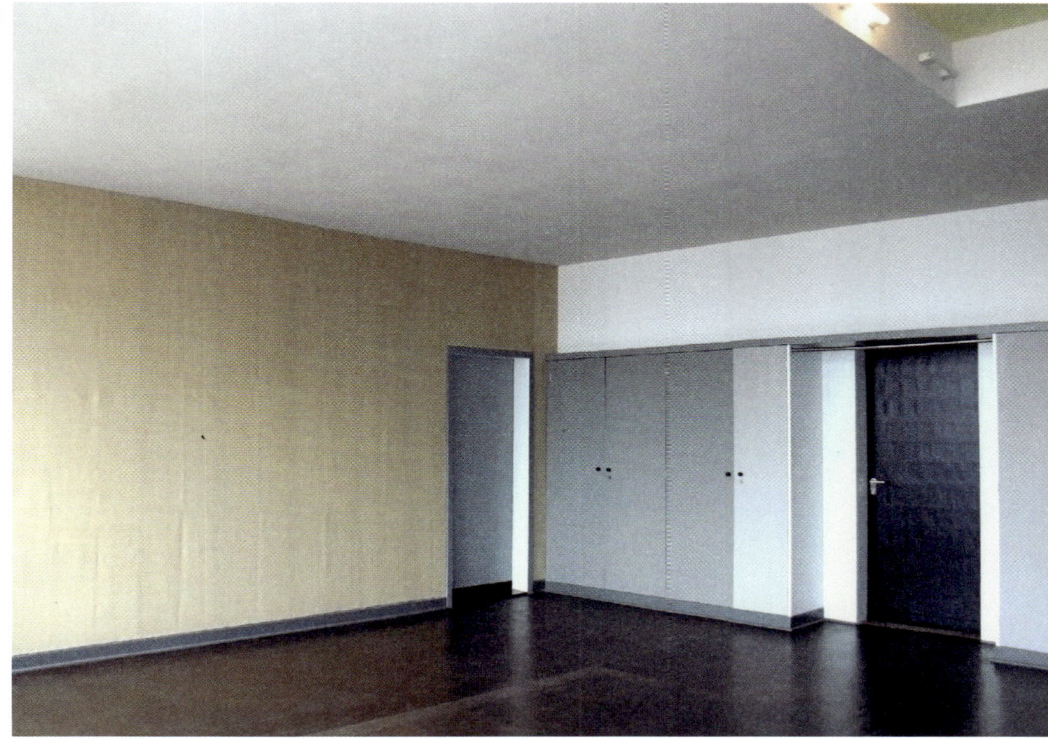

115)
Fragment of Triolin flooring (1926), 2019

116)
Advertisement for Triolin, 1925

117)
Historic director's office with Triolin flooring, 2006

118)

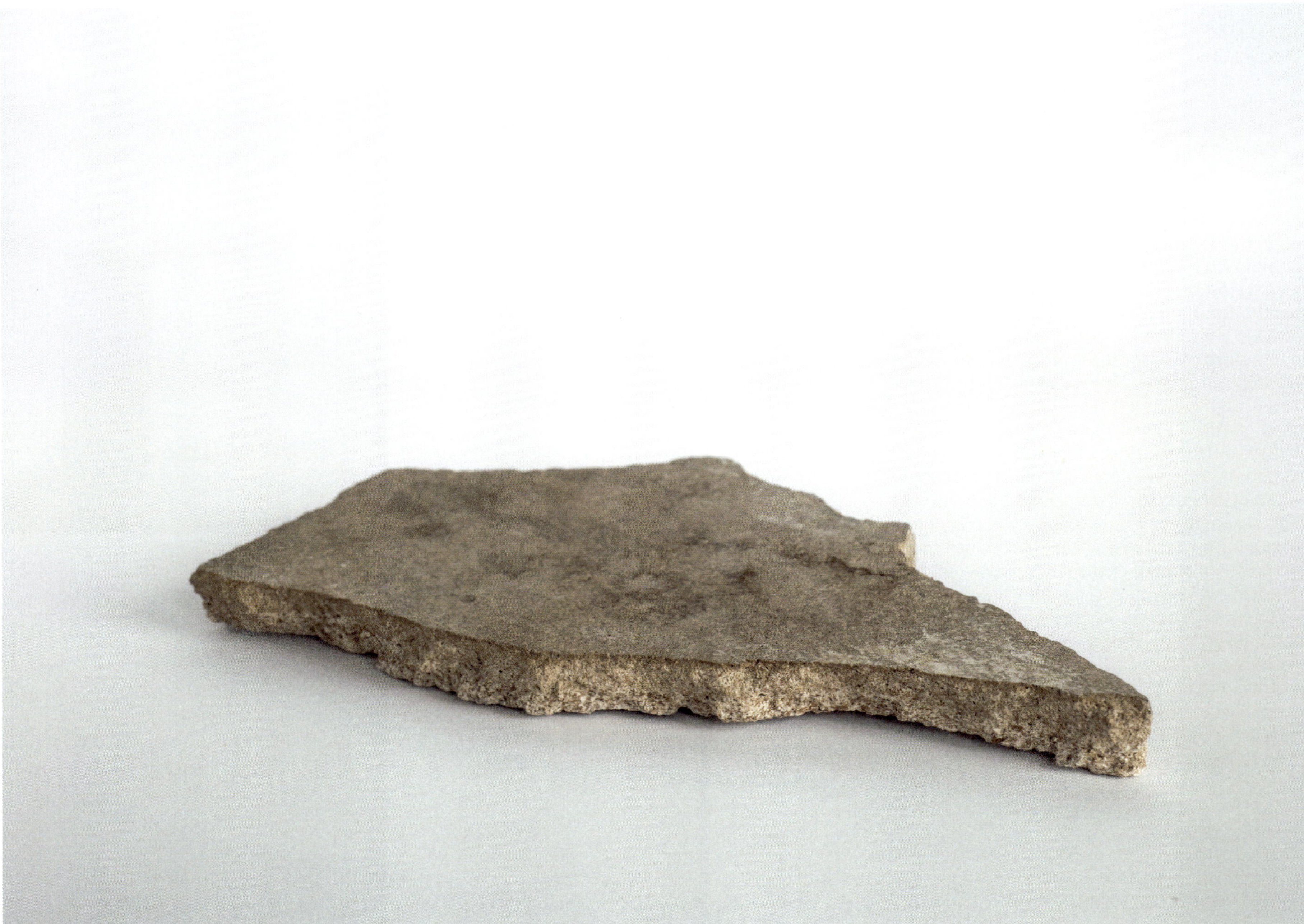

19)

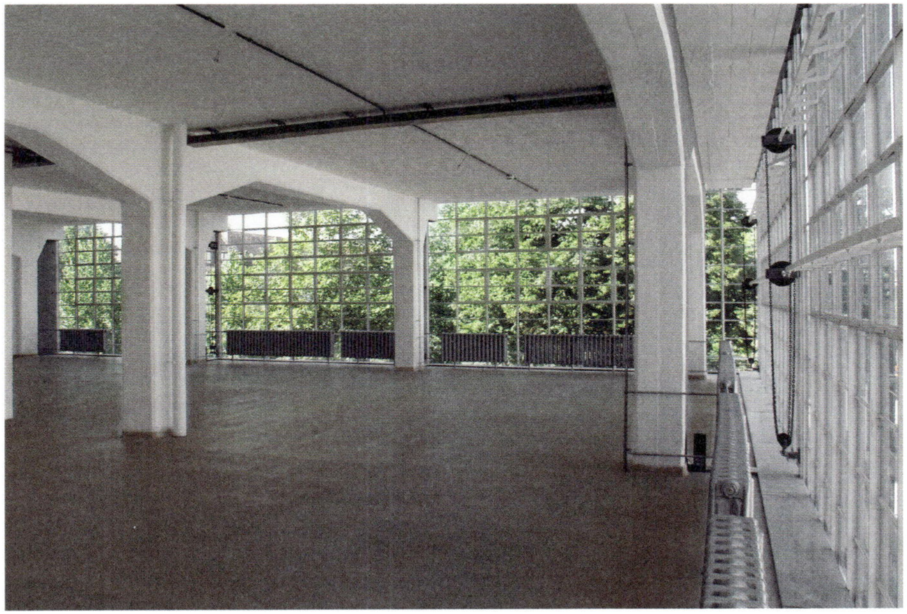

120)

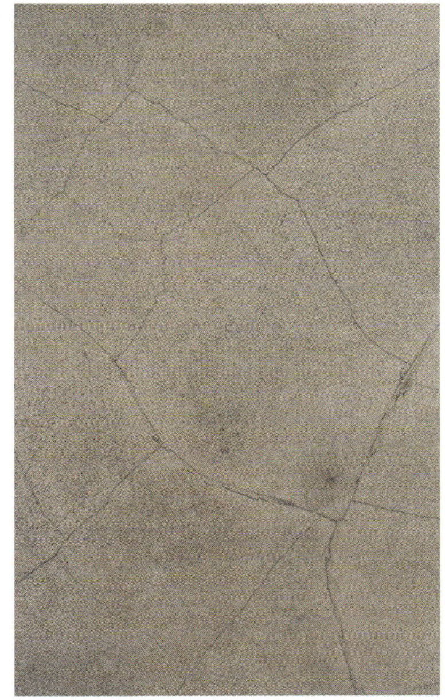

118)
Fragment of stonewood screed (1926), 2021

119)
Stonewood screed floor, workshop wing, 2006

120)
Stonewood screed (1926), 2021

Stonewood Screed

Stonewood screed is a seamless flooring material with a hard, glossy surface made of a mix of magnesite as a binding agent, wood shavings, and other aggregates. Developed in the late nineteenth century, it has better sound and heat insulation properties than stone flooring. The bottom layer has a higher proportion of wood shavings, is therefore more porous, and has good insulating properties. The top layer is denser and hence more robust. An integral cove base forms the equivalent of a skirting board. With the addition of pigments, the flooring may be produced in different colours. The surface is protected and maintained using oil and wax.

A nonpigmented stonewood screed was originally used in the Bauhaus Building although pigmented floors dating from later phases are also present. During the maintenance and renovation of the floors, imperfections, cracks, and indentations in the floor are treated to prevent further crumbling and the eventual loss of original material.

During the renovation of 1996 to 2009, non-original flooring materials such as carpets or PVC flooring on top of the stonewood screed were first removed to enable the original spatial impression to rematerialise. At that time, thorough cleaning entailed several stages of grinding and sanding. But because these methods eventually lead to the loss of original material, more circumspect techniques for the long-term conservation and maintenance of the stonewood floors[26] involving the use of compressors were investigated and established in 2020.[27]

Cracks in stonewood screed can have different causes and may vary in size. While smaller hairline cracks are left untreated, larger cracks are filled to prevent a loss of substance due to continued abrasion. Here, the following steps are taken: the crack is enlarged, a micro-grinder (a dental tool) is used to roughen the edges; the crack is cleaned, holes are drilled along the inner length of the crack to allow the insertion of the filler, and the filler (which contains pigments to match the original) is injected.

121) 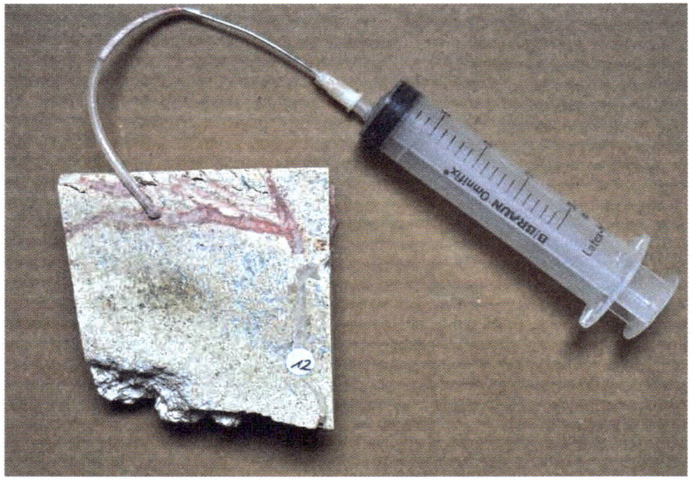

122) 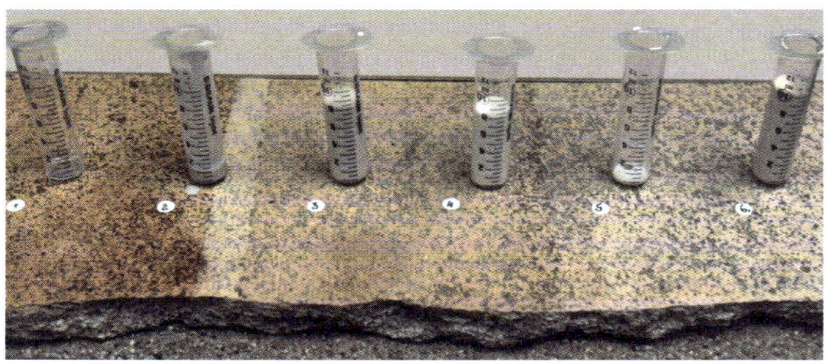

121)
Experimental repair of cracks in stonewood screed, 2018

122)
Experimental backfilling of cavities, 2020

Finally, the surface is trowel filled, and the edges of the crack are sanded by hand.[28]

Cavities are caused by the malformation of the substructure or the construction and by movement in the stonewood screed. Cracks form on the cavities, and the continued movement of the screed around them leads to abrasion and loss of substance along the edges of the cracks. Because backfilling with magnesite, an ingredient of stonewood screed, proved unsuitable, a different concept was developed. Accordingly, the approach to the cracks differs depending on their location in the building, the degree of wear and tear, and the condition of the screed and includes a package of recommendations for steps ranging from no intervention to isolated or selective backfilling.

If the stonewood screed flooring is no longer there but can be proven to have existed in situ originally, it may be reconstructed, as is the case in the historic canteen. Here, extensive repairs and reconstructions are carried out using identical materials based on analyses of the original stonewood screed.[29] The colour of the contemporary material deviates from the original, for example because it is stripped from other locations. Because the historic material has gained a dark and irregular patina which is not only superficial, repairs to defects and cracks cannot be made entirely invisible. Stark differences in colour are temporarily blended in using small amounts of umber pigments mixed into the surface care product. Slight discrepancies in the structure and colour of the repair are accepted, particularly as the differences fade over time due to the formation of a patina on the new material. In conclusion, continuous and skilled maintenance is essential for the long-term conservation of the original floors, for which detailed recommendations have been formulated.[30]

1
Gropius 1965, p. 25

2
Cf. Markgraf 2019

3
Schmidt 1998, p. 43

4
For more information on the preservation of modern historical monuments, see also Wüstenrot 2011

5
Mörsch 2003, p. 140

6
Two research projects were funded by the federal state of Saxony-Anhalt: 'Wissenschaftlich-Technische Untersuchung 1998–2001: Bauforschung Bauhausbauten Dessau, Schwerpunkt Siedlung Dessau-Törten' (project management: Margret Kentgens-Craig / Monika Markgraf, editing and promotion: Andreas Schwarting) and 'Wissenschaftlich-Technische Untersuchung 2002–2004: Bauforschung Bauhausbauten Dessau, Architekturoberflächen' (project management: Omar Akbar / Monika Markgraf, editing: Bettina Lietz).

7
The archive was established in the scope of the research project 'Bauforschung Bauhausbauten Dessau'. It dates back to an initiative of Prof. Berthold Burkhardt of TU Braunschweig and was built up by Andreas Schwarting and Monika Markgraf. Cf. Schwarting / Markgraf 2002; Markgraf 2019

8
Paul 1978, p. 48

9
Gropius 2021, p. 15

10
Quoted in Graf 2010, p. 207

11
Völkers 1948, p. 22 et seqq.

12
Korn 1928 (1968)

13
Berger 1976, p. 725

14
Cf. e.g., Gropius 2021, p. 15; Rehm 2005, p. 33 et seqq.

15
Special thanks to Ruggero Tropeano, who donated the fragment to the Bauhaus Building Archive.

16
Letter from Robert Richter to Walter Gropius, 12 June 1926, in Stadtarchiv Dessau, SB 1, fol. 140

17
Letter from the Dessau municipal administration, 18 June 1926, in Stadtarchiv Dessau, SB I, fol. 154

18
Gropius 2021, p. 15

19
Bauwelt Katalog 1929 / 30, p. 359 et seqq.

20
According to data provided by the Eduard Dyckerhoff Torfoleum works in *Bauwelt Katalog* 1929 / 30, p. 361

21
An overview of the floors is found in Lietz / Markgraf 2004.

22
Cf. Lietz 2005

23
Linke 2020, p. 96 et seqq.

24
The Triolin flooring was restored by Dietmar Linke of Restaurierungsatelier Linke, Berlin.

25
Cf. Lattermann 2009

26
The conservation concept for the stonewood floors was developed in the framework of the Getty Foundation's programme 'Keeping It Modern!' and as part of a project funded by the state of Saxony-Anhalt for the development of a conservation management plan for the Bauhaus Building in Dessau; cf. Schöne 2020

27
The conservation concept was developed by Restaurierungsatelier Schöne, Halle / Saale.

28
Schöne 2018

29
Schöne 2002

30
Linke 2020; Schöne 2020

Spatial Design

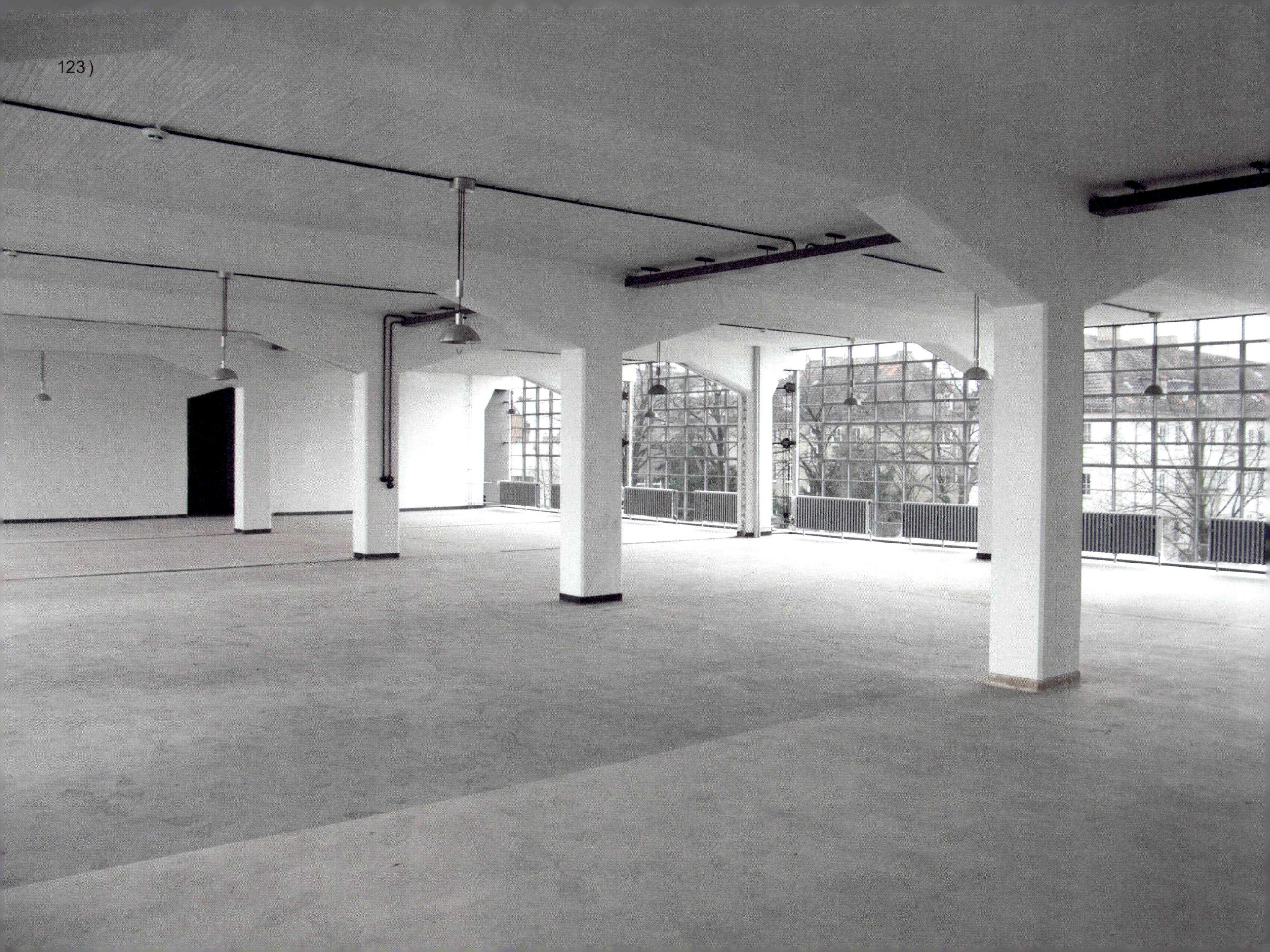

123)

24)

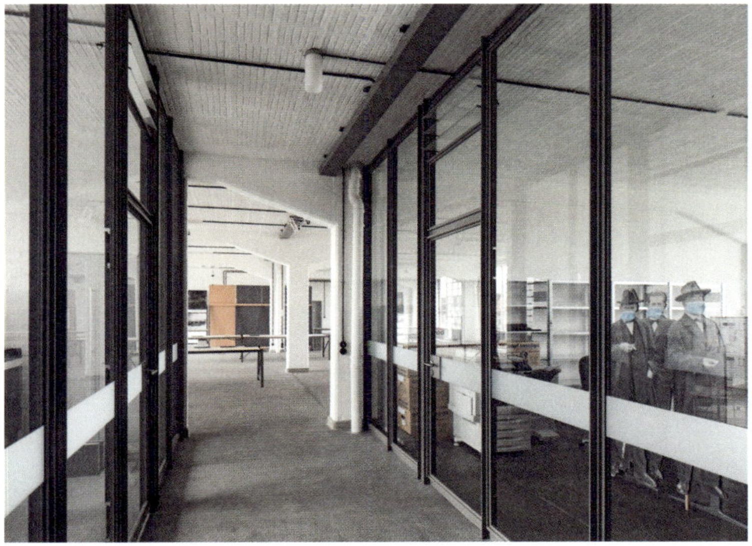

25)

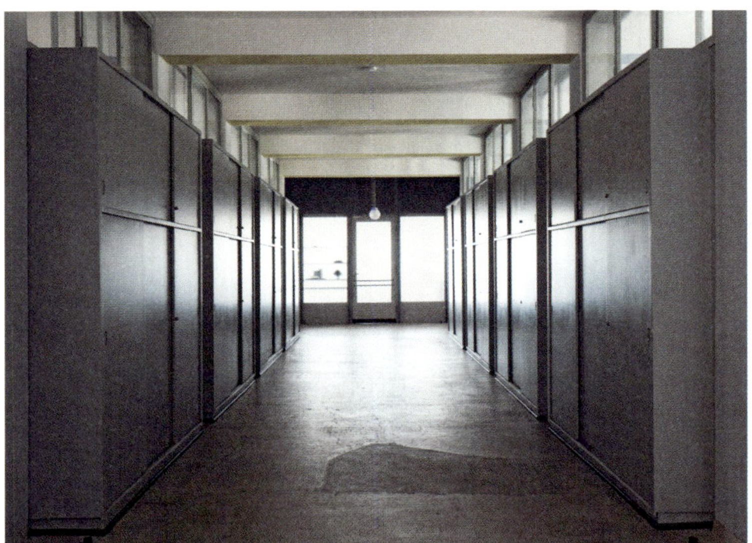

123)
Large spaces in the workshop wing, 2012

124)
Retrofitted glass partitions in the workshop wing, 2021

125)
North wing with built-in cupboards, 2018

The spatial design of 1926 varies significantly in the different parts of the Bauhaus Building. There are therefore different guidelines for usage or modifications, which are documented in the conservation objectives of 1999/2014.

The workshop wing, the 'laboratory of ideas' containing the Bauhaus workshops, is enveloped and informed by the extremely thin membrane of the curtain wall. The interior features not only large, bright, and airy workshop spaces but also smaller rooms, e.g., to store materials, as offices for the masters, or for specific tasks such as galvanising or soldering. The partition walls in the workshop wing were practically arranged according to use. Some were brick-built, others lightweight dividers; others again were formed using built-in cupboards. Over the decades, walls were added and removed. Today, the room layout reflects the historic mix of primarily large and some small rooms but differs in the detail from the historically rather practical spatial structure. In 2005, for example, rooms were divided off using modern glass partitions.

The north wing, by contrast, is consistently divided into classrooms by way of masonry partitions or built-in cupboards with transom windows on the corridor side. Or, in the words of Walter Gropius: 'economic solution for a school corridor enclosed on two sides. illumination of the longitudinal corridor wall by double-glazed sound-insulated skylights above the drawing-board cupboards. cross ventilation through the classrooms opposite and through the windows in the staircase.'[1] Over the decades, this crisp structure was obscured by partitions installed

126)

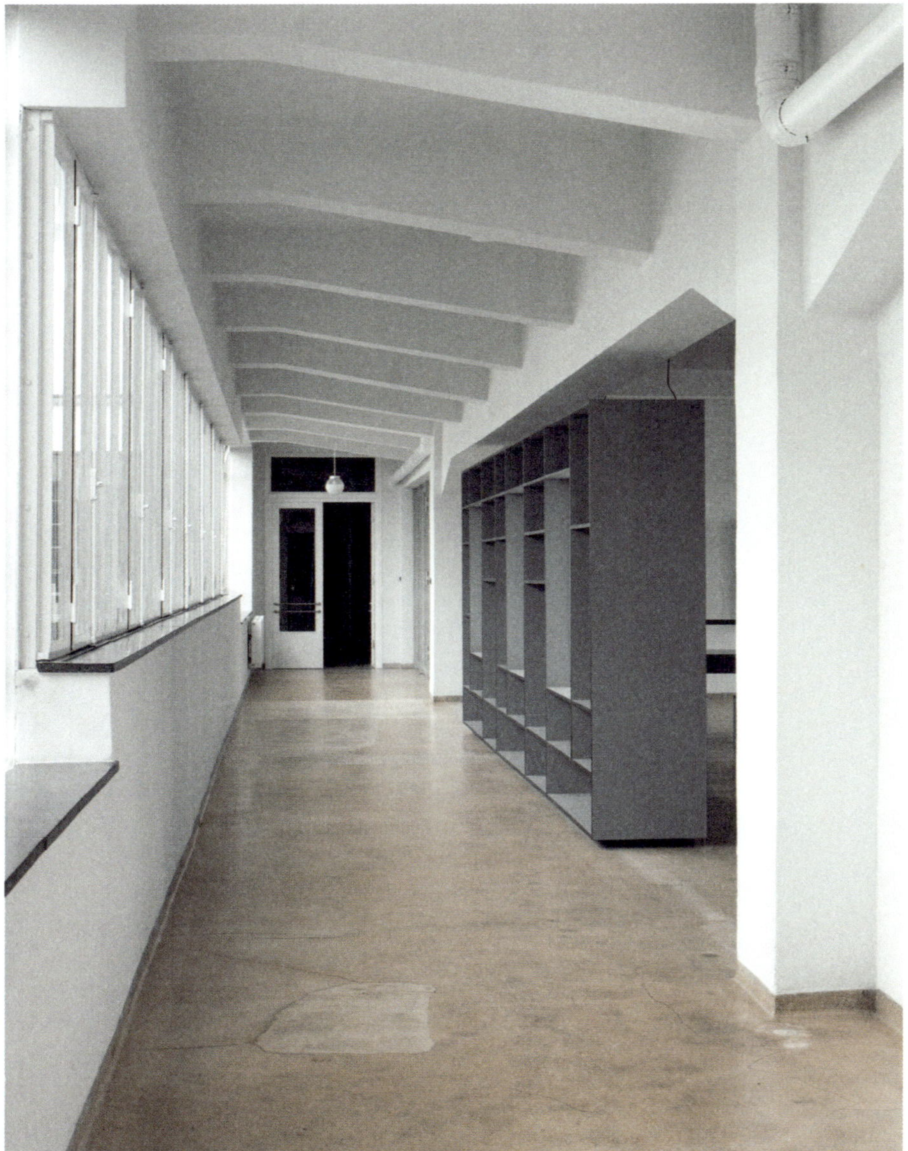

127)

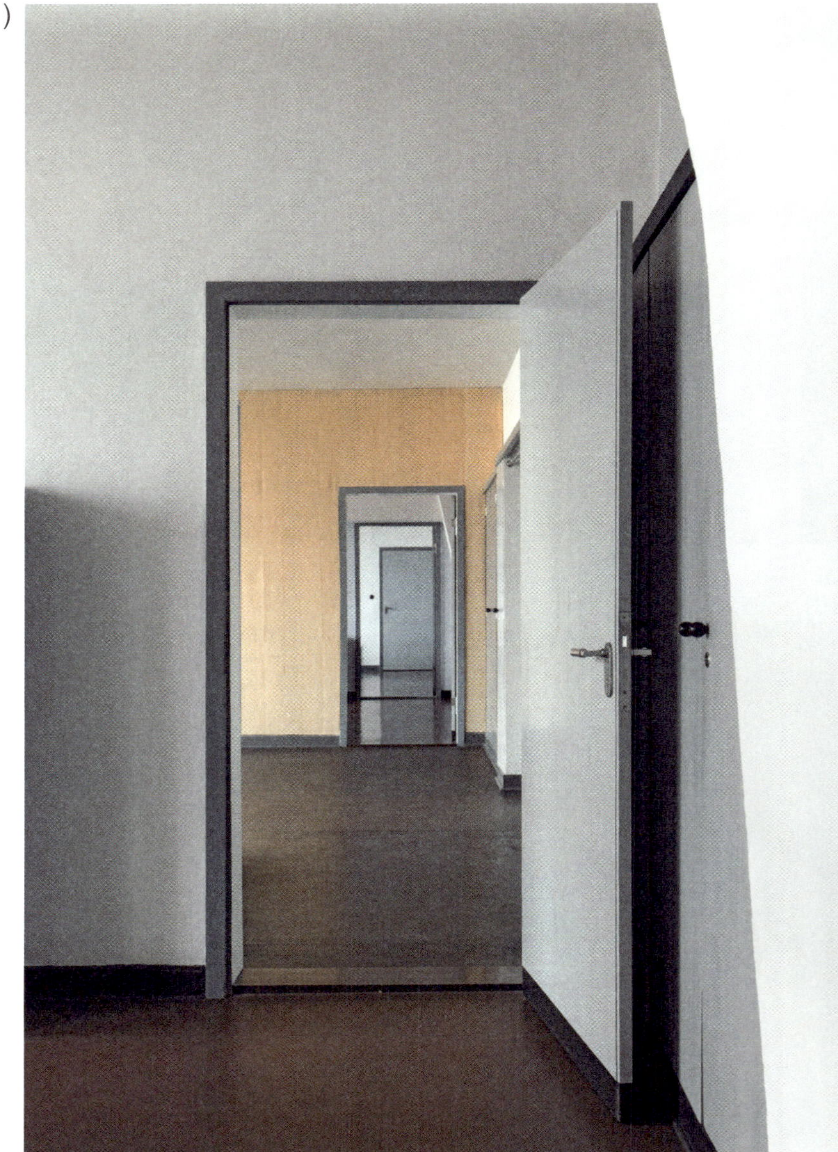

28)

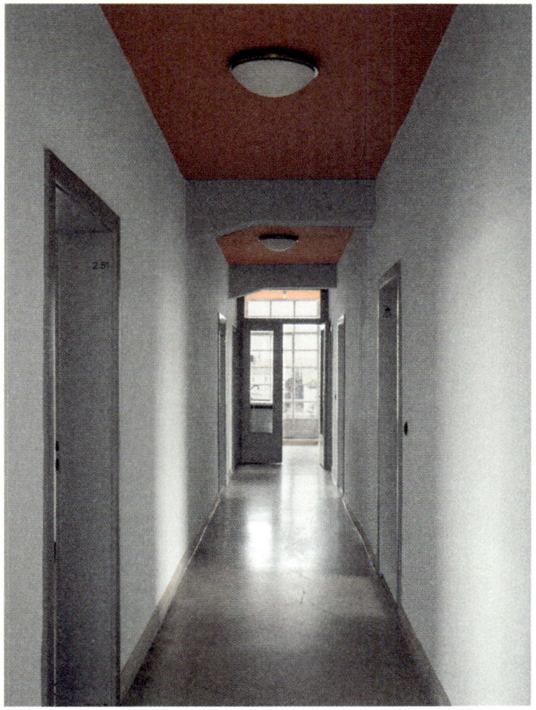

126)
Bridge, second floor, 2021

127)
Sequence of rooms on the bridge, first floor, 2021

128)
Corridor, studio building, 2021

to create smaller rooms. Moreover, very little light entered the access corridor because some of the doors were no longer glazed or new partitions were placed behind the glass doors. In these areas, it is important to preserve the distinct and consistent room layout of this part of the building and to ensure the corridors are flooded with natural light.

The bridge connects the workshop wing and the north wing. On the lower floor, the rooms for the administration are arranged symmetrically on both sides of the centrally placed director's office. The sizes of these rooms differ according to their functions; the rooms are interconnected by internal doors and feature built-in cupboards along the wall facing the corridor. The top floor of the bridge is dominated by one large room which, when occupied from 1926 to 1928 by Gropius's architecture office, was divided off by a wall unit running the length of a connecting corridor. Following Walter Gropius's departure from the Bauhaus, the Bauhaus's building department utilised the room without the wall unit. This historic structure in the bridge was significantly changed by room partitions after 1932 but was restored during the renovation of 1996 to 2009, recreating the original arrangement of rooms on both floors.

The structure of the studio building comprises rooms of equal size designed as private spaces which are accessed from a central corridor with a kitchenette. Here, the original fittings comprising built-in cupboards instead of partition walls and recessed beds which structure the space were partly changed as early as 1932. During the renovation of 1976, the original spatial design was restored as a distinctive attribute, but the historic built-in cupboard, bed recesses, and other details were not. With the exception of the third floor, where the historic built-in fittings were reinstated in two rooms in 2015, the arrangement created in 1976 is to be preserved. It is based on the original example and is moreover a testament to the renovation of 1976.

129)

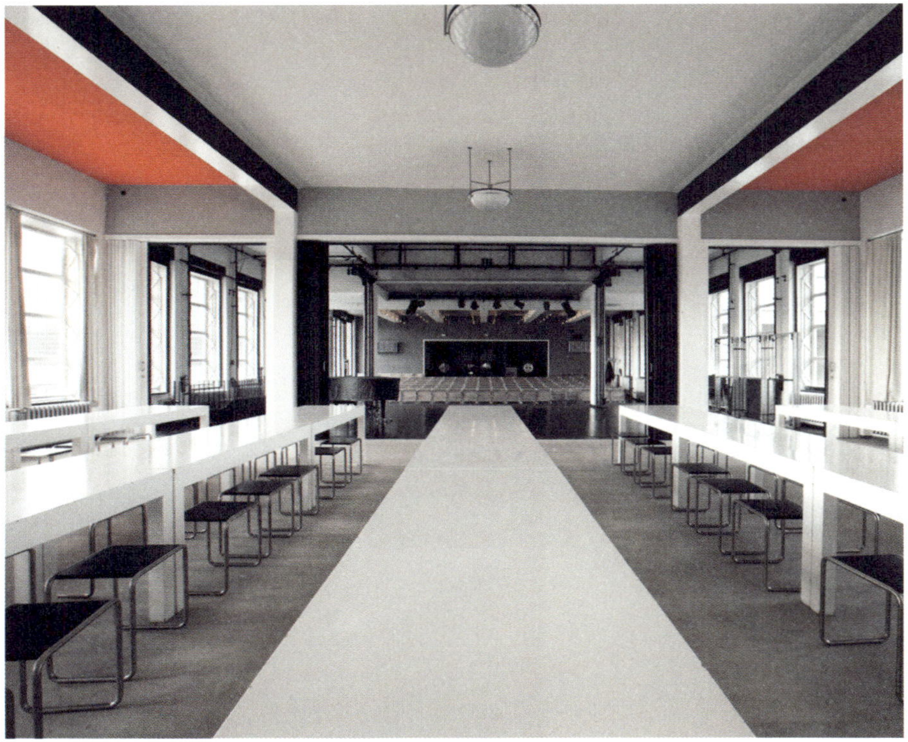

130)

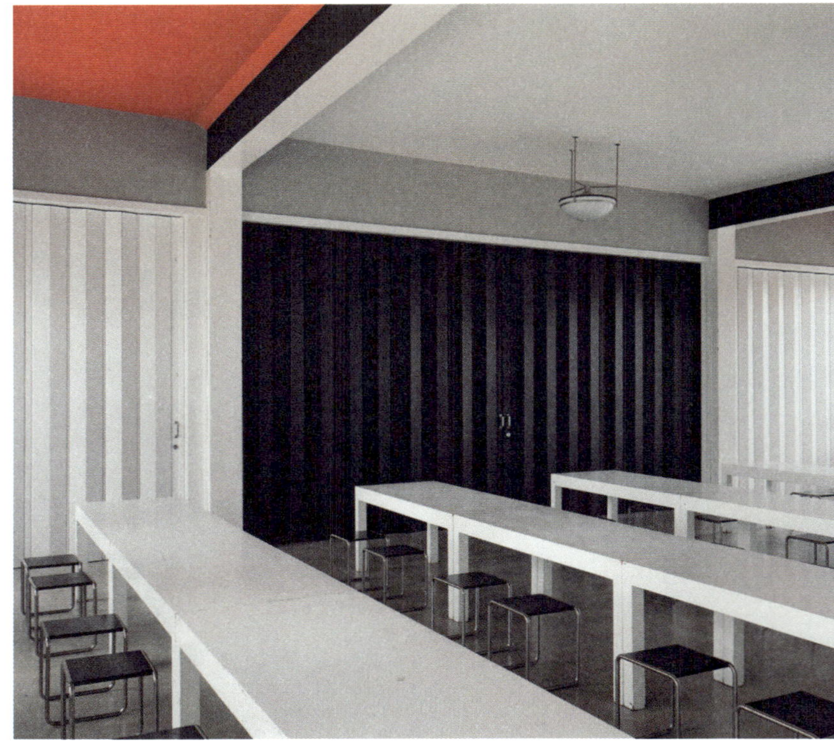

129)
Festive area, canteen with open folding wall, 2021

130)
Festive area, canteen with closed folding wall, 2021

131)
Festive area, stage and auditorium, 2021

The spatial structure of the festive area in the connecting building is defined by its versatility: the large doors between the vestibule and the auditorium and the mobile folding walls between the stage and the historic canteen may be opened or closed. This permits the spaces to be used separately or together as an interconnected festive area, as required. This spatial design was completely transformed by new fittings following the closure of the Bauhaus and reinstated during the renovation of 1976. Since then, the clean-cut and striking original structure has been preserved unchanged.

The stairways in the Bauhaus Building have very different features. The two facing stairways of the workshop wing and the north wing look the same from the outside. But inside, the stairway in the workshop wing leads to a representative vestibule with extensive glazing which opens up the space to reveal a view of the curtain wall. By contrast, the stairway in the north wing leads to an access corridor with a striking, intensive colour design. The stairways on the south side of the workshop wing

1)

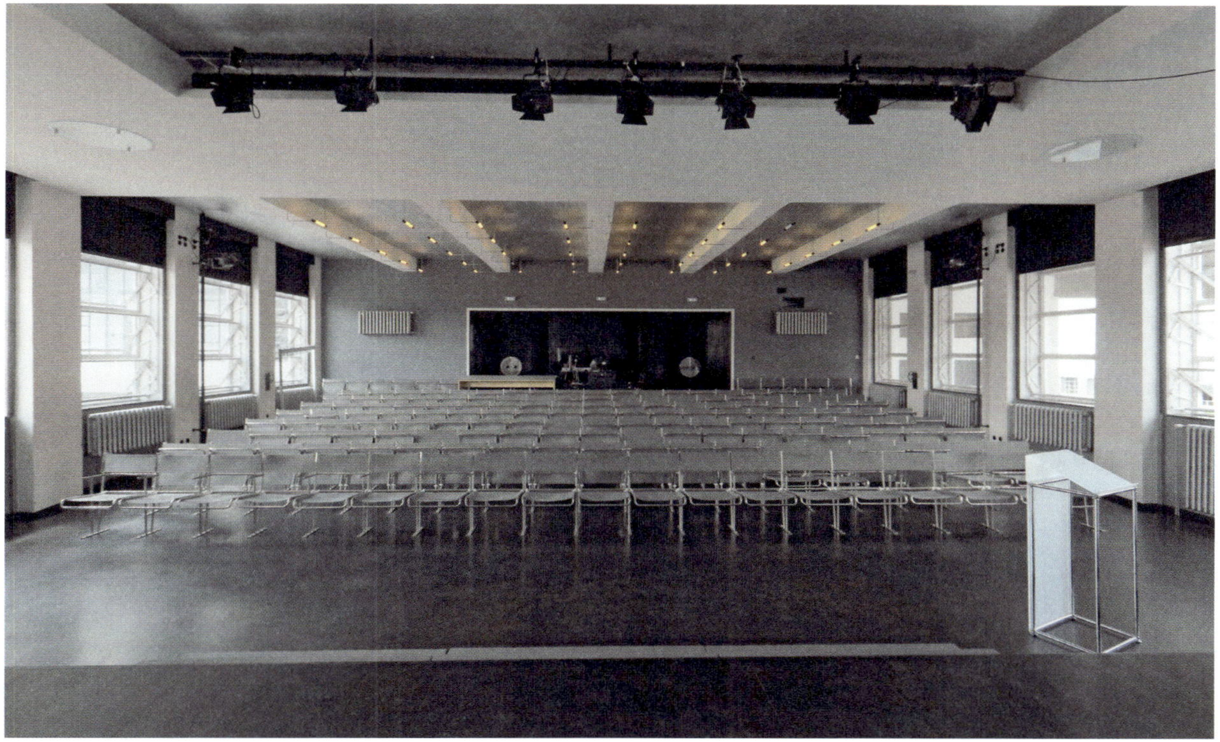

are shaped by individual windows and a vivid red wall, while the stairs in the studio building are distinguished by vertical ribbon windows and colour-coded floors.

Because the spatial assemblage of the Bauhaus Building is so complex, the restoration of the historic rooms' spatial situation does not invariably involve the reconstruction of the original layout. In some instances, the restoration of the differentiated spatial arrangement is prioritised. The aim therefore is to preserve the original layout in the north wing and the bridge, maintain the structure from 1976 in the studio building, and, within a set framework, to permit changes to the spatial distribution of the workshop wing.

1
Gropius 2021, p. 62

132)

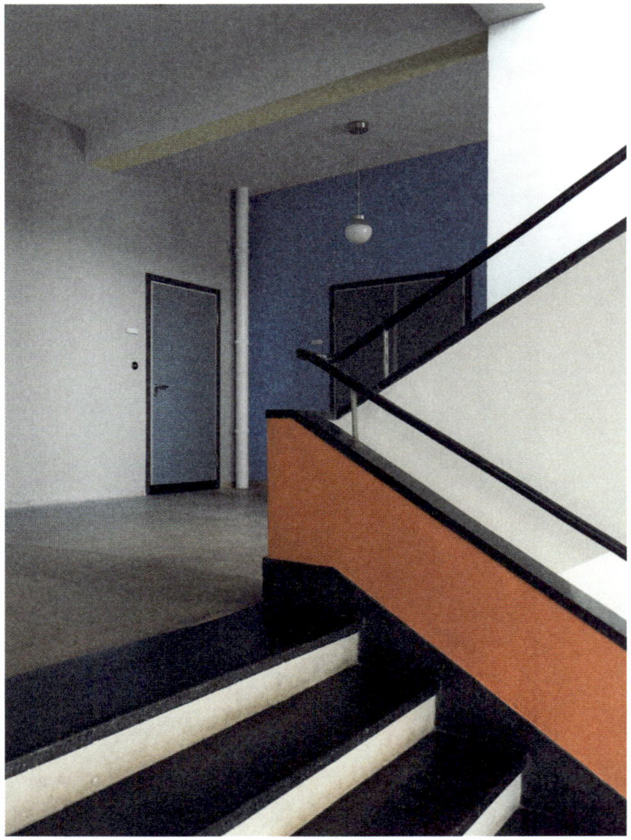

133)

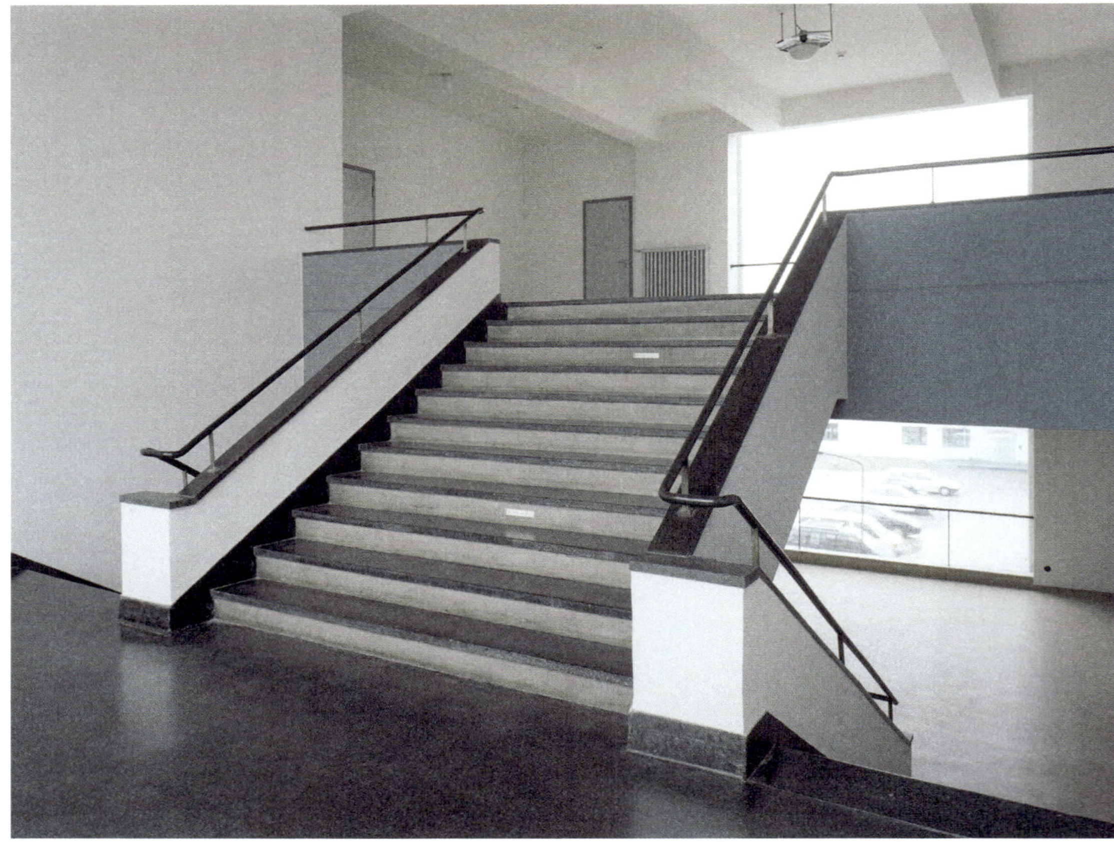

132)
Stairway, north wing,
2017

133)
Stairway, workshop wing,
2006

4)

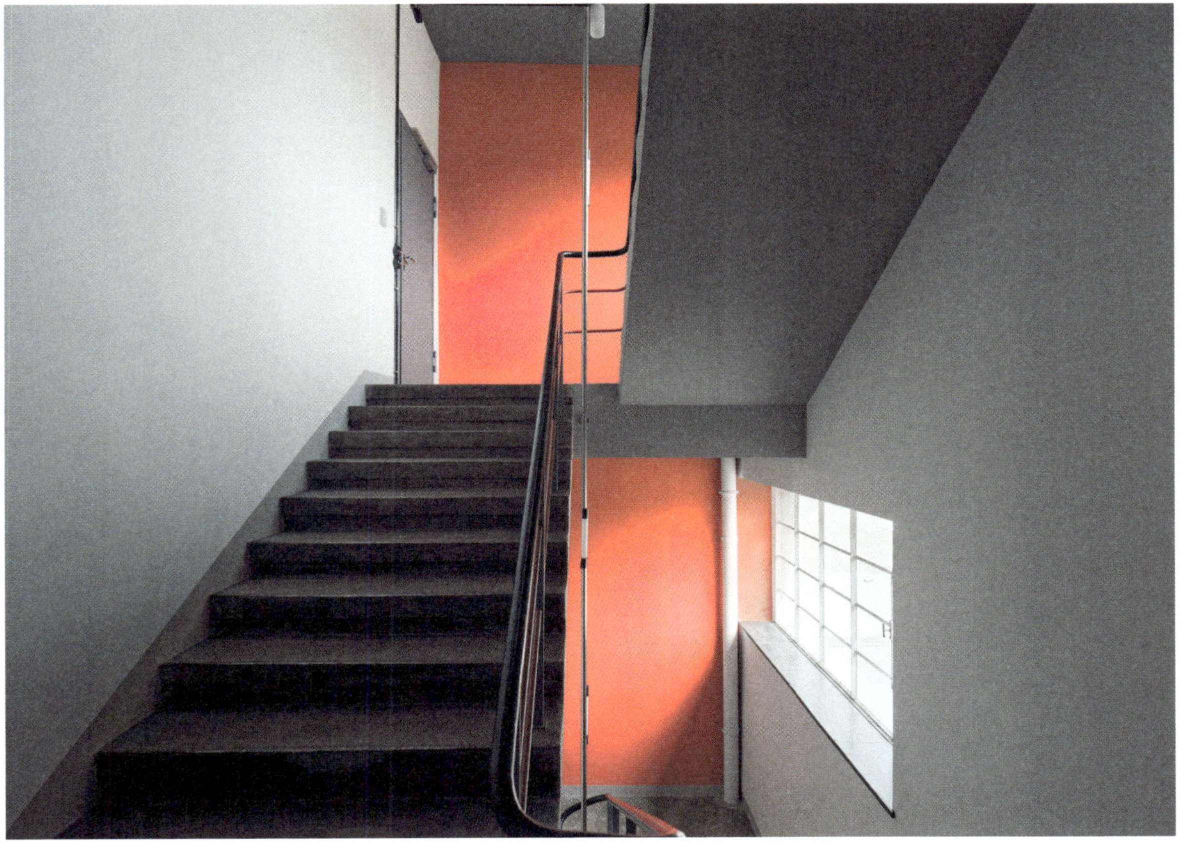

135)

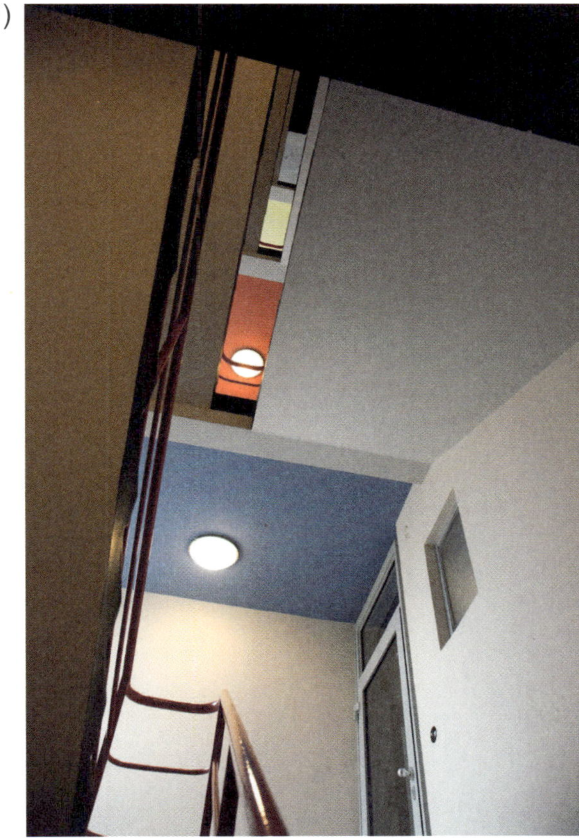

134)
Southern stairway, workshop wing, 2018

135)
Stairway, studio building, 2010

Colour and Surfaces

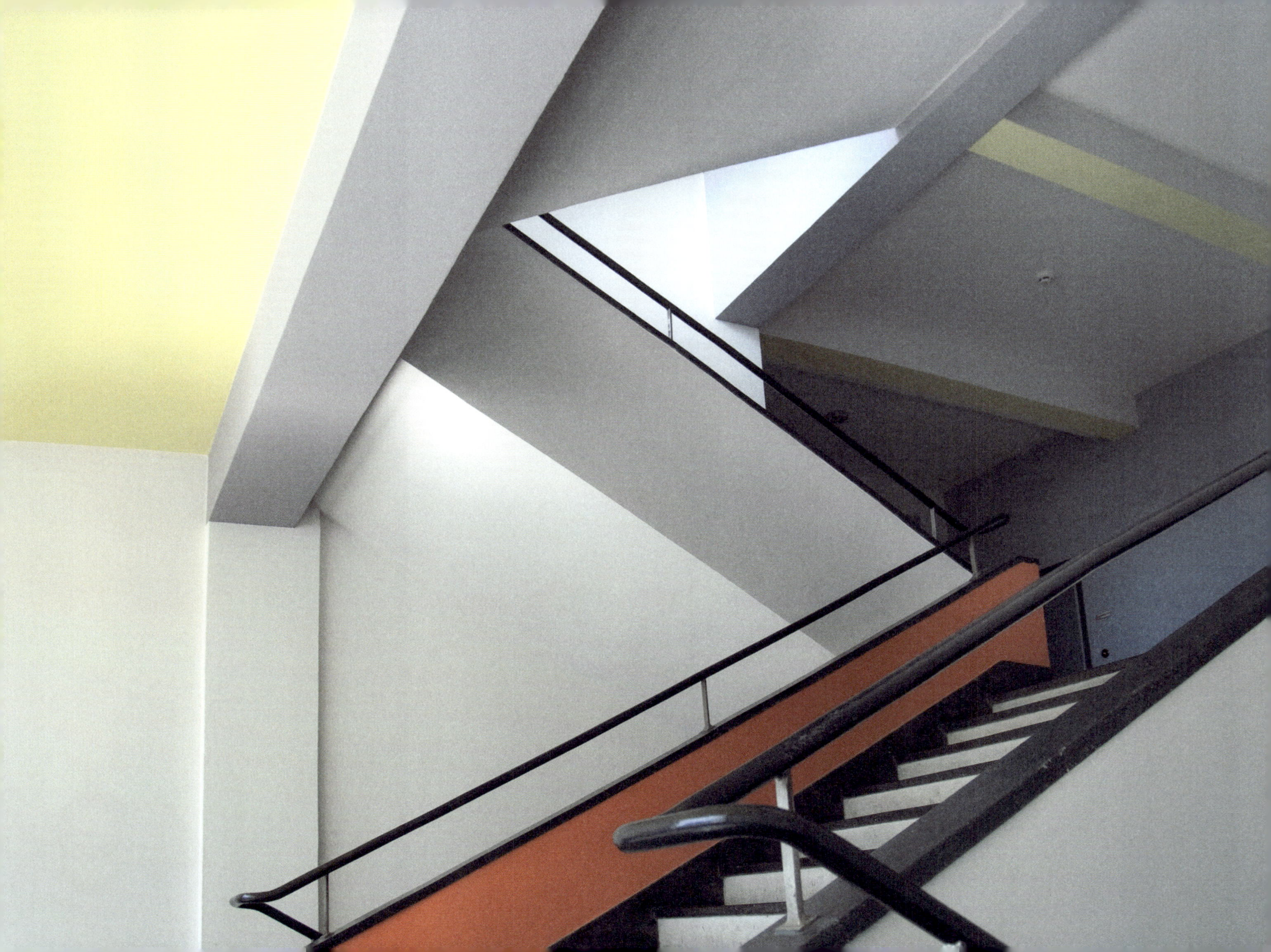

136)
Colours in stairway, north wing, 2011

The treatment of surfaces plays a particularly important role in the Bauhaus Building as it does in other buildings of classical modernism. With its clear and minimal forms, lack of ornaments, and play of light and shadows, the architecture enhances the effects of colours, materials, and surfaces as critical components of the architectonic design, which have a distinct aesthetic impact. As Thomas Danzl highlights: 'The colour treatment of surfaces emerging from the wall painting classes at the Bauhaus is presented in the mid-nineteen-twenties as a contemporary variant of the historic mural, not merely as a distinct work of (artisanal) craftsmanship, and is, rather, to be understood more as an original and autonomous artistic manifestation, albeit assimilated in the *Gesamtkunstwerk* of the building.'[1]

The colouration of a surface is achieved through the colour of the material itself or by means of a surface finish.[2] The latter may be used to decorate, to protect the construction, or to articulate the architecture while many surfaces or elements may be informed by a visible material colour, such as concrete, terrazzo, or textiles. The Dutch painter and architect Theo van Doesburg describes the dramatic import of the architectural surface thus: 'Ultimately, the surfaces alone are essential to the architecture; man does not live in the construction, but in the atmosphere which the surfaces evoke!'[3]

The Bauhauslers engaged with many and varied aspects of colour and surfaces.[4] In relation to the Bauhaus Building, the main points of reference here include László Moholy-Nagy, who was head of the preliminary course and who collaborated on the colour design of the Bauhaus, Wassily Kandinsky, who directed the wall painting workshop until 1925, and Hinnerk Scheper, who headed the same workshop from 1925 and was responsible for the Bauhaus's colour design.

Moholy-Nagy introduced the terms 'structure' to describe the manner in which the material is built up, 'texture' to describe the organically resulting outward surface, and 'facture' (or 'surface aspect') as the effect of the working process.[5] The structure of the background, the texture created by the materiality of the colour, and the facture resulting from the technique provide a plethora of opportunities for exceptionally nuanced designs that play a vital role in the impact of the architecture. Because these surfaces appeal not only to the eye, but also to all other senses—for instance by affecting acoustics or exuding an odour—the preliminary course entailed exercises that appealed to all the senses, for instance using texture boards which were explored through touch. Finally, Moholy-Nagy was interested in light as a design element: 'One aims to create a new space … with light directly, subordinating even paint (pigment)—or at least sublimating it as far as possible.'[6]

Further inspiration came from Kandinsky who analysed the effect of colour and concluded: 'At any rate, it is proved that colour embodies an enormous though unexplored power which can affect the entire human body as an organism.'[7] He not only studied the effects of colours in isolation, such as the cooling and profound nature of blue, yellow's spiritual warmth, or the restful quality of green, but also their effects on colour and form combined.

137)

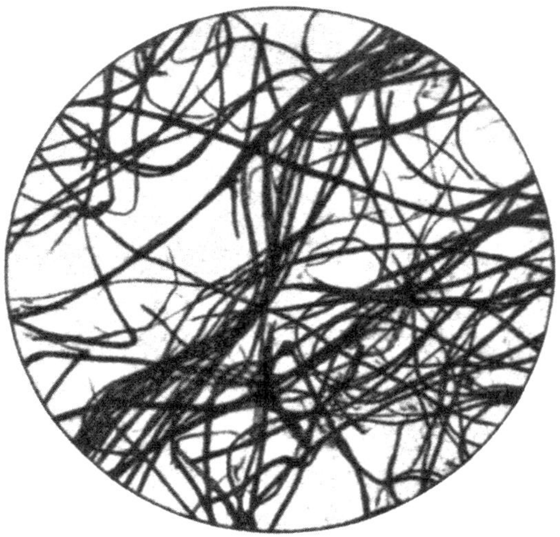

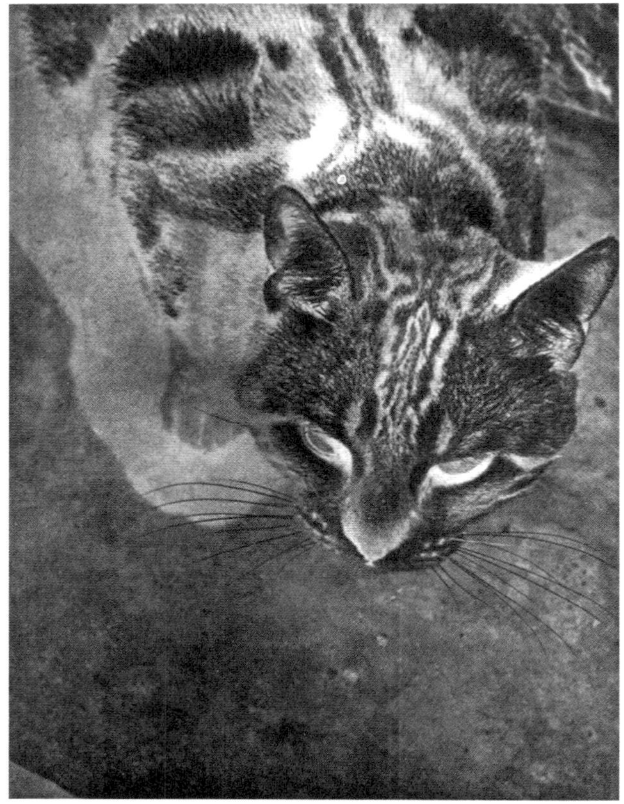

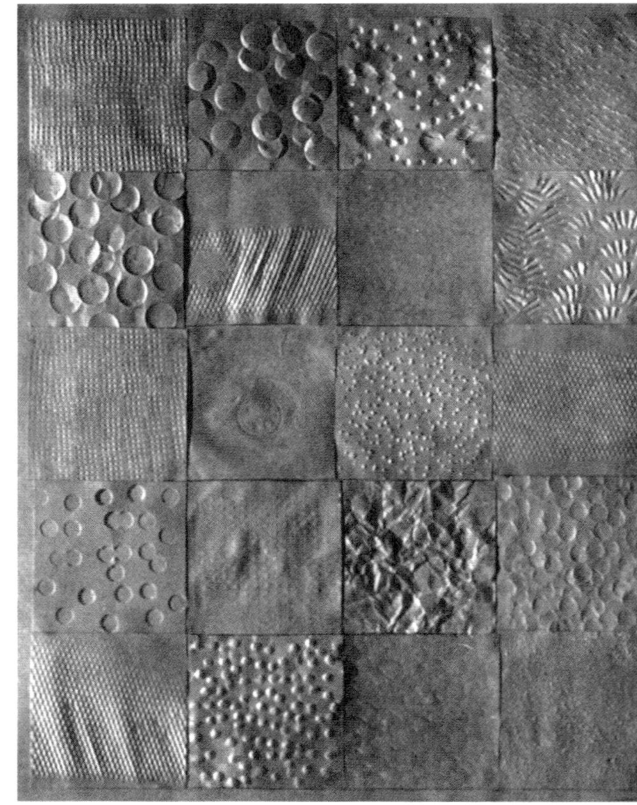

38)

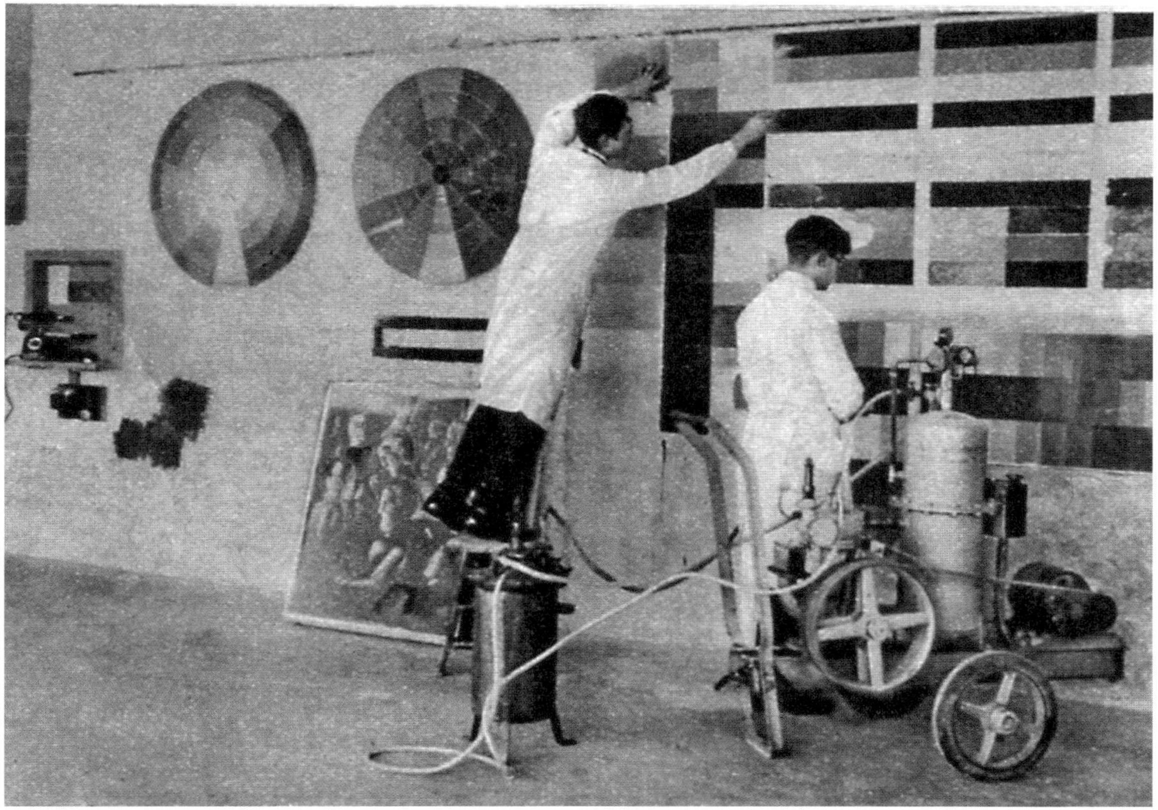

137)
Structure, texture, facture (surface aspect), 1929

138)
Wall painting workshop, ca. 1929

Here, the material essence, the chemical-physical properties of a colour as well as its psychological qualities—its creative powers, so to speak—were of paramount importance.

By contrast, Hinnerk Scheper not only taught the basic knowledge and skills of the craftsman but also trained the capacity to develop and realise creative and experimental intentions. Design was therefore approached from both technical and formal standpoints. Scheper describes the purpose of colour design as follows: 'Colour in architecture cannot be the product of a personal, individual taste. On the contrary, it is aesthetically linked with the formal and technical regularities of the building in question. Here, it is not a matter of decorative painting as such, but of fleshing out a given space according to its architectonic nature. Wall painting can and must not supplant the architectonic form and lose connection with it … In short, the colour should not serve to mask the exterior, but should be an integral feature of the architecture.'[8] Accordingly, the role of colour design is to lend greater expression to the architecture; it is also functional to the extent that it is understood and implemented as an element of the *Gesamtkunstwerk.* As such it is an integral element of the New Architecture.

The material character of the colour itself, the properties of the base on which it is applied, the technique used to do so, and the way in which the surface is finished were important media of spatial design for Scheper for they shaped the architectonic expression of individual components. Hans Fischli described teaching the required manual skills as follows: 'Paint from the same pot on paper, on a door panel, on a plaster wall resulted in three

139)

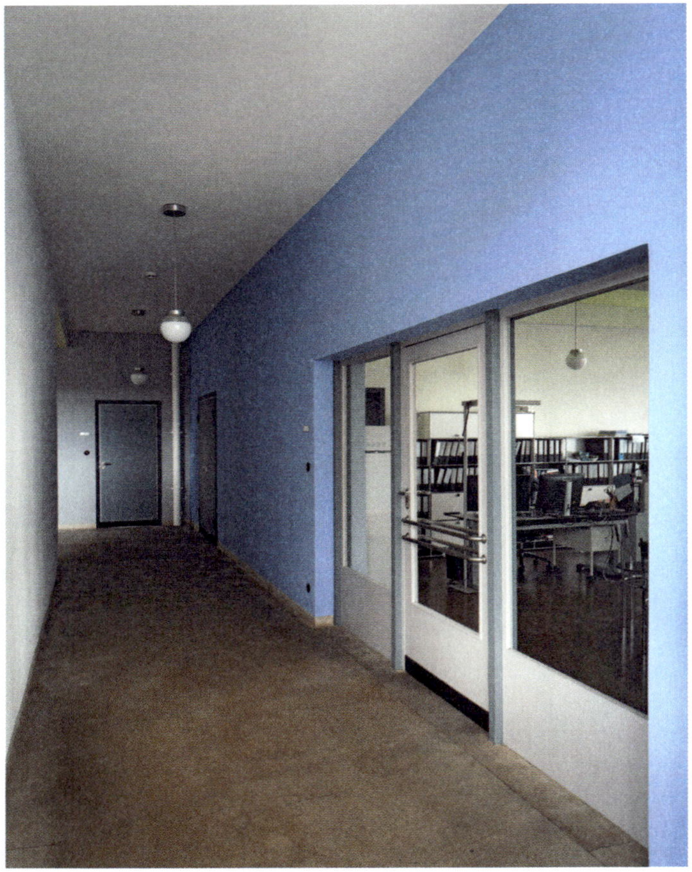

140)

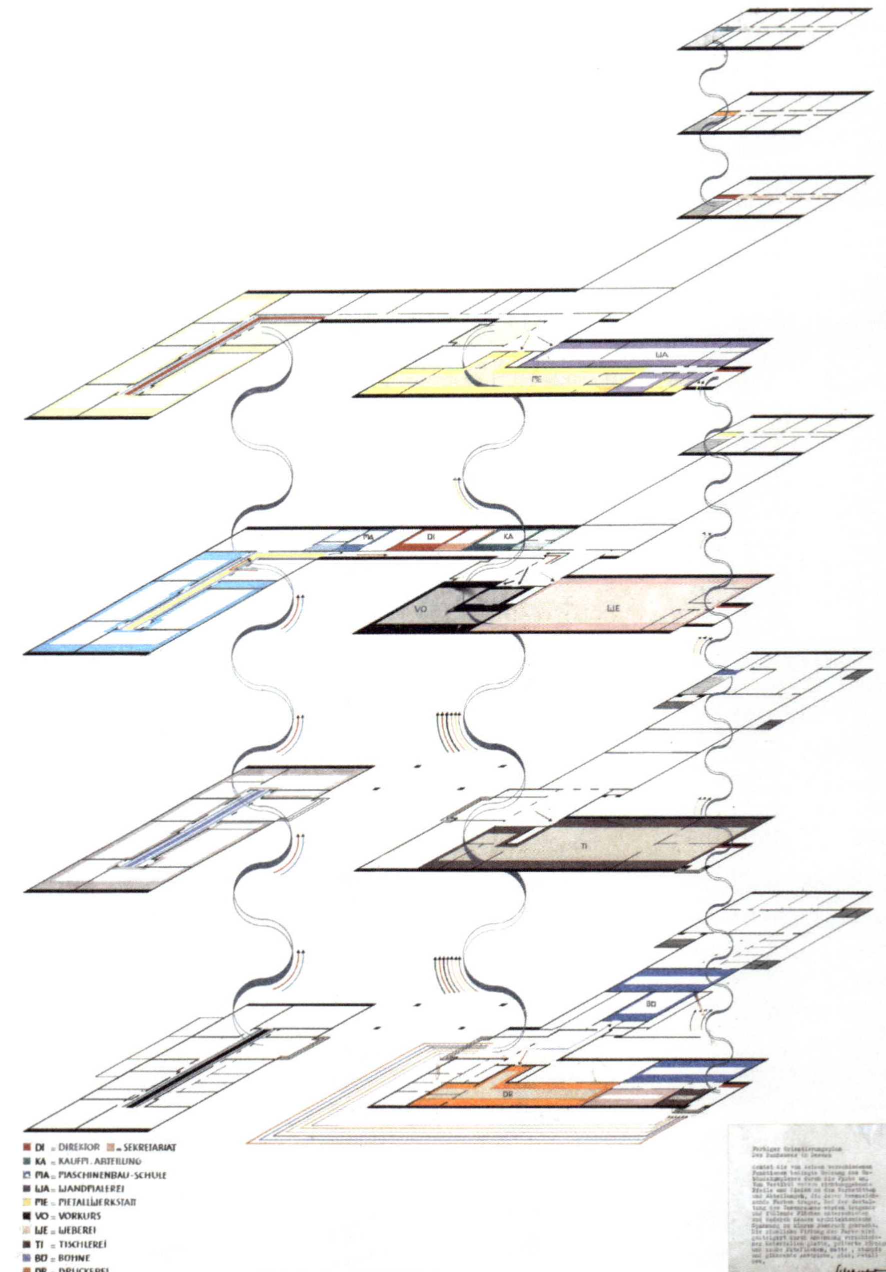

139)
Interplay of blue wall, white and yellow ceiling sections, grey doors, metallic and glazed surfaces, and pigment-free floor, 2021

140)
Hinnerk Scheper: diagram showing the organisation of colours in the Bauhaus Dessau, 1926

different shades because of the different backgrounds. The language of the painter is ripe in imagery: burnt earth, sienna, English red, madder lake, signal red, lead white, Cremnitz white, zinc white, vine black, ultramarine, green earth provoke analogies, and surfaces can be made even more lustrous with silky gloss, eggshell, with all manner of finishes, or subdued so that they become dull or matt. … You developed a heightened sense of smell for this varnish, this acid, that oil, and all the binders; the nose became refined, like the palate of the chef in a hotel kitchen.'[9] Scheper's concepts also considered the physiological and psychological effects of colour; he implemented soothing or uplifting hues, painted dark rooms yellow or sunny rooms a cool green.

The surface treatments and colour designs for the Bauhaus Building were for the most part conceived and executed by the wall painting department led by Hinnerk Scheper.[10] The vestibule in front of the auditorium is one exception: here, László Moholy-Nagy contributed to the colour design.[11] With his approach, Scheper had a significant influence on the colour design of not only this building but also other Bauhaus buildings including the Masters' Houses and the Dessau-Törten Housing Estate. In Scheper's plan, the colours emphasise the architectural layout, aid orientation in the building, and are modified by the different materialities and structures of the surfaces. On the coloured floor plan of the Bauhaus, he noted in 1926: 'In the design of the interior, a differentiation is made between load bearing and infill walls, thus bringing their architectonic tension clearly to the fore. The spatial effect of colour is enhanced by the use of various materials: smooth, polished, gritty, and rough plaster surfaces, dull matt and glossy finishes, glass, metal, etc.'[12] The colour finish is as a rule applied to whole walls or to a specific surface of a component such as the underside of a girder, and thus underlines the architectonic impact.

The articulation of the Bauhaus Building is therefore determined not only by function, volumes, façades, and spatial structure but also by the treatment of surfaces and colour design.

In order to implement restoration measures, comprehensive analyses of the building were required: the existing plans for the colour design (dated 1926 and signed by Scheper) do not show all areas, omit locations such as the main vestibule, details such as doors or built-in elements, and information on the materials and structures of surfaces. In addition, the question of whether the colour design had been executed as intended required clarification. In the evaluation of findings, aspects of the materiality and composition of colours and their ageing behaviour also require examination. The final joint report drafted by restorers, architects, architectural historians, and heritage conservationists also contains information on workmanship, the interactions of colour and architecture in the building, and comparisons with other buildings and Scheper's collected works.

141)

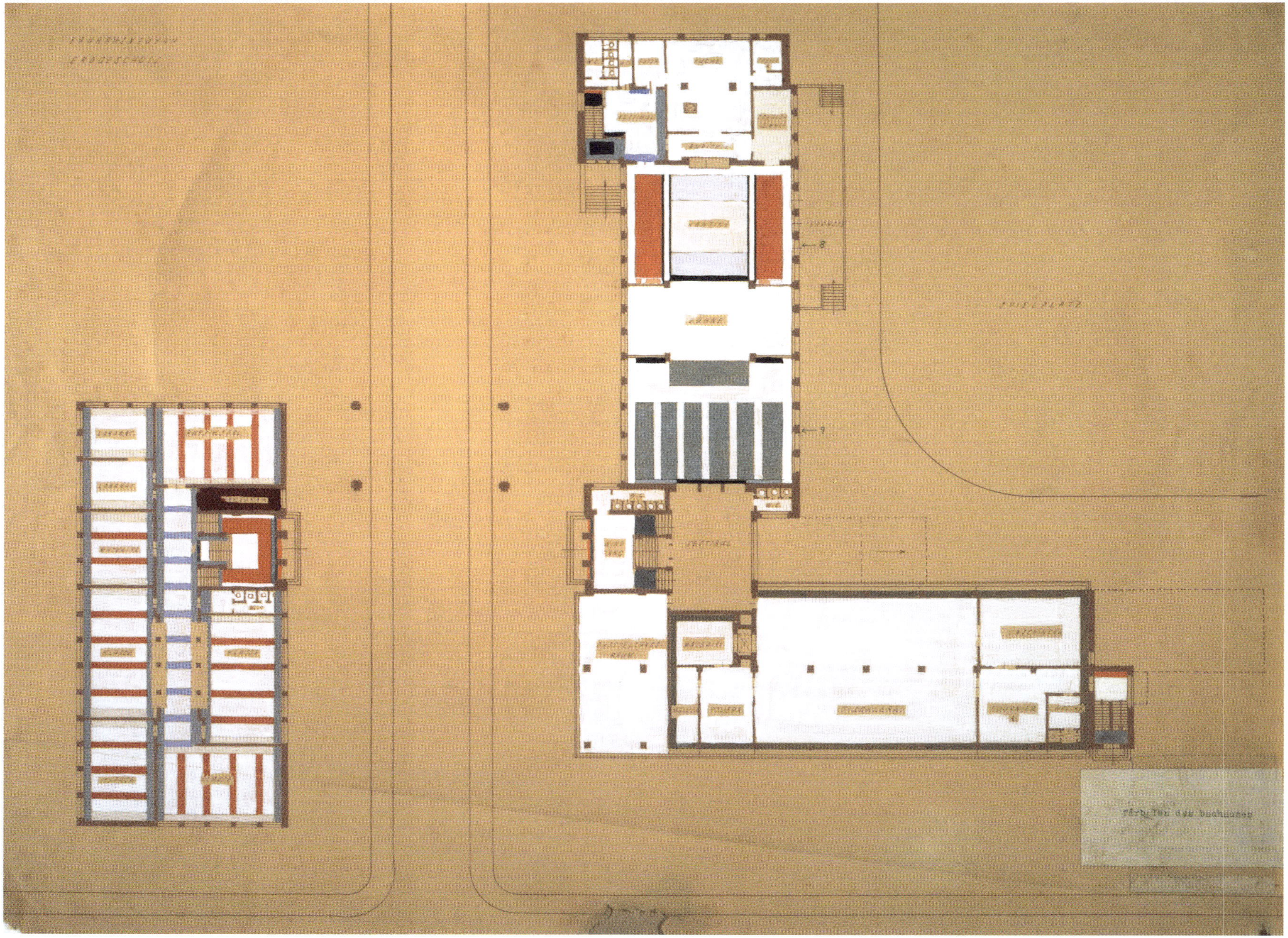
ERDGESCHOSS
KANTINE
BÜHNE
SPIELPLATZ
VESTIBUL
MATERIAL
TISCHLEREI
MASCHINEN
FURNIER
färbplan des bauhauses

141)
Hinnerk Scheper: new Bauhaus Building, ground floor, colour plan of the Bauhaus, 1926

142)
Colours of ceilings and walls, ground floor, 2021

42)

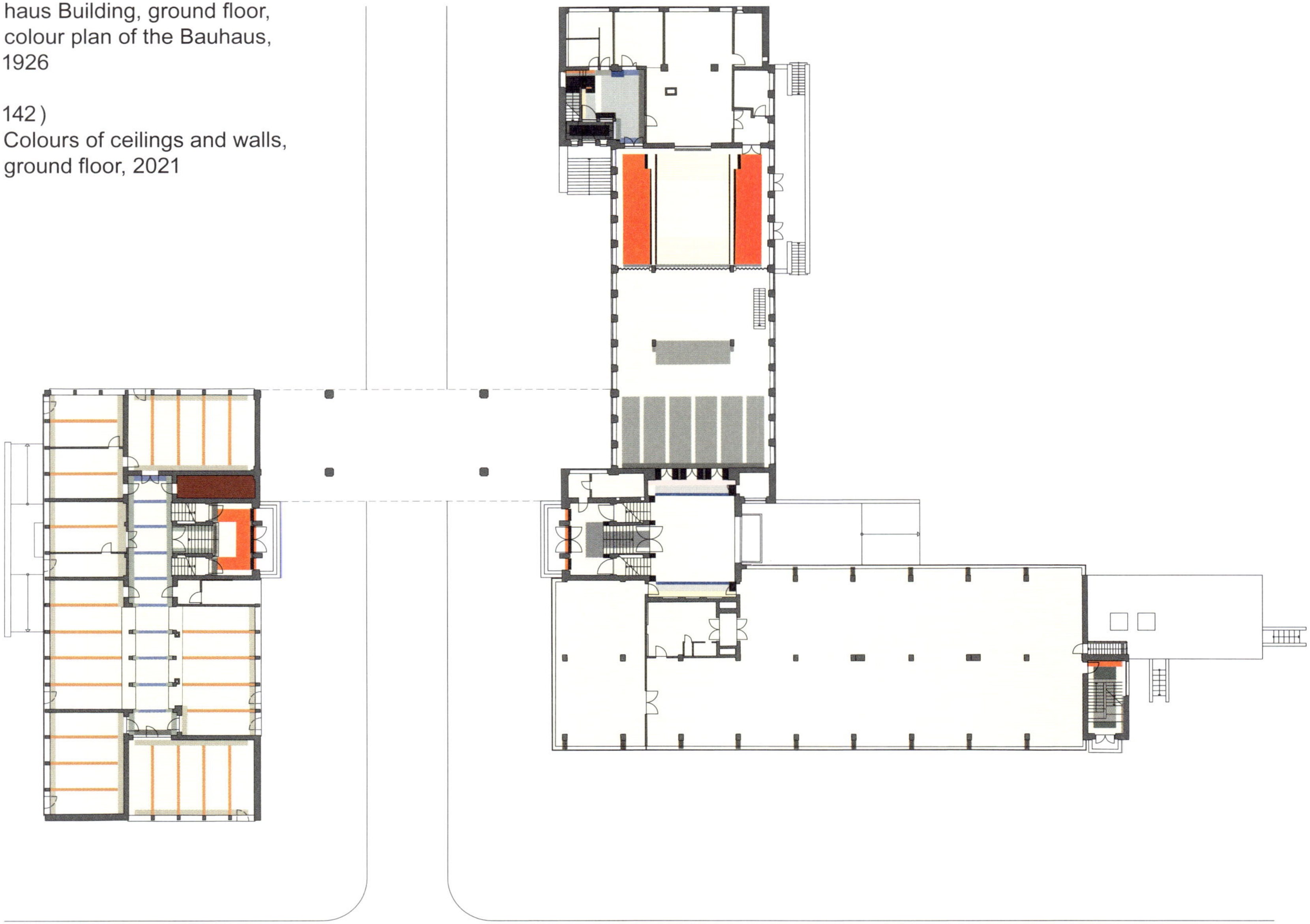

143)

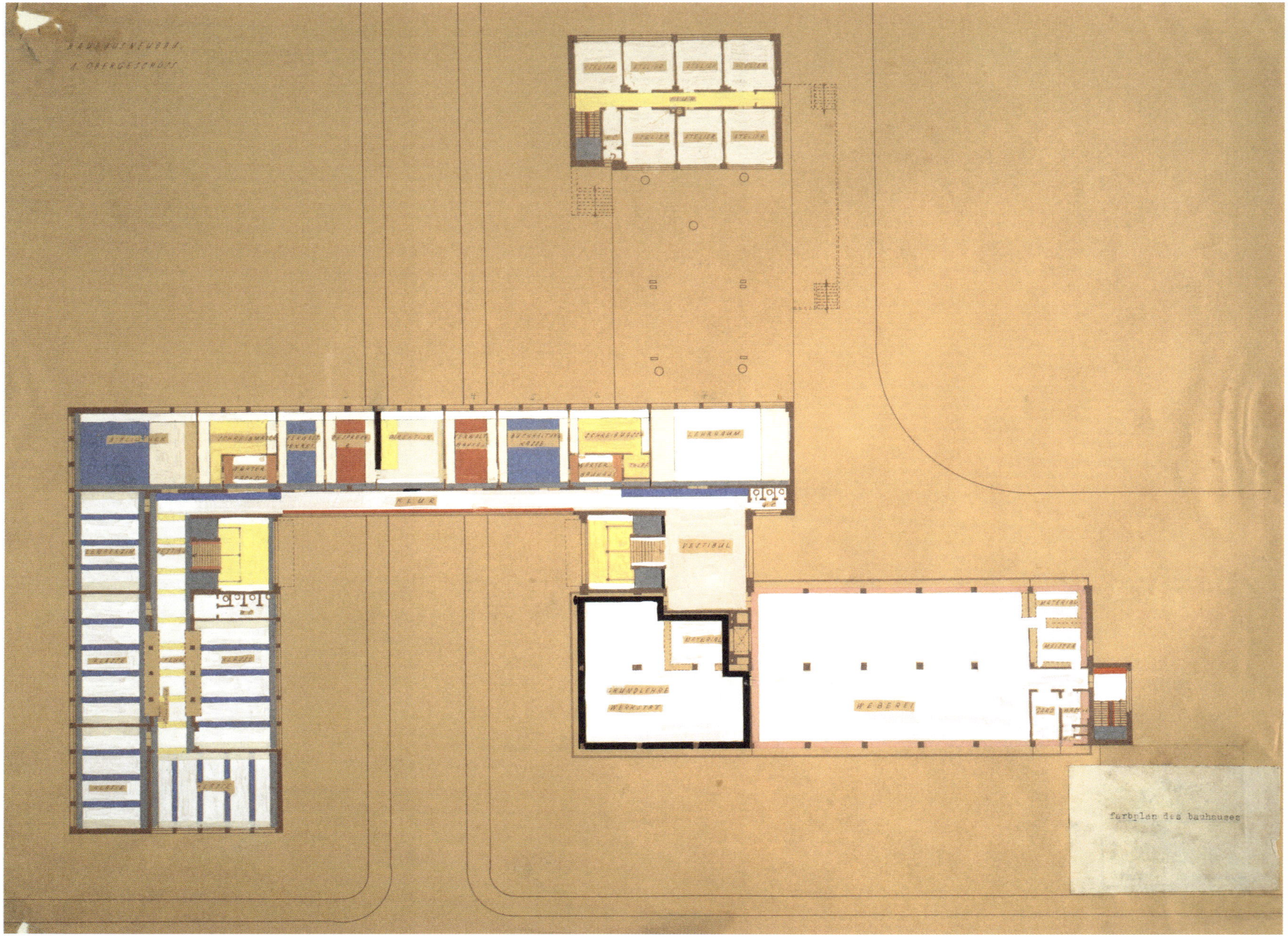

143)
Hinnerk Scheper: new Bauhaus Building, first floor, colour plan of the Bauhaus, 1926

144)
Colours of ceilings and walls, first floor, 2021

144)

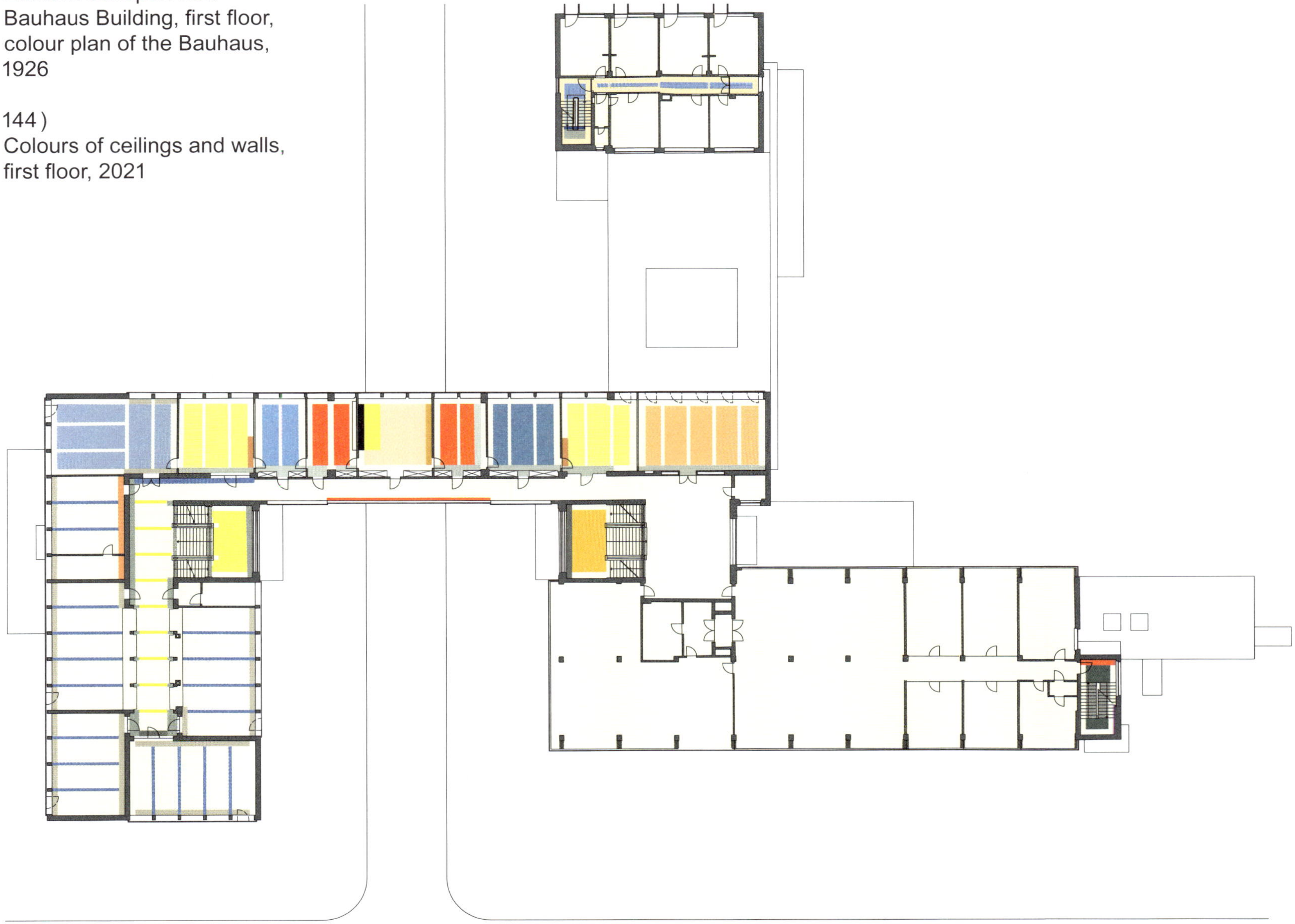

145)

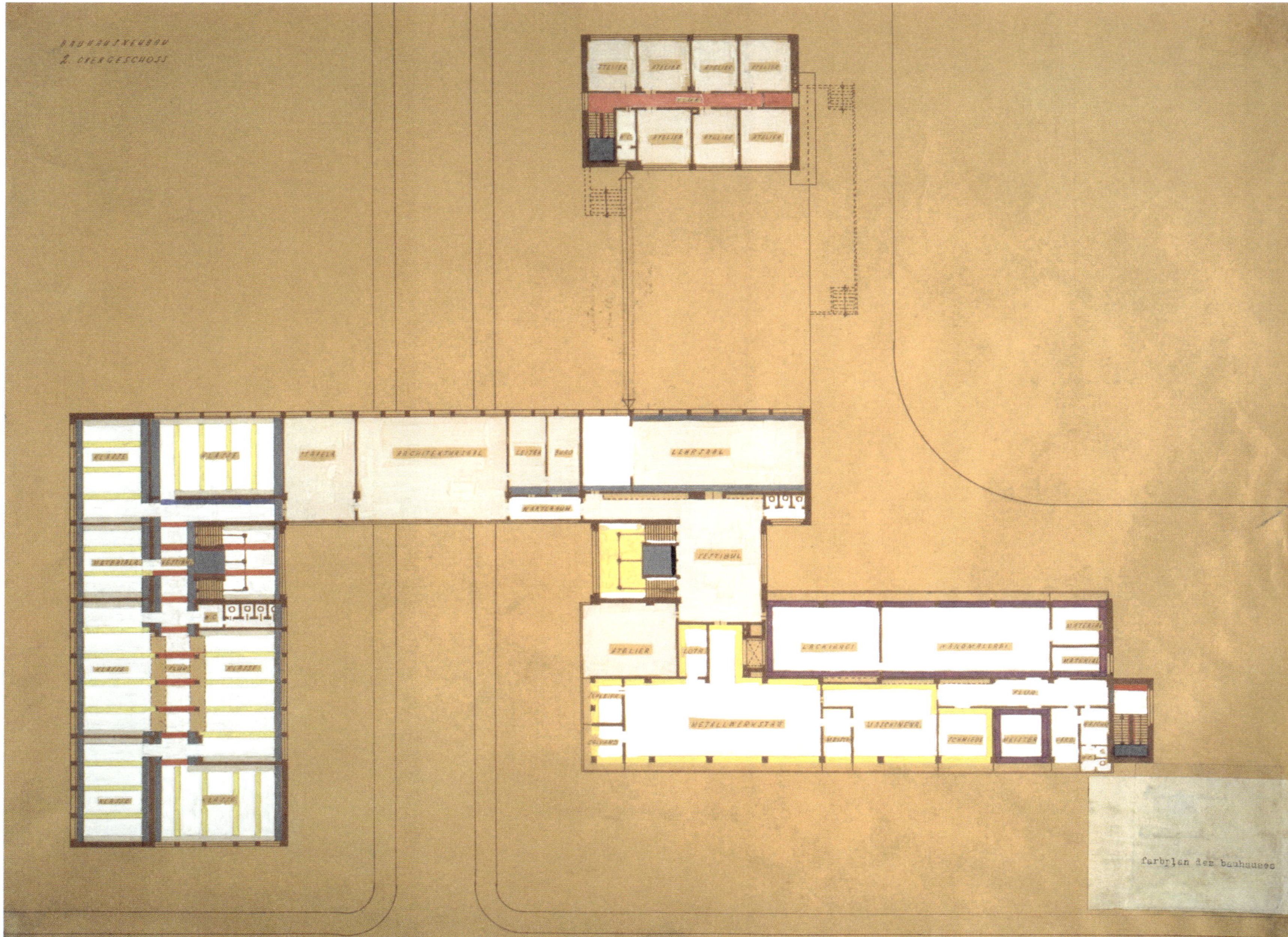
BAUHAUSNEUBAU
2. OBERGESCHOSS
ATELIER
LEHRSAAL
farbplan des bauhauses

145)
Hinnerk Scheper: new Bauhaus Building, second floor, colour plan of the Bauhaus, 1926

146)
Colours of ceilings and walls, second to fourth floor, 2021

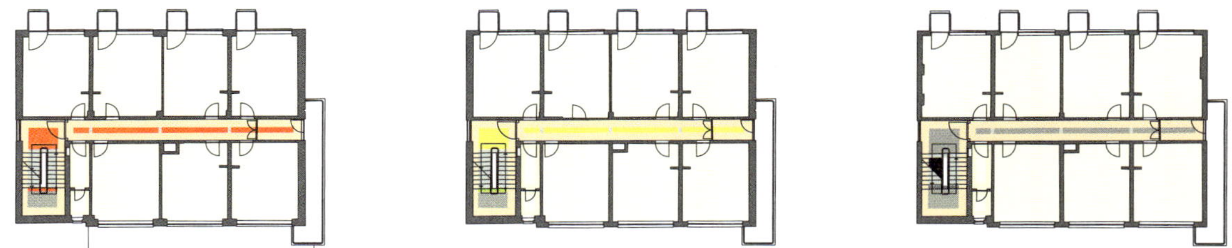

6)

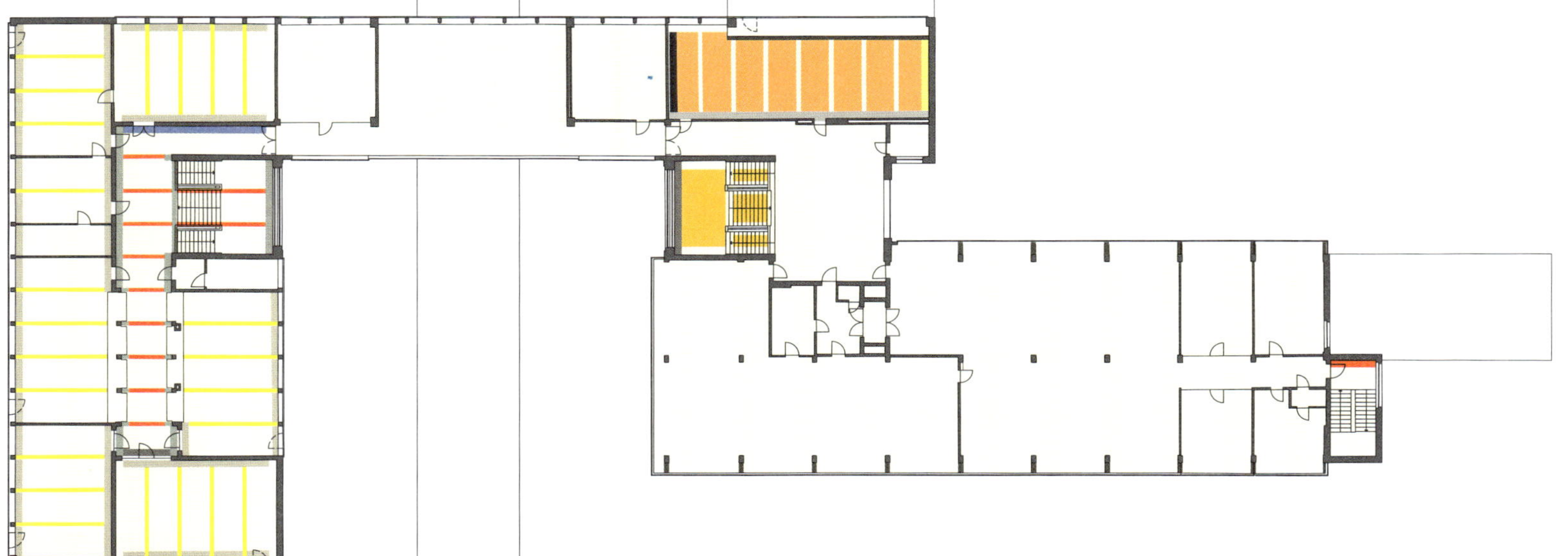

147)

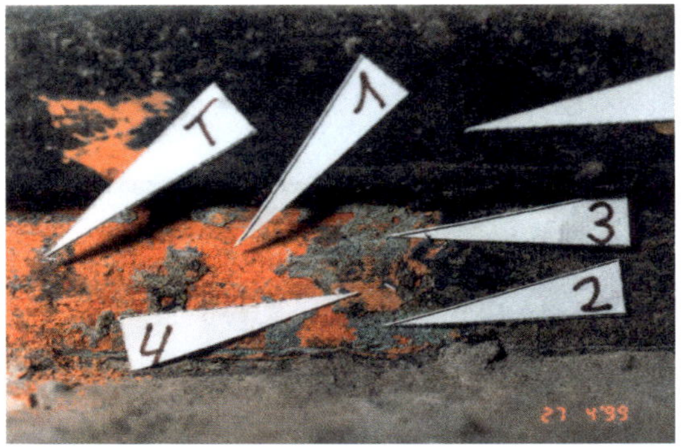

148)

SCHÖNE
DIPLOM-RESTAURATOR
Atelier für Konservierung
und Restaurierung
Ulestraße 20, 06114 Halle (S.)
Telefon: +49 345 - 388 04 50
Telefax: +49 345 - 388 18 51

Dessau, Bauhaus, Fachschule (FS), R 2.14 (Bibliothek)
Tabelle der bewerteten Farbtöne für Flächen mit historischem Befund

Bauteil	Farbtonbeschreibung	Ausm.	Farbaufstrich
Ostwand, einschließlich Wandpfeiler und Fensterlaibungen	Weiß; Leimf., DA, m	Keim 9870	
Ostwand - Standort Bücherregel	vormals ziegelsichtig belassen, keine gerade Beschneidekante zum historischen Putz vorhanden		
Ostwand - Fensterbrüstungen	Grau; Leimf., DA, m	Ausm. 68	
Nord- und Südwand, einschl. der Fensterbrüstungen in der Nordwand	Weiß; Leimf., DA, m	Keim 9870	
Westwand, einschl. Laibungsfläche des Wandversatzes	Grau; Leimf., DA, m	Ausm. 68	
Westwand - Ölsockel neben Türanlage	Grau; Emulsion, DA, m	Ausm. 68	
Westwand - Standort Bücherregel	vormals ziegelsichtig belassen, keine gerade Beschneidekante zum historischen Putz vorhanden		
Wandpfeiler - fensterseitige Sirnflächen	Grau; Leimf., DA., m	NCS - S 6000 - N	
Deckenfelder	Ultramarinblau, hell; Leimf., DA., m	Ausm. 17	
Unterzüge	Weiß, gebr.; Leimf., DA, m	Keim 9870	
T 2.01.07 - Rahmen	Grau; Ölf., DA, sg	NCS S 5005 - R80B	
T 2.01.07 - Blatt	Schwarz; Ölf., DA, sg	Sik ON.00.10	
Fußboden	unpigmentierter Steinholzestrich		

147)
Restoration research into colours of original window frame, 1999

148)
Evaluated colours for areas with historic findings, 1999

149)
Colour specifications for building parts, built-in elements, and technical installations, 2005

49)

Stiftung Bauhaus Dessau
Gropiusallee 38, 06846 Dessau,
Tel: 0340/ 6508-0 Fax: 0340/ 615 222

Generalsanierung des Bauhausgebäudes
Nordflügel – Fachschule

Farbangaben zu den Bauteilen

Bibliothek – restauratorischer Bereich
Raum FS 2.14

Nachtrag 02.11.2005

Bauteil	Farbton Material	Ausmischung Näherungswert	Glanzgrad Oberfläche	Aufstrichproben
Wand a1 Standort Bücherregal	Weiß, Leimfarbe	Keim 9870	matt	
Wand a2	Grau, Leimfarbe	Ausmischung 68	matt	
Wand a3 Ölsockel	Grau, Alcyd- bzw. Kunstharzfare	Ausmischung 68	matt	
Wand b, d	Weiß Leimfarbe	Keim 9870	matt	
Wand c1, c2 Fensterleibung, Pfeiler	Weiß Leimfarbe	Keim 9870	matt	
Wand c2 Brüstung	Grau, Leimfarbe	Ausmischung 68	matt	
Deckenfelder	Hellblau Leimfarbe	Ausmischung 17	matt	
Unterzüge dreiseitig	Weiß Leimfarbe	Keim 9870	matt	
Boden / Sockelleisten	Unpigmentiert Steinholz			
Wandpfeiler außen fassadenseitig	Dunkel Grau Leimfarbe	NCS – S 6000 N	matt	

Stiftung Bauhaus Dessau
Gropiusallee 38, 06846 Dessau,
Tel: 0340/ 6508-0 Fax: 0340/ 615 222

Generalsanierung des Bauhausgebäudes
Nordflügel – Fachschule

Farbangaben zu den **Einbauelementen**

Bibliothek – restauratorischer Bereich
Raum FS 2.14

Bauteil	Farbton Material	Ausmischung Näherungswert	Glanzgrad/Oberfläche	Aufstrichproben
Türanlage T2.01.07	**Türblatt** Alcyd-bzw. Kunstharzfarbe	SIK ON.00.10	seiden-glänzend	
	Türrahmen Alcyd-bzw. Kunstharzfarbe	NCS-S 5005-R80B	seiden-glänzend	
Türanlage T2.14.01	**Türblatt** Alcyd-bzw. Kunstharzfarbe	RAL 7044	seiden-glänzend	
	Türrahmen Alcyd-bzw. Kunstharzfarbe	RAL 7044	seiden-glänzend	
Fensteranlagen (Innen)	Weiß Alcyd-bzw. Kunstharzfarbe	NCS-S 0500-N	seiden-glänzend	bereits ausgeführt 4. BA
Fensterbank Bestand	materialsichtig Terrazzo	Bestand		

Farbangaben zu **technischen Einbauelementen**

Bibliothek – restauratorischer Bereich
Raum FS 2.14

Bauteil	Farbton Material	Ausmischung	Glanzgrad/Oberfläche	Aufstrichproben
Installationsrohre Heizleitungen	Reinweiß Alcyd- bzw. Kunstharzfarbe	RAL 9010	seiden-glänzend	
Heizkörper	Reinweiß Alcyd- bzw. Kunstharzfarbe	RAL 9010	seiden-glänzend	
Elektrotrassen Boden- und wandseitig falls Aufbodentrasse	Quarzgrau Pulverbeschichtung	RAL 7039	seiden-glänzend	
Lichtschalter Steckdosen Fa. Berker / Serie 1930 Unterputzmontage Ringplatte u. Schalter	Schwarzbraun	RAL 8022		

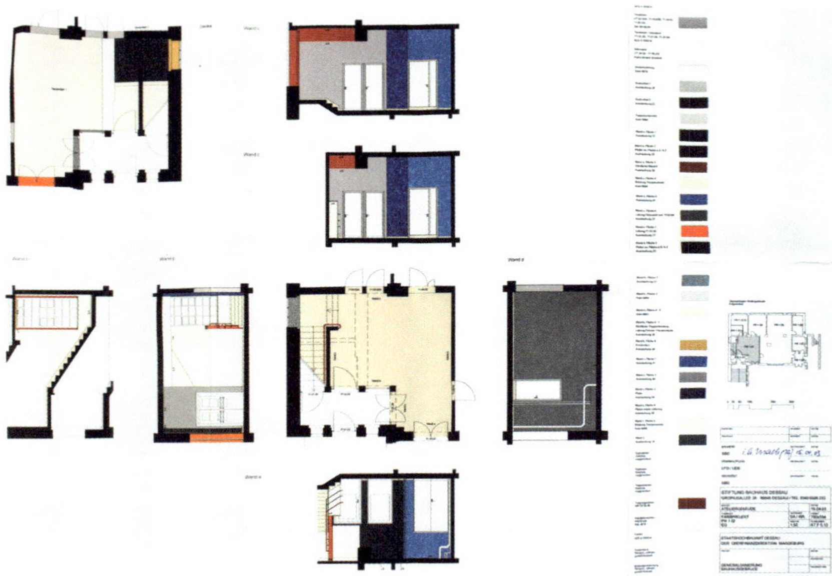

150)
Colour project for vestibule, studio building, 2003

To restore the historical colour design, it is important to not only identify the right colour but also investigate the background, materiality, and structure of the surface. To create a surface that reproduces the original as faithfully as possible, it is crucial to consider both material composition and workmanship since traces of how it was made, or the nature of a patina, can also be integral to the design.

At present, the original colour design has not been restored throughout the building. Firstly, because evidence of the original colouration is incomplete in, for example, the studio building's guest rooms or parts of the semi-basement, where historic walls or defining original built-in fittings are missing. Here, the original colour fragments have been preserved under a protective layer and overpainted with a 'neutral' colour. This is not only due to the fact that the original colour scheme cannot be reconstructed in its entirety but also because new building components such as glass partitions or fittings are being introduced. Bearing in mind that there can be no neutral colours in a colourful setting, a range of four colours was defined for these areas, which impinge as little as possible on the historical colour design: the RAL colours black (8022), quartz grey (7039), silk grey (7044) and pure white (9010). Should minimal deviations from the original colour design arise, the overall spatial effect is more important than finding the exact colour. Windows and doors from different decades in one room or façade therefore receive the same colour finish. Functional modifications or additions for utility reasons such as cable ducts should be identifiable as such, but not adversely affect or dominate the overall impression. They are therefore painted with one of the four colours in the RAL range so that they blend into the overall picture.

Up to 2006, a number of architects collaborated on the production of a comprehensive colour project,[13] which is being updated as required with new information, fresh insights, etc. The colour project is based on the studies and assessments of restorers, includes new elements such as the fittings or cable ducts, and presents an overview of both historic and more recently applied colours and materials in charts and explanatory texts. To restore the original colour design, chalk paints are being used on the external walls, a modified distemper on the internal walls, and alkyd resin paint on the windows, doors, and other fittings.

The historical layers of paint have been revealed and fully protected by restorers in just a few selected locations in the Bauhaus Building. Only parts of the original surfaces have been preserved, and the intensive use of the building presents such a risk that original, sensitive historic layers could be irretrievably lost. A protective layer also evens out significant flaws in the plaster, creating a surface that corresponds with the original in both materiality and structure. In most parts of the building, a removable, thin, mineral plaster slurry is therefore applied to ceiling and wall surfaces after first treating the existing original lime plaster on those surfaces. Here, loose fragments of paint and plaster and cement fillings are removed and stabilised with injections of filler where necessary. The damaged areas are fixed with a modified double layer of lime plaster, after which the entire area is covered with a thin layer of lime plaster containing methylcellulose, into which glass fibre matting is incorporated. Finally, the modified lime plaster is smoothed with a felt board and painted wet-on-wet with whitewash. Under the resulting surface, which corresponds with the original finish, the historic remnants of plaster and paint are protected and conserved. The final layer comprises a modified chalk paint based on the findings of restoration research. The original surfaces of fittings such as doors are also protected.

A comparison of Scheper's 1926 plan and the historic colour design that was revealed during research and subsequently restored proves conclusively that the original plan was not fully realised. The findings of the colour project are now integrated in the conservation objectives and the conservation management plan.

The surfaces of ceilings and walls are rendered in most of the parts of the Bauhaus Building (north wing, bridge, connecting building, studio building) as is the visible reinforced concrete construction with its pillars and girders. The workshop wing and semi-basements differ in character: here, the ceilings and walls, props and joists are render-free, as was customary at the time for workshops and ancillary rooms. These rough surfaces feature traces of the concrete formwork, visible under a thin slurry on props and joists, the structure of the ceiling cavity bricks or plain bricks. The visible installation of conduits in this render-free area of the building likewise accentuates its character. Notable places like the festive area and the director's office are treated differently: here, sections of the reinforced concrete girder structure, which is visible elsewhere in the building, are hidden from view.

The original colour design for the Bauhaus Building is complex. The rooms on the first floor of the bridge feature coloured ceilings and white joists—an intense colour scheme which convenes symmetrically on the director's office in the centre. By contrast, the rooms on the second floor are painted plain white. The picture in the north wing is defined by the white and grey walls and by the undersides of the joists, which are painted in different colours on each floor and depending on whether they are in public or private areas. In the rooms in the workshop wing only whitewash has been found. The coloured markers on the workshops in Scheper's plan thus aided orientation on the plan only and did not refer to the actual colours in the building. All connecting routes throughout the building are accentuated by strong colours on the ceiling or walls. In the stairway in the north wing, for example, the scene is set by the bright red of the stairway stringers, different colours on the landing ceilings, and grey and blue walls in the corridors.

151)

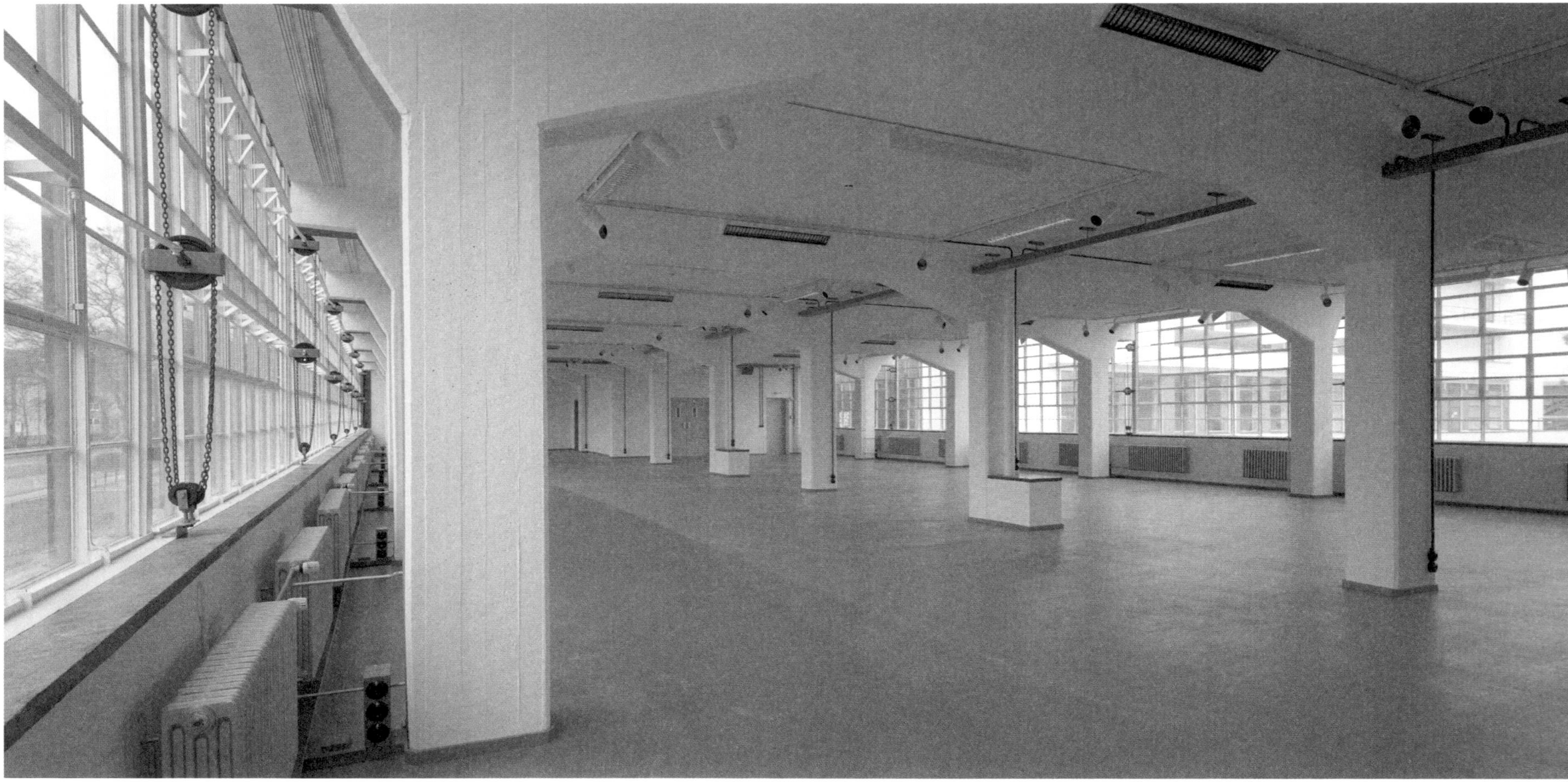

151)
Plaster-free surfaces, workshop wing, 2006

152)
Colour in the studio building, 2021

152)

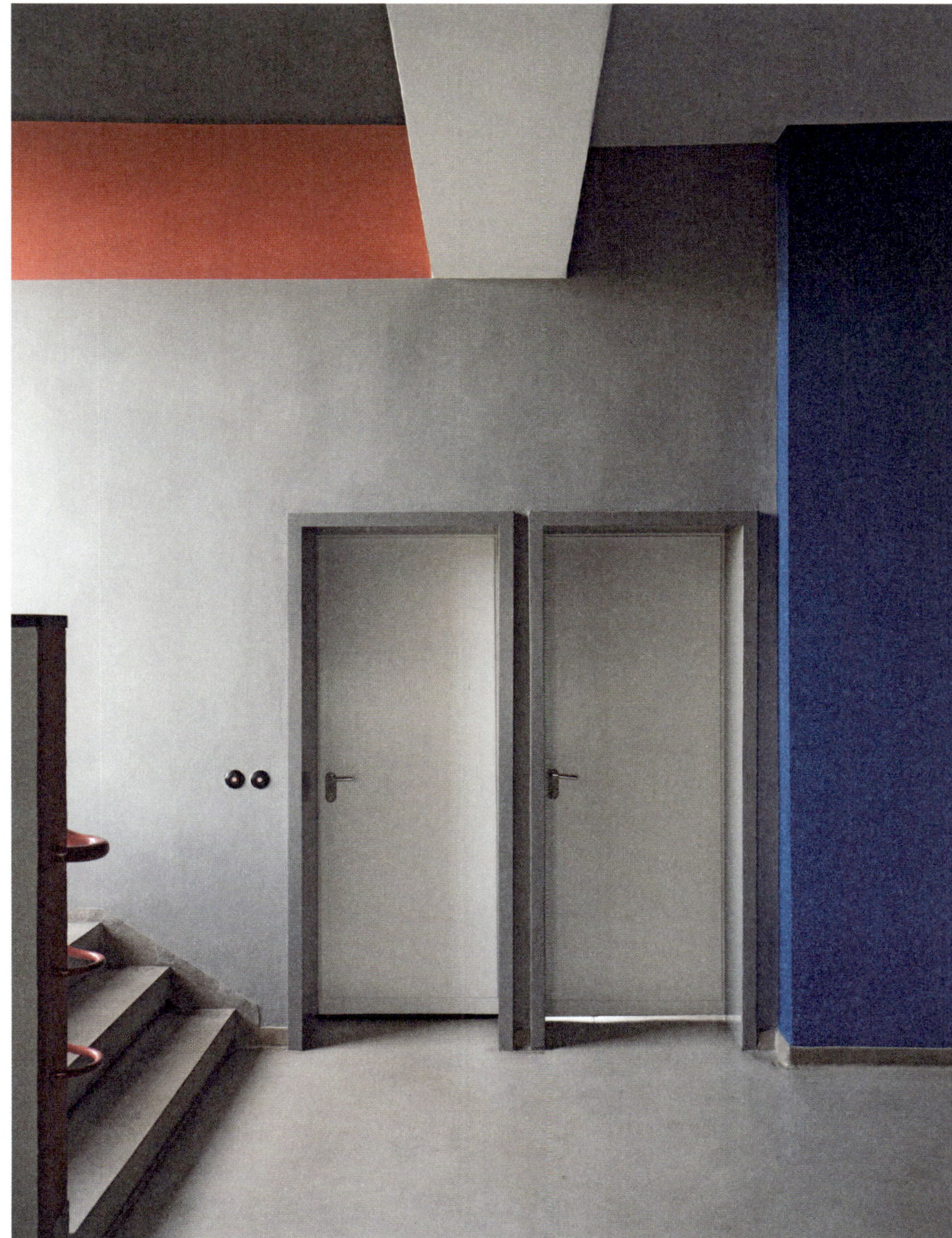

153)

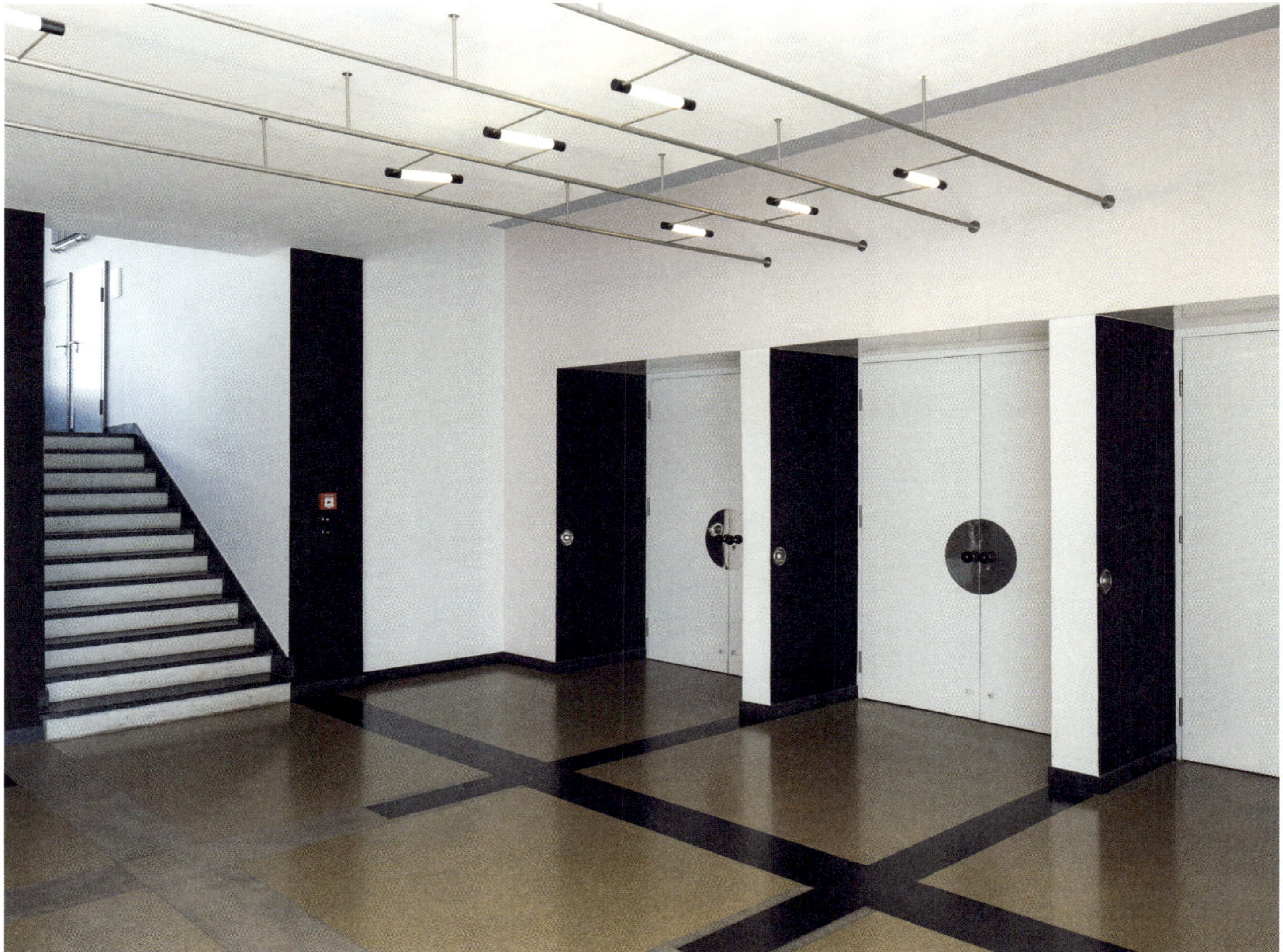

153)
Colour in the vestibule of the workshop wing, 2018

154)
Metallic, reflective surface of the auditorium ceiling, 2017

155)
Rough, smooth, gloss and matt surfaces, historic canteen, 2021

54) 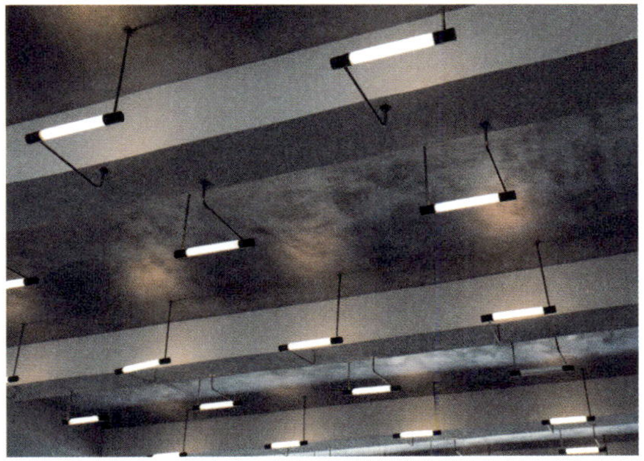

55) 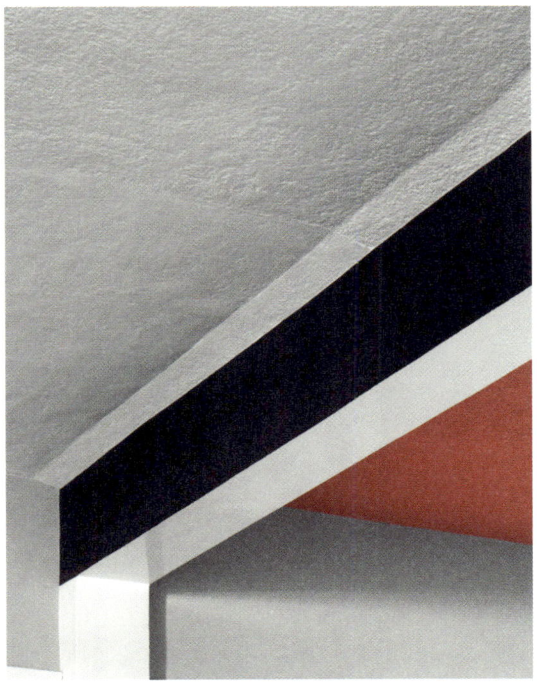

In the public areas of the studio building, colour is used in an exemplary way to aid orientation: a strong red colour in the vestibule shows the way forward, the ceilings on each floor are painted in different colours, and the underside of each stairway landing is painted the same colour as the floor to come. The uniform colours on each floor's stairway, floor, and kitchenette ceiling demonstrate their spatial cohesion. The grey joists stand out on the colourful ceilings, thus emphasising the constructive elements and the role they play in structuring the space. Today, modern smoke protection doors installed between the stairways and corridors interrupt the spatial flow of stairways, corridors, and kitchenettes, but constitute a necessary fire safety measure.

In prominent rooms, the design becomes even more complex: the colours used have a specific material quality and the surfaces are finished in different ways. In the director's office, for instance, the spatial impression is governed by the coloured surfaces of ceilings and walls, the fittings, the Triolin flooring, and a wall covering made of woven raffia. This very lively, handcrafted surface establishes a singular spatial tension and quality, illustrating the interface of the aesthetic of industrial perfection and artisanal production.

The festive area in the Bauhaus Building comprises the vestibule, auditorium, stage, and canteen. This multifunctional space is a representative area for events, a platform on which the Bauhaus presented itself to the public. The design may therefore be regarded as programmatic. The striking colour design of the vestibule is the result of a collaboration with László Moholy-Nagy and was described as follows in 1927: 'But the final and principal factor is colour, used in the Bauhaus as often as not for the purposes of light reflection. I recall a pink with light yellow and grey in combination with plate glass and black window blinds in the vestibule, a composition as bright as it is elegant.'[14] The findings of restoration research confirm the original finishes of most features: black and white for the auditorium door reveals, light ochre, black, and white for the walls, and grey and ultramarine for sections of the ceiling. Unfortunately, not all of the vestibule's original components have survived and there are no original findings for the doors, the main ceiling area, or part of the south wall; proper restoration and reconstruction is thus impossible. Even with a report to hand on the reconstruction of the original colour design based on a greyscale analysis of original photographs, only an approximation is possible.[15] However, because a 'neutral' colour was not a coherent choice for the entire space, especially in connection with the festive area as a whole, the original colour design was restored where possible and enhanced by the range of colours for areas for which there is no historical evidence, the aim being to create a harmonious overall architectural impression.

The structure and colour design of the original surfaces of walls and ceilings in the auditorium, stage, and canteen exemplify Hinnerk Scheper's design and are reconstructed based on original findings. The colours on the ceiling areas in the auditorium are of particular note. The areas between the white joists feature a matt, colourful base coat under a sprayed-on 'silver bronze' paint, which derives its pigmentation from tiny aluminium flakes. It reflects daylight and the light from the tubular lamps

156)

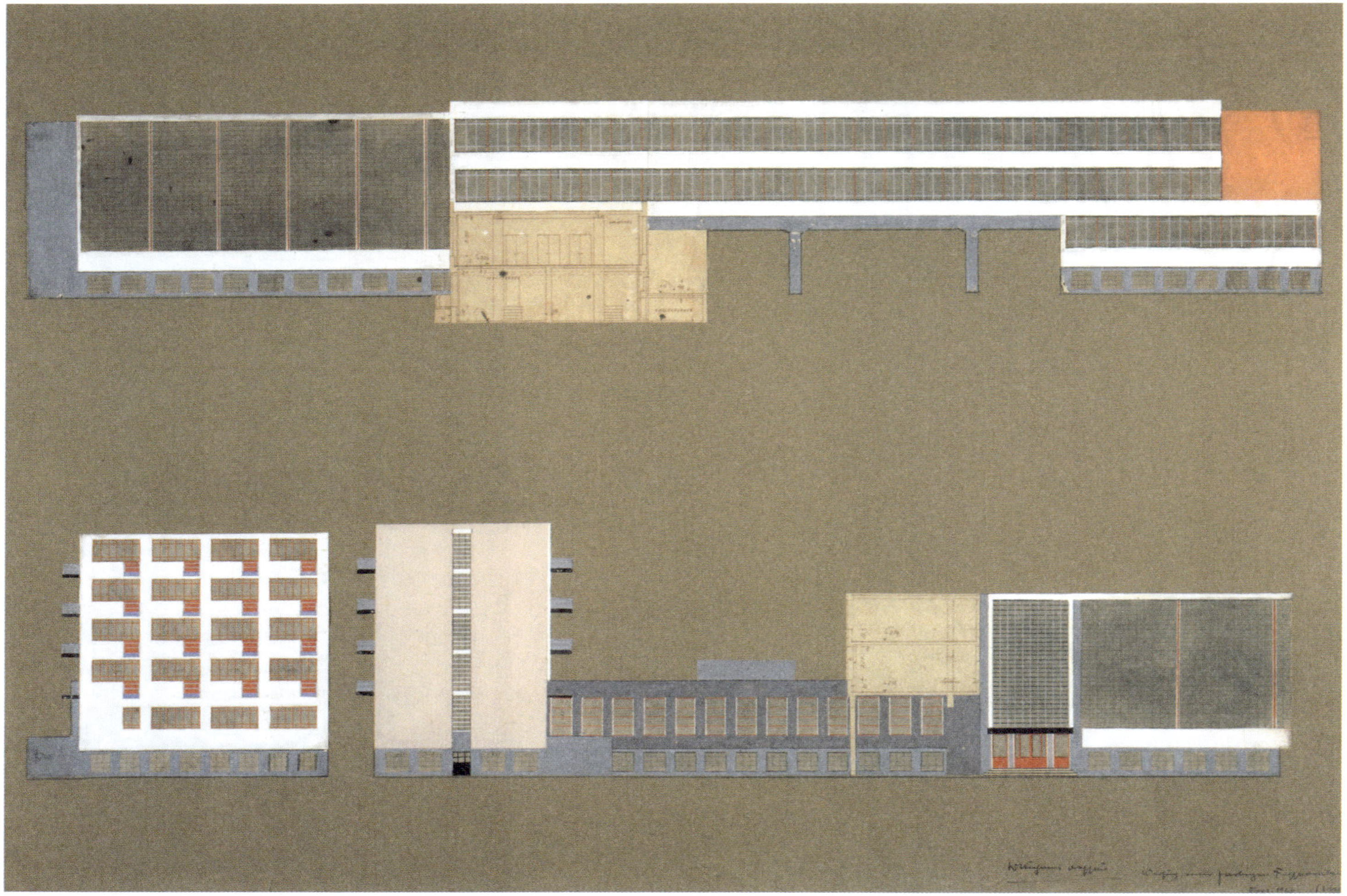

156)
Hinnerk Scheper: coloured façade experiment, 1926

157)
Colour scheme of façades, 2021

157)

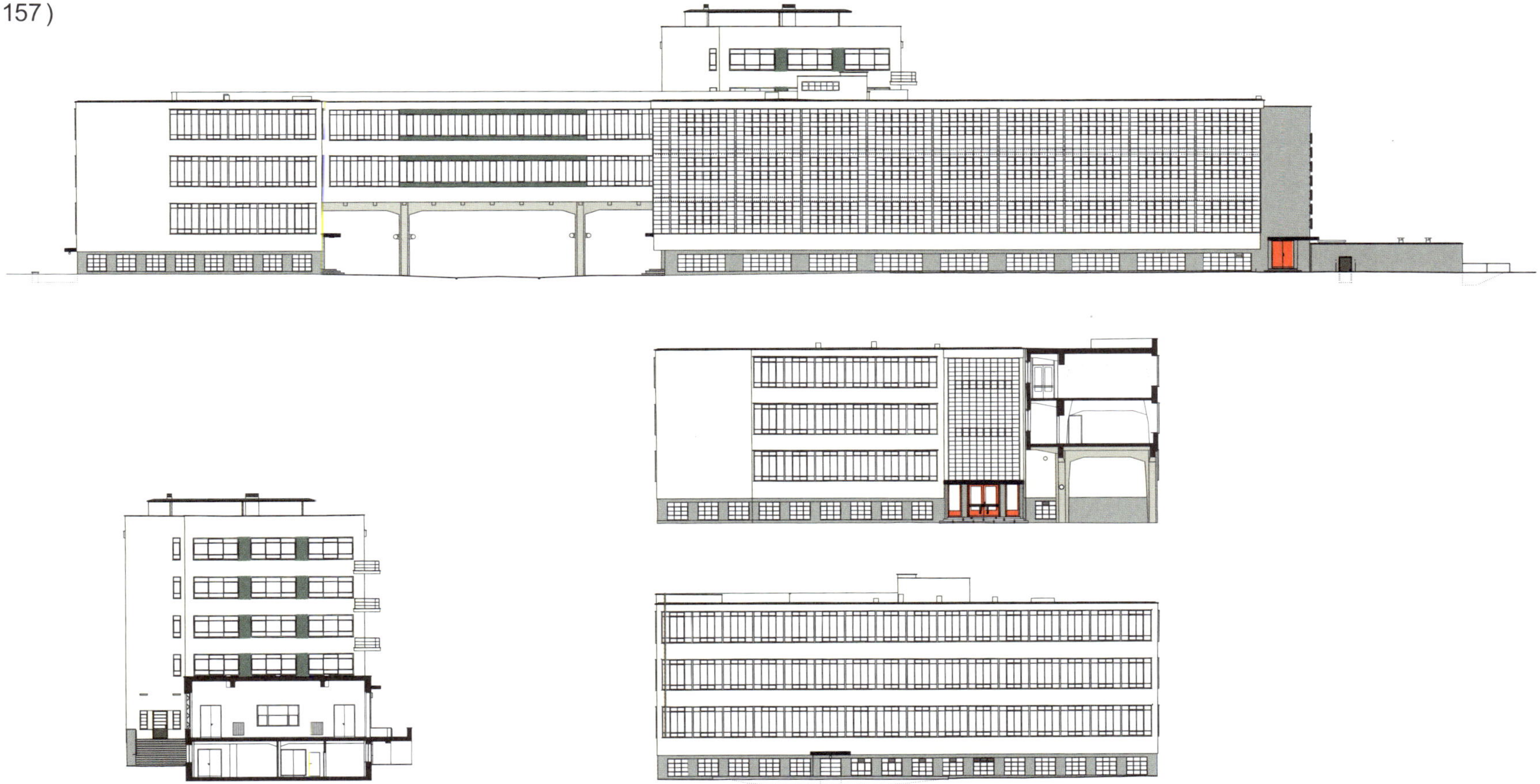

158)

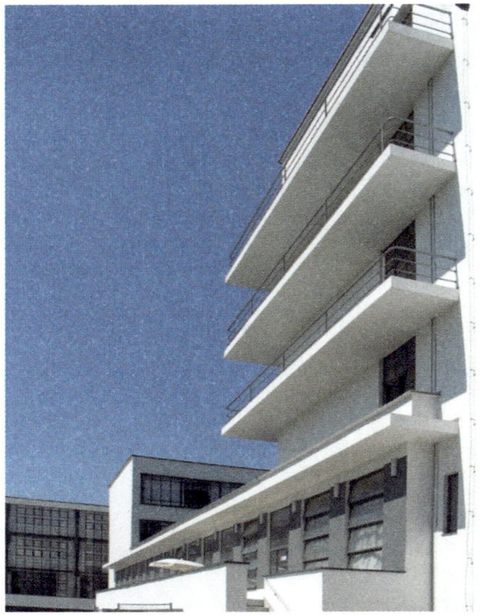

159)

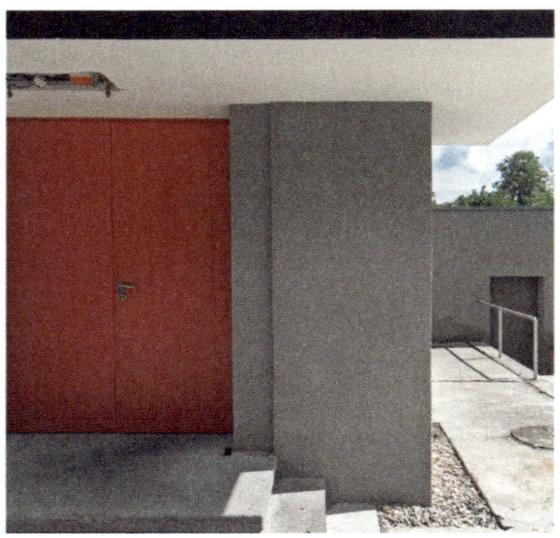

158)
Rendered façade, painted white, 2006

159)
Grey render with mica content, 2006

on the ceiling, resulting in a highly animated surface that is constantly transformed by the incidence of light. The festive atmosphere is also shaped by the interplay of matt wall surfaces and high-gloss door panels, the gleaming surfaces of the nickel-plated metallic elements, the silver radiators, and matt textiles. There is no surviving material evidence of the original flooring, or any other clear proof such as invoices dating from the building period. For this reason, the floors were covered with linoleum in a colour taken from the RAL range, which blends in with the historic colours and the overall picture.

The walls and ceilings of the stage feature the original white paint, thus emphasise the way the auditorium, stage, and canteen of the festive area work together as a whole. An option to create a black box theatre for special performances is realised by covering the white walls with fabric. No firm evidence of the original flooring has been found, and it has therefore been painted with the black RAL colour from the range for areas which lack historical evidence.

The historic canteen, too, provides a textbook example of the diverse surface designs produced by the wall painting workshop under Hinnerk Scheper. The colours accentuate the articulation of the building parts, and the impact of the surfaces is enhanced by their rugged and refined, rough and smooth, matt and glossy finishes. Using wire mesh, the materiality and structure of the original surface structure of the canteen ceiling was reconstructed based on the findings of restoration research. Fragments of the original surface remain protected and preserved under this surface. The well-preserved original render on the walls was restored. The colour finishes on the walls and ceiling were applied by restorers using a modified chalk paint with historic pigments. The original stonewood screed flooring was extensively reconstructed based on the original compound. The restored or reconstructed surfaces thus conform with the original versions in terms of structure, materiality, and colour.

The windows of the Bauhaus Building establish a connection between interior and exterior and are painted grey on the outside and white on the inside, based on historic findings. From the outside, the contemporary coat of grey paint allows the steel profiles to blend in almost entirely with the dark-looking glazed surfaces, lending the façade a light and elegant look. From the inside, the bright white profiles interact with the white walls, taking a secondary role in the overall appearance.

Hinnerk Scheper developed colour designs not only for the interiors of the Bauhaus Building, but also for the exterior.[16] Here, he had devised a concept which envisaged strong colour accents on the outside of the building; however, both historic photographs and the findings of restoration research show that these designs were not realised. The exterior of the Bauhaus Building, too, is shaped by diversely treated surfaces: the handcrafted surfaces of the exposed concrete construction under the bridge, the rough, grey render containing mica on the semi-basement level, the south stairway, and the southern addition, and the smoothly finished, white, rendered walls. During restoration research, evidence of white paint was found on remnants of original plaster, and grey paint on the columns between some of the windows. Only the ceiling areas on the underside of the bridge are known to have been painted a pale yellow tone, and the entrance doors were painted red.[17]

With the discovery, restoration, and reconstruction of the complex colour design and the nuanced surface designs, the original aesthetics of both interior and exterior of the Bauhaus Building are again revealed.[18]

1
Danzl 2003, p. 153

2
Cf. Markgraf 2017, p. 325 et seqq.

3
Van Doesburg 1928 (1984), p. 221

4
For basic information on colour at the Bauhaus, cf. Düchting 1996

5
Moholy-Nagy 1928, p. 25–26

6
Moholy-Nagy 1928, p. 38–39

7
Kandinsky 1946, p. 68

8
Scheper 1930 (2012), p. 66

9
Fischli 1968, p. 72

10
Scheper studied at the Bauhaus Weimar 1919–1922 and taught at the Bauhaus Dessau 1925–1932. Post-1945 he was head of the antiquities and monuments office in West Berlin and later professor at the Technical University of Berlin.

11
Gropius 2021, p. 64

12
Hinnerk Scheper, coloured map of the Bauhaus Dessau, 1926. Scheper estate, on permanent loan to the Bauhaus-Archiv Berlin

13
The concept was developed by the following architects: Brambach und Ebert Architekten, Halle, Pfister Schiess Tropeano Architekten, Zurich, and Johannes Bausch of the Bauhaus Dessau Foundation. It was based on restoration analyses and colour evaluations completed by Restaurierungsatelier Schöne, Halle.

14
Schwalacher 1927

15
The approximation of the original colour design was based on an assessment of two photos taken by Erich Consemüller in 1927/28, most likely using the same film stock he used to take photos of the vestibule in the Bauhaus Building and a wall hanging by Gunta Stölzl. Because the original wall hanging still exists, using complex methods it was possible to assign approximate colours to the grey tones on both photographs. Accordingly, the ceiling was painted a very pale yellowy white; cf. Pollmeier 2005

16
Hinnerk Scheper, Bauhaus Dessau. Versuch einer farbigen Fassadenbemalung (Trial colour façade design), 1926, in Scheper Estate, on permanent loan to the Bauhaus-Archiv Berlin

17
The restoration analyses and assessments of colour findings and colour concepts were completed by Restaurierungsatelier Schöne, Halle/Saale. The colour projects for the façades and semi-basement of the workshop wing were produced by Brambach Architekten, Halle/Saale. The colour projects for the interiors were developed by Johannes Bausch (Bauhaus Dessau Foundation).

18
In addition to the Bauhaus Building, other Bauhaus buildings have been renovated following restoration research, most recently by the Wüstenrot Stiftung 2020. Still pending is a cohesive scientific study of the use of colour in the Bauhaus buildings (which to date has primarily been considered in connection with specific building measures) contributing to the creation of a basis for the categorisation and evaluation of the Bauhaus buildings in twentieth-century architectural history.

Interior Design

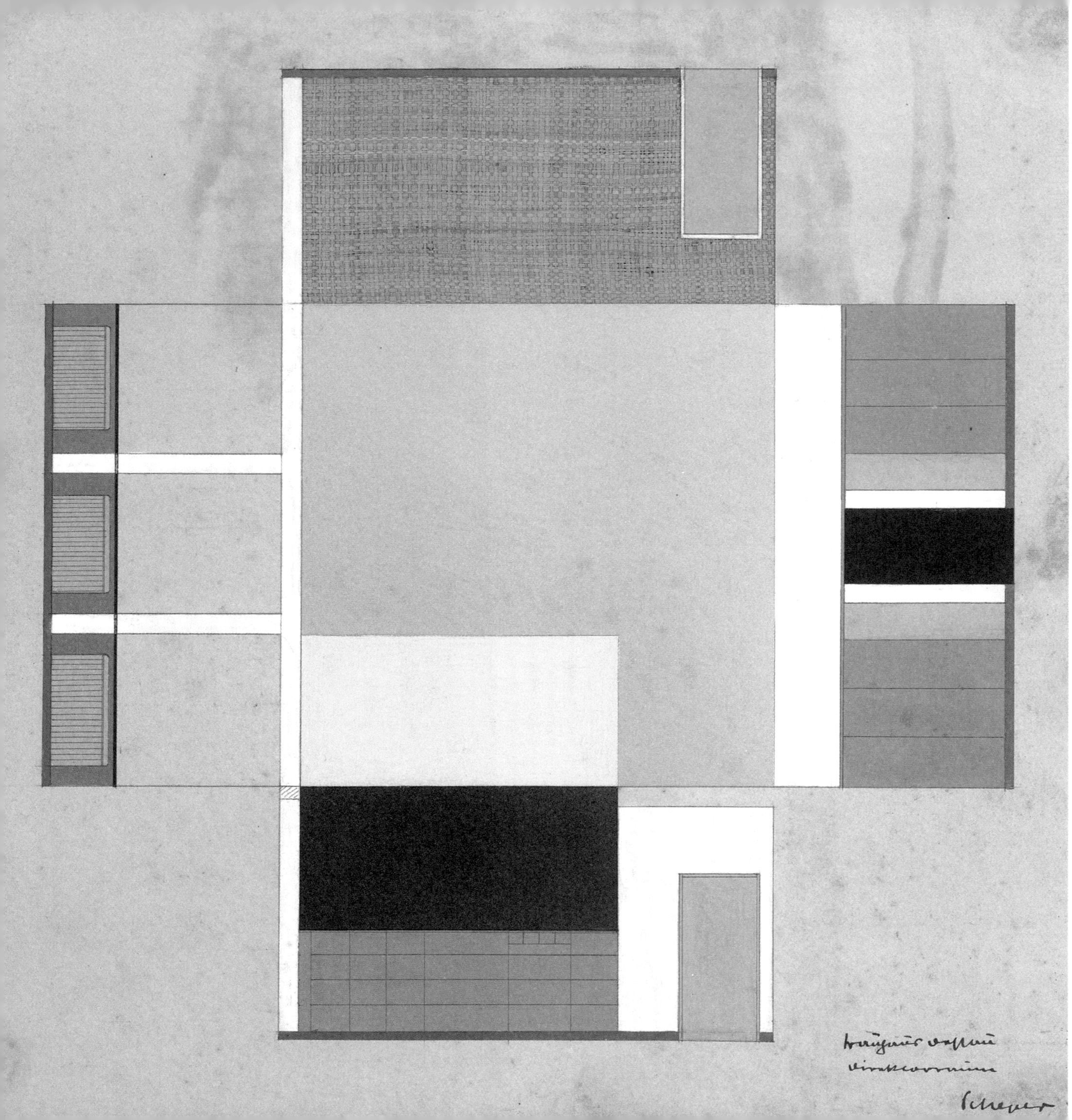

160)
Hinnerk Scheper: Bauhaus Dessau, director's office, 1926

Interior Design
Furnishings and Fittings

The interior design in the Bauhaus Building also comprises built-in furniture, lettering and signs, or door fittings that Walter Gropius and the Bauhaus workshops created especially for it. These elements are preserved as a matter of principle. In some areas, the reconstruction of missing original components regarded as integral parts of the building is also envisaged and outlined in the conservation objectives. In other areas in which scientifically substantiated reconstruction is not possible due to insufficient evidence, a recreation is undertaken. A recreation does not meet the rigorous scientific demands placed on a reconstruction, but can be a useful way of conveying an impression of relevant spatial contexts to visitors. Such recreations include the configuration of the director's office, two rooms in the studio building, and the furniture in the auditorium. All were meticulously executed based on historic records such as photographs or written descriptions and in coordination with the monument conservation authorities.

Historic Director's Office

The historic director's office, the appointments of which were designed by Walter Gropius in 1926, is a programmatic part of the building's design. A detailed sketch of the colour design for the office by Hinnerk Scheper, then head of the wall painting workshop, is on hand.[1] The recreation aims to convey the historic design, usage, and significance of the director's office.

Surviving original features including built-in cupboards on the corridor side of the office, the original Triolin flooring, and the coloured surfaces of walls and ceilings were meticulously restored in 1997 and 2014. Historic Junkers radiators from another modern building were installed for heating purposes. The raffia wall covering[2] was replicated based on a small original sample and Hinnerk Scheper's sketch. Further reconstructions were initially vetoed on the grounds of insufficient scientific evidence.

The space is informed by the idea of a 'room within a room', which is realised by means of one ceiling area which is higher than the rest, the positioning of a glass display cabinet and a desk, and the colour design. This was Walter Gropius's place of work, and as public interest in the Bauhaus grew over the years, so too did the desire to experience the full impact of the space and its décor. In the nineteen-nineties, a reconstruction of the desk was made. The original desk, found in Gropius House in Lincoln, Massachusetts, USA,[3] provided a detailed, true picture as a basis for the reconstruction. A lighting fixture comprising tubular bulbs was originally situated above the desk; however, because this original element is missing, modern strip lights were initially installed in its place in 1997. In line with the aim of restoring the room to its original condition wherever possible, these will in future be replaced by tubular lamps.

The spatial quality of the director's office is also significantly shaped by the glass cabinet placed upright in the room, in which products from the Bauhaus workshops including Otto Lindig's ceramics, an ashtray by Marianne Brandt, or tea infusers by Hans Przyrembel were showcased, and by the built-in shelves and cupboards behind the desk. Gropius's design had envisaged a niche in the north wall

161) 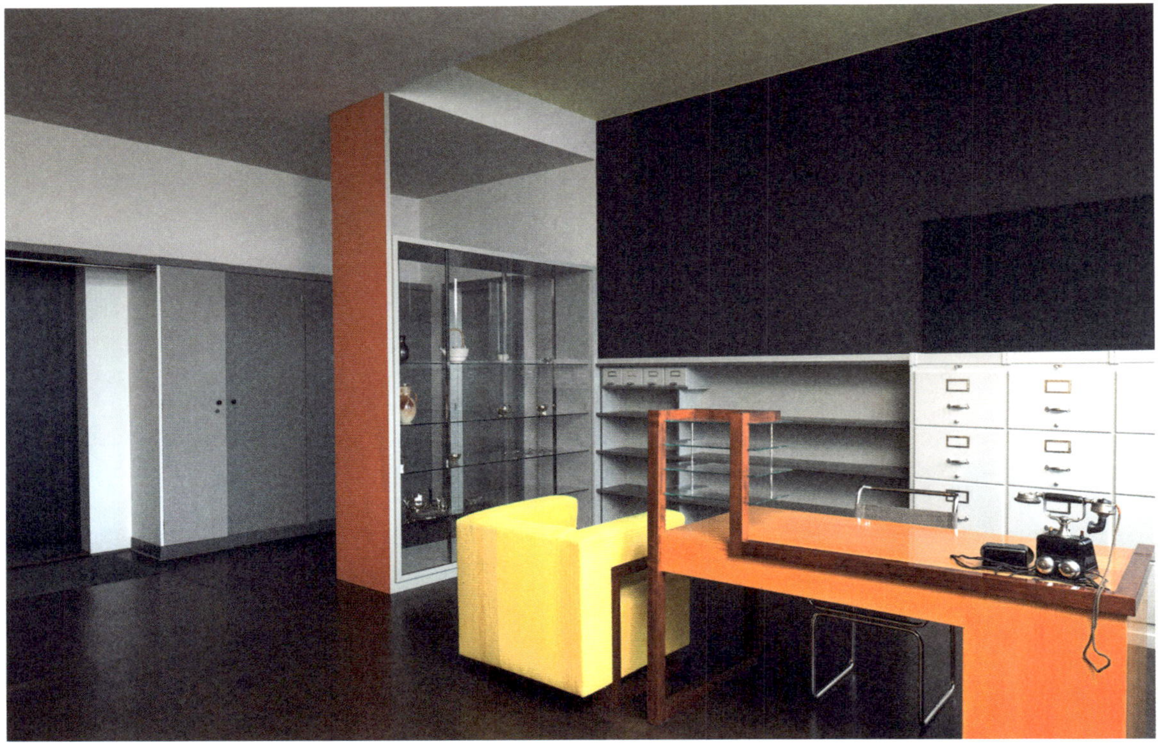

for the built-in shelves and filing cabinet. The recreation of the office complete with these built-in features was based on an analysis of informative historical photographs, Hinnerk Scheper's colour design sketch, and research into individual objects such as the filing cabinets. The room was painted using shades from the range of colours for areas for which there are no historical findings. Only the bright red colour on the room-facing wooden side of the glass display cabinet is based on concrete evidence, in this instance found on the ceiling during restoration research. No unambiguous proof was found as regards the original furniture or lighting in the opposite part of the room and as such, its recreation was not feasible.[4]

161)
Historic director's office, 2015

162)
Plans for the reconstruction of the original built-in shelving and file cabinets in the director's office, 2014

162)

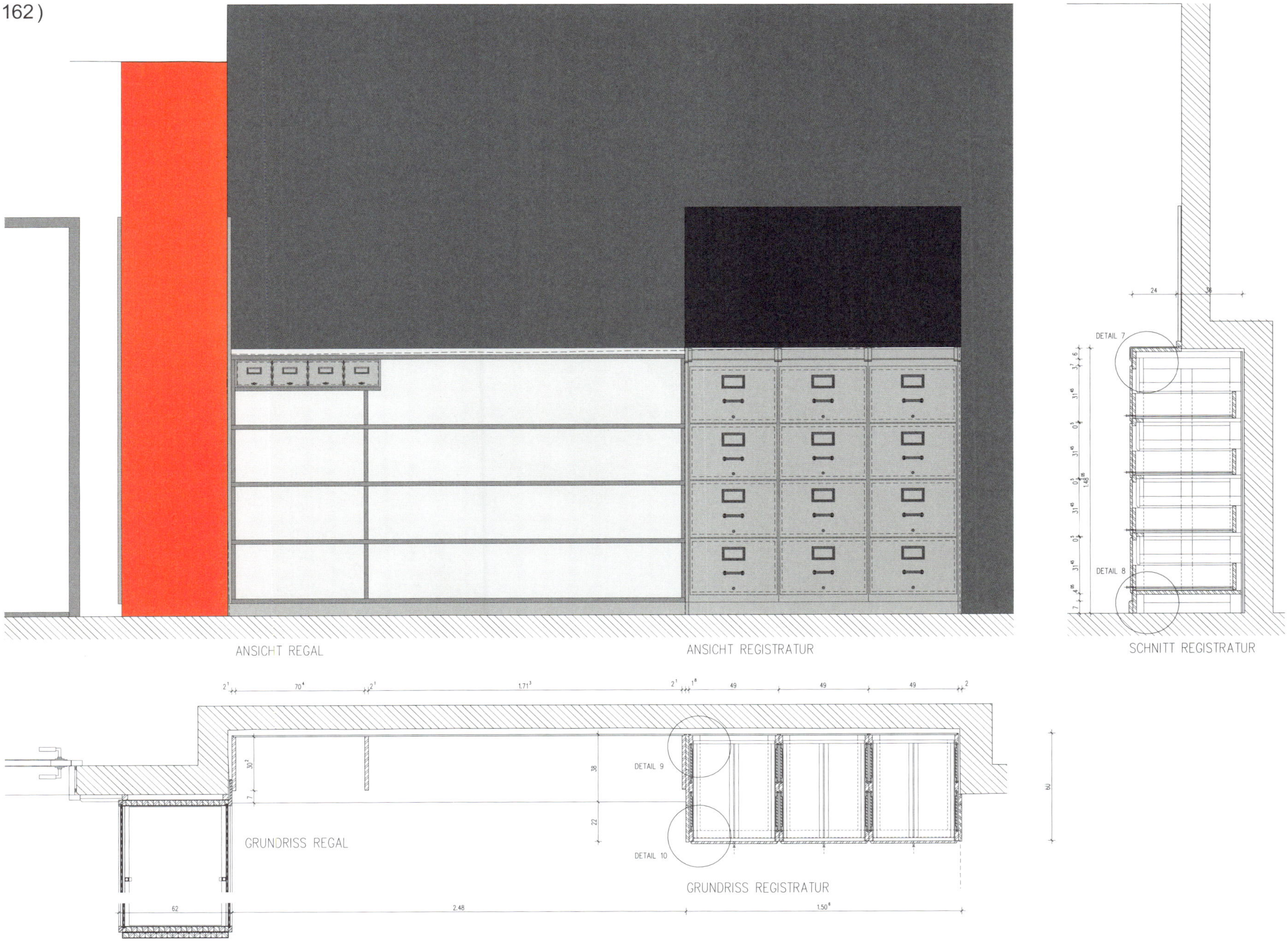
ANSICHT REGAL
ANSICHT REGISTRATUR
SCHNITT REGISTRATUR
DETAIL 7
DETAIL 8
DETAIL 9
DETAIL 10
GRUNDRISS REGAL
GRUNDRISS REGISTRATUR

163) 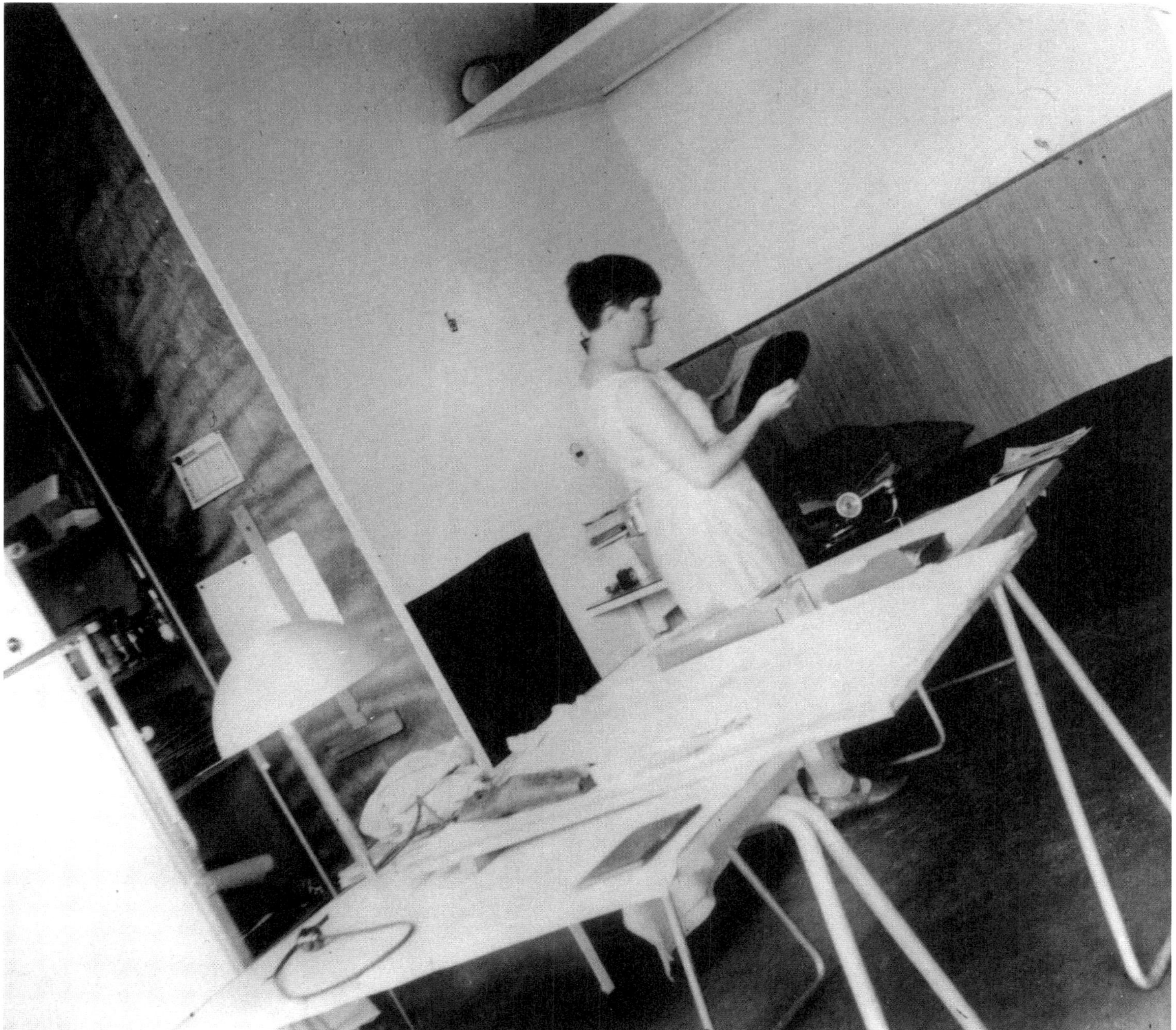

163)
Marianne Brandt in her studio, 1928 / 29

164)
Recreated studio, 2014

64)

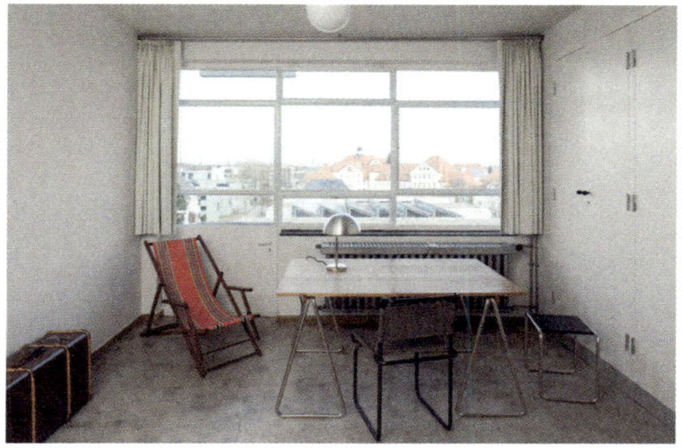

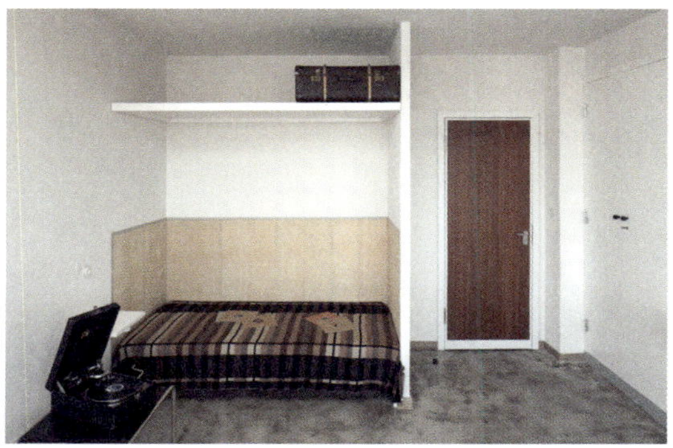

Studio Building

In the studio building in which the Bauhaus's students and junior masters lived, Walter Gropius showcased his vision of a modern way of living. The rooms were fitted with built-in furniture including a bed recess with a suitcase stand, folding table, and cupboards. The built-in cupboards were arranged in such a way that one formed the dividing wall between two rooms; the inside of one section of the cupboard was entirely accessible from one room, the inside of the second from the other room. These built-in fittings meant the rooms were well-suited for short-term use and thus also ideal for the modern, mobile generation. In this way, the architecture sought to improve people's lives, as Walter Gropius said: 'The standardization of the practical machinery of life implies no robotization of the individual, but, on the contrary, the unburdening of his existence from much unnecessary dead-weight so as to leave him freer to develop on a higher plane.'[5] The studio building was altered even during the Bauhaus era in order to add extra classrooms. Other modifications led to the loss of almost all the built-in elements apart from one bed recess and one built-in cupboard on the top floor, as records from 1964 show.[6] Over the course of the renovations which began in 1976, around 1980 the original uniform spatial design of the studio building was restored by installing simple partition walls between the rooms, which were then used as guest rooms. In the process, the bed recess and built-in cupboard which had survived until then were destroyed and with them the last evidence of the original built-in furnishings. Because the simplified structure created in 1980 corresponds with the original cell-like structure of this part of the building and also meets functional requirements, it is also conserved as proof of the renovation of 1976.

With the increased public interest in the Bauhaus World Heritage site, the need arose to convey the historic design, use, and significance of these interiors more effectively to visitors. In 2013, two rooms in the studio building were therefore recreated in an exemplary manner. One of these was inhabited by Marianne Brandt and is especially well documented. The recreation was based on analyses of traces of the built-in fittings found on preserved original surfaces such as the stonewood floor, walls, and ceilings. Based on historic photographs and other records,[7] the preparatory work also entailed detailed research into individual objects such as a comparative study of other original built-in cupboards in the Bauhaus Building and Masters' Houses. The recreation encompassed the demolition of non-original partition walls, the construction of new walls between the rooms to create recesses, the reconstruction of the built-in cupboards, the restoration of the original door openings, door frames, and doors, and the reproduction of the bed recess with suitcase stand, raffia wall covering, and small folding table next to the bed. Junkers radiators salvaged from another modern building (and thus saved from the rubbish tip) were installed for heating purposes, and an old washstand, consistent with the original, completes the recreation. The original stonewood flooring was cleaned, repaired, and polished, and walls and ceilings were painted white based on evidence found on the original walls and ceilings. The new built-in furnishings were painted white using one of the range of colours for areas without historical evidence.[8]

165)
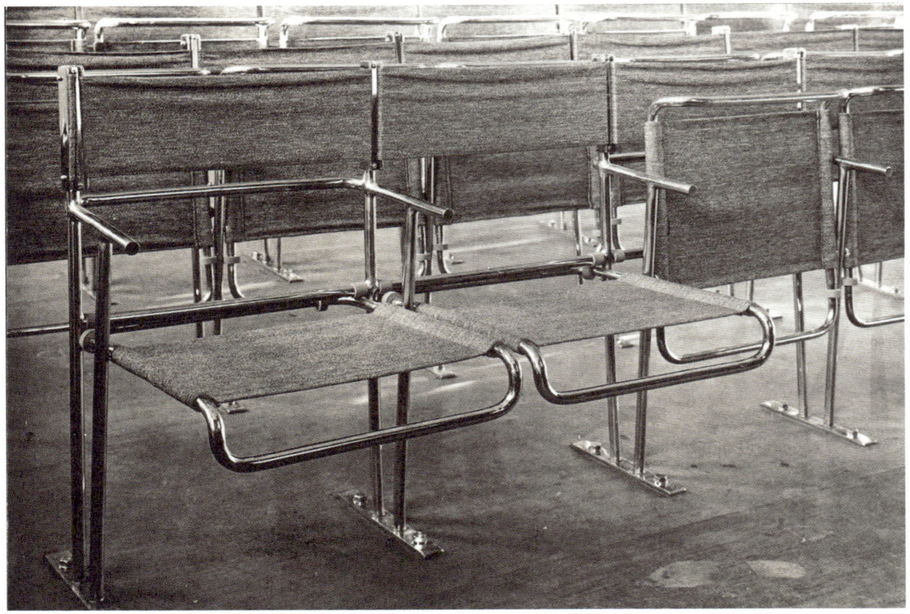

166)
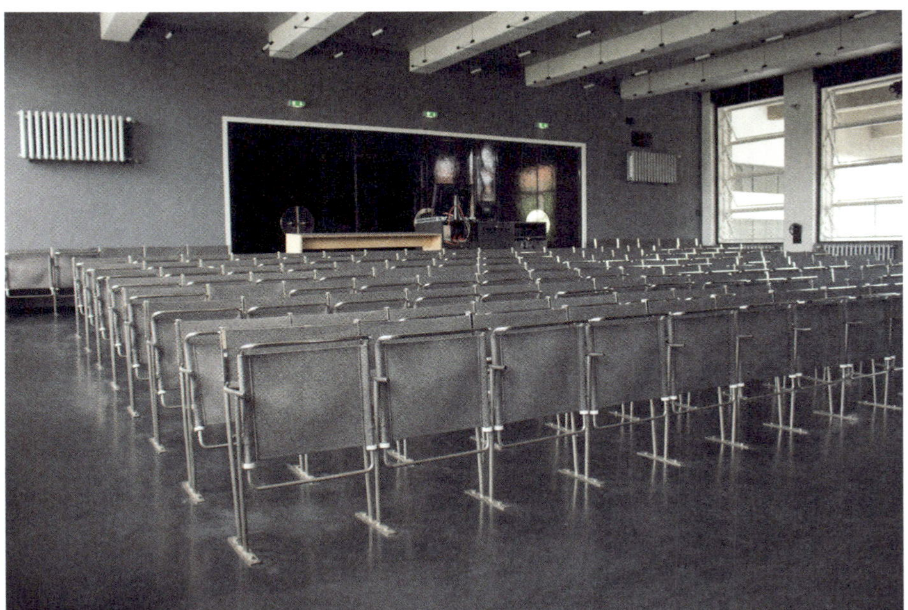

165)
Folding seat model B1 in the auditorium of the Bauhaus Dessau (design: Marcel Breuer, 1926), ca. 1927

166)
Auditorium with new textile covers on the tubular steel frames, 2019

Auditorium

The auditorium is part of the emblematic festive area. Accordingly, the décor has a programmatic character. The then highly contemporary seating comprising 162 chairs which are connected to the floor or each other was designed by the Bauhausler Marcel Breuer. The frames are made of lengths of nickel-plated tubular steel pieces which are welded, screwed, and plugged together with screws.[9] The folding seats can be locked in place using rubber pads. The seats were upholstered with a robust blended cotton, supplied in 1926 by the Berlin-based company Teppich Bursch.[10]

The extensive space was used for different purposes and modified over the decades. As a result, the original frames and textile covers no longer exist. Thus, the renovation of 1976 included not only the restoration of the historic sequence of rooms, but also the reconstruction of the furniture. Based on further research and findings, a new reconstruction of the nickel-plated tubular steel construction was made in 1991. Because the auditorium is intensively used, the textile covers are exposed to a great deal of wear. They have therefore been replaced about every fourteen years since 1976, which is not unusual for heavily used textiles in public spaces. In 1991, the covers were made from *Eisengarn,* although this material was first made at the Bauhaus in 1927/28 and was not part of the 1926 furnishings. But because the festive area is defined as a location[11] in which the original condition of 1926 is to be restored wherever possible, the textile must be based on the original blended cotton. Unfortunately, no fragments of the original textile covers have survived, and comparable fabrics from the collection of the Bauhaus Dessau Foundation must therefore serve as models.[12] These blended textile samples were used in 1926 to upholster tubular steel chairs made at the Bauhaus and, based on current information, they match the textile used in the auditorium.

The recreation of the textile in 2018 was therefore based on restoration research, analyses, and assessments and aimed to achieve as much likeness as possible to this historic model in terms of structure, texture, and facture (or surface aspect). Due to the auditorium's role as a fundamental programmatic space, the objective is to achieve as much likeness as possible to the original materiality, haptics, and appearance of 1926. At the same time, lasting colourfastness, stability, and durability is sought because the auditorium is widely used for events and the seating is thus constantly in use. Another important issue is the way in which the textile responds to light over time since the textile recreated in 2004 had become strongly discoloured by exposure to light. Yarns of appropriate thickness, twist, and colour were first sourced and tested and the materials deemed most suitable were subsequently used to make woven samples. The sample that best replicated the vibrant look of the historic model finally served as a template for the recreation of the textile used to make the covers.[13]

1
Hinnerk Scheper, Bauhaus Dessau, director's office, no year, privately owned by Dirk Scheper and the Bauhaus Dessau Foundation

2
This kind of raffia wall covering was also used in the studio building and the Masters' Houses, where it was known as a 'Madagascar wall covering'.

3
Cf. Bauhaus LAB 2016 (2017)

4
Planned by Brenne Architekten, Berlin

5
Gropius, 1965, p. 90

6
Schlesier/Püschel 1964, p. 25

7
Werner 2014/II

8
Planned by Brenne Architekten, Berlin

9
Information about the tubular steel furniture in the Bauhaus Building in Rehm 2005, p. 70 et seqq.

10
Municipal archive, Dessau, SB/2, folio 20, 27

11
ARGE Bauhaus 1999; Pro Denkmal 2014

12
According to Lutz Schöbe and Rüdiger Messerschmidt, 2018

13
The reconstruction of the textile was managed by Bettina Göttke-Krogmann, professor of textile design at Burg Giebichenstein Kunsthochschule Halle; cf. Göttke-Krogmann et al. 2018

167)

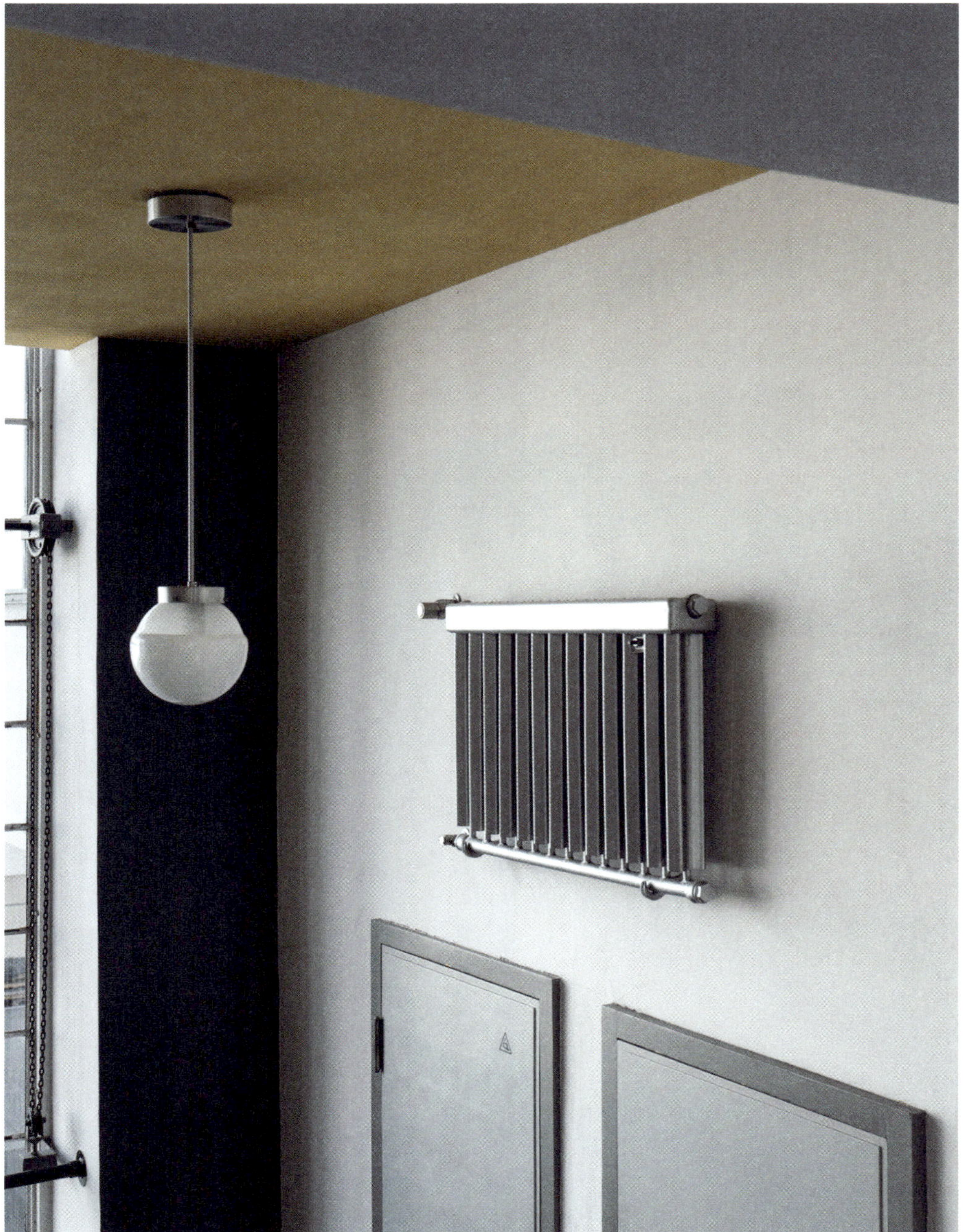

168)

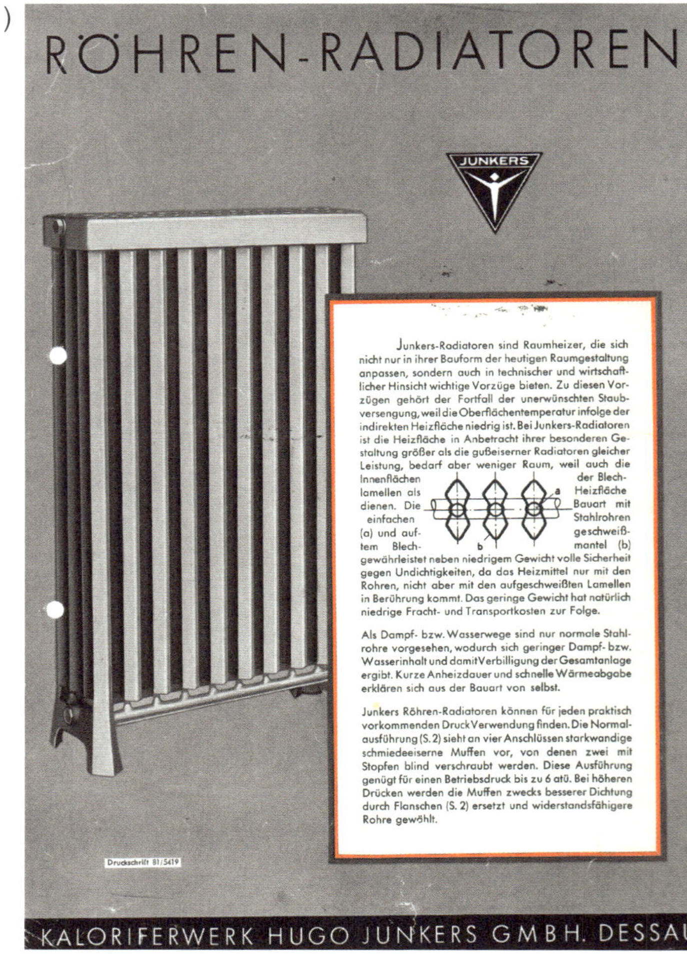

167)
Radiator and glass pendant lamp in the stair landing of the workshop wing, 2021

168)
Advertising brochure for Junkers tube radiators, n. y.

Interior Design
Building Services

Technical features play an important role in architecture: elements such as lighting or radiators which are essential to a building's use not only fulfil a function, but also influence the impact it makes. As such it is especially important to examine the technical features of the Bauhaus Building, for which Walter Gropius coined the maxim 'Art and technology–a new unity'.

In modern buildings, the constituent parts of the building services including radiators, conduits, or lifts are rarely regarded as objects worthy of conservation which must be protected as features of the historic monument. By contrast, the need to preserve the hypocaust heating system of a medieval cloister or the tiled stove of a Jugendstil house has long been acknowledged.[1] The appliances of then modern building services seldom conform to modern standards and are regarded as expendable parts which are simply removed and replaced by newer elements as required. Thus, only a few of the original technical features in the Bauhaus Building have been preserved.

Heating System

In 1926, a central heating system providing two million thermal units[2] was installed in the Bauhaus Building by the Dessau-based company Karl Plöger. The boiler room[3] with five boilers was located in the semi-basement under the festive area; the flue passed through a horizontal skimmer to a vertical chimney located next to the lift in the workshop wing. The coal bunkers were situated next to the boiler room, therefore outside the building and underground, partly under the bridge. The concrete bunker lid complete with hatches for coal deliveries is still visible outside the Bauhaus Building today. Additional rooms for the heating system included a woodchip bunker, a workshop, and a small room for the boilermen. Later, the coal was delivered to the boiler room from the south using a ramp. With the gradual conversion of the system[4] to a hot water heating system by 1978, the changes made during the renovation of 1976, the district heating system connected in the 1990s and, finally, the general renovation from 1996, both the heating equipment and aesthetically impactful objects such as pipes, regulators, or radiators were replaced by new components. The rooms previously occupied by the heating system are currently used as sanitary facilities and cloakrooms for visitors.

The radiators play an especially effective role in the design of the heating system. In 1926, innovative radiators made by the Junkers works were installed in the building. These featured steel pipes and indirect heating areas in the form of uniquely shaped sheet metal fins. Their advantages included a steady and economic heat build-up and their relative lightness in comparison with conventional cast iron radiators. These modern radiators show their aesthetic impact in the stairway of the workshop wing, where they are hung in such a way that they resemble works of art. Most of the original Junkers radiators were removed, apart from those that may still be seen in the vestibule and the workshop wing stairway. Because such radiators are no longer made, other models are now used in the building.

During the renovation of 1976, column radiators such as those still found in the auditorium were installed. With the connection to district heating in the 1990s, a large number of then common panel radiators were installed, the aim being to provide low-temperature, energy-efficient heating. In the meantime, the number of panel radiators on the bridge has been reduced again in order to improve the sense of space. In other areas such as the north wing and the workshop wing, column radiators of a similar design to the original Junkers radiators were installed and painted silver. Selected areas in which the aim is to restore the original context of 1926, such as the director's office or in the recreated room in the studio building, now again feature historic Junkers radiators. These were recovered from other modern buildings and stored in the archive before being used in the Bauhaus Building.

A look at the history of the radiators in the building illustrates how the exchanges happened in order to meet the respective requirements but also depended on the way the perceived value or conservation-worthiness of the original Junkers radiators changed over time. While the original radiators were discarded in the nineteen-seventies, today similar radiators from other modern buildings are being restored and reinstalled in selected parts of the building. This history may be traced today in the building, where original Junkers radiators, GDR-era column radiators, panel radiators from the post-reunification period, the column radiators currently in use, and the Junkers radiators from other modern buildings are found side by side. Specifications regarding which radiators should in future be fitted in which rooms are listed in the conservation objectives. In order ensure the radiators are harmoniously integrated in the overall architectonic picture, the column radiators are painted silver based on evidence found on the original radiators, while the panel radiators in front of white walls are painted with the white RAL colour for areas for which no historical precedence exists.

169)

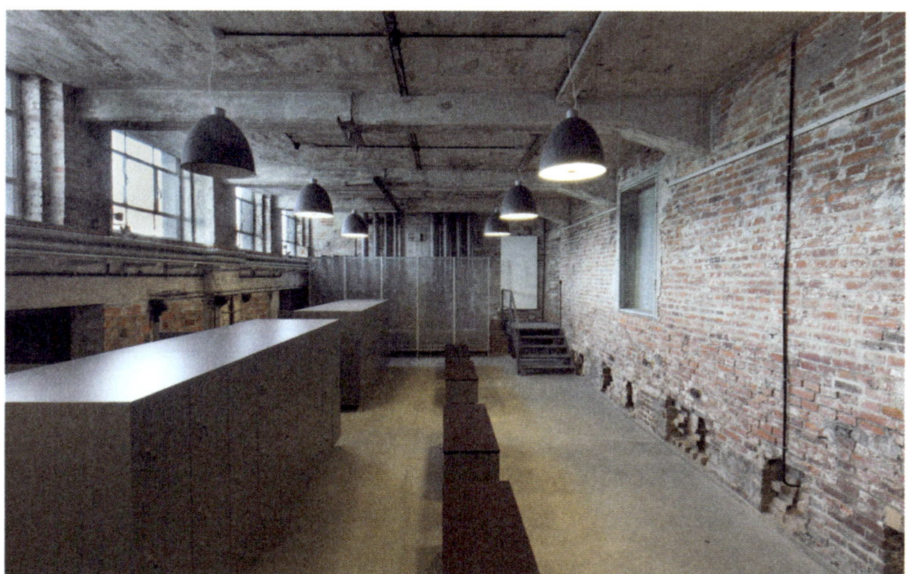

169)
Cloakroom in the former boiler room, 2016

170)
Two-zone glass pendant lamp ME 94 (design: Marianne Brandt, 1926), 2018

70)

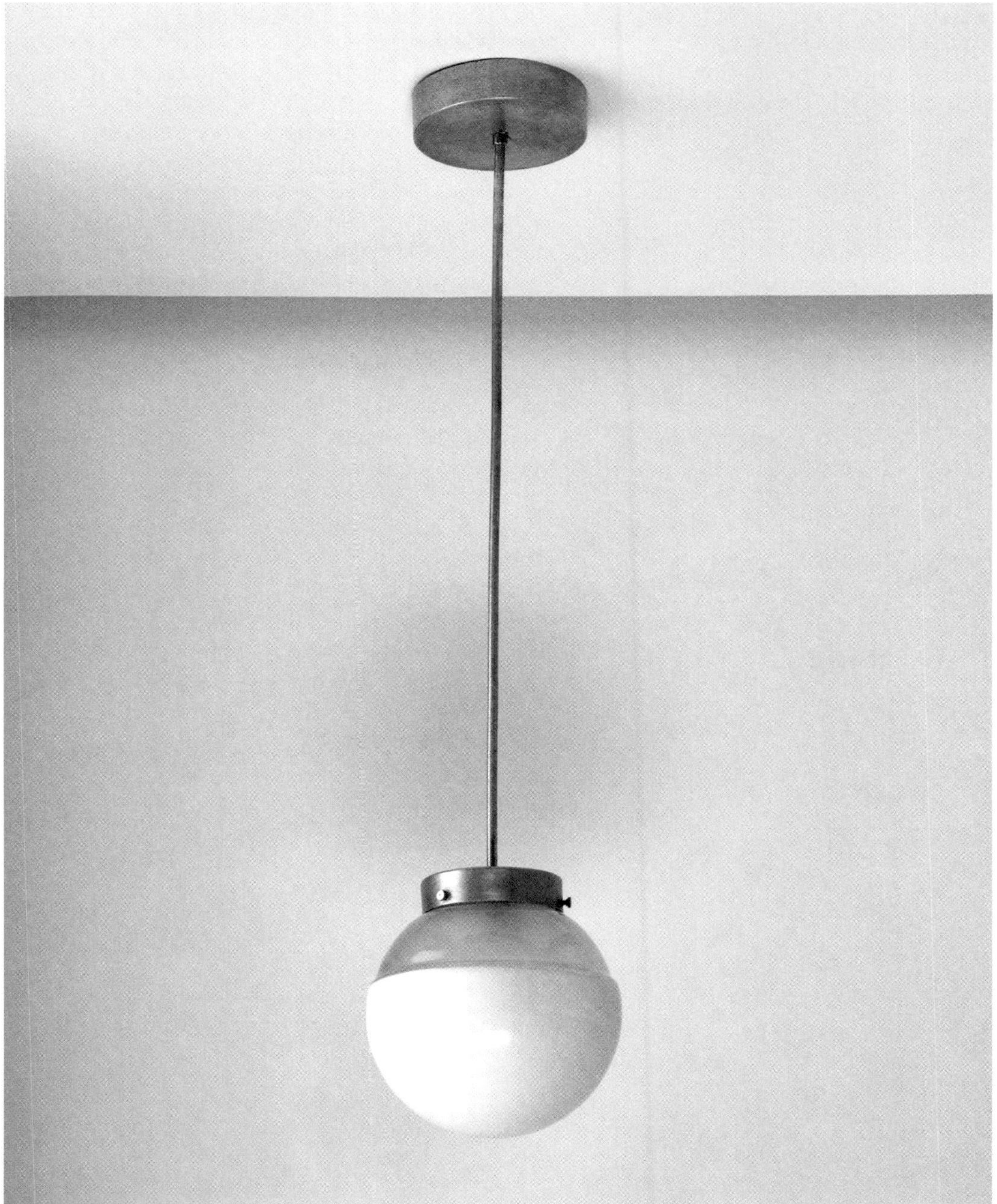

Lighting Fixtures

Many of the electrical lighting fixtures installed in the building in 1926 were designed and made in the Bauhaus's metal workshop. They bear witness to the work in the workshops and likewise play an important part in the identity of the historic space and in the overall appearance of the building. Their impact builds from their design and the way the light they emit is perceived both inside and outside the building. In many rooms, the original lighting fixtures and their locations may be discerned based on historic photographs and the examination of ceilings. The rooms in which reproductions of the original light fixtures are found are specified in the conservation objectives.

Original objects, drawings from 1925/26, and historic photographs serve as a basis for the accurate reproduction of light fittings.[5] Examples include the two-zone glass ceiling lamp ME 94, which was designed by Marianne Brandt in the metal workshop and later manufactured by Schwintzer & Gräff in Berlin. The lower half of the globe is made of opal glass, which prevents glare, and the upper part of transparent matt glass so that the light shines onto the ceiling and is reflected. Beading conceals any irregularities that arise where the two materials meet. The bulb holder and rod attached to the globe, which is twenty-four-centimetres in diameter, are made from aluminium. In 1926, this lamp was used in many parts of the building including offices and classrooms and plays a meaningful role in its impact. For this reason, a number of copies were made in 1986 and again in 2004.

171)

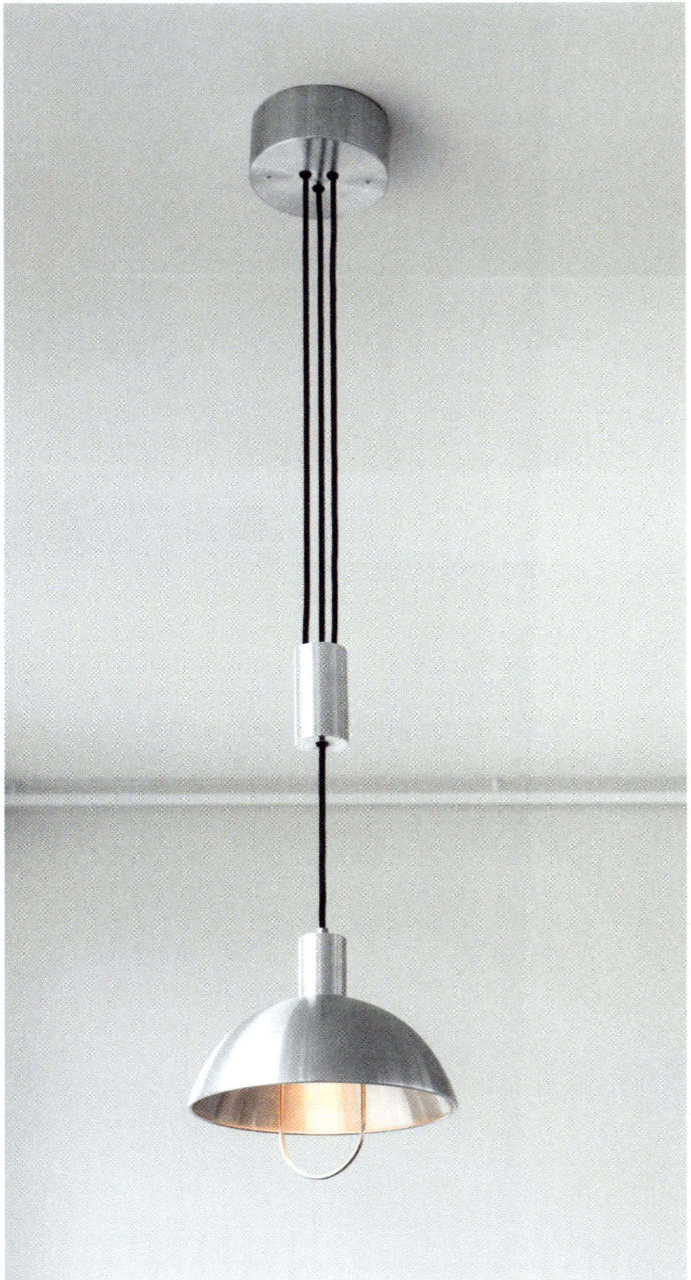

171)
Adjustable aluminium pendant lamp (design: Marianne Brandt and Hin Bredendieck, 1926), 2021

172)
Metal workshop, Bauhaus Dessau: Marianne Brandt (left) and Hin Bredendieck working on designs at their drawing tables, ca. 1927/28

173)
Auditorium with tubular light fittings, 2004

174)
Tubular light bulbs, 1976/2016

The adjustable aluminium pendant luminaire designed by Marianne Brandt and Hans Przyrembel has different qualities. Several variants of this lamp, among them a simple pendant lamp, were used in the Bauhaus workshops in 1926. Their robust practicability suits the character of the workshops. The lamp was reconstructed in 2004 and installed in the original locations in the workshop wing and in Gropius's former architecture office on the top floor of the bridge. Other reconstructions of original light fittings are found in the building, including the large ceiling lamps in the vestibules in front of the workshop wing and the historic canteen, the cylindrical lamp ME 79 in the corridor on the bridge, and the tubular lights.[6]

The historical lighting fixtures provide general lighting in public spaces and workrooms. This lighting does not always meet current requirements and additional high-performance spotlights are therefore used in, e.g., exhibition areas and workplaces. In some areas, the

172)

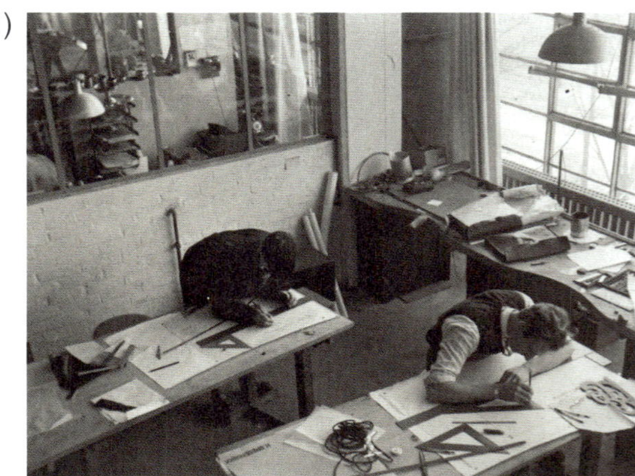

73) 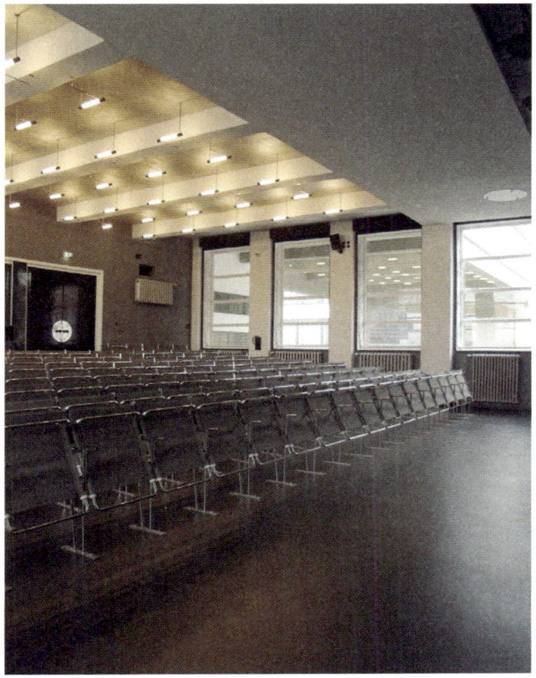

74) 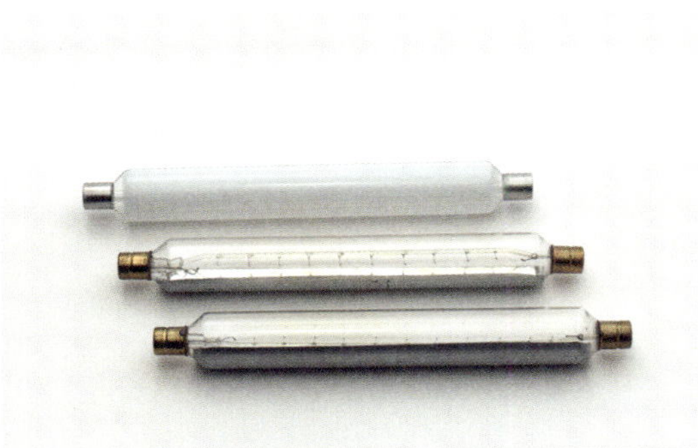

required security lighting is integrated in the historic lighting fixtures.

A unique situation prevails in the festive area, a programmatic part of the Bauhaus Building in which the restoration of the original condition of 1926 is prioritised. In the historic canteen, two original ceiling lamps designed by Max Karajewski are well preserved and have been restored. A third lamp did no longer exist but could be reconstructed based on the others. Other lamps designed by Marianne Brandt and Hin Bredendieck in the Bauhaus's metal workshop and installed later were documented in the same area in 2000.[7] These were however designed in 1930 and were therefore not part of the original décor in 1926. They were thus removed and placed in the archive for safekeeping.

The vestibule and auditorium are characterised by area lighting featuring tubular lamps, which was reconstructed in 1976 and replaced in 2004. Originally, a tubular lamp comprised an incandescent bulb connected on both ends to a socket fitting. It generated light by heating a wire filament. In the festive area, these tubular lamps are arranged on one part of the ceiling using nickel-plated fittings which complement the other nickel-plated elements in the space, such as the door finger plates or the tubular steel frames of the theatre-style seating. The warm light of the incandescent lamps leaves a singular stamp on the building and in this area especially, it is a crucial component of the innovative design: without lamp shades or casings, the tubular bulbs remain visible as technical elements and define the room impression. Since Commission Regulation (EC) No. 244/2009 came into force, the manufacture of incandescent lamps has been prohibited in the interests of energy efficiency and climate protection. LED tubular lamps are meanwhile available as a substitute for the traditional model. These look similar but emit a completely different kind of light and thus significantly alter the spatial impact as a direct comparison shows. It is therefore especially important that the surviving tubular lamps with wire filaments are archived in order to document the historic lighting effect and as templates for future developments. Not only the lighting fixtures but also their effects and the contemporary perspectives on historic lighting must be examined from the standpoint of heritage conservation. This field of investigation, which is vitally important to the architecture, is still in its infancy.[8]

175)
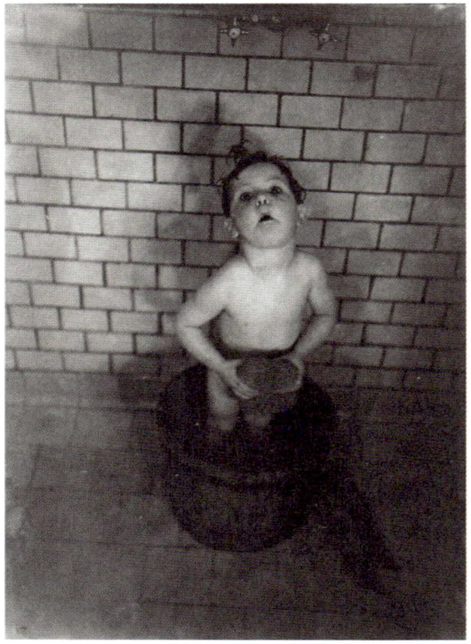

176)
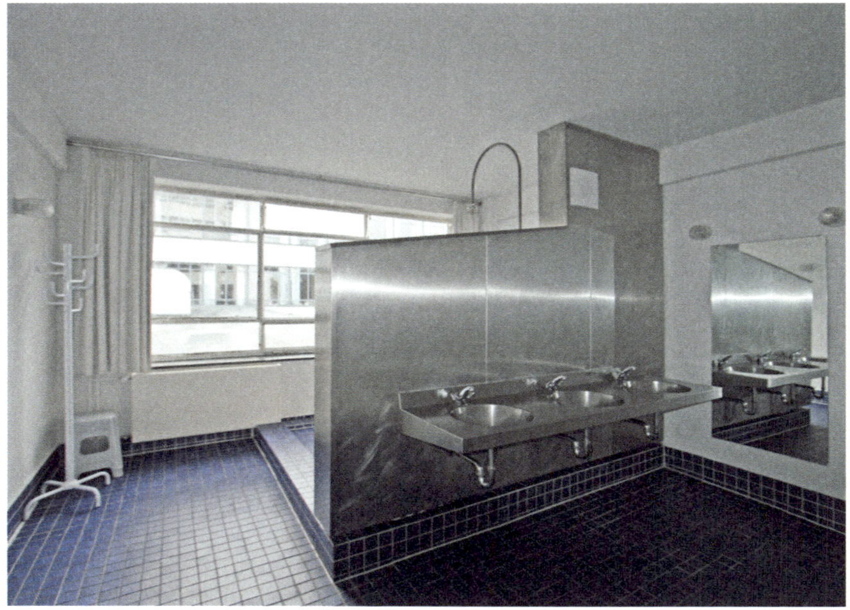

177)
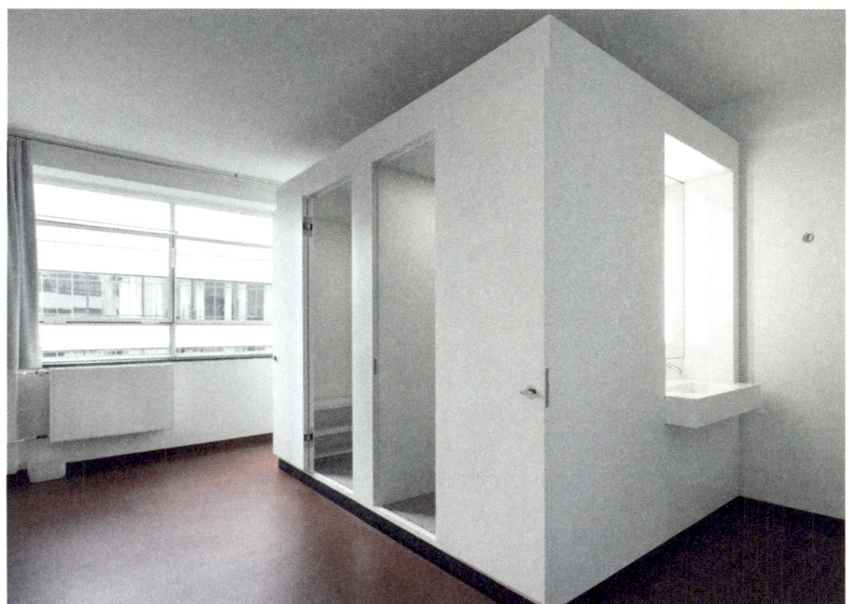

175)
Joost Siedhoff in the showers in the basement of the connecting building, ca. 1929

176)
Showers in the studio building, 1989–2016

177)
Showers in the studio building, 2017

178)
New sanitary facilities in the semi-basement, beneath the festive area, 2016

78)

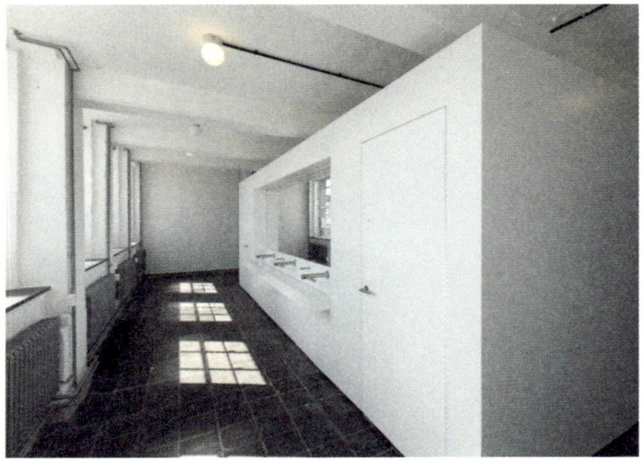

Sanitary Facilities

The sanitary facilities in the Bauhaus Building have been modified several times since 1926 to meet various requirements and uses. The few pieces of historical evidence to hand include a fragment of terrazzo flooring, which was discovered in the vicinity of the original toilet facility in the semi-basement of the north wing. All the toilet facilities in a historical location have been fully upgraded—including flooring, wall tiles, partition walls, fixtures, fittings, and lighting—since 1995. The only exceptions are the two cubicles in the semi-basement of the connecting building, which have been preserved complete with high, wall-hung toilet cisterns, glass tiles, and plastic tapware as evidence of use in the GDR-era.

Due to increasing visitor numbers in the Bauhaus Building in the early 2000s, more toilet facilities and cloakrooms were required. After examining different options in the building or elsewhere, such as in the flat-roofed building on the Bauhaus grounds, a new location in the semi-basement under the festive area was agreed in coordination with heritage conservation authorities including ICOMOS. In 2015, a freestanding monochrome box structure comprising matt mineral panels in the RAL colour 9010 from the range for areas without historical findings was installed in the space. The box is equipped with WC cubicles with tiled floors. The washstand on an external wall of the box is designed for use by both men and women, therefore saves space. The original room, formerly a workshop next to the historic boiler room, was left largely untouched, the historic surfaces of the rendered walls and ceilings and asphalt tiles were refurbished. Cloakrooms for visitors were installed in the former boiler room directly adjacent to these facilities. These are also freestanding structures, which means that traces of the former heating system are still visible on the walls.[9]

In early October 1990, a closed meeting with international guests was held at the Bauhaus Dessau in order to prepare for a symposium on plans for the future development of Berlin. With this in mind, new showers were installed for the guests on each floor of the studio building and the toilet facilities were refurbished, based on plans by the architect Inken Baller.[10] Originally each of the rooms for the students and junior masters of the Bauhaus era was equipped with a wash basin. There was also one WC per floor and communal shower facilities and bathtubs were found in the semi-basement. Now the shower facilities comprised a freestanding metallic block in the centre of the room with three open showers on the one side and washbasins on the other. As guest rooms with integrated WC and shower became the norm, in 2001 the option of installing bathroom units in the rooms in the studio building was discussed. The idea was rejected on the grounds that installing the necessary pipes and cables would constitute a massive intervention in the fabric of the walls and ceilings, and the installation of the units would significantly detract from the spatial qualities of the historic rooms.

However, because the open showers installed in 1989 led to building physics problems, two shower cubicles were installed in their place in 2017. The resulting smaller volume of air enables it to be extracted through the narrower historic shafts. Much like the new WC facilities for guests in the semi-basement, these shower cubicles were installed in the room in a freestanding box comprising white, jointless mineral panels. In the process, it was possible to more or less meet modern demands while making allowances for the historic building fabric, structure, and spatial quality.[11]

179)

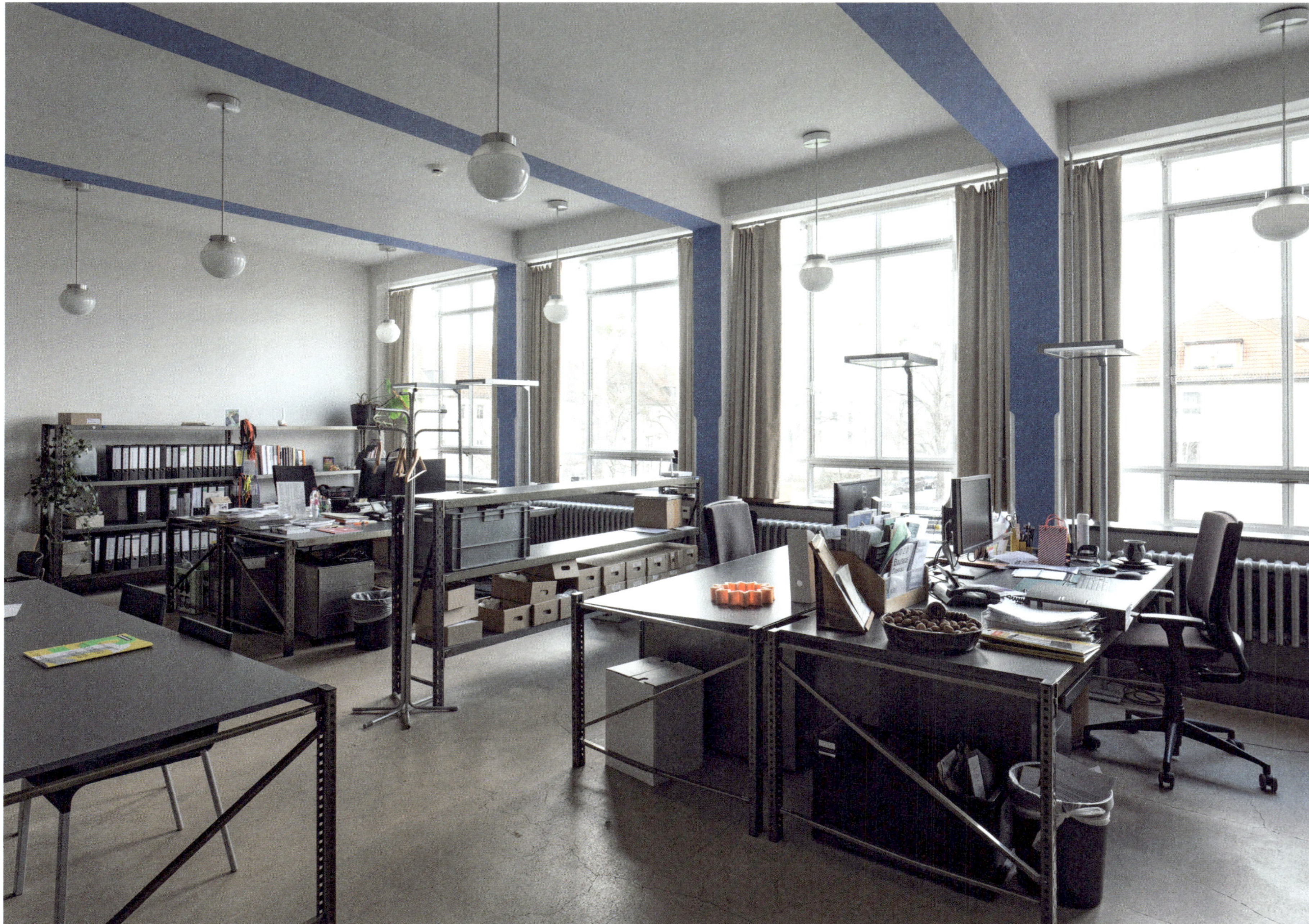

Workspaces and Classrooms

Even though some of the rooms in the Bauhaus Building were designed as classrooms and offices in the nineteen-twenties, today the demands placed on office spaces are very different from those of ninety-five years ago, especially as regards indoor climate or the installations required for data technology, lighting, or emergency routes. Despite efforts to minimise the technical installations in the historic building, it is still necessary to establish the cable runs, ducts, and openings needed to route modern data technology and to install the central server rooms, network cabinets, and ventilation and cooling systems for these. Technical installations are frequently updated, and they should therefore intrude as little as possible in the building fabric and be reversible, i.e., it should be possible to uninstall them at will without causing more damage. At the same time, existing routing should be used wherever possible so as not to undermine the aesthetics of the building. In the unrendered parts of the building such as the workshop wing and the semi-basements, the routing for the technical installations is by necessity visible, as in the nineteen-twenties. In order to minimise the cable routing on the ceilings and walls, some of the cables run through routing on the floor.

1
BDA 2018, p. 14 et seqq.

2
bauhaus dessau, n. d., n. p.

3
Stein 1926, p. 278

4
Blomeier 1994, p. 19 et seqq.

5
The original light fittings were reconstructed by Mr Richard of Lichtsysteme Halle. Tubular light fixtures were also installed in the director's office and south stairway.

6
Cf. Weber 1992

7
Kandem ceiling lamp no. 740, design: Marianne Brandt, Hin Bredendieck, 1930. These lamps were installed in various places in the building around 1930, including the rooms in the studio building adapted for use as classrooms.

8
This issue was discussed during the renovation of the Kandinsky/Klee Masters' House; cf. Blieske 2020, p. 148–57

9
Planning by Brenne Architekten, Berlin

10
Blomeyer/Milzkott 1990, p. 6 et seqq.

11
Planning by AADe (Atelier für Architektur & Denkmalpflege), Dessau/Köthen/Leipzig

180)

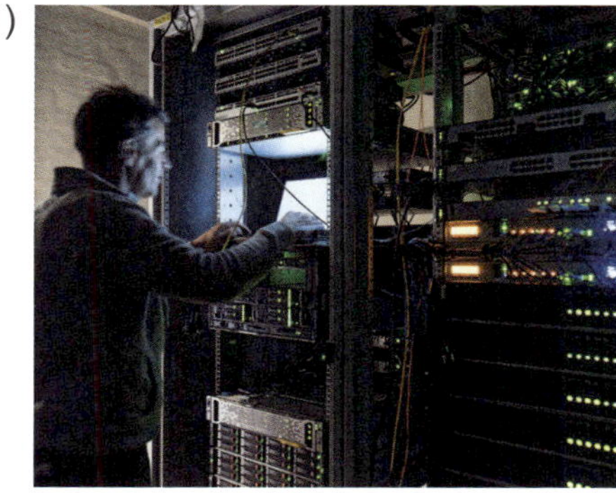

181)

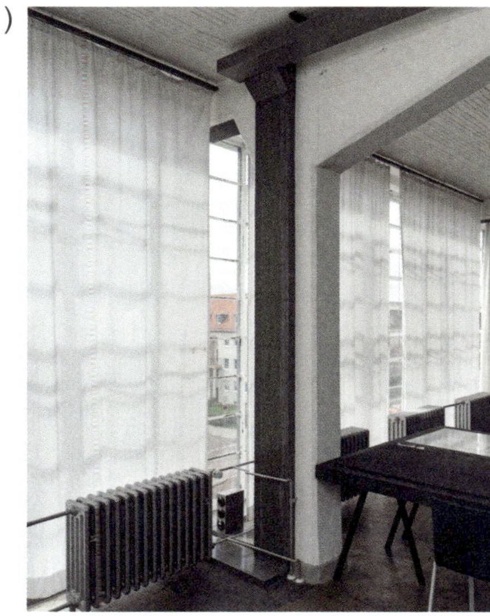

179)
Work room in the north wing, 2021

180)
Central computer system, 2021

181)
Cable routing in the workshop wing, 2021

Outdoor Area

182)
Site plan, 1926

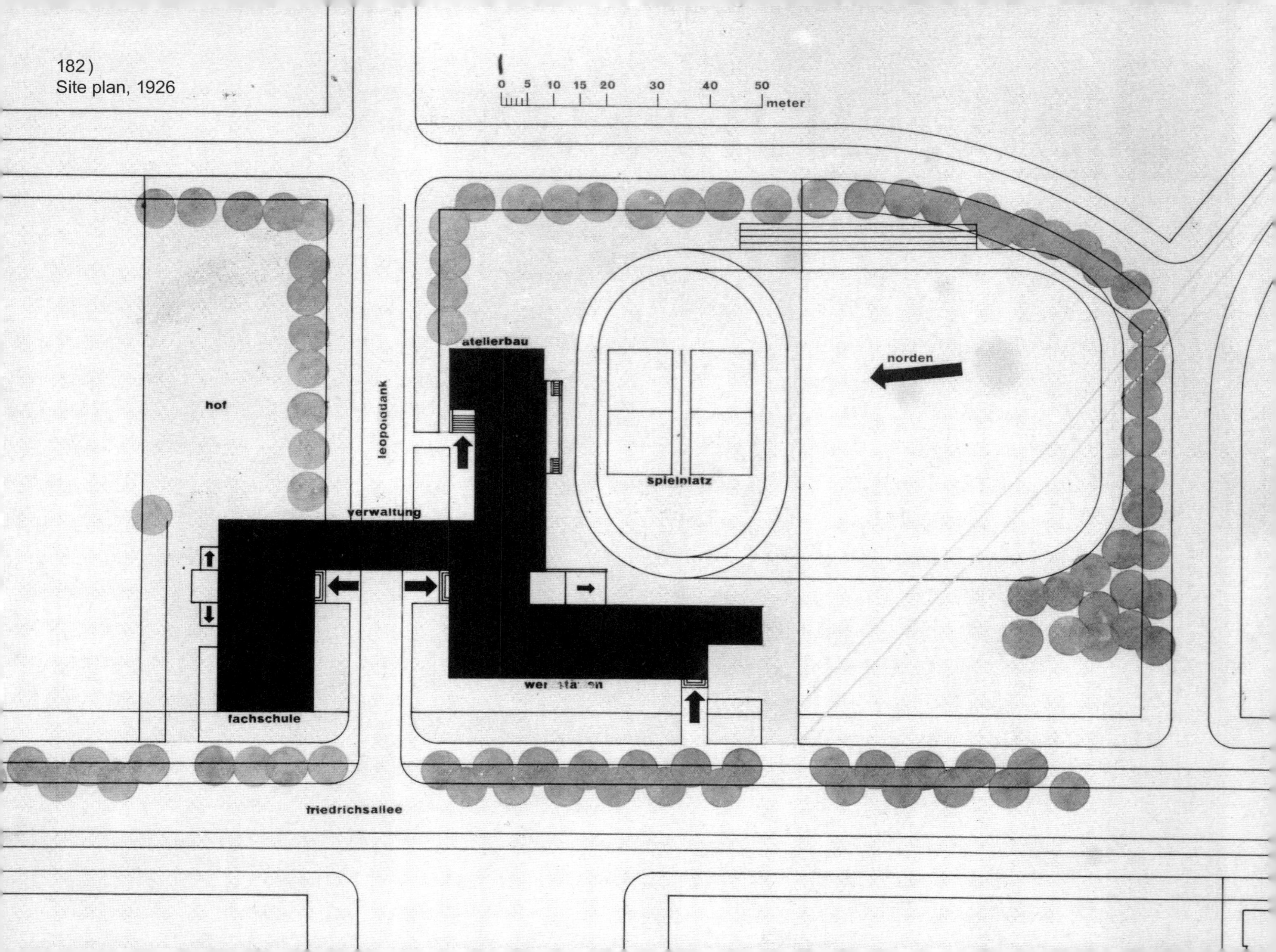

83)

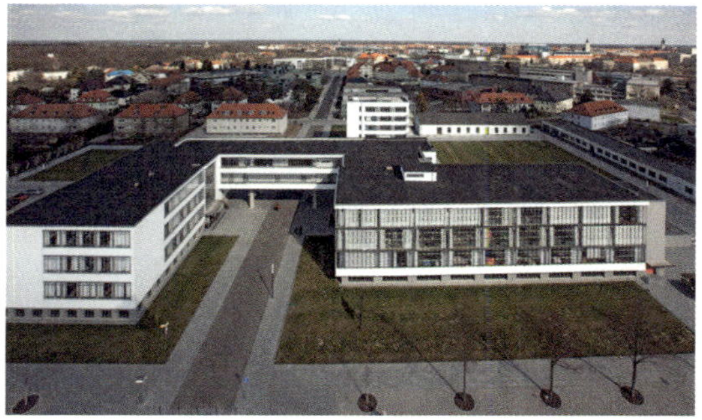

84)

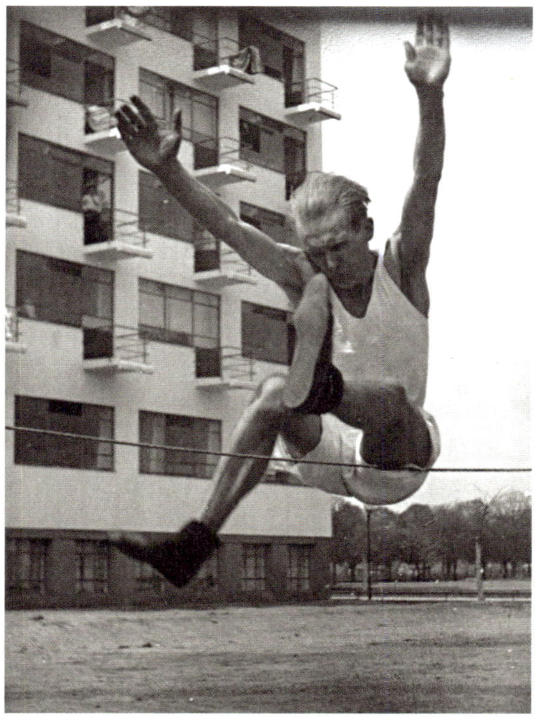

183)
Aerial photograph, 2010

184)
High jump in front of the Bauhaus, ca. 1928

The complex layout of the Bauhaus Building also informs its setting. There is no obvious front and back but rather a composition of complex building blocks and open spaces. Walter Gropius describes the concept as follows: 'a building born of the spirit of our times moves away from the imposing manifestation of the symmetrical facade. you have to walk right around the building to grasp its physicality and the function of its parts.'[1] The building opens up to establish a natural connection between interior and exterior as an important part of the design concept. This connection is also strengthened by the complex layout and by elements such as stairways, ramps, and terrace which reach into the exterior space. The building is arranged on two sides of a public road; the two parts are connected by a building which bridges the road. It fits into the existing road infrastructure and simultaneously redefines the exterior space. With their transparency and reflections, the extensive glass surfaces reveal many layers of the building, the surroundings, and the relationships between them: 'Perceiving the transparency invariably involves crossing a threshold or barrier between interior and exterior, public and private, light and shade, seeing and hiding, and warmth and cold, too.'[2] Then again, the reflections which form on the extensive glass surfaces close in the building and mirror the surroundings. A complex interaction thus evolves, linking interior and exterior. The building is part of the setting; the setting is likewise part of the building.

The outdoor facilities of the Bauhaus were designed according to their functions, just like the building: the Bauhausstraße was bordered by lawns, there were roofed bicycle stands north of the building, a school yard for the vocational school east of the north wing, and sports grounds south and east of the building, which were used by the Bauhauslers.[3]

Today's Bauhausstraße[4] is an important part of the complex. The road provides access to the building and links it to the surrounding neighbourhood not only literally, but also through the overall design. According to the conventions of the day, this comprised pavements with small mosaic pavers and kerb flanking the lower road paved with natural stone. Lawns in front of the buildings, trees planted along the road, and street lighting completed the picture in the Bauhausstraße and integrated the Bauhaus Building in its environment. But the design near the Bauhaus Building differed from that of the area around it in one important respect: here, the road was surfaced with asphalt, a material then associated with notions of motorisation, speed, and modernity. The asphalt strip corresponds with the horizontal ribbon window on the bridge, which likewise symbolises momentum and modernity.

To this day, outdoor facilities are often neglected during the research and conservation of modern buildings. Due to their sometimes unusual qualities, among them functionality, plainness, or emptiness, they are not recognised as historico-cultural documents.[5] Open areas designated as usable spaces or simply designed lawns are frequently regarded as 'lacking garden design quality'[6] and are transformed at will over the years according to changing requirements or contemporary tastes.

185)

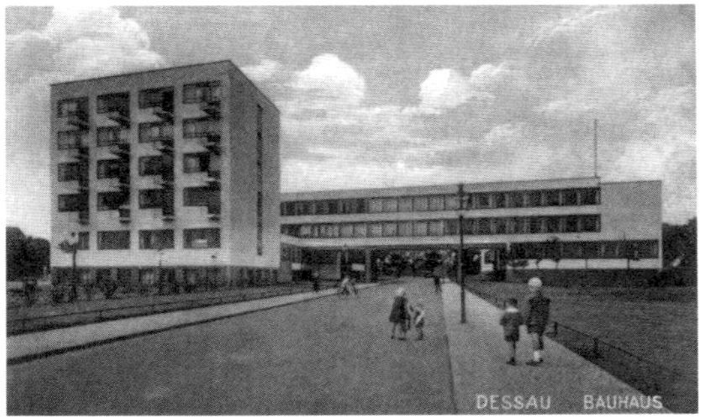

186)

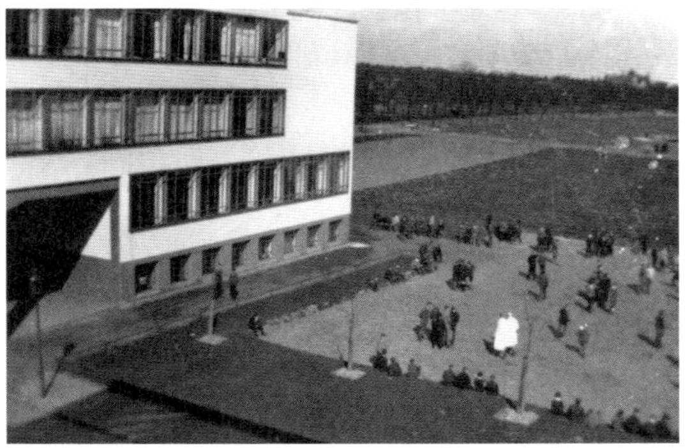

187)

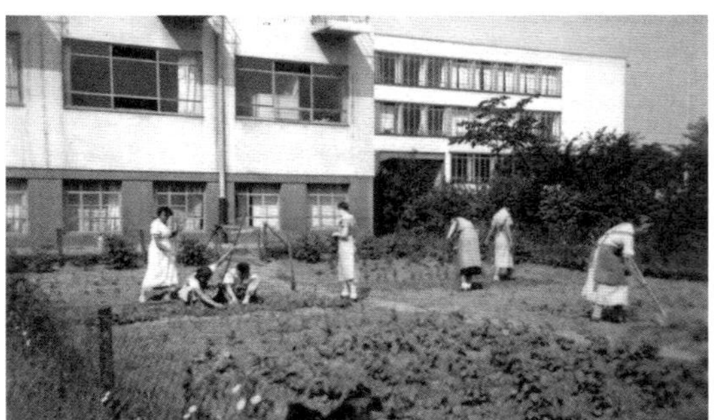

But the setting of the Bauhaus Building is a fundamental part of the building concept and is meanwhile listed alongside the building itself.[7] UNESCO, too, takes the protection of the setting of a World Heritage site into consideration.[8] The 'core zone' defines the World Heritage site and includes the grounds of the Bauhaus. In this area, the protection of the World Heritage site has absolute priority. The broader 'buffer zone' marks an area in which planned building or other measures must be reviewed with respect to their impact on the World Heritage site. In both zones, changes must show special appreciation for the outstanding universal value of the Bauhaus World Heritage site.

Over the decades, not only the Bauhaus Building but also its setting changed a great deal.[9] In addition to the structural modifications, in the immediate vicinity of the building these included the construction of supplementary buildings, use by the *Landesfrauenarbeitsschule* including vegetable cultivation,[10] other planting on the grounds, and the transformation of the Bauhausstraße. During the renovation of 1976, a new design incorporating large concrete slabs rendered the road unidentifiable as the axis of the Bauhaus design. Thus, the arrangement of the two entrances on the two sides of one road as well as the connecting function of the bridge were no longer apparent to the observer.

During the renovations of the outdoor area completed from 2006 to 2009, the aim was to bring the artistic and historic qualities of Walter Gropius's design visibly to the fore rather than reconstruct the historic status.[11] Owing to the existing close connection between the grounds of the Bauhaus Building and the Bauhausplatz and the link between the railway station, the Bauhaus, and the campus of the Anhalt University of Applied Sciences, a general plan was developed for this area. Today, the historic route is defined by an asphalt surface, rather than the original road surface; it runs from the Bauhaus via Seminarplatz to the railway station and is lined by modern lampposts designed as light steles. Together with the lawns and trees alongside it, the road still shapes the character of the area today. It incorporates the Bauhaus Building in the urban context and is a key component of the complex.

At the Bauhaus Building, the functions of road and bridge and the close relationship between building and open areas may be understood using modern means. The hard surfaces are uniformly paved with grey concrete slabs. The positioning and dimensions of the lawn areas are based on the historic situation, as is the low tubular steel railing around them, although its location and design are not reconstructed but new. Furthermore, functional improvements were made to essential processes including deliveries, waste disposal, or parking; opportunities that enable visitors to walk unhindered around the building and to observe it from all sides were also created. The historic vocational school yard and sports ground were not reconstructed, firstly due to insufficient background knowledge and secondly, because these functions no longer reflect current uses. Instead, a network of paths and seating areas enables visitors and users to not only walk around and experience the Bauhaus Building undisturbed, but to contemplate it for longer from selected locations.

Coupled with the modern design elements, the focus on creating a network of paths for visitors as an alternative to the sports areas

88)

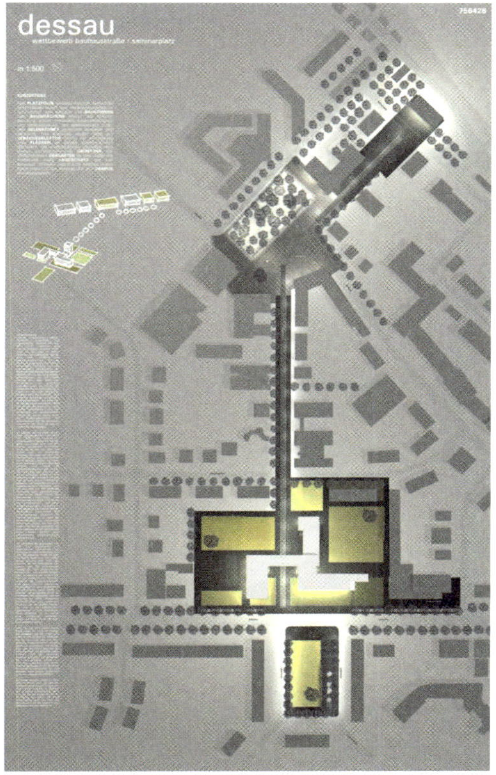

189)

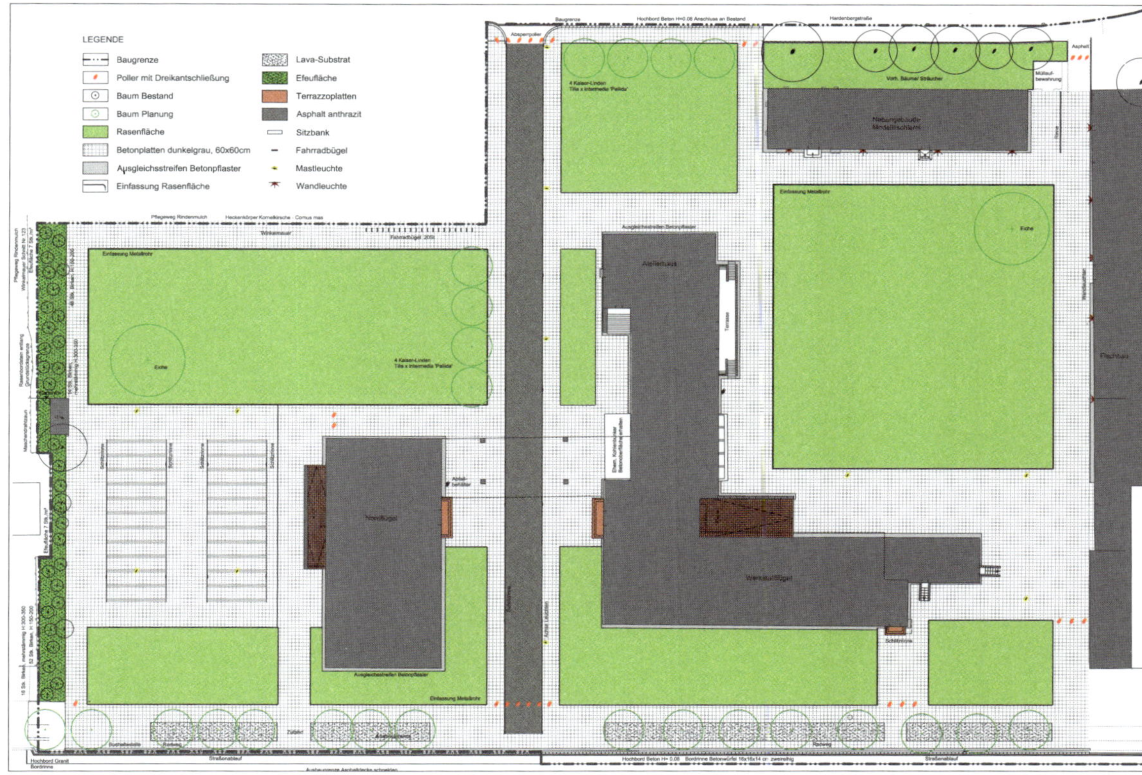

185)
Bauhausstraße from the east, ca. 1927

186)
School yard of the vocational school, ca. 1930

187)
Students of the *Landesfrauenarbeitsschule* gardening in front of the Bauhaus, 1935

188)
Winning entry in the competition 'Design of the Bauhausplatz, Bauhausstraße, Seminarplatz and the area of the western exit of the main station' in Dessau, 2004

189)
Conservation objectives for the outdoor area, 2014

for the students document a shift in the role of the Bauhaus Building from its use as a school of design and a municipal vocational school to a World Heritage site visited by people from all over the world. Above all, with its reserved design the outdoor area enables visitors to appreciate the corporeality and function of the parts of the building as well as the unique connection between architecture and environment.[12]

1
Gropius 2021, p. 19

2
Loebermann 1998, p. 100

3
Cf. HORTEC GbR 1998; Fischer-Leonhardt 2005

4
The road was originally called Leopolddank.

5
On the special qualities of the exteriors of Bauhaus architectures, cf. Müller 2004

6
Mader 1999, p. 92

7
§1 (1) the heritage protection act of the state of Saxony-Anhalt of 21 October 1991, revision of 22 December 2004, states: 'The protection extends to the entire substance of a cultural monument including its setting, provided this is important to conservation, impact, accessibility and scientific research.'

8
https://whc.unesco.org/en/list/729/multiple=1&unique_number=2158 (accessed 15 February 2021)

9
The changing names of nearby roads and thus the address of the Bauhaus also reflect the shifting political landscape. Following a short period as Ebertallee (1931–34), the former Friedrichsallee, on which the Bauhaus Building was erected in 1926, was renamed Schlageterallee (1934–47) during National Socialist rule after Alfred Leo Schlageter, who was stylised as a martyr during the Third Reich. In the GDR era it was renamed Thälmannallee (1947–90) in honour of the leader of the communist party of Germany during the Weimar Republic, Ernst Thälmann, who was murdered in Buchenwald concentration camp. Following German reunification, the name was changed to Gropiusallee.

10
The *Landesfrauenarbeitsschule* was based in the Bauhaus from 1933 to 1940; cf. Werner 2014/I

11
Kimmel 2011, p. 18–21

12
Planning courtesy of Mann Landschaftsarchitekten, Kassel

190)
Bauhausstraße from the west,
2021

191)
Open space at the Bauhaus,
2019

190)

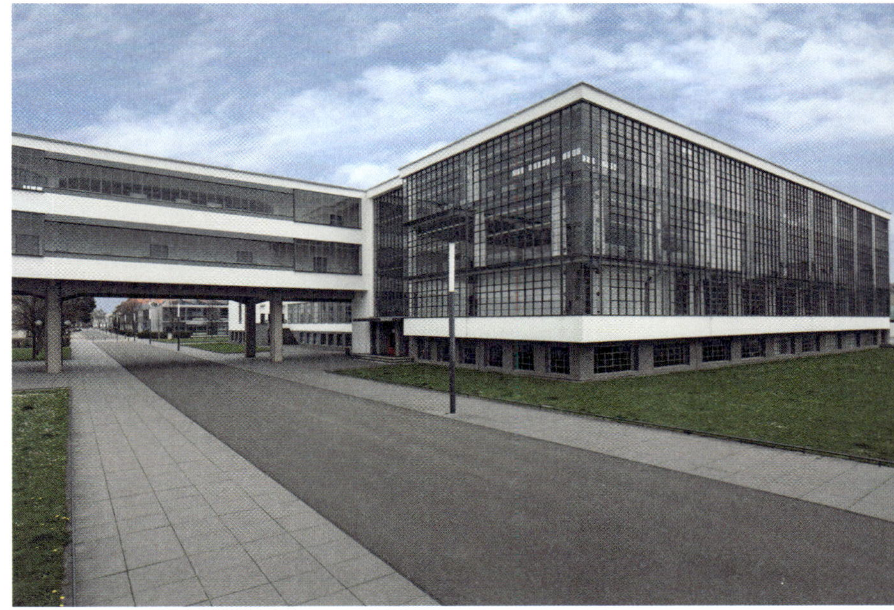

191)

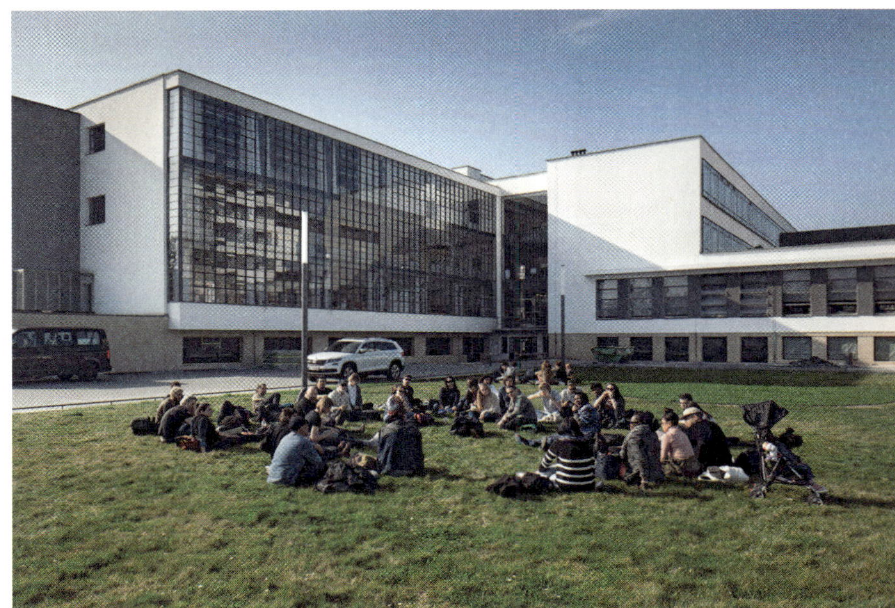

Usage

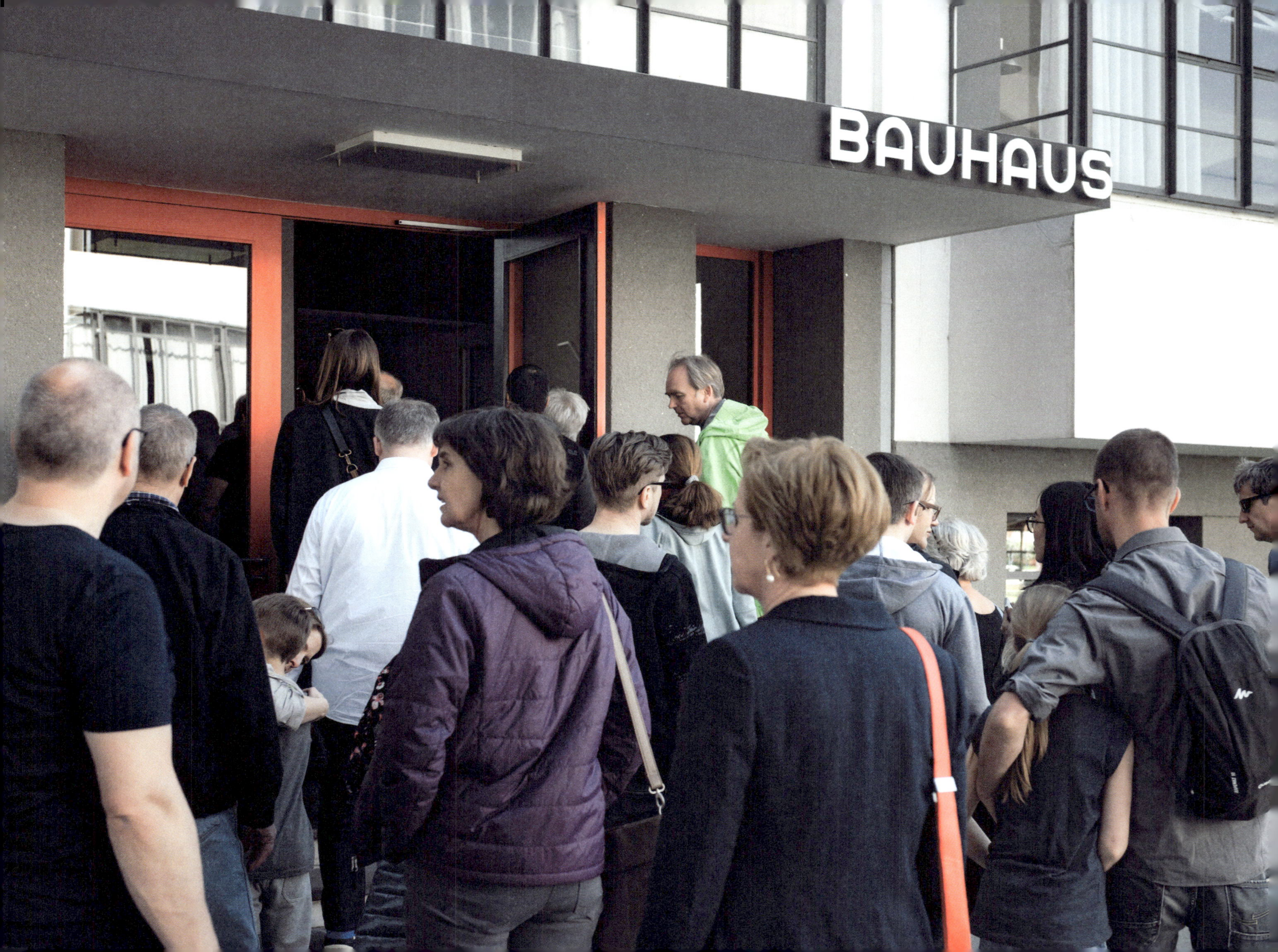
BAUHAUS

192) Guided tour of the Bauhaus, 2019

The Bauhaus Building is currently used by the Bauhaus Dessau Foundation, which was established in 1994. The artistic-scientific foundation is funded by the German government, the state of Saxony-Anhalt, and the municipality of Dessau-Roßlau. Its mission is to research, preserve, and pass on the ideas and theses of the Bauhaus. The foundation's work is historically reflexive and simultaneously investigates the present-day relevance and contemporary potentials that may be derived from the Bauhaus heritage for the twenty-first century. The Bauhaus Building is a locus of research, education, and experimental design. Like the Masters' Houses and the Steel House in Dessau, it is owned by the Bauhaus Dessau Foundation.

The ground floor of the workshop wing, formerly the Bauhaus's exhibition space and the main domain of the carpentry workshop, currently houses a visitor information centre and a shop which sells books and other Bauhaus-related products. Here, visitors can not only learn something about the Bauhaus's themes or the work of the Bauhaus Dessau Foundation, but also discover the building by experiencing the unique architectonic impact of the workshop wing. The first floor, formerly the preliminary course room and the weaving workshop's main place of work, is available for temporary exhibitions. The light-filled and ample rooms are used for temporary activities and presentations, for which the given spatial and climatic conditions are well-suited. The second floor of the workshop wing once occupied by the metal and wall painting workshops is now used by the Bauhaus Dessau Foundation for artistic, scientific, and research programmes which explore the legacy of the Bauhaus in Dessau and for education and outreach projects. In the semi-basement of the workshop wing, the rooms of the former printing workshop and the packing area provide additional spaces for exhibitions without conservational aspirations. Where there was once a caretaker's flat, there is now a café.

The first floor and part of the second floor of the bridge are used for administrative purposes, as in the Bauhaus's day. Gropius's former architecture office, later the Bauhaus's architectural workshop, is now used to communicate the Bauhaus's cultural heritage.

In the north wing, the rooms formerly used by the vocational school are now workrooms for the Bauhaus Dessau Foundation; lecturers and students from the Anhalt University of Applied Sciences work on the ground floor. Additional workspaces and rooms for museum education are available in the semi-basement. The festive area is utilised much as it was in the Bauhaus era: the auditorium and stage for varied events including lectures, conferences, experimental stage productions, or festivities and the historic canteen to feed people who work in the building and guests. Storerooms, dressing rooms for the stage, additional ancillary rooms, and central building services are located in the semi-basement. Sanitary facilities, cloakrooms, and information point provide the necessary infrastructure for the building's many visitors. Guests are able to stay overnight in the studio building, in which the Bauhaus's students and junior masters once lived.

The Bauhaus Building also bears the imprint of the norms and standards of its day, which

193) 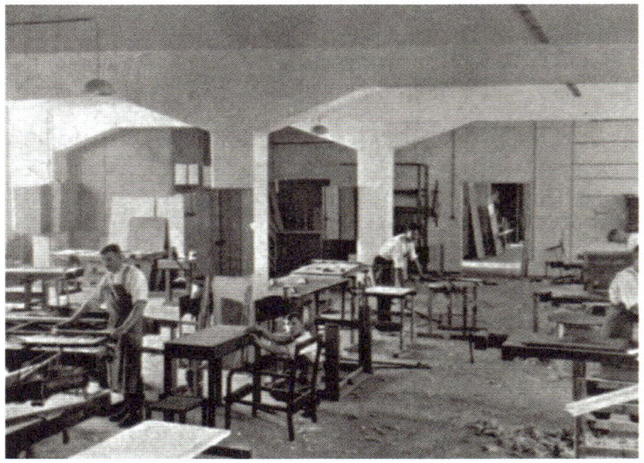

194) 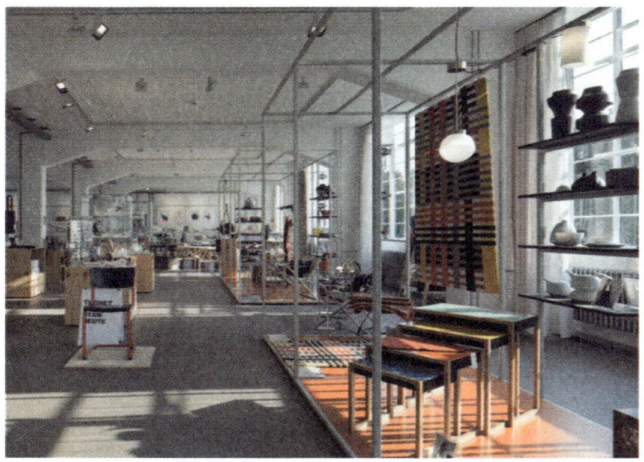

influence structure, construction, and design. In architecture as in society, norms and standards are in a constant state of flux, and a historic building can thus only approximately comply with the respective fluctuating concepts or requirements. These include different expectations of comfort as regards cold, heat, noise, or lighting, or they relate to technical equipment or compliance with legal requirements, e.g., for workplaces or emergency escape routes. Against the backdrop of the building's major cultural and historical significance and the constantly changing demands placed on it, these must be regularly reassessed to find a healthy balance. Given that all modifications will be questioned within a few years and subsequently changed yet again, they should be implemented with sensitivity and must above all be reversible. As the Venice Charter specifies, the use must be adapted to suit the building rather than the building to suit the use.[1]

Cultural monuments, especially a World Heritage site of outstanding significance, can also assume a useful social function above and beyond a use for administration purposes, as a shop, or a café. Such cultural monuments can also serve a cultural, aesthetic, or historic role, for instance as an urban or historic point of reference.[2] It is self-evident that the use of older monuments such as churches or castles must respect their unique features. However, modern buildings are so closely connected to our world that they are expected to be fully usable and meet contemporary requirements. The Bauhaus Building too is used intensively for the work of the Bauhaus Dessau Foundation and must satisfy contemporary requirements; at the same time its use is attuned to its significance as a preeminent World Heritage site.

193)
Carpentry workshop, ground floor, workshop wing, ca. 1928

194)
Visitor information and shop, ground floor, workshop wing, 2014

195)
Weaving workshop, first floor, workshop wing, ca. 1927

196)
Metal workshop, second floor, workshop wing, ca. 1928

197)
Temporary exhibition, first floor, workshop wing, 2019

95)
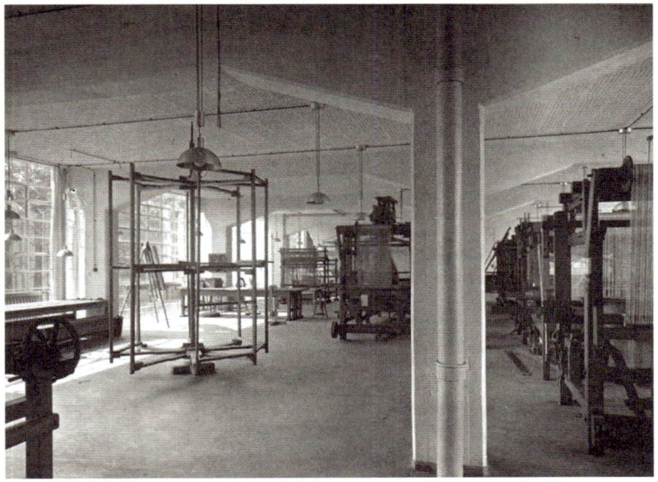

196)
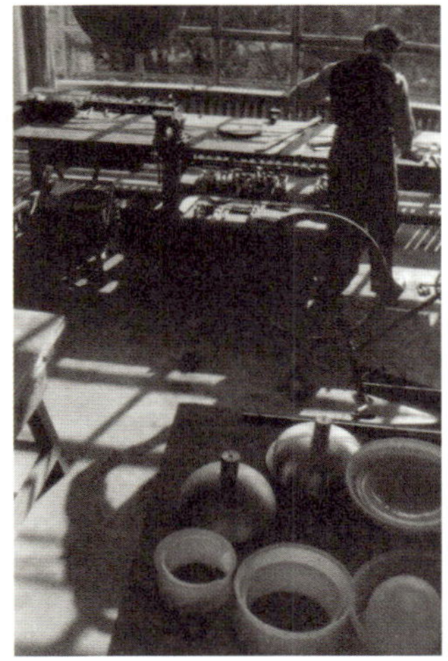

97)
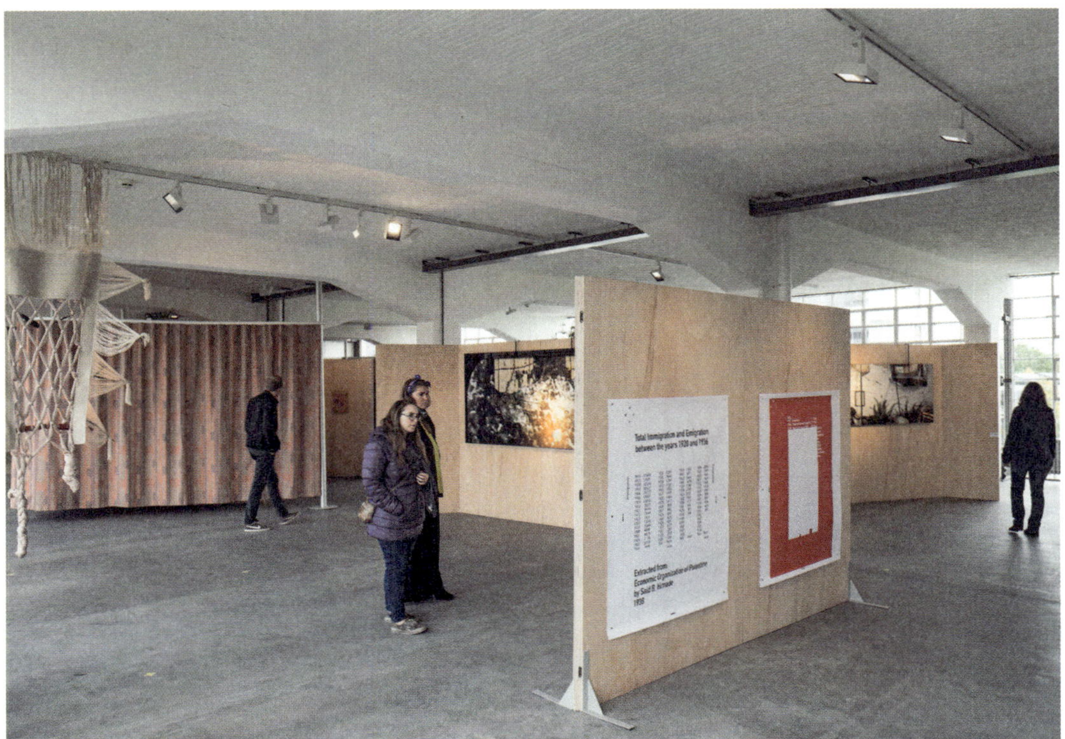

Exhibitions

Since the nineteen-seventies, preliminary course work, artworks such as paintings, drawings, and photographs, items made in the workshops, and other articles that document the historic Bauhaus have been collected, stored, and exhibited in the Bauhaus Dessau. But while the building's characteristic glass façades permit light, air, and sun to flood into the depths of the rooms, these valuable objects must be protected from the very same elements. The extensive glazed surfaces also cause extreme temperature fluctuations in the building while the works of art must be kept at specific, preferably even temperatures. The installation of air conditioning and safety equipment would significantly compromise the transparency of the building and the clean lines of the construction and make damage to the fabric of the building inevitable. Since 1999, the Bauhaus Dessau Foundation has therefore acknowledged that from a technological standpoint, the Bauhaus Building is not an appropriate place to store and exhibit artworks and archive materials, but an 'authentic testimony of the history of the Bauhaus Building, which is to be maintained intact if possible', as stated in a 1999 report by the ICOMOS expert group.[3] The opening of the new Bauhaus Museum Dessau in 2019 provided a new, suitable space to showcase the Bauhaus Dessau Foundation's excellent collection, and as a result the last of the installations for art exhibitions could be removed from the historic building.

The use of the rooms in the workshop wing for guided tours, presentations, workshops, or seminars means they can as a rule be presented with a relatively basic set of fixtures

198)

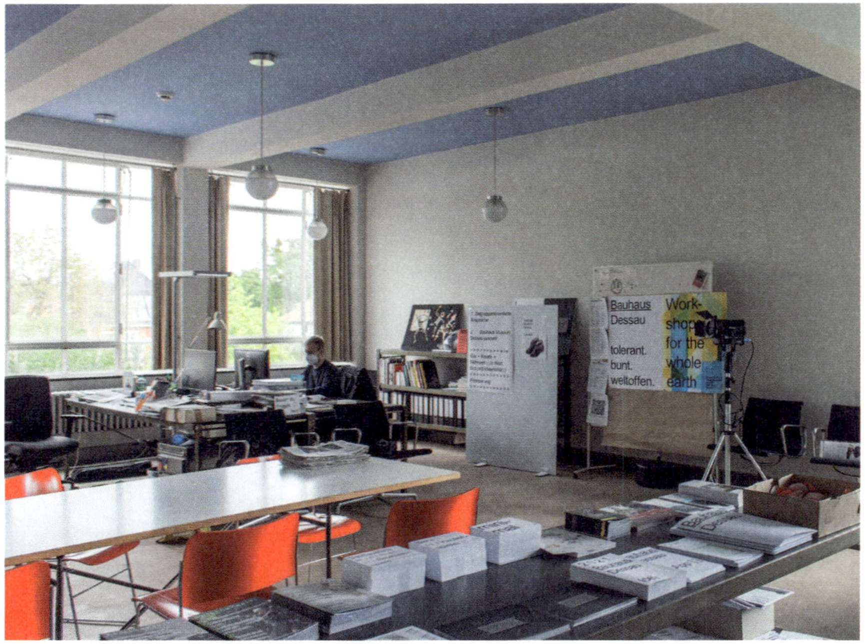

199)

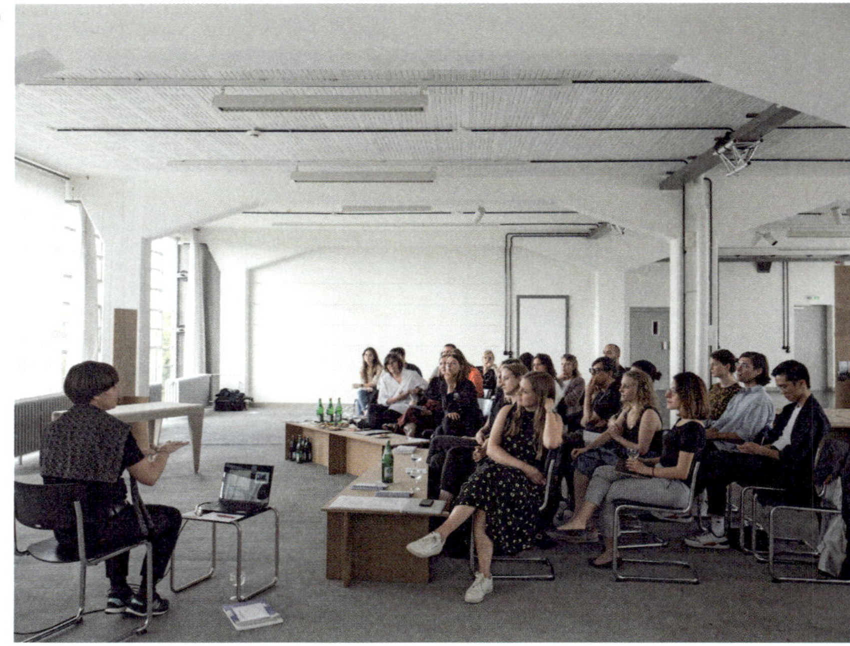

and fittings. The more moderate temperatures which can be maintained also reduce structural and building physics problems, e.g., the production of condensation, thus supporting the long-term preservation of the building fabric.

Offices

Permanent office workstations in the workshop wing were moved out of this part of the building as part of a general plan to reduce energy consumption because a significant amount of heating energy is lost through the extensive surfaces of the curtain wall. Here, instead of using energy-saving measures to upgrade the workshop wing and thus alter its authentic character, its use was changed rather than the historic building itself. Relocating the workstations to the north wing also allows technical installations to be concentrated in one location and enables short distances between one workplace and the next. The need for interventions to accommodate workstations is thus reduced in other parts of the building such as the workshop wing.

Work rooms and classrooms in all parts of the building are exposed to temperature fluctuations caused by the extensive glazing. Even though the expectations of levels of comfort have grown over the ninety-five years since the building's construction, reduced levels of comfort are accepted under extreme weather conditions given that the conservation of the Bauhaus Building as a monument of international relevance must be prioritised.

Events

Numerous events are hosted in the Bauhaus Building. These include the foundation's own programmes for children, young people, career entrants, postgraduates, or others who organise small exhibitions or alternative activities here. Large-scale events such as the Bauhaus Festival or concerts are held on a regular basis and attract a wide audience. In addition, rooms are rented out for seminars, festivities, and other occasions. Great respect for the historic

200)

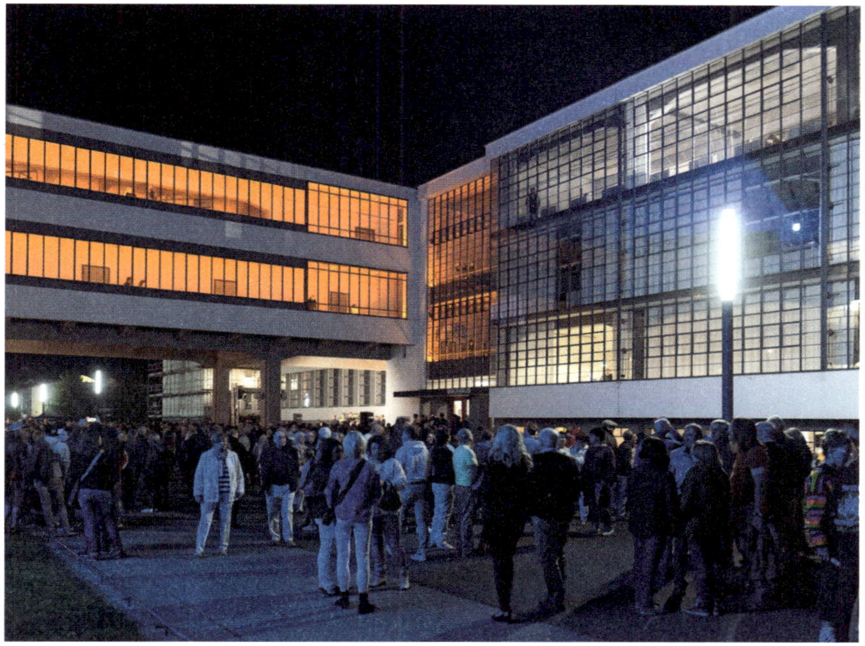

201)

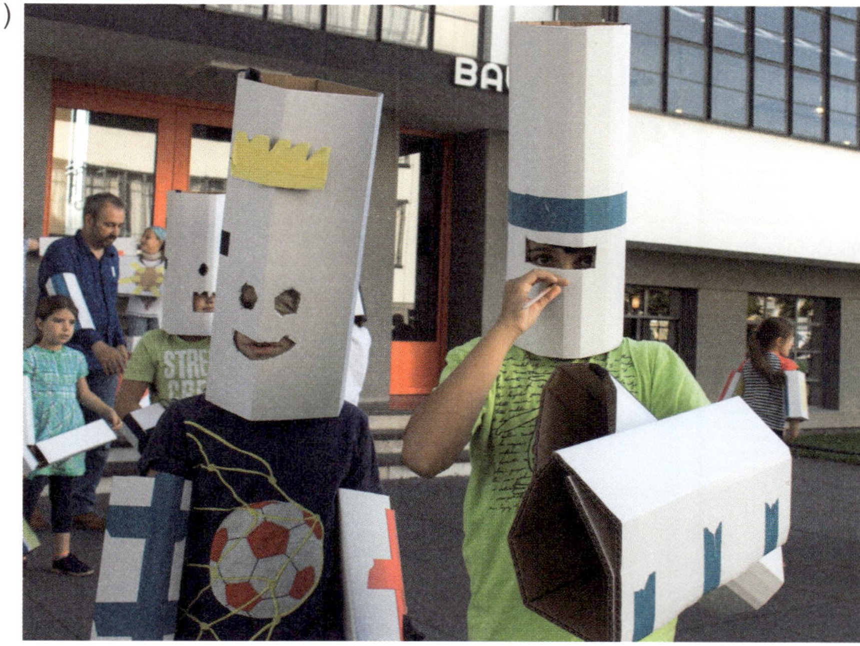

building and its sensitive surfaces must be maintained during all events; a set of rules and regulations therefore provides information on the necessary safeguards for the use of the building. Regulations set out in black and white are indispensable but nonetheless often insufficient. Therefore personal reminders of the need to protect and value the building's unique qualities remain an important tool for its protection.

198)
Workstations,
north wing, 2021

199)
Bauhaus Lab
symposium, second floor,
workshop wing, 2019

200)
Bauhaus Festival
Yellow-angled, 2018

201)
Workshop with school
pupils, 2017

202)
Usage, semi-basement (detail of the conservation objectives, 2014)

203)
Usage, ground floor (detail of the conservation objectives, 2014)

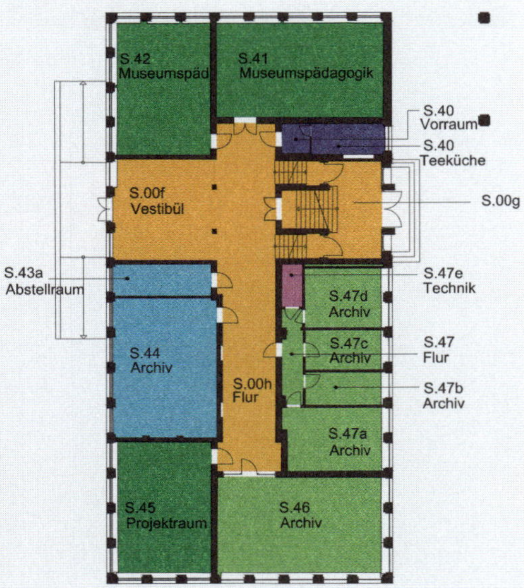

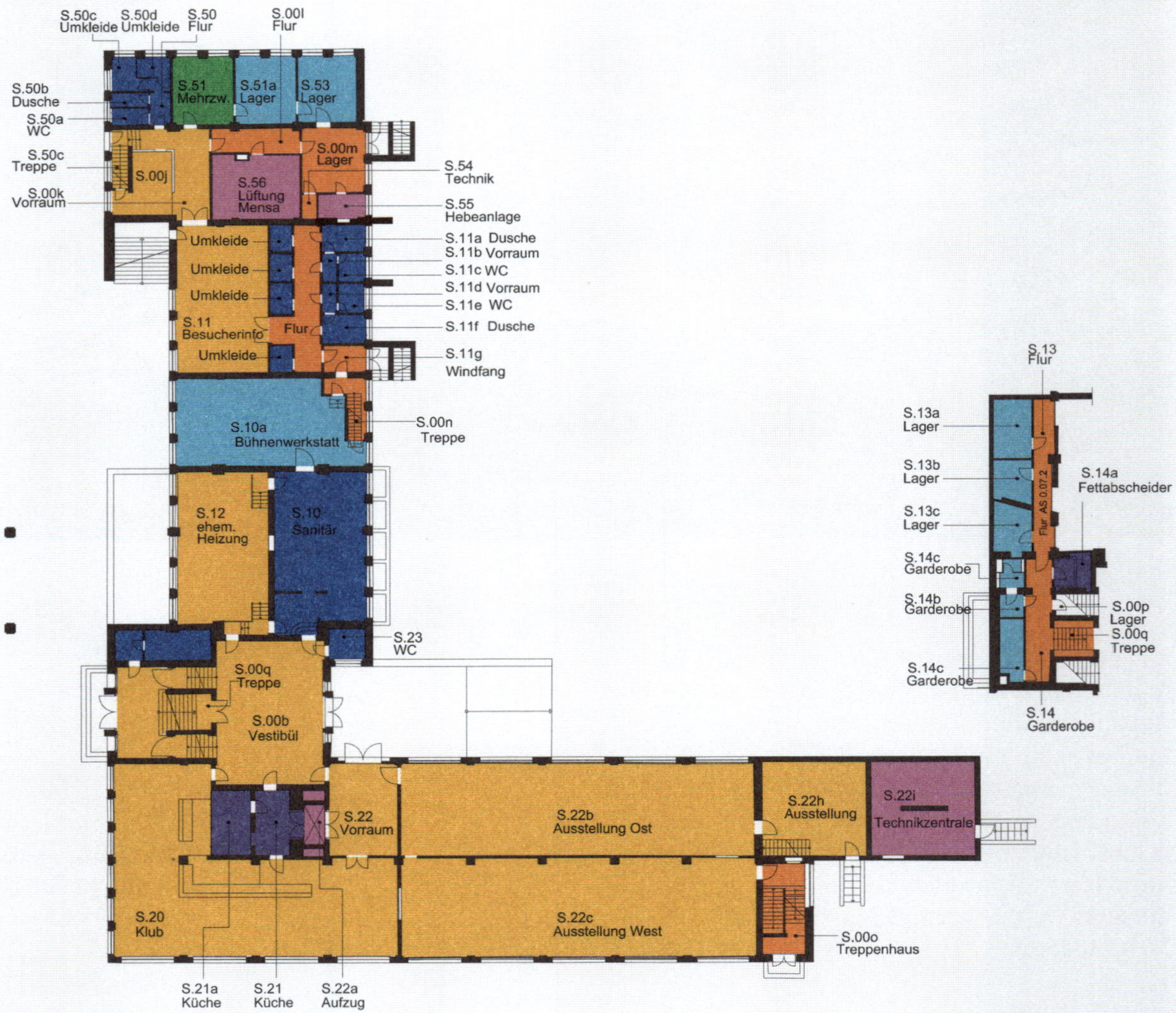

202)

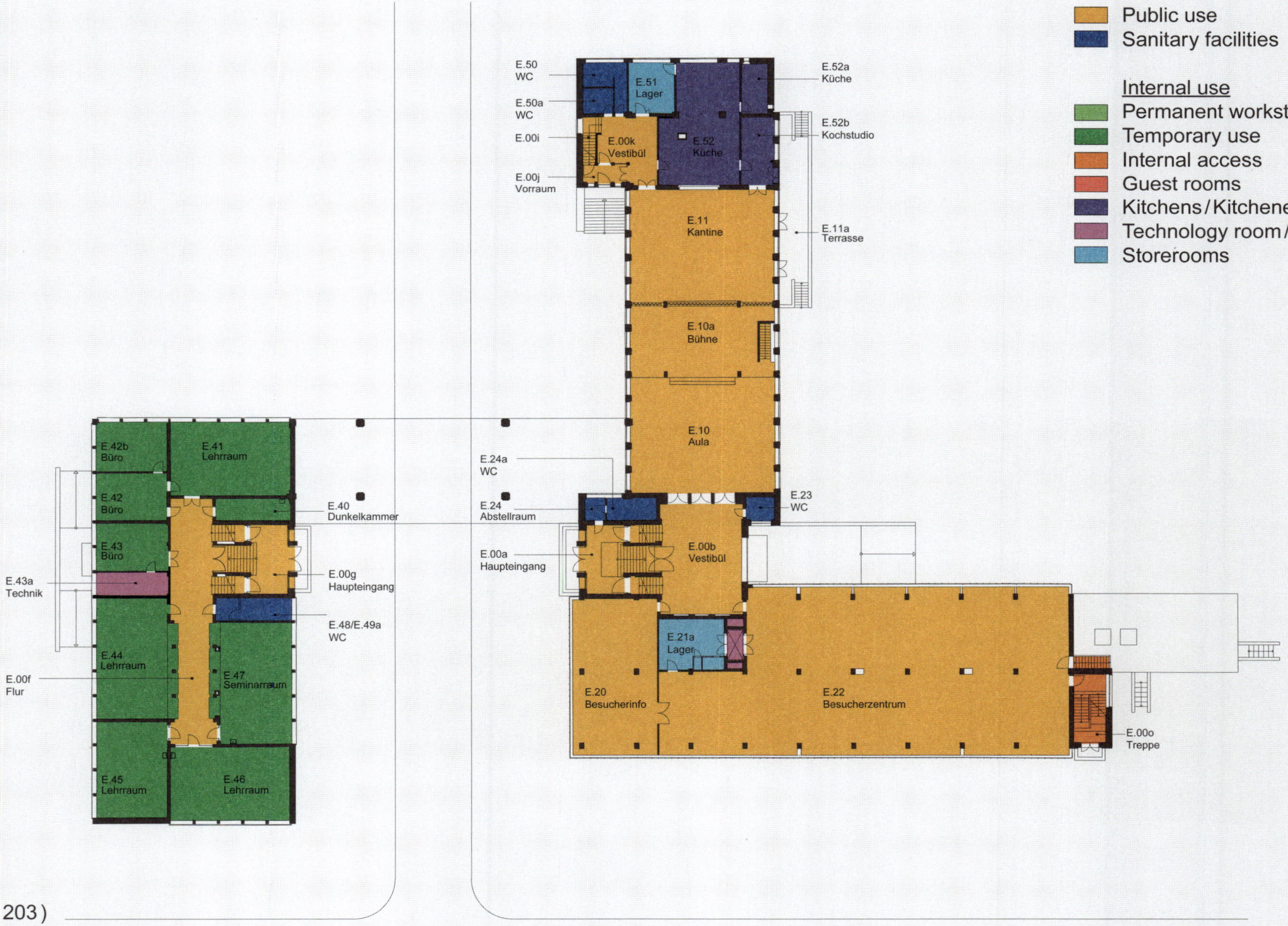

Key

- Public use
- Sanitary facilities

Internal use

- Permanent workstations
- Temporary use
- Internal access
- Guest rooms
- Kitchens / Kitchenettes
- Technology room / Lift
- Storerooms

204)
Usage, first floor (detail of the conservation objectives, 2014)

205)
Usage, floors 2–4 (detail of the conservation objectives, 2014)

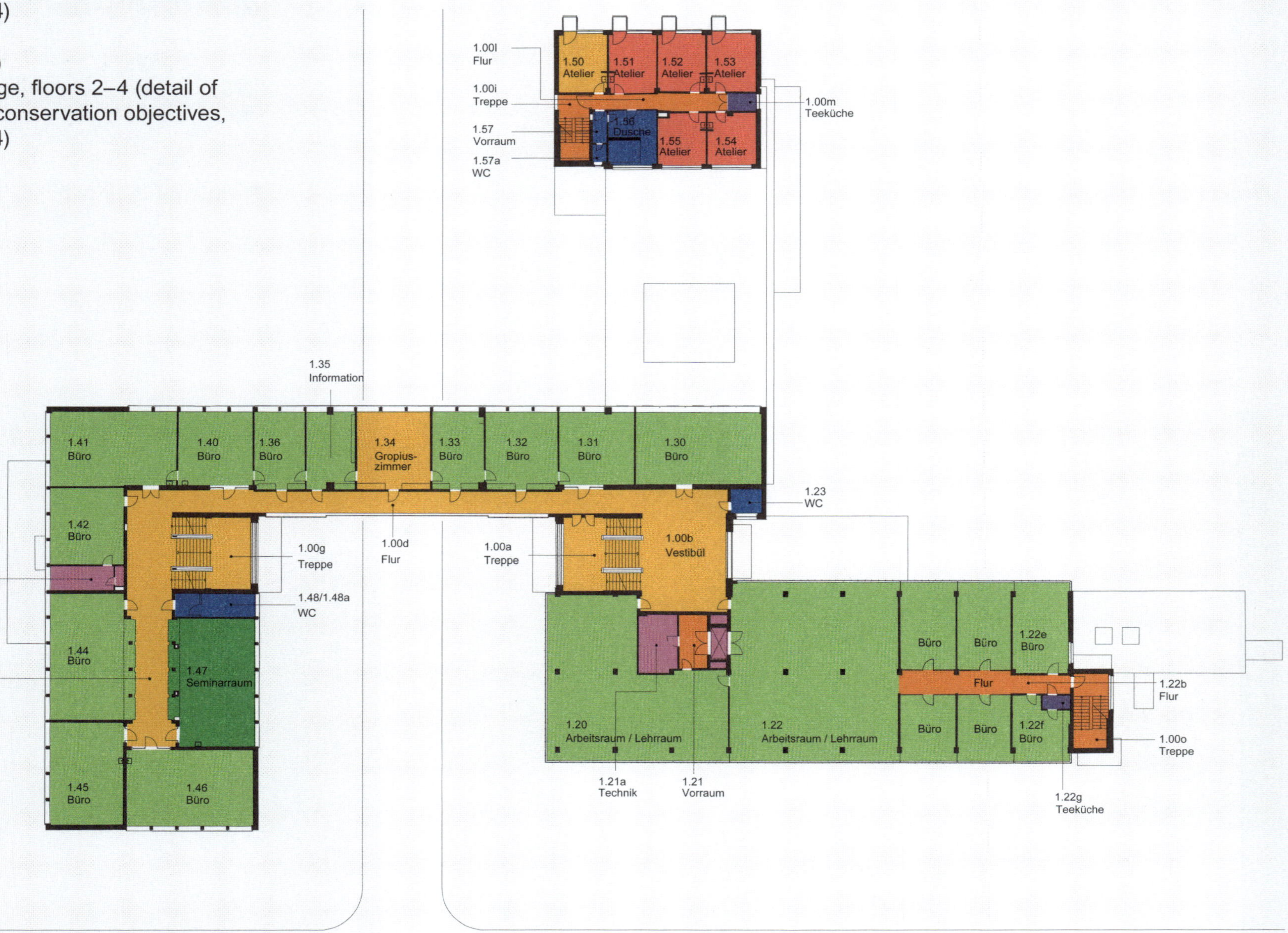

204)

Key

- Public use
- Sanitary facilities

Internal use

- Permanent workstations
- Temporary use
- Internal access
- Guest rooms
- Kitchens / Kitchenettes
- Technology room / Lift
- Storerooms

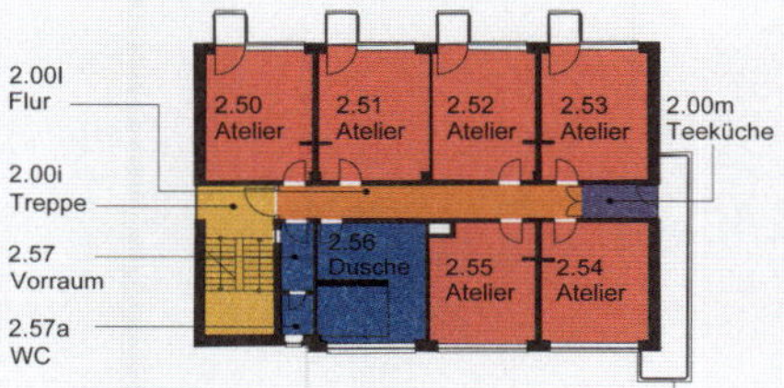

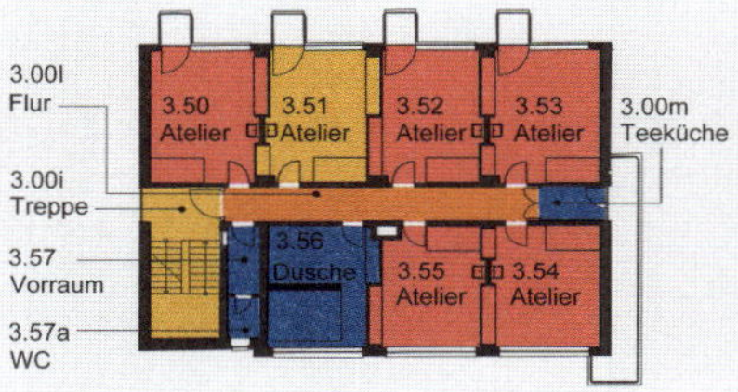

3rd floor

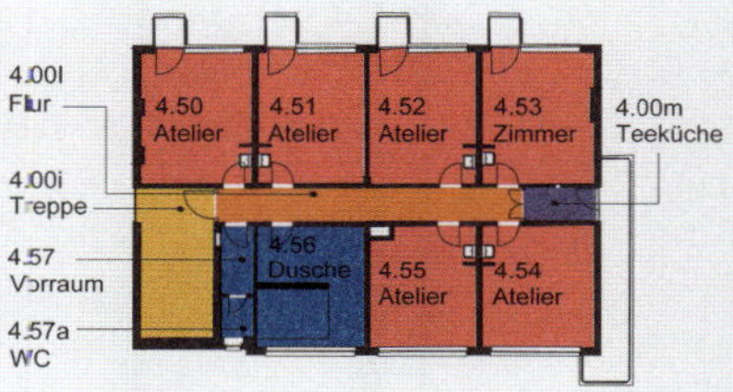

4th floor

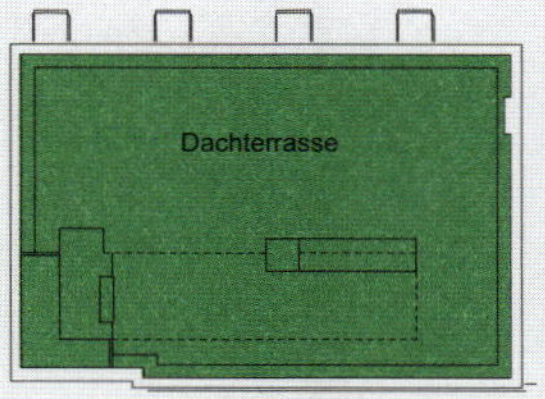

Roof plan

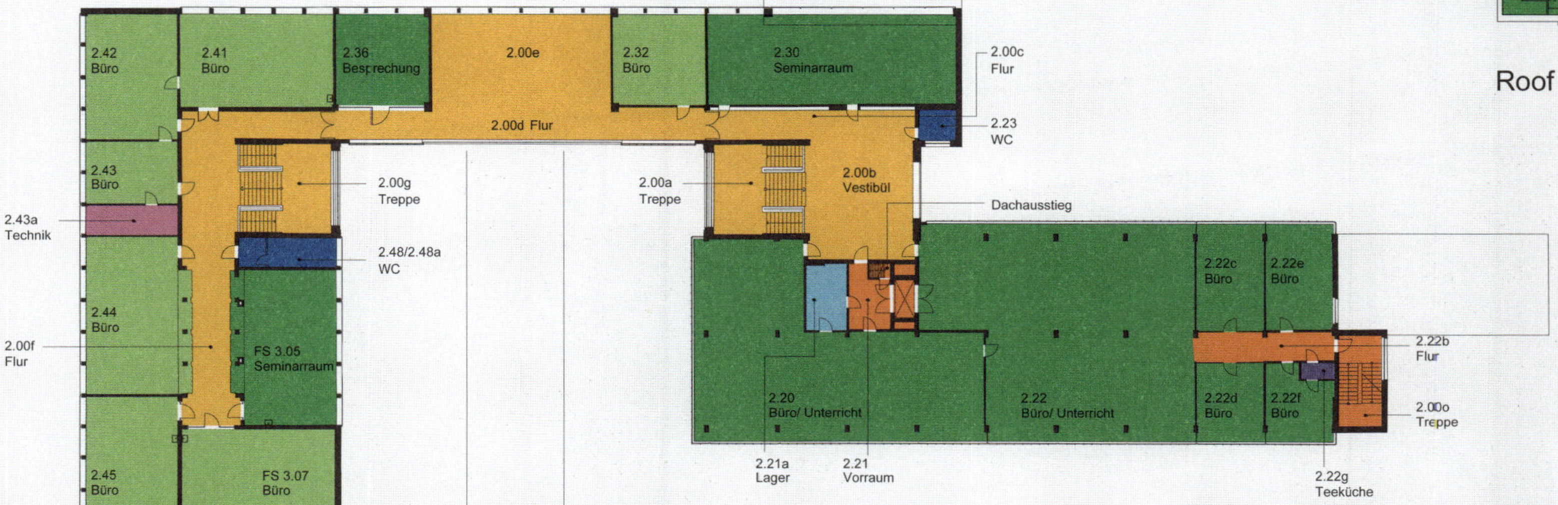

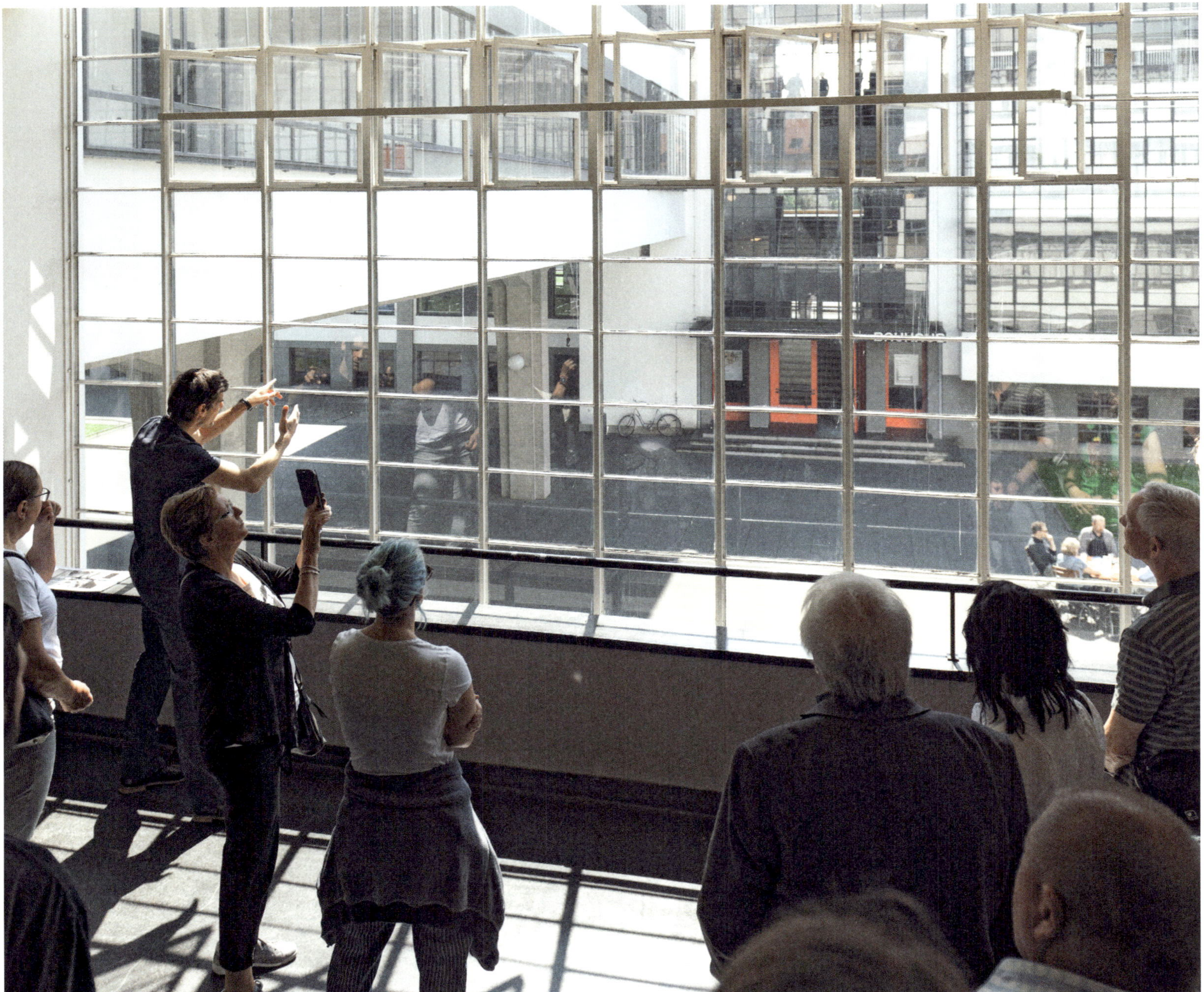

206)
Guided tour of
the Bauhaus,
2019

Tourism

The growing number of visitors to the Bauhaus Building is an encouraging trend, but at the same time it places an increasing burden on the building, as became clear most recently during the centenary "100 Years of Bauhaus" in 2019.[4] The many individuals and groups not only place ever-greater demands on the infrastructure, but also damage surfaces such as floors, walls, or doors, which must consequently be protected or repeatedly repaired. In order to limit damage to the original building fabric caused by increased wear and tear or negligence, the original surfaces in the building are revealed or displayed only in exceptional circumstances and are usually preserved under a protective layer. The necessary expansion of the infrastructure to include visitor information, signage, sanitary facilities, cloakrooms, bicycle racks, and garages was implemented with respect to the historic building.

The public interest in the building remains a double-edged sword: it boosts the Bauhaus and its buildings but also places a burden on them. Because the increasing recognition of modern buildings as cultural monuments and World Heritage sites means visitor numbers are expected to continue to rise, a greater focus must be placed on managing visitors, limiting their numbers, outsourcing service functions, and the systematic continuous maintenance of the building with a view to safeguarding the original fabric.

As a 'built manifesto of the Bauhaus's ideas', the Bauhaus Building has also always been an exhibit. But now the building is changing not only due to the visitors, who wish to be directed and provided for, but also in terms of its value, which is being reassessed. Its meaning as a framework for a specific use is increasingly being supplanted by its relevance as a place of public interest. 'It [the space] stops being a repository of real experiences and memories. The haptic and routine perception of the owner is replaced by the new visitors' mainly visual impression. The space … transforms itself into an object of study, an object of curiosity. … The outsider's view is comparative; it measures the unknown against the known. Thus what was never intended as art becomes sculpture. And places that were never laid out according to the rules of the game become (adventure) playgrounds. According to this outlook, the visitor behaves like a gallerist or like a child.'[5]

1
Venice Charter, Article 5: 'The conservation of monuments is always facilitated by making use of them for some socially useful purpose. Such use is therefore desirable but it must not change the lay-out or decoration of the building. It is within these limits only that modifications demanded by a change of function should be envisaged and may be permitted.'

2
Petzet 2004, p. 9

3
ICOMOS Preventive Monitoring 1999

4
The number of visitors to the Bauhaus Building rose from 26,631 in 1998 to 35,101 in 2005. During the centenary year 2019, 285,000 guests visited the Bauhaus World Heritage site. In 2020, the visitors numbers reached 146,000, despite the pandemic restrictions.

5
Mazzoni 2004, p. 66

Long-term Conservation

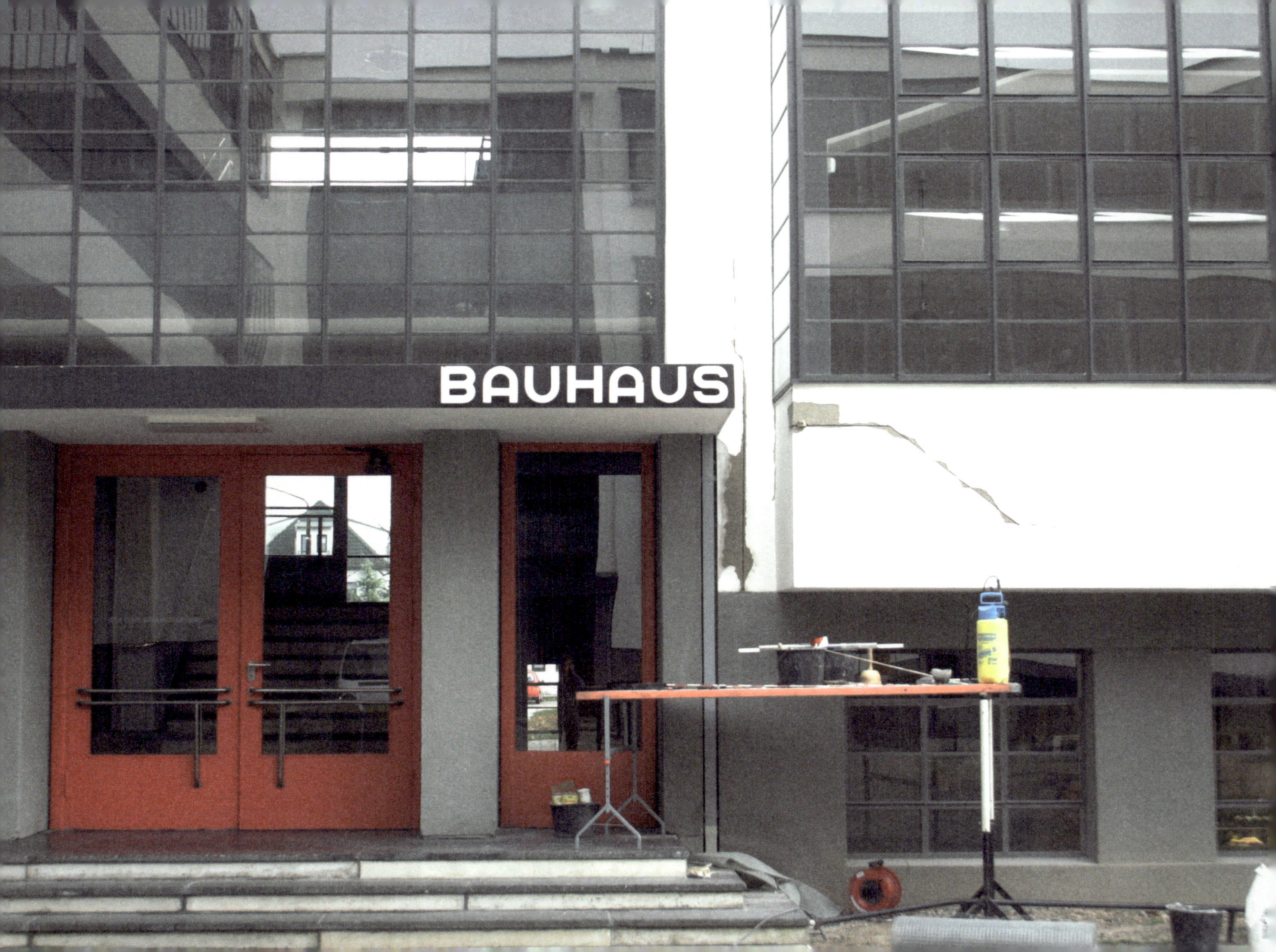
BAUHAUS

Long-term Conservation

207)
Repair work on rendered façade, 2006

Heritage Conservation Concepts

Continuous, preventative, systematic, and specialised care and maintenance are vital in order to safeguard the original fabric of the Bauhaus Building for the future, especially in respect of its uniquely modern forms, surfaces, constructions, and materials. The planning and implementation of measures to protect the building, which have in the past frequently resulted in significant damage to the original building fabric, must focus on the preventive conservation of the original material.

One of the challenges that modern buildings often face today is that, unlike older buildings such as medieval half-timbered houses or baroque churches, they are not seen as unique, irreplaceable cultural monuments but as belonging to the present day. As such, they are expected to meet contemporary requirements—even though they comply with the norms and standards of the time they were built. Modifications thus often lead to the deterioration of the historic material or aesthetic qualities of the architecture. But the materiality of buildings and their surfaces, the traces of use and age which mark them out as witnesses of the past are unparalleled and indispensable components of modern monuments too.

The preservation of design elements including the sensitive, hand-worked lime render surfaces, monochrome floors, nickel-plate metal elements, many steel and glass constructions, as well as the impression and impact of the architecture for future generations calls for preventive and meticulous care. Experimental materials and constructions that are no longer produced today and therefore cannot be replaced present an additional challenge. Moreover, skimpily built building components and details rarely satisfy contemporary requirements as regards structural engineering and statics. This easily leads to damage and rapid wear and tear. Above and beyond this, even minimal modifications have already caused damage to a building which is distinguished by balanced proportions, meticulously planned details, and considered surfaces. Thus, systematic and permanent care informed by scientific research and an appreciation of the architecture's unique qualities is essential for the long-term conservation of the Bauhaus Building and other Bauhaus buildings alike.

With the conservation objectives and the conservation management plan, the Bauhaus Dessau Foundation has established principles for the management of systematic and preventive conservation measures for the Bauhaus Building. The conservation objectives set out fundamental specifications for protection and preservation, for example regarding the use of individual parts of the building, time layers deemed worthy of conservation, or possible changes to the glass façades. The conservation management plan goes into greater detail and provides access to in-depth information on the care and maintenance of individual building components in a database.

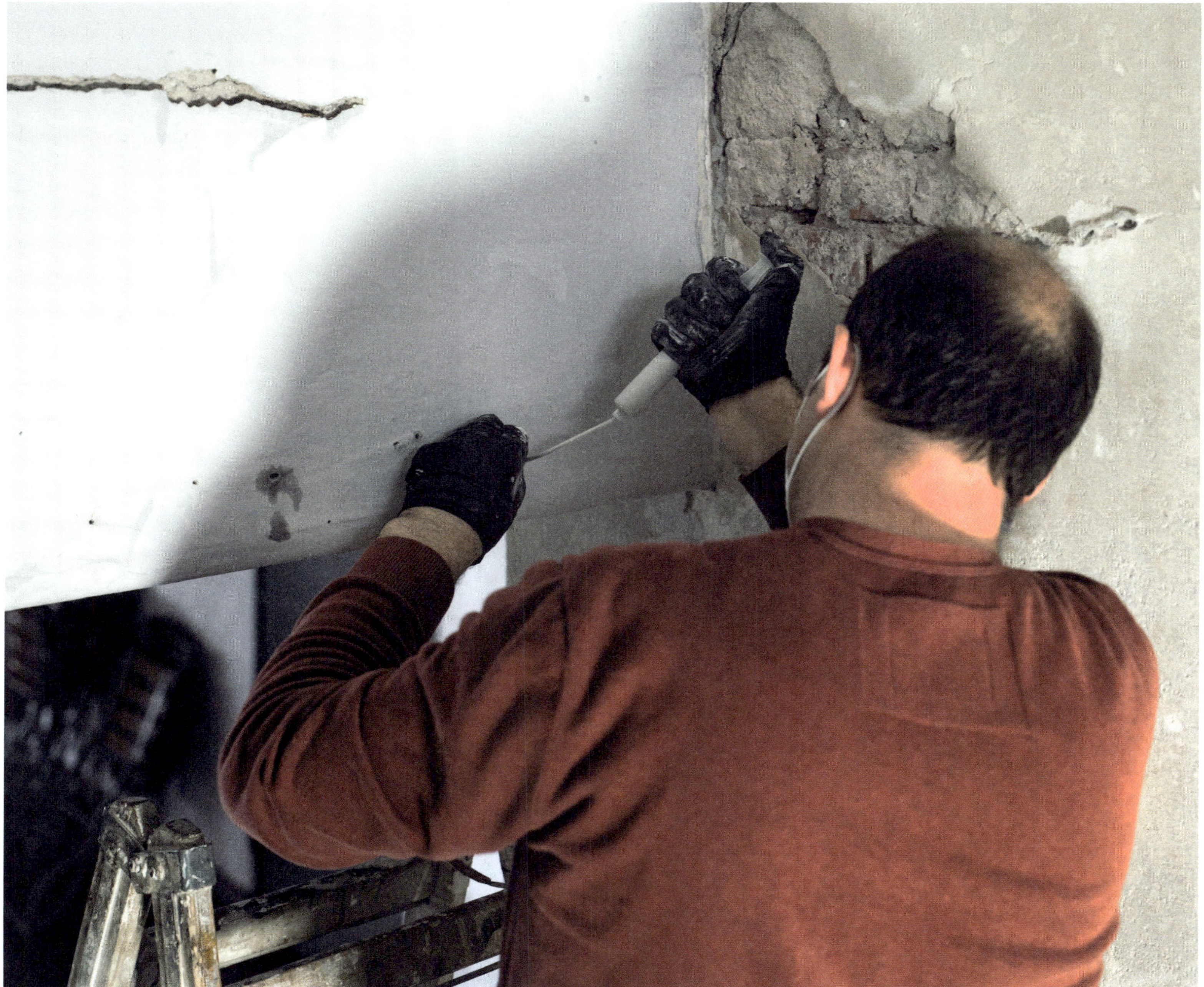

208)
Restoration of
plaster surfaces,
2021

Conservation Objectives

'The conservation objectives are specialised guidelines for a conservation-orientated approach to the historical monument that take under consideration the requirements of use and the structural context. They make no reference to planning or funding, but outline the objectives of a long-term, scientifically substantiated approach to the World Cultural Heritage.' They serve as a standard for the planning of maintenance measures, modifications, or changes of use.

The conservation objectives take a nuanced view of the building's relevance as a cultural monument, that is, as a material witness to the way people once lived the preservation of which is in the public interest. They comprise aspects of monument preservation, on energy-related problems, or requirements arising from current use. To enable coherent evaluation and planning, the various interests must be addressed and evaluated in context.

With reference to the Venice Charter,[3] the intention is not to fully restore the building to its original state as in 1926 but to preserve or recreate the fundamental structure of the building including the exposed construction, the spatial coherencies, and the colour design. However, the traces of age, use, and modifications that reflect the ninety-five-year history of the building are to be respected, not erased, provided they do not compromise the building's artistic expression.

However, before describing the objectives in greater detail, the relevant terminology must first be clarified:[4]

Renovation:

A comprehensive package of measures which includes reconstruction, restoration, recreation, repair, maintenance, upkeep, and replacement. With renovation, the aim is to safeguard and preserve the building over the long term. It also takes under consideration requirements arising from use, such as the modernisation of technical installations or compliance with building regulations. Interventions should be reduced to a minimum where possible, be reversible, and blend into the overall architectonic context.

Reconstruction:

Accurate reproduction, using identical materials, of original building components which are missing but which are essential to an understanding of the overall impact of the building or the space. The term also applies to the precise recreation of a spatial situation. Reconstructions are only permissible in exceptional circumstances and provided there is an adequate scientific basis. Only original building elements dating from 1926 are reconstructed in the Bauhaus Building.

Recreation:

A replication of an original spatial situation, which is not obliged to meet the rigorous requirements imposed on a scientifically founded reconstruction. Yet it is important to convey an impression of original spatial setting, and it approximates the original situation.

Restoration:

Measures that restore the original condition of a historical building component and preserve it long-term by eliminating later changes and making small amendments. During the restoration of doors, for example, the original layer of paint is revealed, protected, and amended following the removal of later layers above the reference layer and the repair of any damage to the wood.

Repair and maintenance:

The elimination of structural damage using basic resources, with repair requiring the more far-reaching interventions. Through continuous care and simple improvements and repairs using identical materials, the current condition is preserved. In the Bauhaus Building, non-original building components worthy of conservation are dealt with and safeguarded in this way (e.g., the steel windows and curtain wall rebuilt in 1976).

Upkeep:

Repairs and maintenance measures in areas in which measures deemed necessary for functional or design reasons are prioritised over the preservation or creation of a specific historic situation. Here as in all parts of the building, the original materials must be respected during implementation of such measures (e.g., the upkeep of the rooms of the Klub in the Bauhaus, a café and bistro established in 1989).

Replacement:

New building components that meet current needs, but blend into the overall context. Examples include the glass partitions in the workshop wing or the additional WC cubicles, which are not in the original location and are distinguishable as new elements. Replacements can include colour finishes on areas for which no historic colour finds exist. In both material and aesthetic terms, replacements should integrate harmoniously with the whole and should also be reversible.

With extensive knowledge of the building and an in-depth understanding of its unique qualities, it is possible to stipulate within it areas with different priorities. Marked as red, green, and blue areas in the conservation objectives, these pinpoint the objectives of future measures:

Red areas:
restoration and reconstruction

Here, the original condition of 1926, which is representative of the building's value as a monument, is to be extensively preserved. In areas of particular significance, not only restoration but also reconstruction (where required and possible) aid the preservation of the monument's aesthetic value or render it accessible.

Green areas:
maintenance and repairs

These areas mostly bear the stamp of the renovation of 1976, in the course of which the appearance of the Bauhaus was restored following previous damage. This renovation marks an important stage in the history of the Bauhaus Building, not least because the picture it created has shaped the perception of the building for the last thirty years and thus bears witness to its history.[5]

Blue areas:
upkeep and replacement

Here, the preservation or recreation of a particular historic context, such as in the semi-basement of the workshop wing and connecting building, is not prioritised. Most of the measures implemented here are required for technical or functional reasons.

As set out in the Venice Charter, the original material must be fully respected in all areas. Modern additions should be distinguishable as such but not impinge on or dominate the overall impression. They should only become apparent under closer scrutiny.[6]

The following guidelines apply to future measures for the care and conservation of the Bauhaus Building:

– Preservation of the structure of the building or restoration of the structure if it is damaged

– Modification of use to suit the building; minimal technical installations

– Preservation of traces of history, provided they do not disfigure the building

– Maintenance and conservation of the building in its current form

– Reconstruction of missing original parts if a reconstruction based on scientific evidence is possible

Interventions in the building fabric and architectural structure are to be reduced to an absolute minimum; every intervention also involves losses and can result in incalculable further damage. All measures in the Bauhaus Building must prioritise the preservation of the original fabric of the building since this is an irreplaceable component of the cultural monument. Original components which are not preserved in the original location or which are covered up following the completion of works are therefore documented in situ or stored in the Building Research Archive. Where possible, processes and findings are to be scientifically documented and evaluated as part of the research work accompanying the restoration. Before work begins on more substantial building measures, sample surfaces are created in order to work out the details of suitable methods and test their feasibility.

The requirements for the individual areas and building components are outlined in the conservation objectives in plans with succinct texts that provide a clear overview of the findings. The first section includes essentials such as a list of rooms, a general plan, a description of the existing historic structures, and an index of studies and reports, etc. The second section comprises an analysis of the building construction with a focus on glass façades, statics, colour design, outdoor facilities, furnishings and fittings, fire safety, use, and spatial structure. This extensive knowledge of the building is essential in order to determine the objectives. The third section includes propositions for the historic allocation concept, usage, glass façades, fittings (radiators and lighting fixtures), colours, surfaces, and outdoor facilities. The conservation objectives were drafted in 1999[7] and updated in 2014.[8] They were approved by the respective experts, the monument conservation services in Dessau, the state of Saxony-Anhalt, and ICOMOS Germany.

1
Cf. ICOMOS ISC20C 2011

2
Arge Bauhaus 1999, 1.1 Zielstellung

3
Article 3: 'The intention in conserving and restoring monuments is to safeguard them no less as works of art than as historical evidence.' Article 11: 'The valid contributions of all periods to the building of a monument must be respected, since unity of style is not the aim of a restoration.' ICOMOS International 1964; see also www.icomos.org/charters/venice_e.pdf (10 May 2021)

4
Definition of terms according to Mörsch 1989, p. 115–41; Petzet 1992, p. 7–45

5
The renovation of 1976 is one of the first far-reaching renovations of a modern building completed in Germany and thus testifies to the recognition of modernism as a subject of heritage conservation.

6
Article 12: 'Replacements of missing parts must integrate harmoniously with the whole, but at the same time must be distinguishable from the original so that restoration does not falsify the artistic or historic evidence.' Article 13: 'Additions cannot be allowed except in so far as they do not detract from the interesting parts of the building, its traditional setting, the balance of its composition and its relation with its surroundings.' ICOMOS International 1964

7
Developed by ARGE Bauhaus: Brambach und Ebert, Halle/Saale, and Pfister Schiess Tropeano, Zurich

8
Updated by ProDenkmal GmbH, Bamberg/Berlin

Historic inventory of walls

209) Semi-basement, 2014

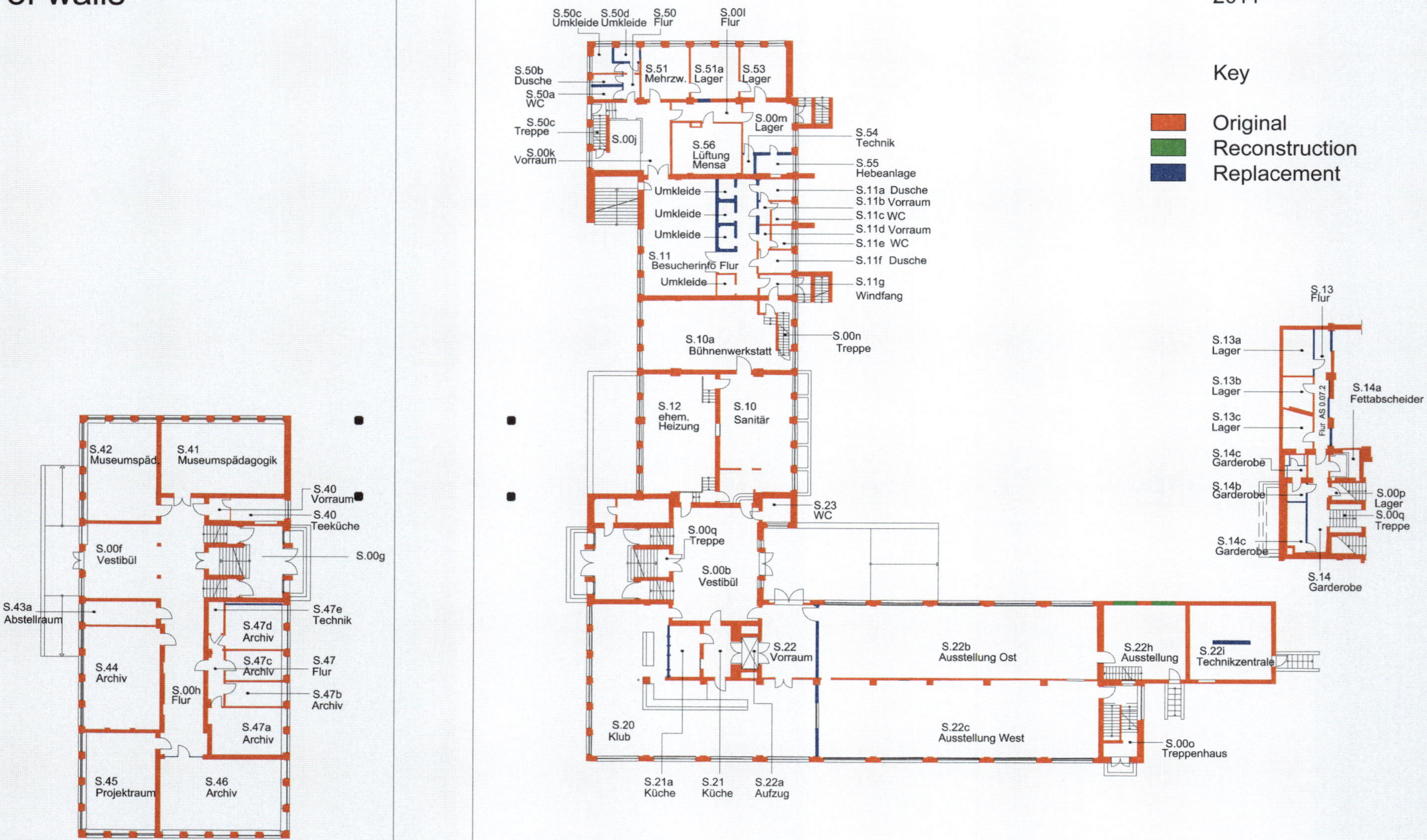

Key

- Original
- Reconstruction
- Replacement

210)
Ground floor,
2014

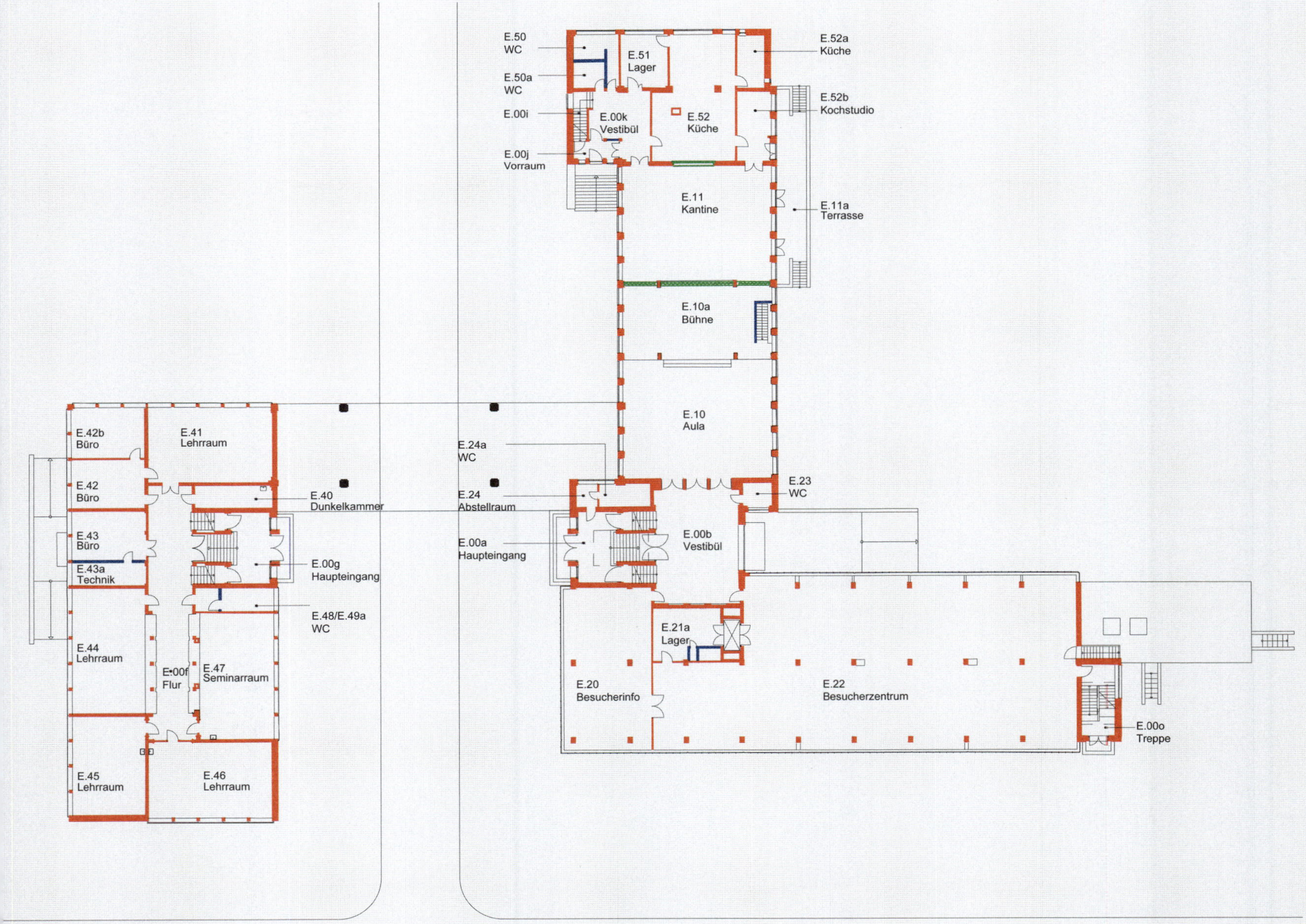

Historic inventory of walls

211)
First floor,
2014

Key

Original
Reconstruction
Replacement

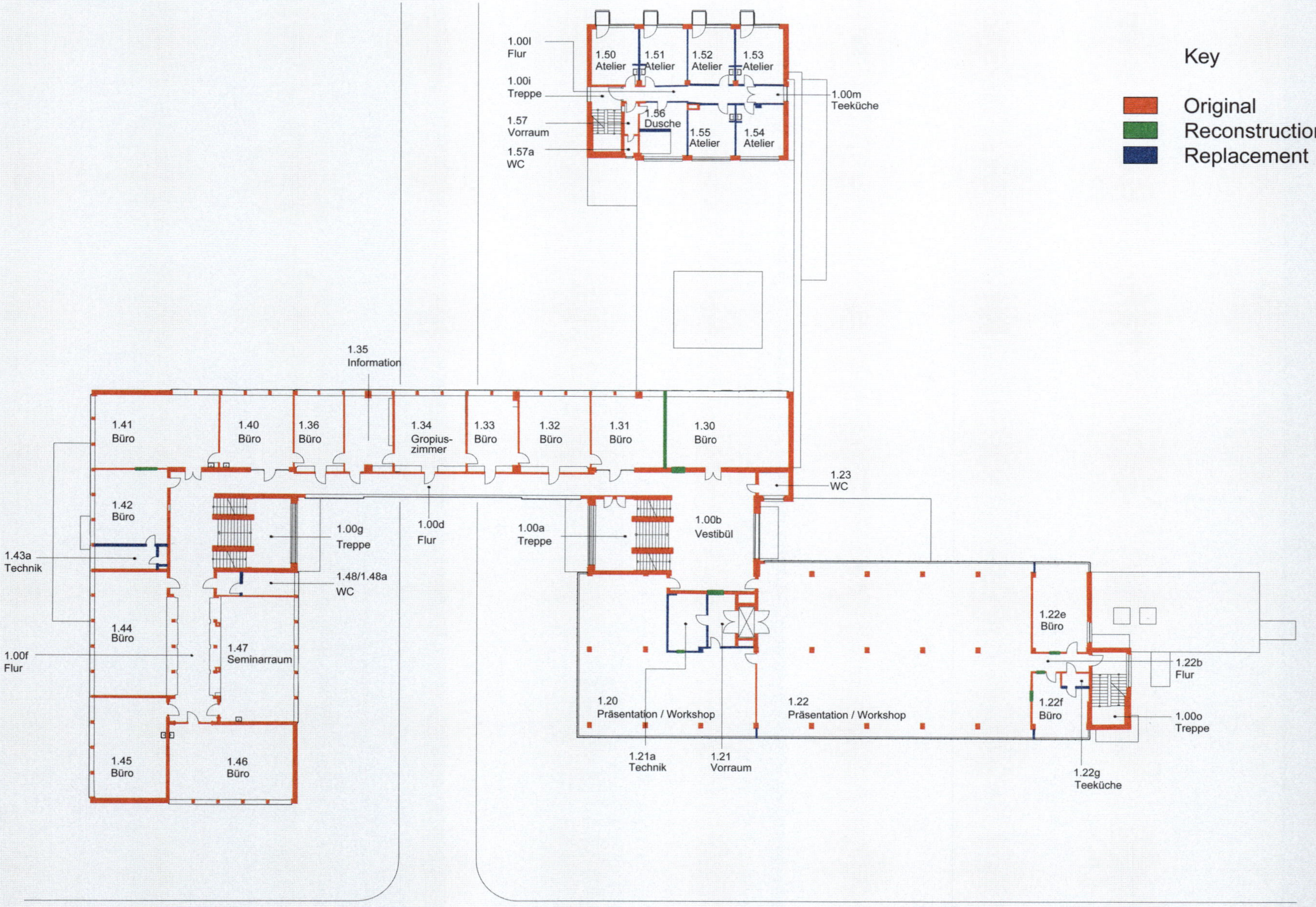

212)
Floors 2–4,
2014

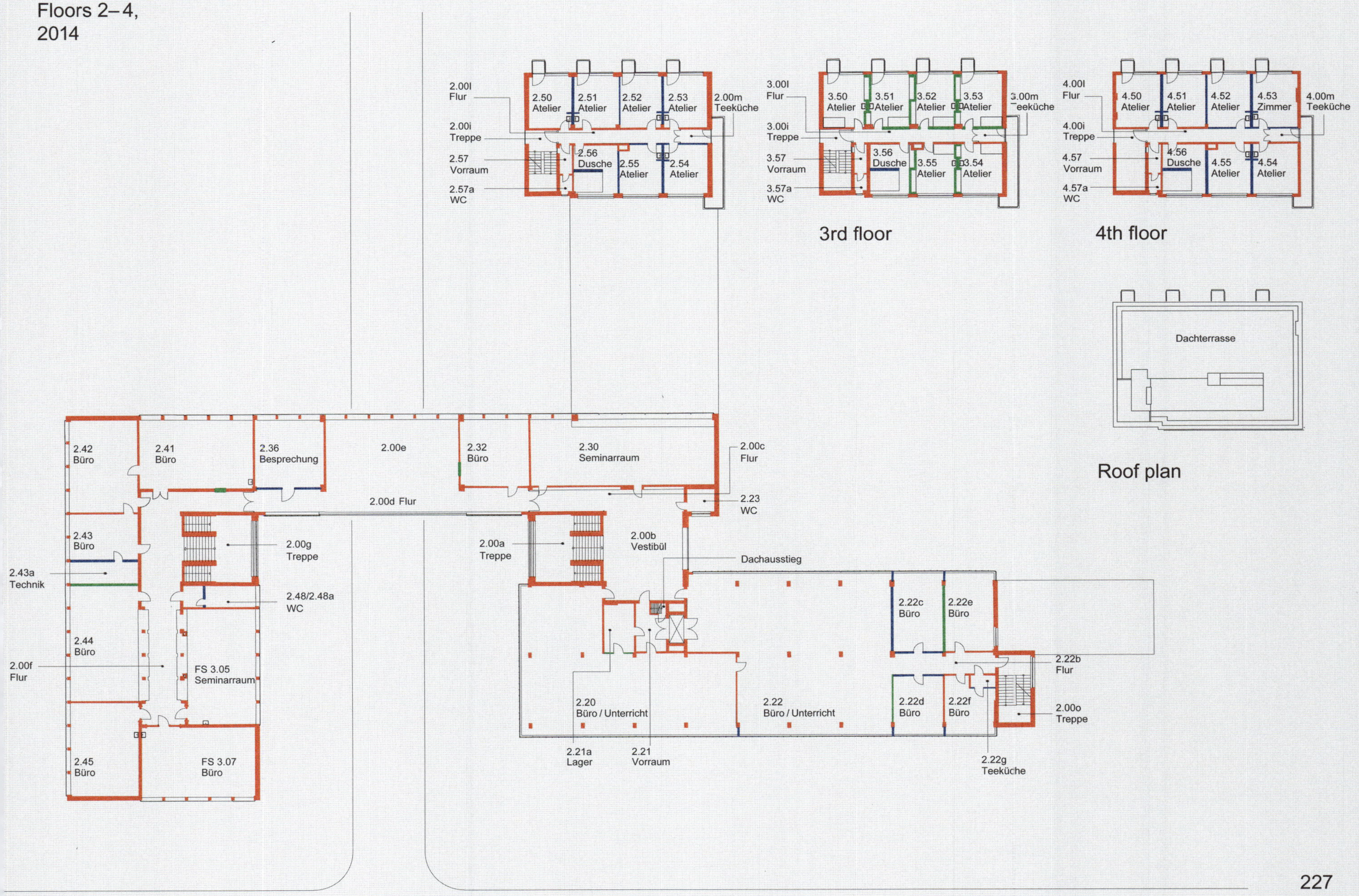

Historic inventory of enclosing walls and fitout elements

213)
Semi-basement, 2014

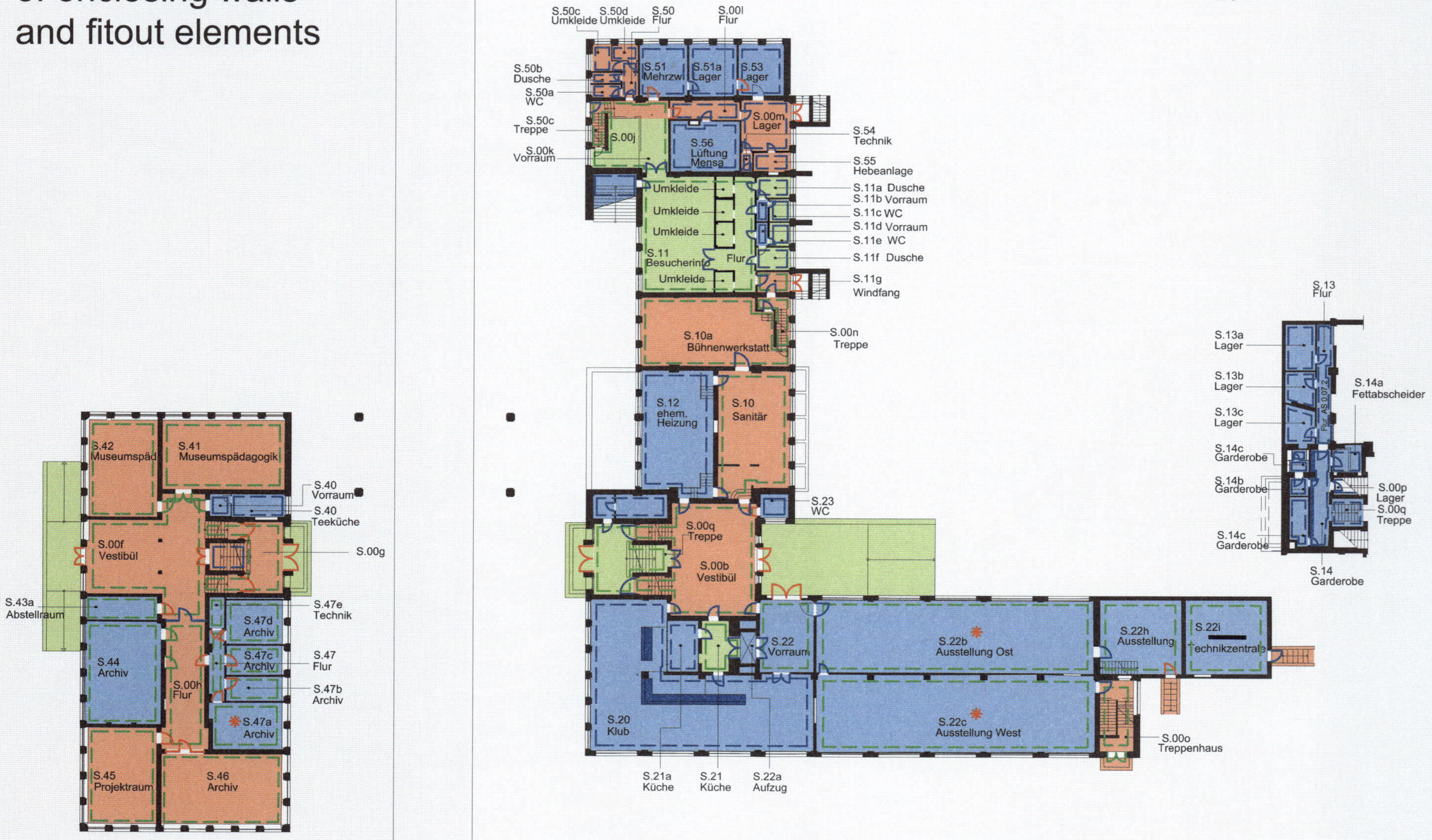

214)
Groundfloor,
2014

Key

- Original
- Reconstruction
- Replacement
- Original wall surface
- Reconstructed wall surface
- Replacement wall surface
- Original floor
- Reconstructed floor
- Replacement floor
- * Original screed and new floor surface

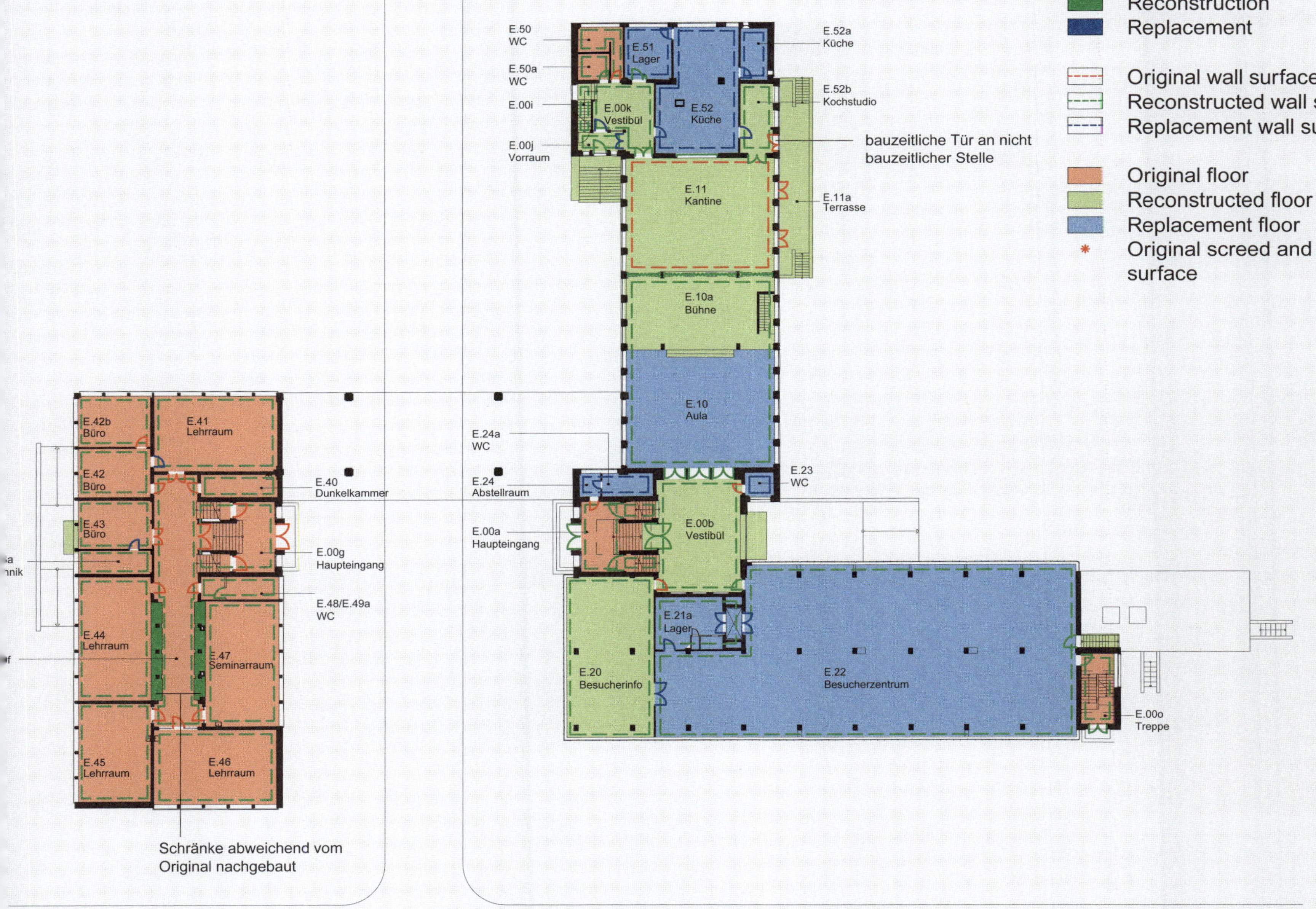

Historic inventory of enclosing walls and fitout elements

215) First floor, 2014

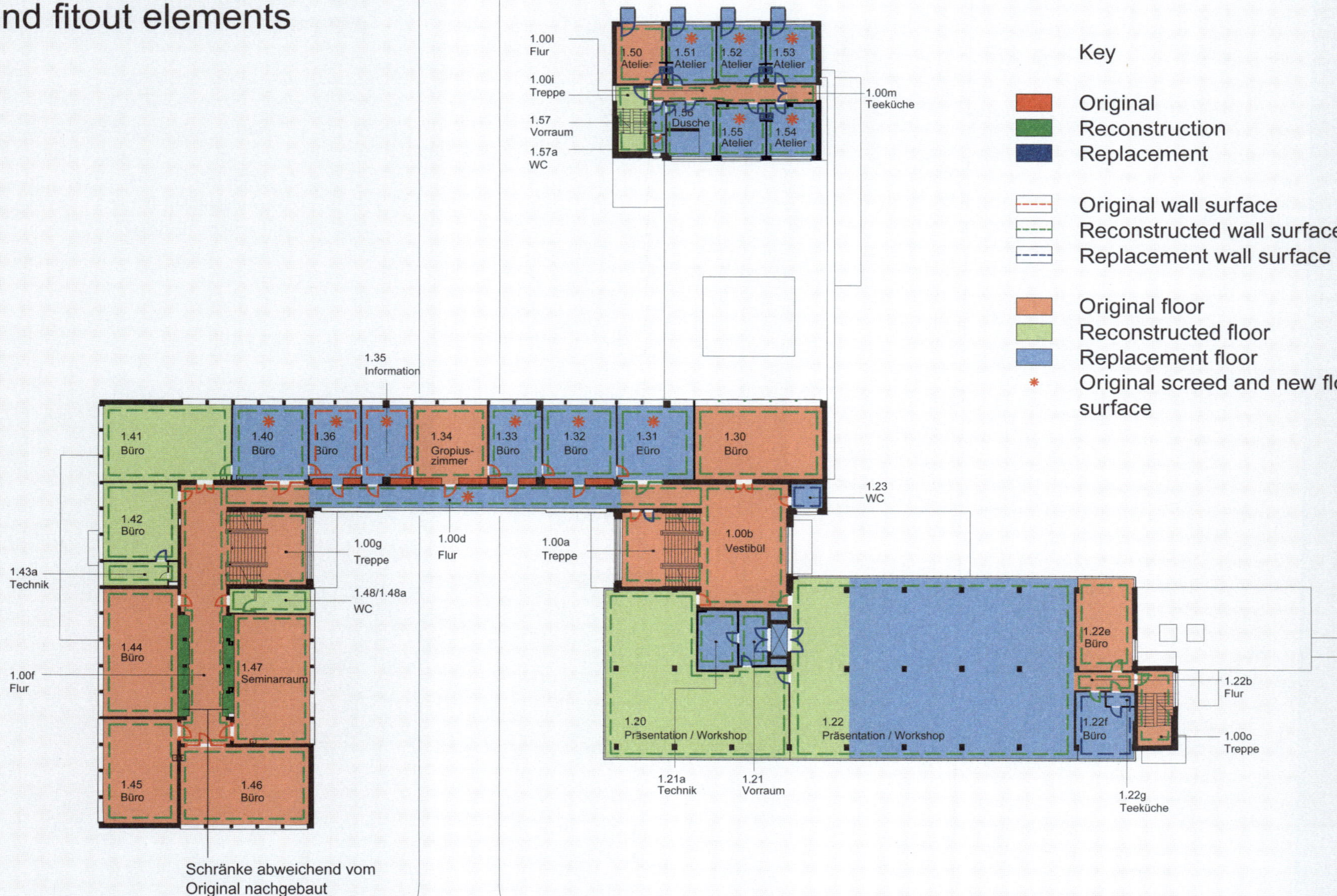

Key

- Original
- Reconstruction
- Replacement
- Original wall surface
- Reconstructed wall surface
- Replacement wall surface
- Original floor
- Reconstructed floor
- Replacement floor
- * Original screed and new floor surface

216)
Floors 2–4,
2014

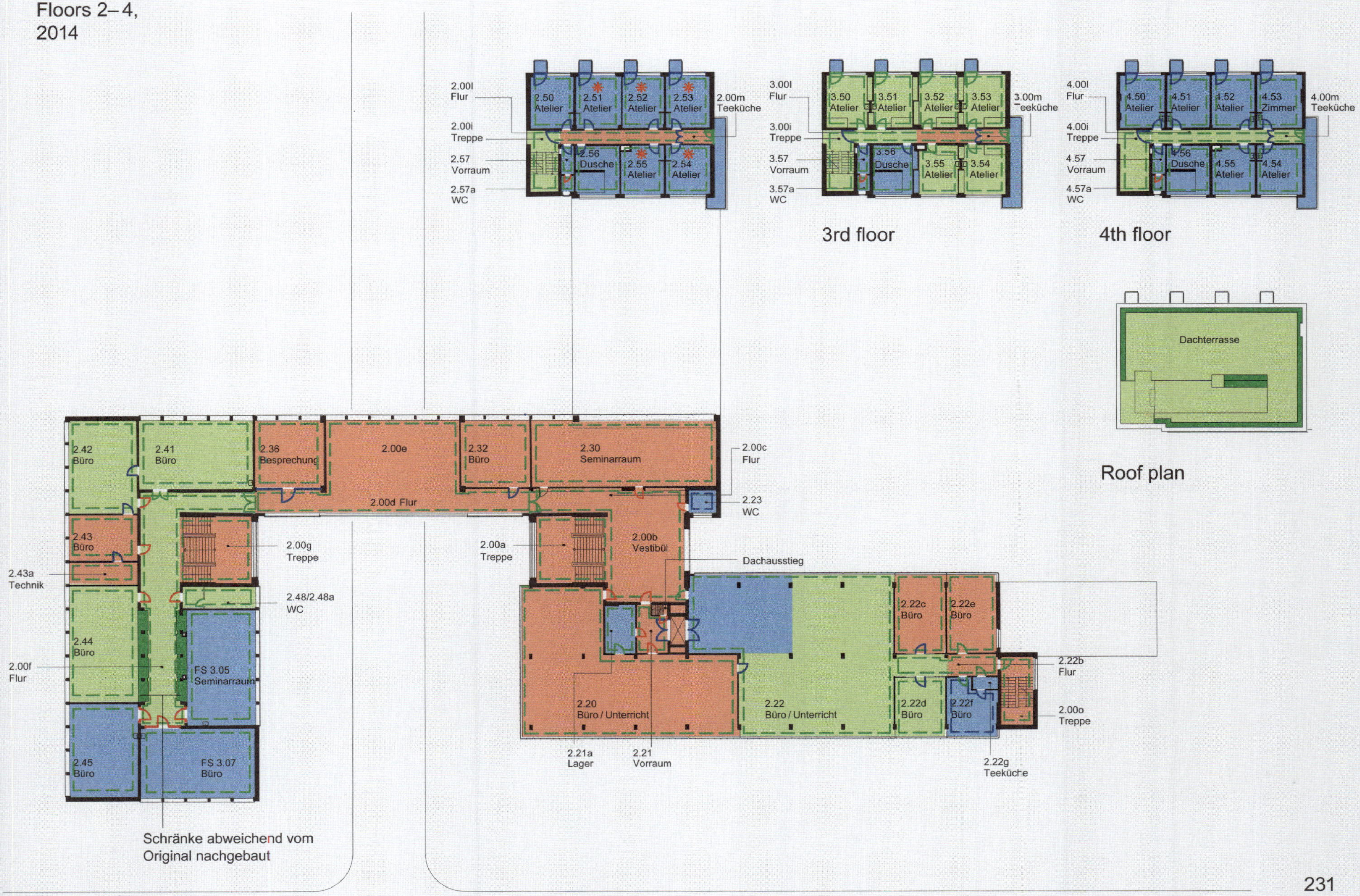

Allocation concept

217)
Semi-basement,
2014

Key

- Priority 1926: restoration and reconstruction
- Priority 1976: maintenance and repair
- No historic priority: upkeep and replacement

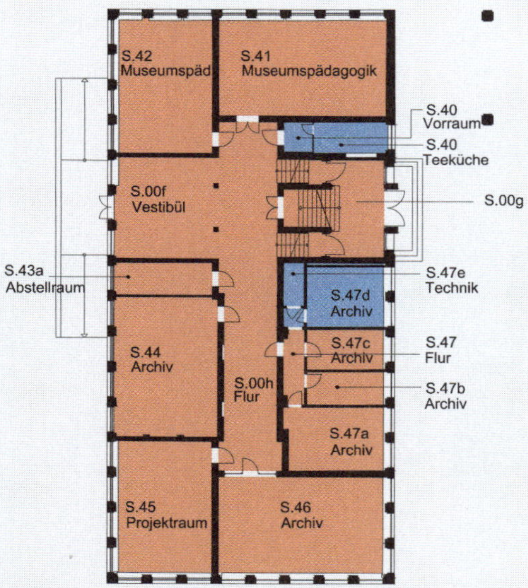

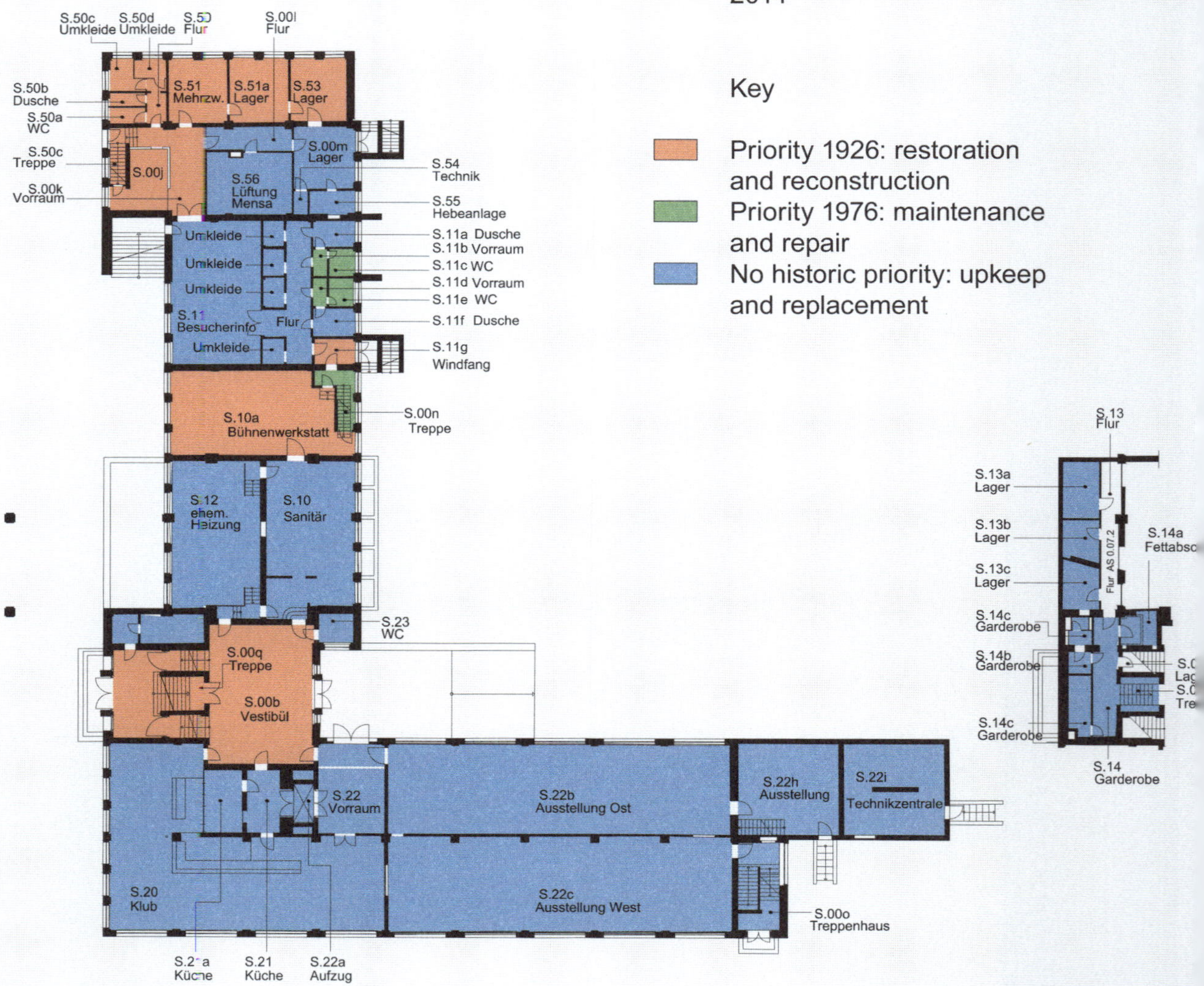

218)
Ground floor,
2014

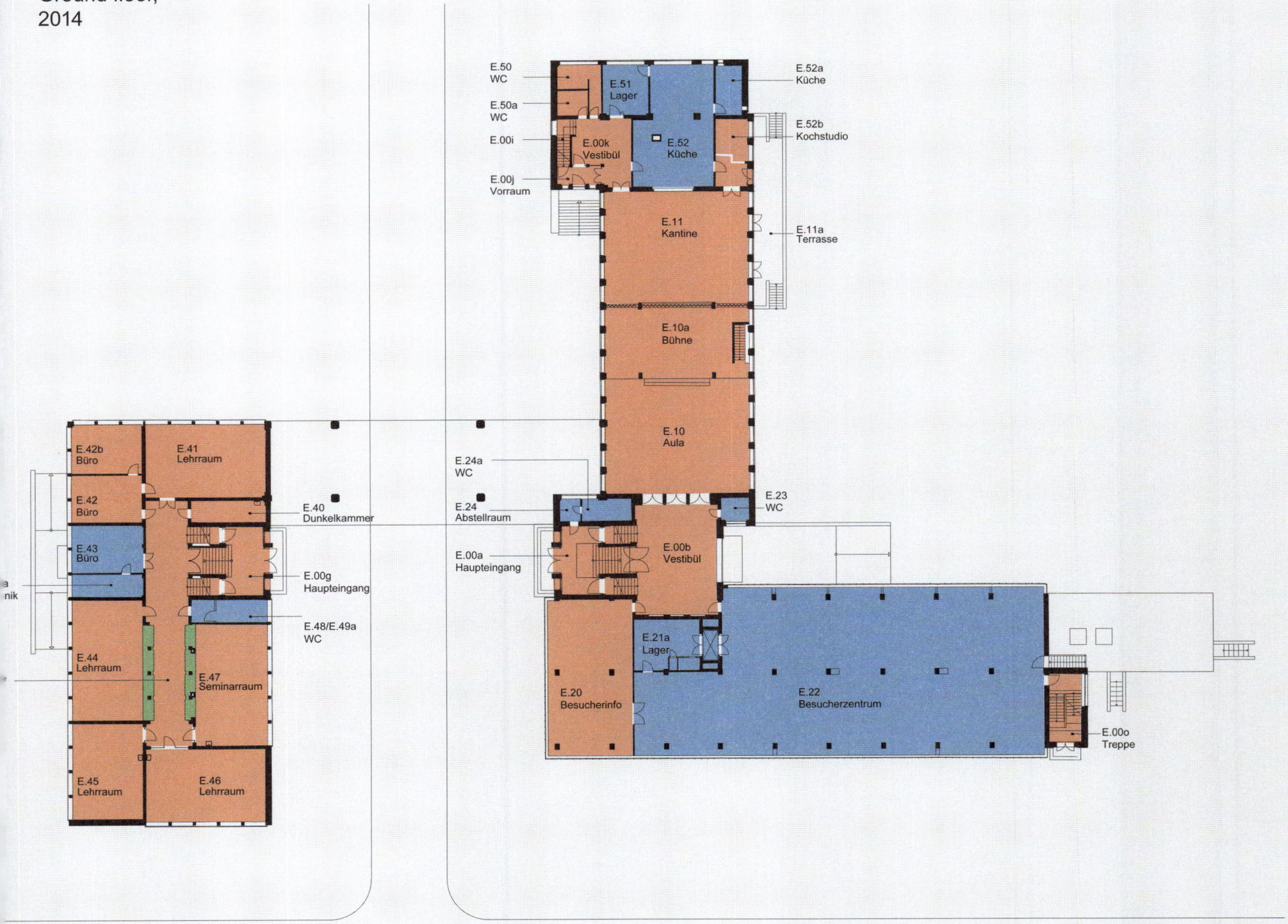

Allocation concept

219)
First floor,
2014

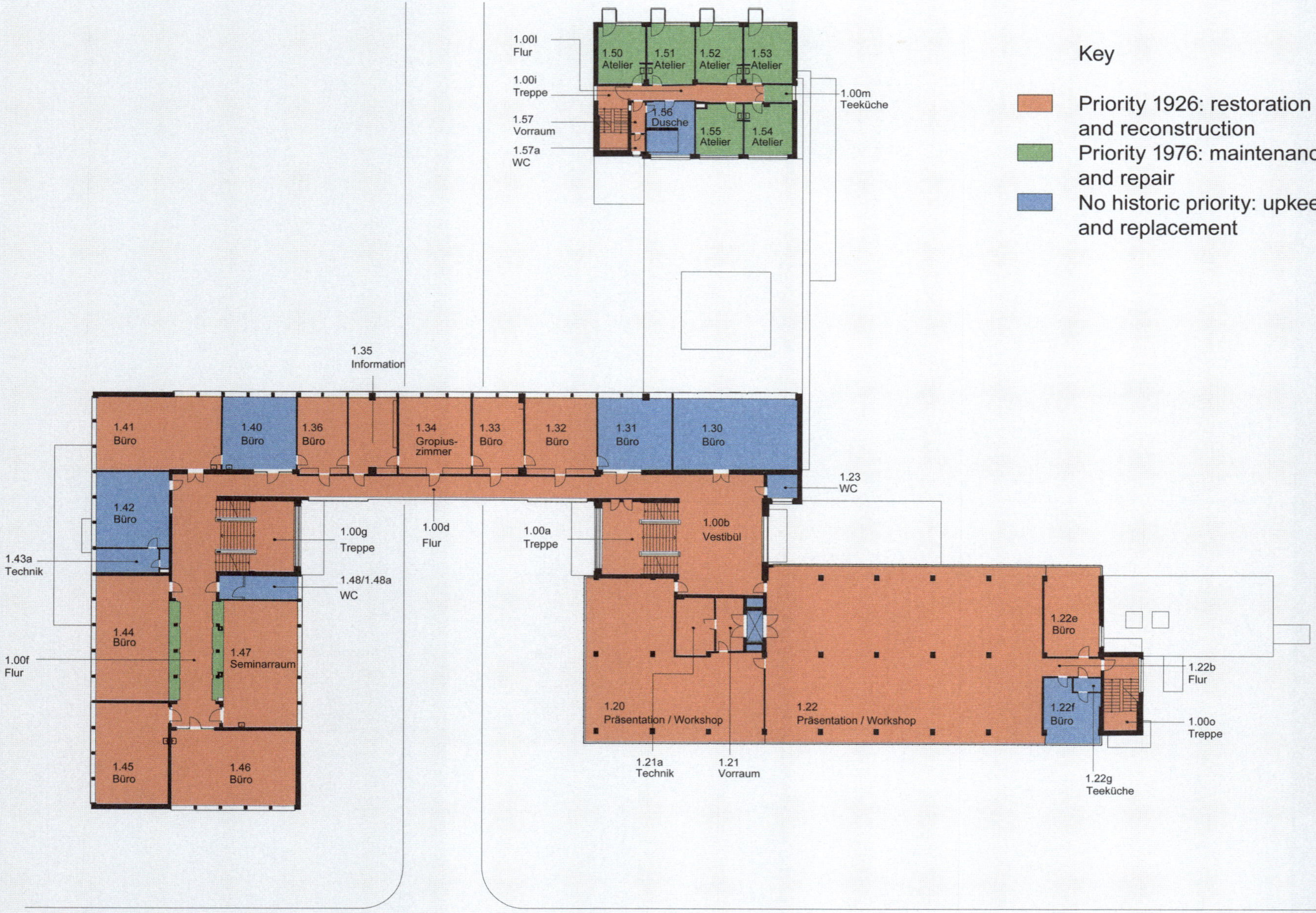

Key

- Priority 1926: restoration and reconstruction
- Priority 1976: maintenance and repair
- No historic priority: upkeep and replacement

220)
Floors 2–4,
2014

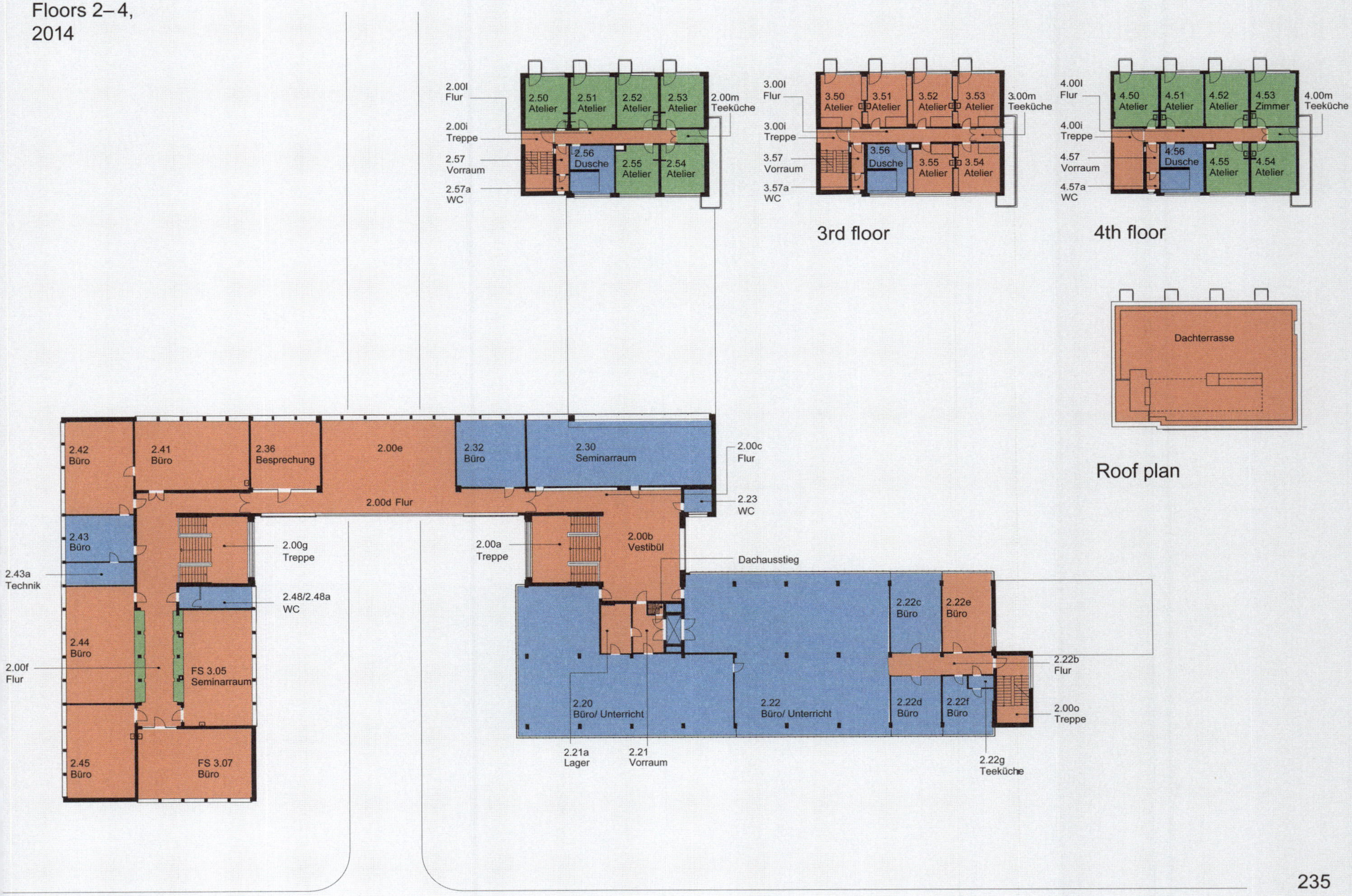

Objectives for light fixtures and radiators

221)
Semi-basement,
2014

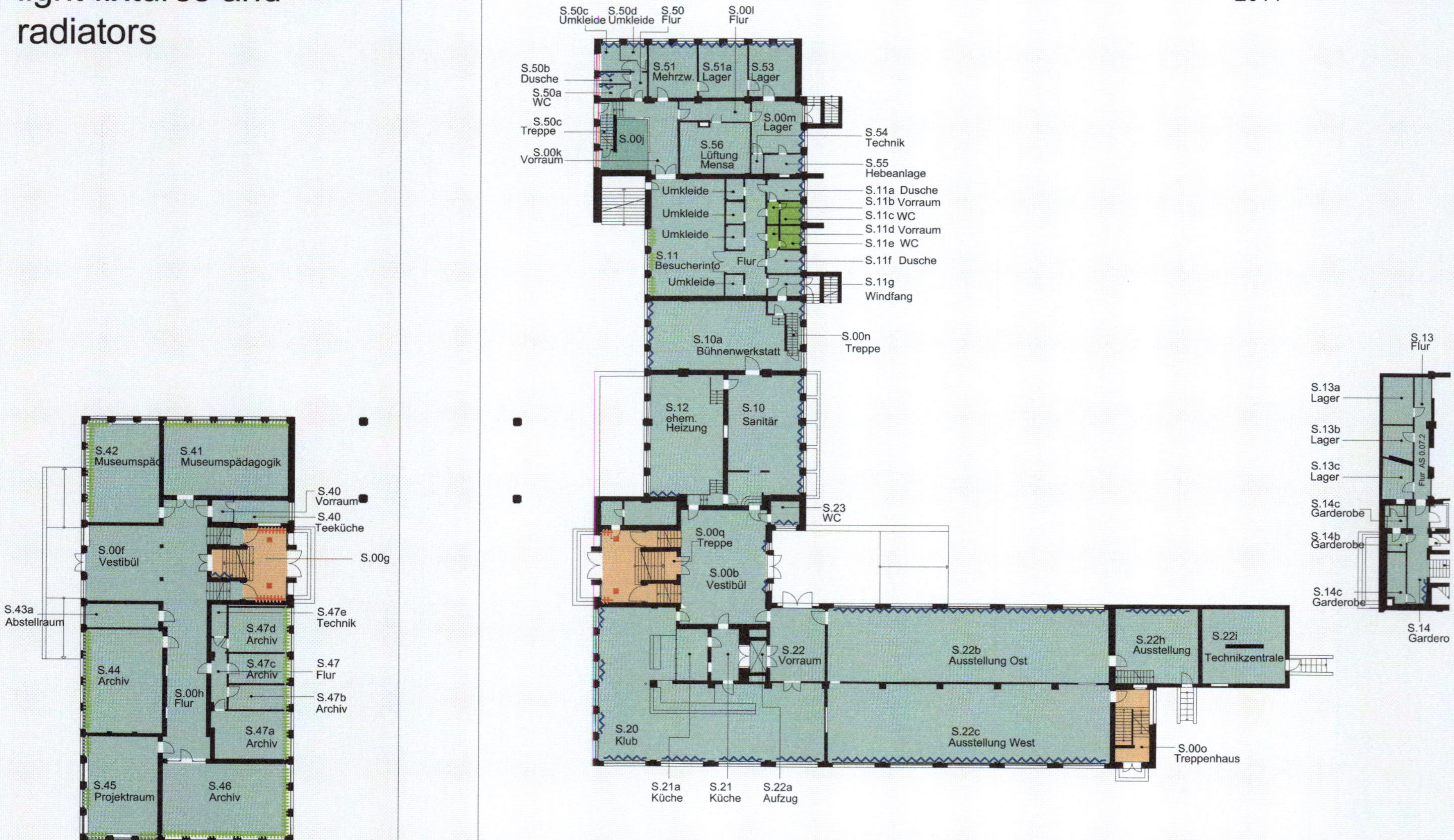

222)
Ground floor,
2014

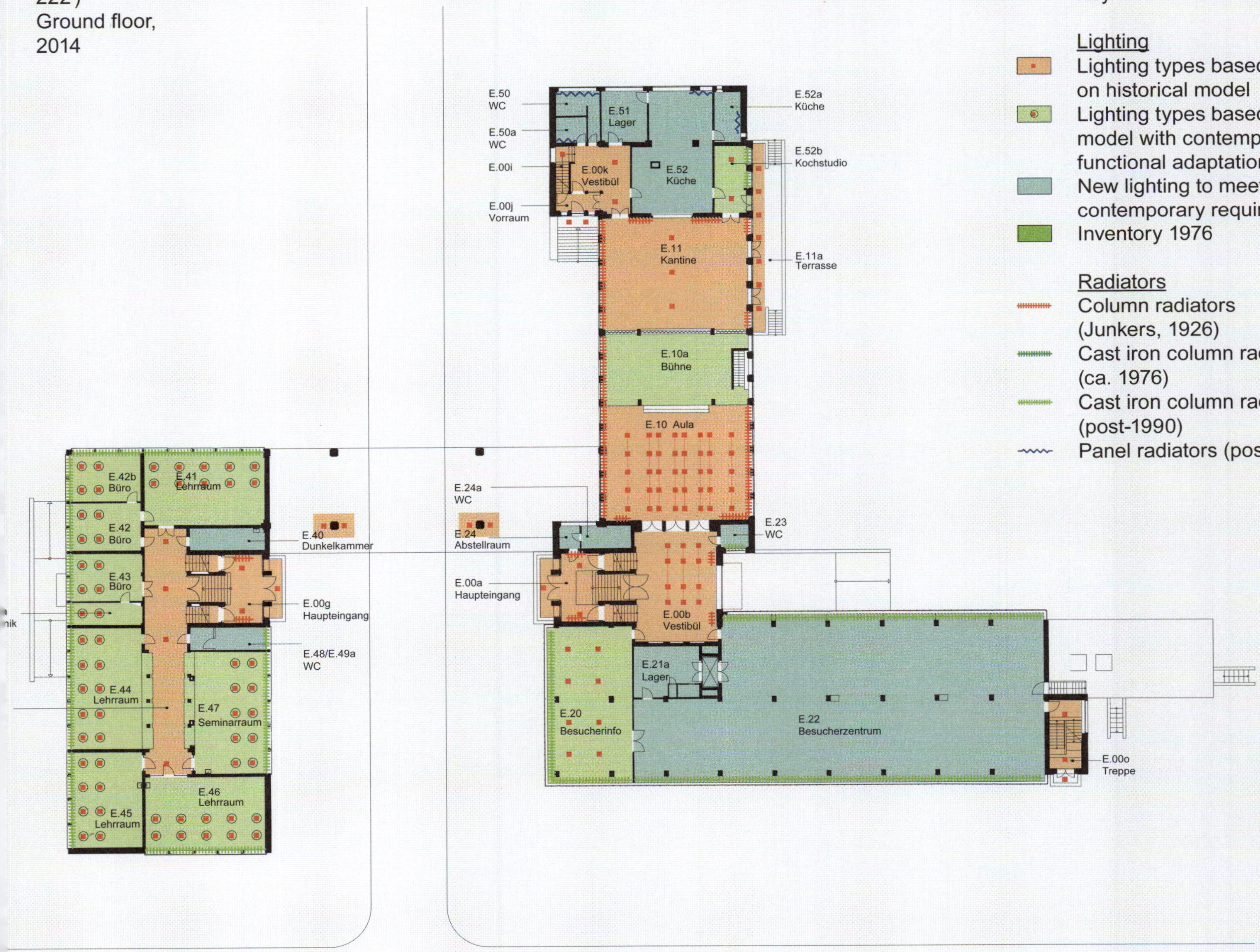

Key

Lighting
Lighting types based on historical model
Lighting types based on historical model with contemporary, functional adaptations
New lighting to meet contemporary requirements
Inventory 1976

Radiators
Column radiators (Junkers, 1926)
Cast iron column radiators (ca. 1976)
Cast iron column radiators (post-1990)
Panel radiators (post-1990)

Objectives for light fixtures and radiators

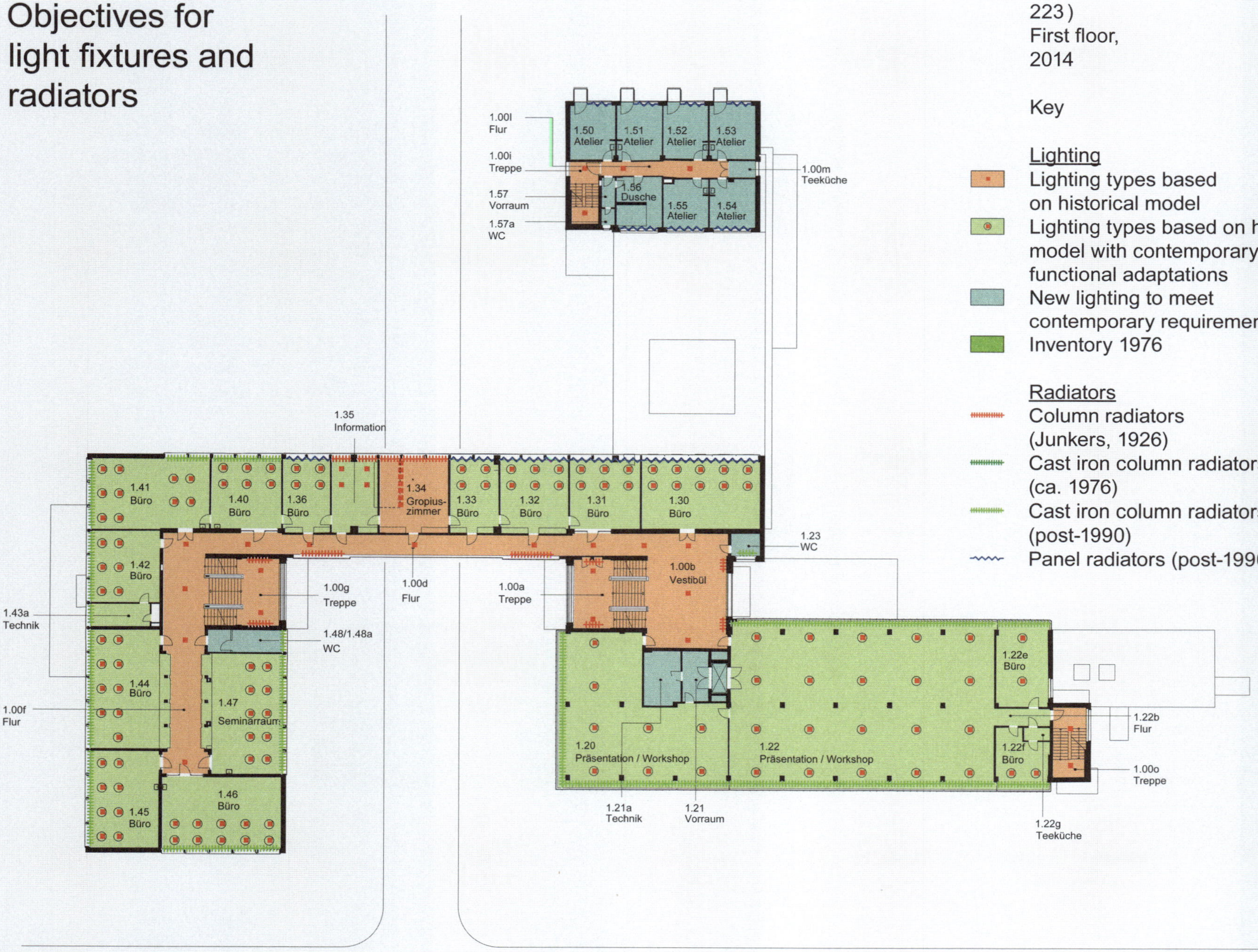

223)
First floor,
2014

Key

Lighting
- Lighting types based on historical model
- Lighting types based on historical model with contemporary, functional adaptations
- New lighting to meet contemporary requirements
- Inventory 1976

Radiators
- Column radiators (Junkers, 1926)
- Cast iron column radiators (ca. 1976)
- Cast iron column radiators (post-1990)
- Panel radiators (post-1990)

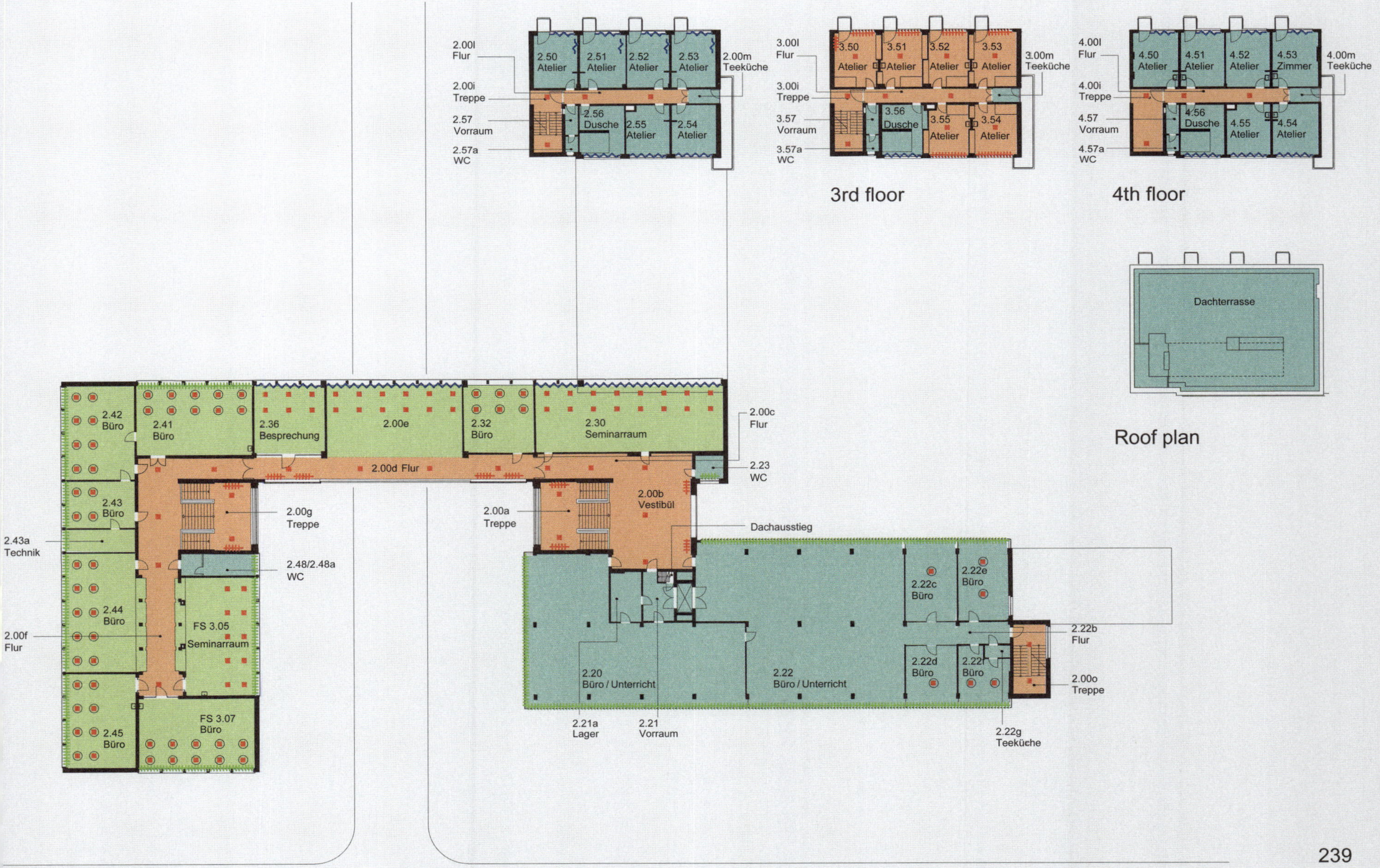

224)
Floors 2–4, 2014

Objectives for glass façades

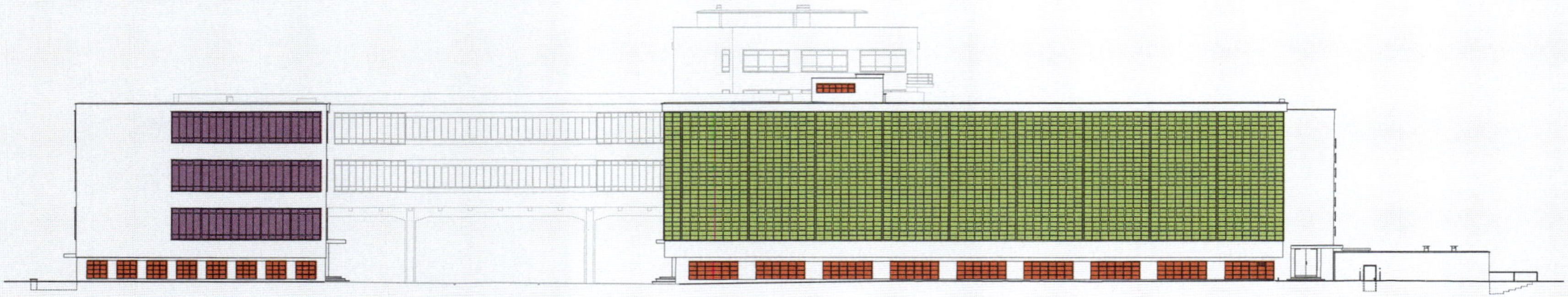

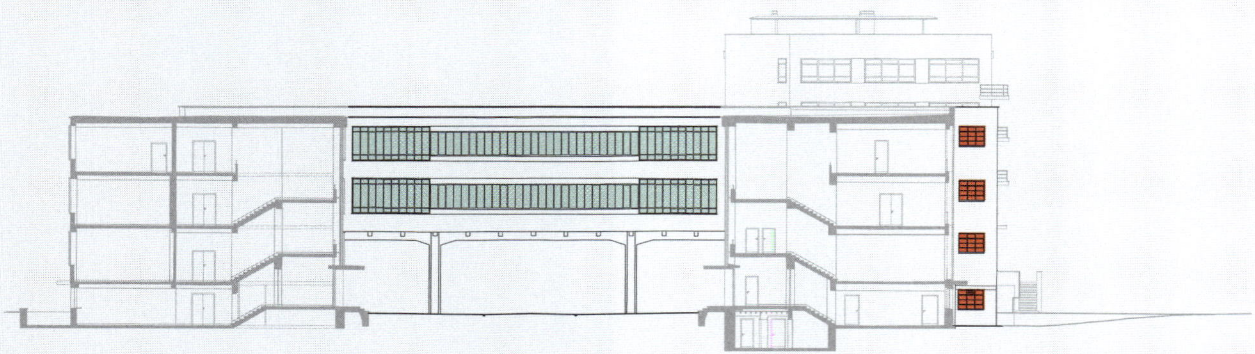

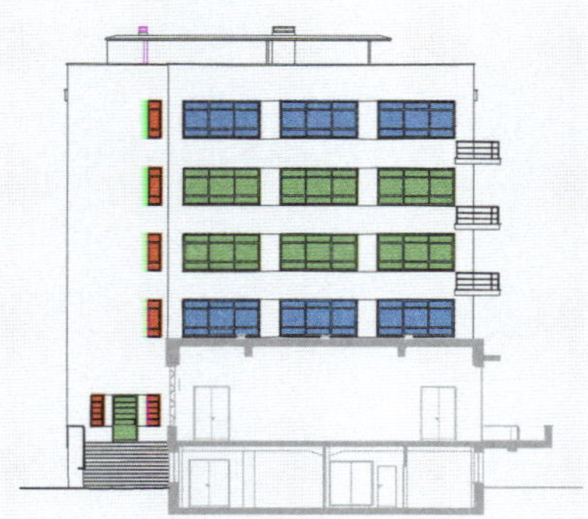

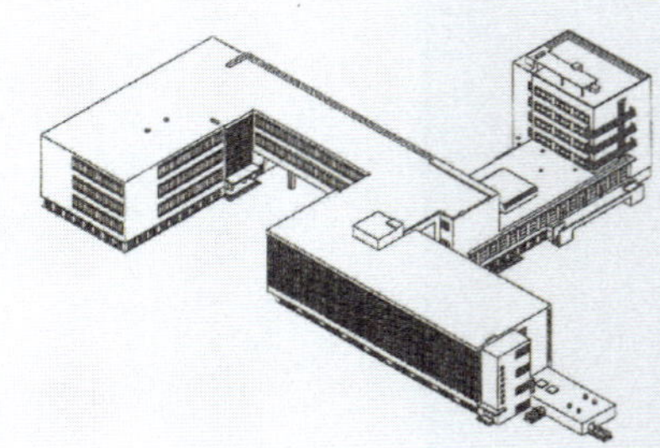

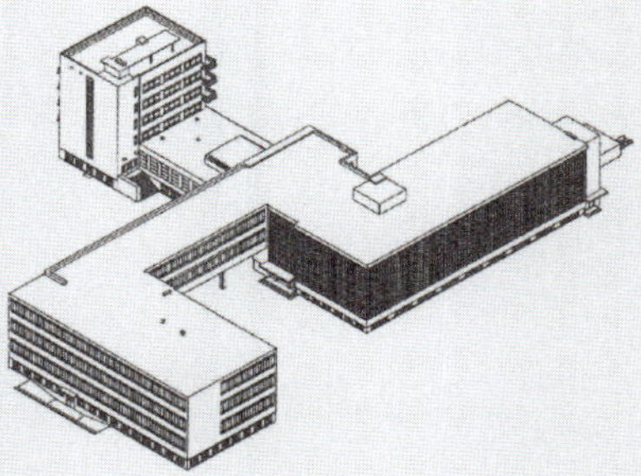

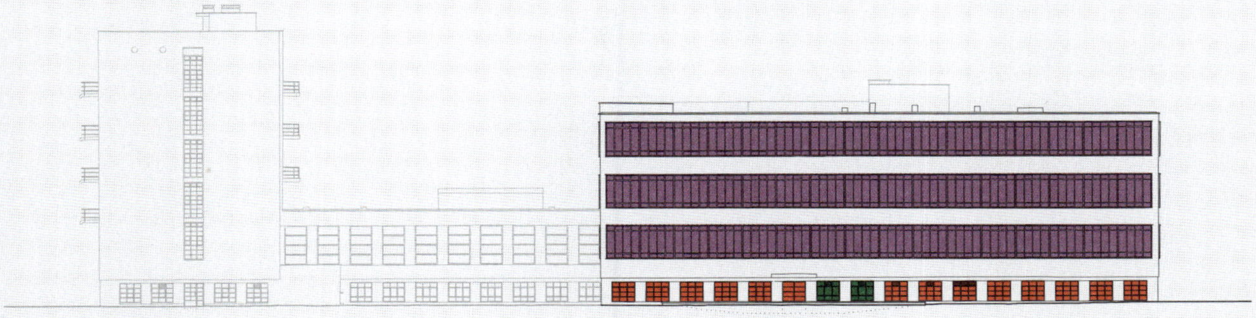

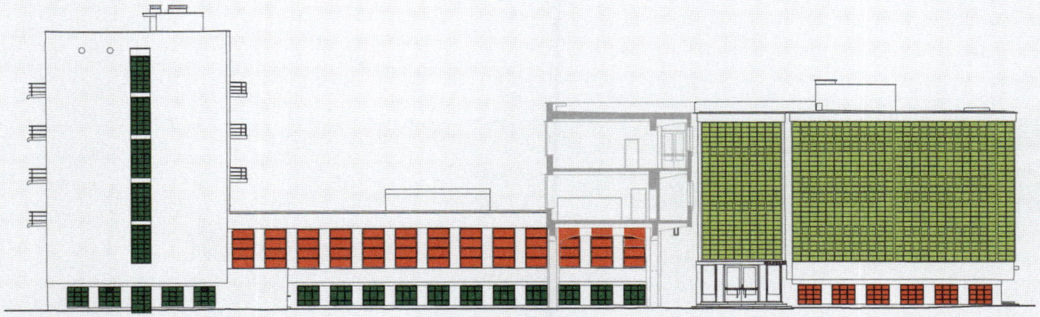

225)
Elevation west

226)
Elevation north

Key

Windows 1926
- Conservation

Windows 1976
- Conservation
- Energy efficiency testing
- Change possible

Windows 2006, reconstructed based on historical model
- Conservation
- Energy efficiency testing
- Change possible

Windows 2012/2014
- Energy efficiency upgrade implemented

226)

Objectives for glass façades

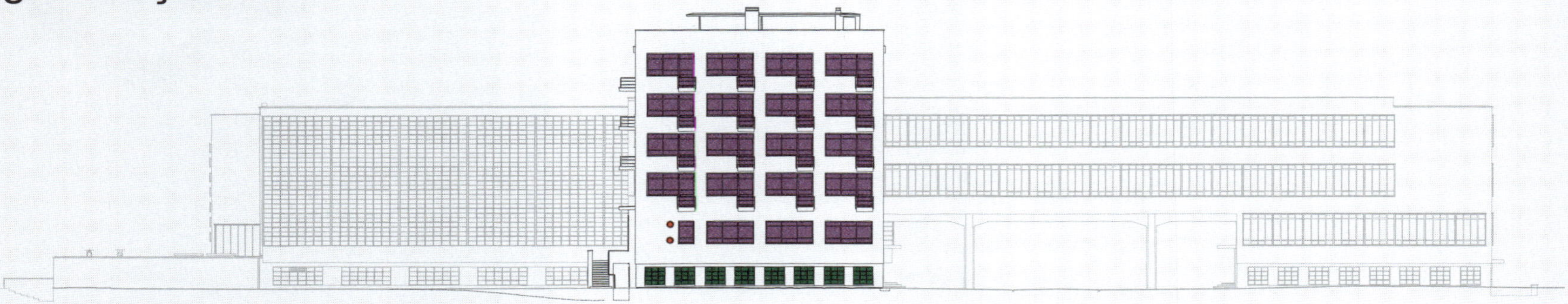

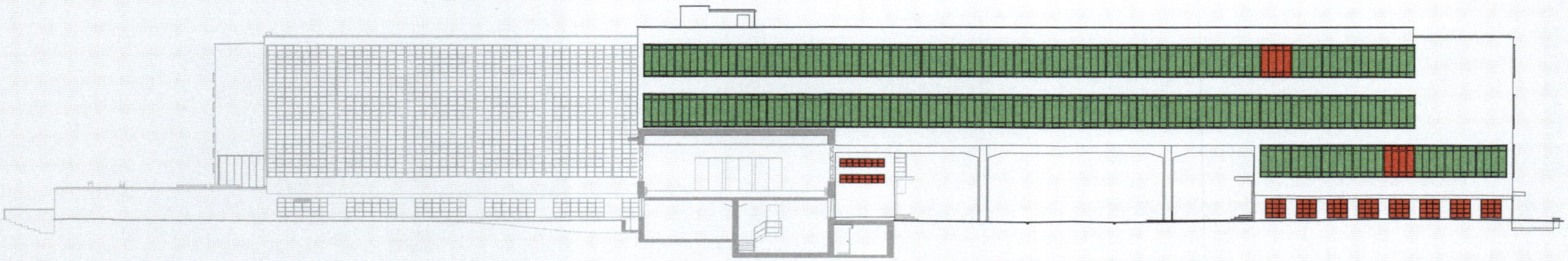

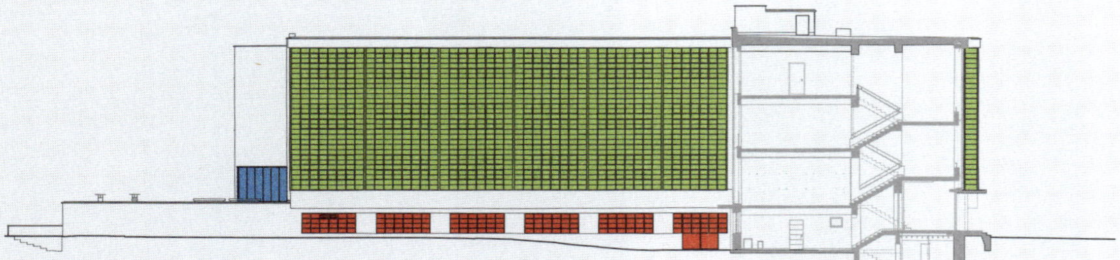

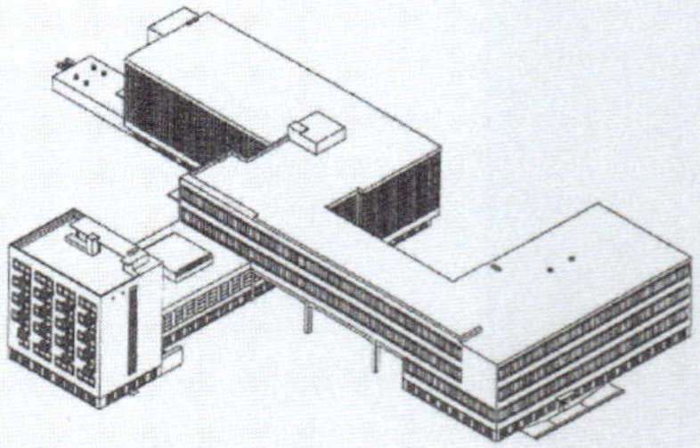

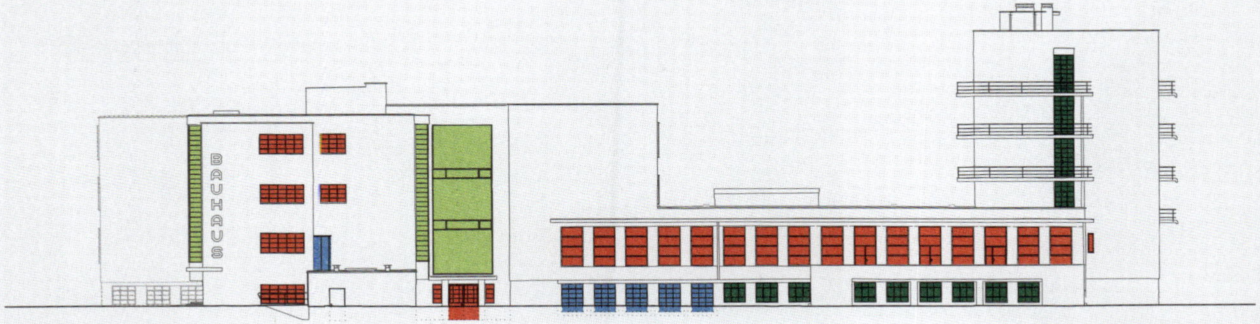

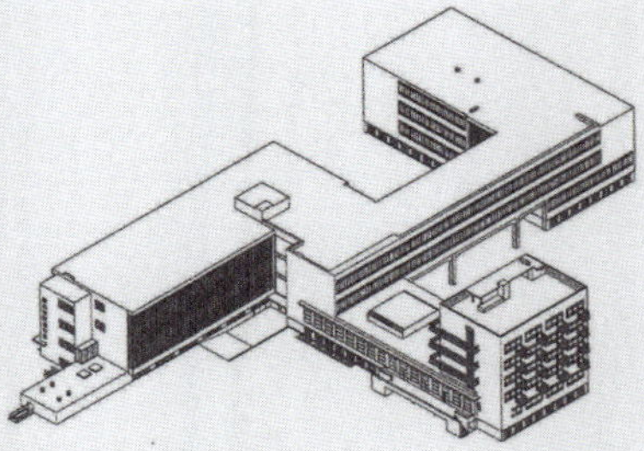

227)
Elevation east

228)
Elevation south

Key

Windows 1926
Conservation

Windows 1976
Conservation
Energy efficiency testing
Change possible

Windows 2006, reconstructed based on historical model
Conservation
Energy efficiency testing
Change possible

Windows 2012/2014
Energy efficiency upgrade implemented

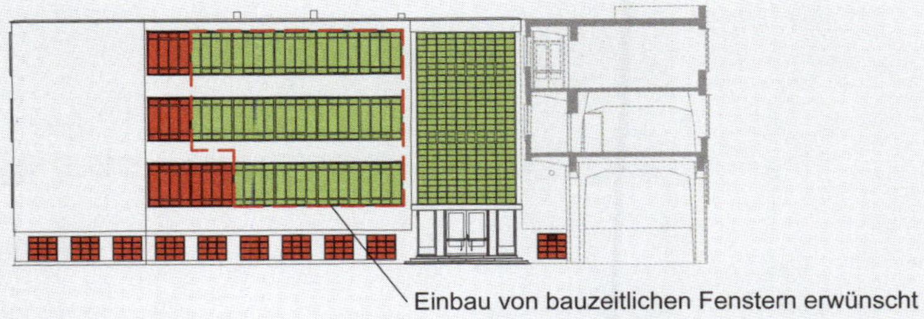

228)

229)

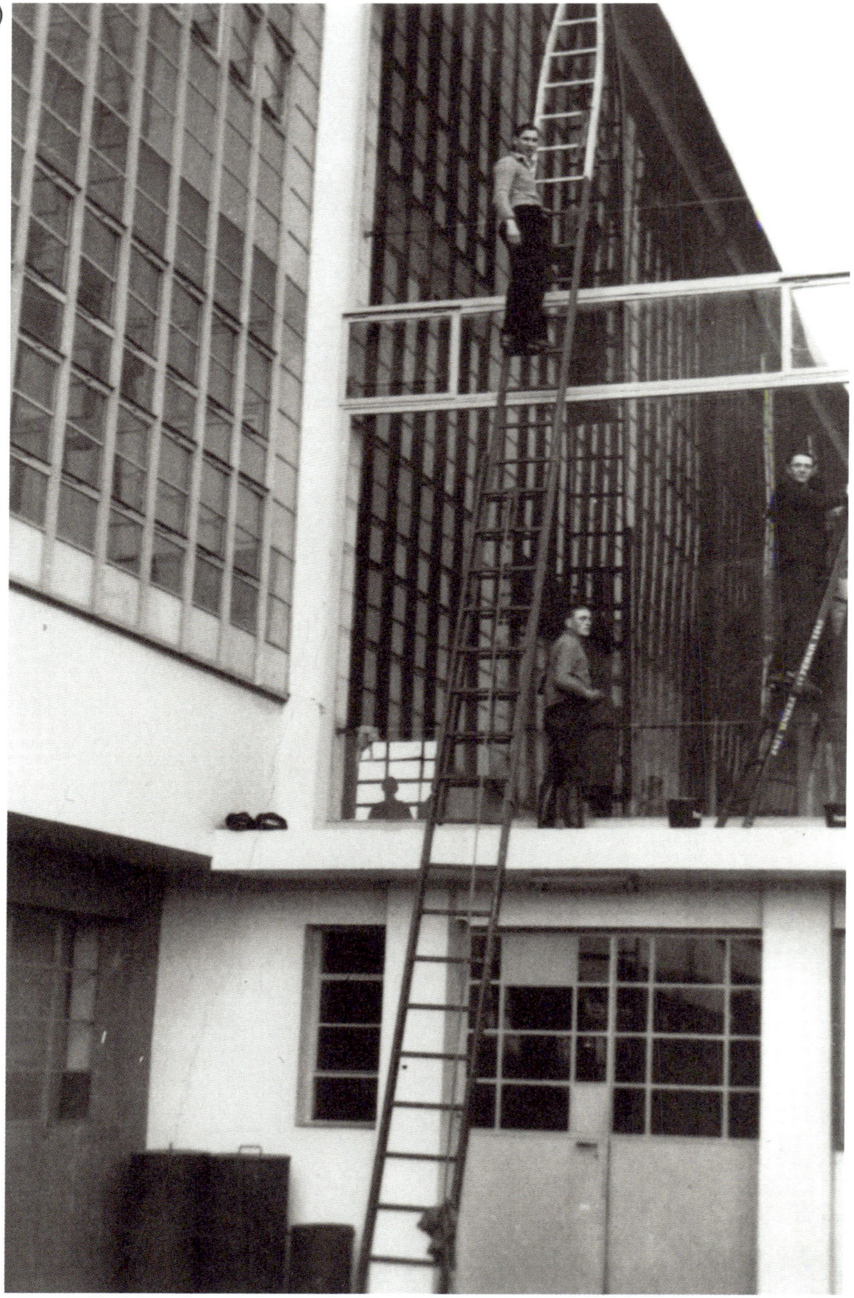

230)

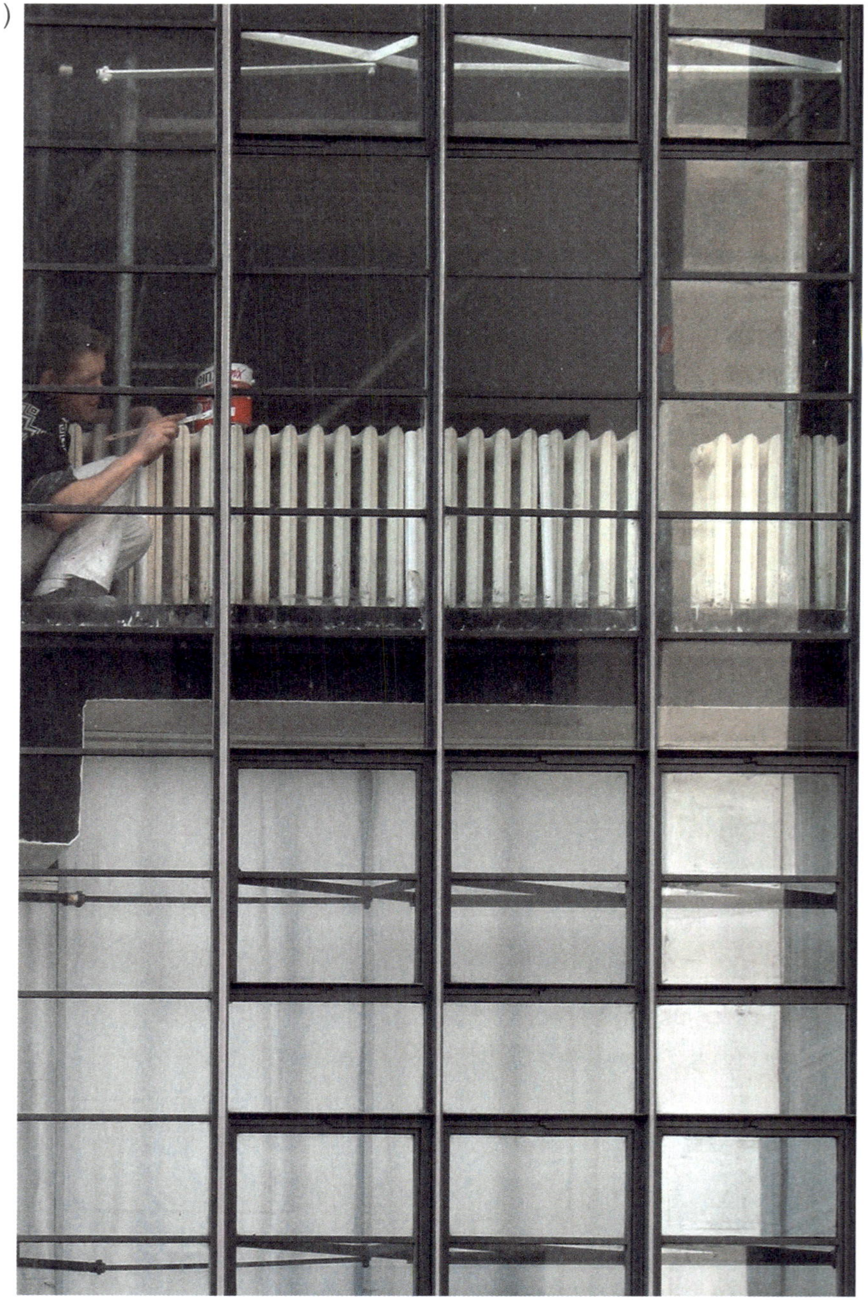

229)
Cleaning the glass façades, late 1930s

230)
Repair work on glass façade, 2004

Conservation Management Plan

In the mid-nineteenth century, the English social reformer and art critic John Ruskin highlighted the need for preventive care as the most effective means of preserving historical monuments: 'Take proper care of your monuments, and you will not need to restore them. A few sheets of lead put in time upon the roof, a few dead leaves swept in time out of a water-course, will save both roof and walls from ruin.'[9]

The traditional ways of looking after buildings are now often overshadowed or forgotten. In contemporary society, the prevailing assumption is that all products are permanently available, and it is frequently cheaper to replace a product than to maintain an existing one. In the Bauhaus Building too, historic building elements have all too frequently been replaced by new ones. Consequently, even this eminent historical monument now features only very few original windows, door handles, rendered surfaces, or lighting fixtures.

Ultimately, the loss of more and more parts of a monument detracts from its authenticity, and as the historic parts and surfaces disappear, so too does the knowledge of the original techniques and materials. However, a monument is without equal and bound to its material existence in all its complexity as a record of a particular historic context, its material, technical, and economic resources, and as a creative accomplishment. Therefore, heritage conservation aims to protect and preserve buildings for as long as possible through continuous, specialised, and preventive care, even if their deterioration cannot be halted.[10]

Continuous monitoring and maintenance focus attention on the building and aspects of its conservation and promotes the understanding of it. Keeping an eye on the building and ensuring small repairs are made in time not only cuts costs but also ensures that the costs for its maintenance in line with heritage conservation guidelines may be planned with confidence. Just as cleaning water courses regularly prevents further damage, hairline cracks in render can be repaired easily and cheaply while more extensive damage can lead to large-scale construction works. Instructions for appropriate cleaning and care are essential: often, the unusual materials found in the building are no longer widely known and must be protected in specific ways. As the German writer Erich Kästner already knew, most breakages are caused not by use, but by cleaning. In addition, skilled and preventive maintenance satisfies the need to conserve resources and the demand for structural measures that are fit for the future.

Care packages including maintenance cycles are common in facility management, and functional systems for efficient and effective maintenance do exist. 'With modifications this model could also be applied to maintenance contracts for the general preservation of historic buildings; restorers or craftsmen specialized in certain fields could look after certain historic buildings, of course in coordination with the state conservation services.'[11]

As long as this responsibility cannot be assumed by the conservation services, as Michael Petzet proposes with reference to the Venice Charter, the owner remains responsible for the continuous maintenance and long-term conservation of the original building fabric and of the quality of workmanship achieved during renovation.

A conservation management plan was therefore developed as a guideline for the long-term and systematic preservation of the Bauhaus Building.[12] The plan is designed to provide speedy and systematic access to relevant information, regulate areas of competence and responsibility, and ensure the quality of future maintenance works. The plan is aligned to the Burra Charter[13] and comprises the following steps: description and importance of the building, collation of information, creation of guidelines, roll-out, and monitoring.

The description of the building draws on existing documents such as the criteria for inclusion on the World Heritage list and applies these in practice to elements of the building including layout, construction, building envelope, building services, colour and surfaces, spatial structures, fit-out, and 'spirit of place'.

A database forms the centrepiece of the conservation management plan. Computer-aided facilities management systems, that is, systems for the effective management of buildings, already exist. However, these are only partly transferrable to eminent historical buildings and their care and maintenance: so far, they fail to sufficiently take into account the complexity of their historic, artistic, and aesthetic significance or their technical and economic characteristics. It is this complexity which gives the essential depth and detail to specifications for the care and conservation of the building, its surfaces and component parts, which the current facility management systems do not provide.

The Bauhaus Dessau Foundation has therefore developed a monument management module as an add-on to an existing facility management database, thus broadening its scope by adding features relevant to monument conservation. For example, the system includes ground plans in which all building parts are clearly defined and can therefore be interlined with detailed information. Room plans featuring layout, ceiling plan, and developed views of walls, in which the building components are also clearly visually identifiable, are likewise available. In this way, the room components may be navigated using the conventional tree structure or using the room plans with a click of the mouse.

Information on care and maintenance is contained in the care catalogue. In the database, this establishes a link between the maintenance management module (with which maintenance works and repairs are managed in the facility management system) and the new monument management module. It is thus possible to inventory damage, allocate contracts, make appointments, and more employing the existing digital tools used by maintenance management. The required information on building components or surfaces, monument value, or maintenance concepts is therefore available in the same database system of the monument management. Information on the building parts and surfaces and how to clean, care for, maintain, and repair them is collated and managed. The requirements specific to heritage conservation are shown here for every building component and surface and include information about certain properties of the materials, techniques, or necessary protective measures in addition to historical information such as construction date, modifications, or colour. The relevant members of staff are already familiar with the use of the database integrated in the facility management system.

The information is organised (and accessed) by room by consulting the building book or catalogues for surfaces, joists, windows, etc., and extends to a care and maintenance catalogue and a document archive. The monument management module contains practical information on how to handle each case, and the availability of relevant documents enables targeted access to more in-depth knowledge. The objective is to conserve the Bauhaus Building in its cultural importance as an outstanding monument and part of the Bauhaus World Heritage, while maintaining the active use of the building. Vitally, the conservation management plan therefore features detailed specifications for the use of the building with regard to the protection of especially sensitive areas such as floors or characteristic wall surfaces. Regulations concerning areas of competence and responsibility form another integral part of the plan.

The conservation management plan also addresses factors that have an impact on the building, including development pressures, tourism, environmental influences, climate change, and worst-case scenarios. Systematic and continuous maintenance and the effects of climate change are notably expected to create additional demands in future. The compiled information also includes a summary of the parties involved in the conservation of the Bauhaus Building, among them the Bauhaus Dessau Foundation with its range of departments, funding agencies, competent authorities, heritage conservation offices, experts, and executive bodies. Also included are the details of involvement in international and national networks such as UNESCO, ICOMOS, or DOCOMOMO and of administrative bodies for the conservation and maintenance of the building.

The guideline for the conservation of the building, including not only specifications and instructions for individual building components or surfaces but also methodologies and the individuals or institutions which must be consulted, is integrated in the database. It is thus systematically incorporated in all maintenance and conservation activities. Pre-existing regulations and specifications like the *Denkmalpflegerische Zielstellung für das Bauhausgebäude* (conservation objectives for the Bauhaus Building) or in-house or operational rules are likewise incorporated in the database. Continuous monitoring sees actions such as damage reporting, observation, or repair tracked in the database. In future, monitoring will focus on the building components and monument values which are referred to in the descriptions and assessments of the conservation management plan.

The systematic processing of information for the conservation of the Bauhaus Building is no substitute for ensuring that all those who work in and on it respect and appreciate the building.

231)

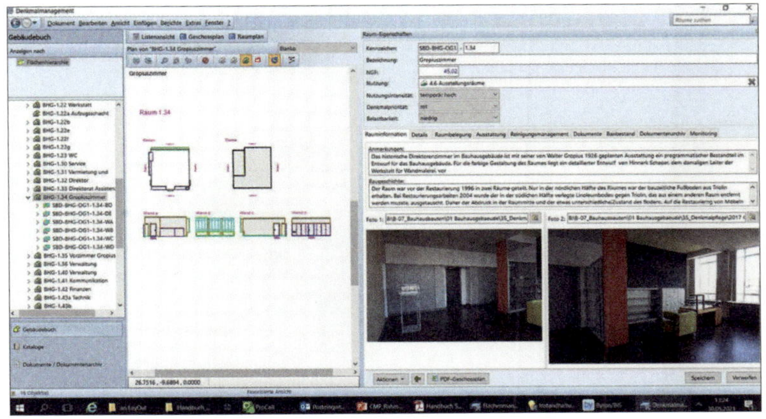

232)

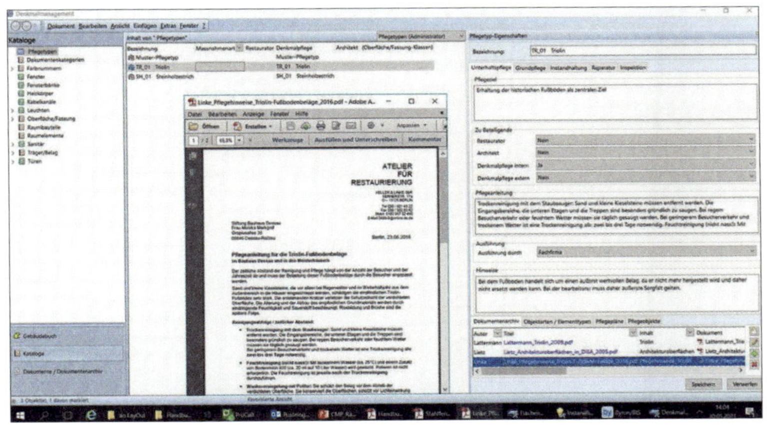

231)
Monument management module, building book, structure: Pro Denkmal, software: Byron BIS, 2021

232)
Monument management module, types of maintenance and care, structure: Pro Denkmal, software: Byron BIS, 2021

233)

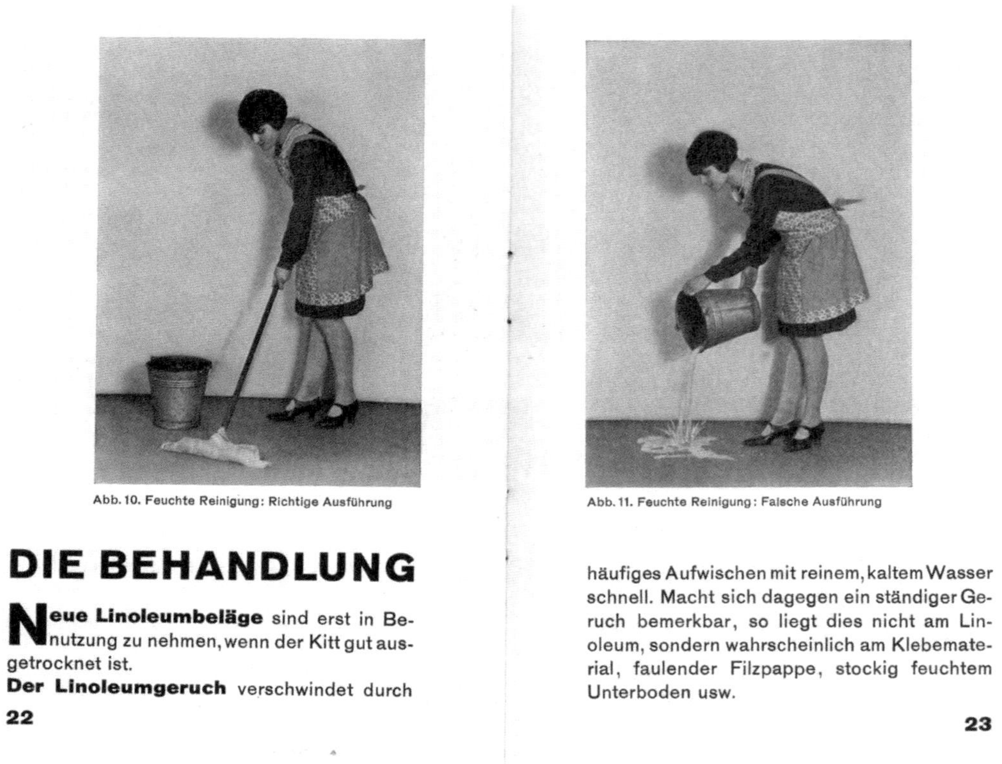

Abb. 10. Feuchte Reinigung: Richtige Ausführung

DIE BEHANDLUNG

Neue Linoleumbeläge sind erst in Benutzung zu nehmen, wenn der Kitt gut ausgetrocknet ist.
Der Linoleumgeruch verschwindet durch

22

Abb. 11. Feuchte Reinigung: Falsche Ausführung

häufiges Aufwischen mit reinem, kaltem Wasser schnell. Macht sich dagegen ein ständiger Geruch bemerkbar, so liegt dies nicht am Linoleum, sondern wahrscheinlich am Klebematerial, faulender Filzpappe, stockig feuchtem Unterboden usw.

23

233)
Cleaning instructions for linoleum floors, also applicable to other historical floors

234)
Maintenance of original stonewood floor, 2021

Understanding the architecture with its unique, not always contemporary qualities and its historic and artistic relevance is fundamental to its long-term conservation. The ICOMOS International Scientific Committee on Twentieth Century Heritage (ISC20C) states: 'More than ever, the architectural heritage of this century is at risk from a lack of appreciation and care. Some has already been lost and more is in danger. It is a living heritage and it is essential to understand, define, interpret and manage it well for future generations.'[14] In this regard, the fastidious and respectful way of dealing with a vintage vehicle may serve to inspire approaches to a historic building, for instance in the way it is used as a matter of course but must not satisfy today's needs for high speeds and comfort, or how it is continuously cared for and maintained in order to prevent damage, not repaired when the damage has already occurred. In this spirit, the understanding and appreciation of the monument are central to all considerations and form the foundations of long-term conservation. As the heritage conservationist Wilfred Lipp ascertained: 'Preventive action begins in the mind.'[15] The historic monument conservation expert Georg Mörsch also emphasises the link between the appreciation of a monument and the care of its material substance: 'For the monument, such care must be both spiritual and material in nature. Spiritual care evokes the message of the monument and makes it socially relevant. But only the preservation of material keeps the possibility of such an encounter alive for good. The fabric of the monument and its importance go hand in hand, like a candle and its flame.'[16]

9
Ruskin 1849, p. 186

10
Cf. Wüstenrot Stiftung 2011, p. 72 et seqq.

11
Petzet 2004, p. 17

12
Developed by ProDenkmal GmbH, Bamberg / Berlin

13
ICOMOS Australia 1999

14
ICOMOS ISC20C 2011, p. 2

15
Lipp 2006, p. 32

16
Mörsch 2003, p. 140

234)

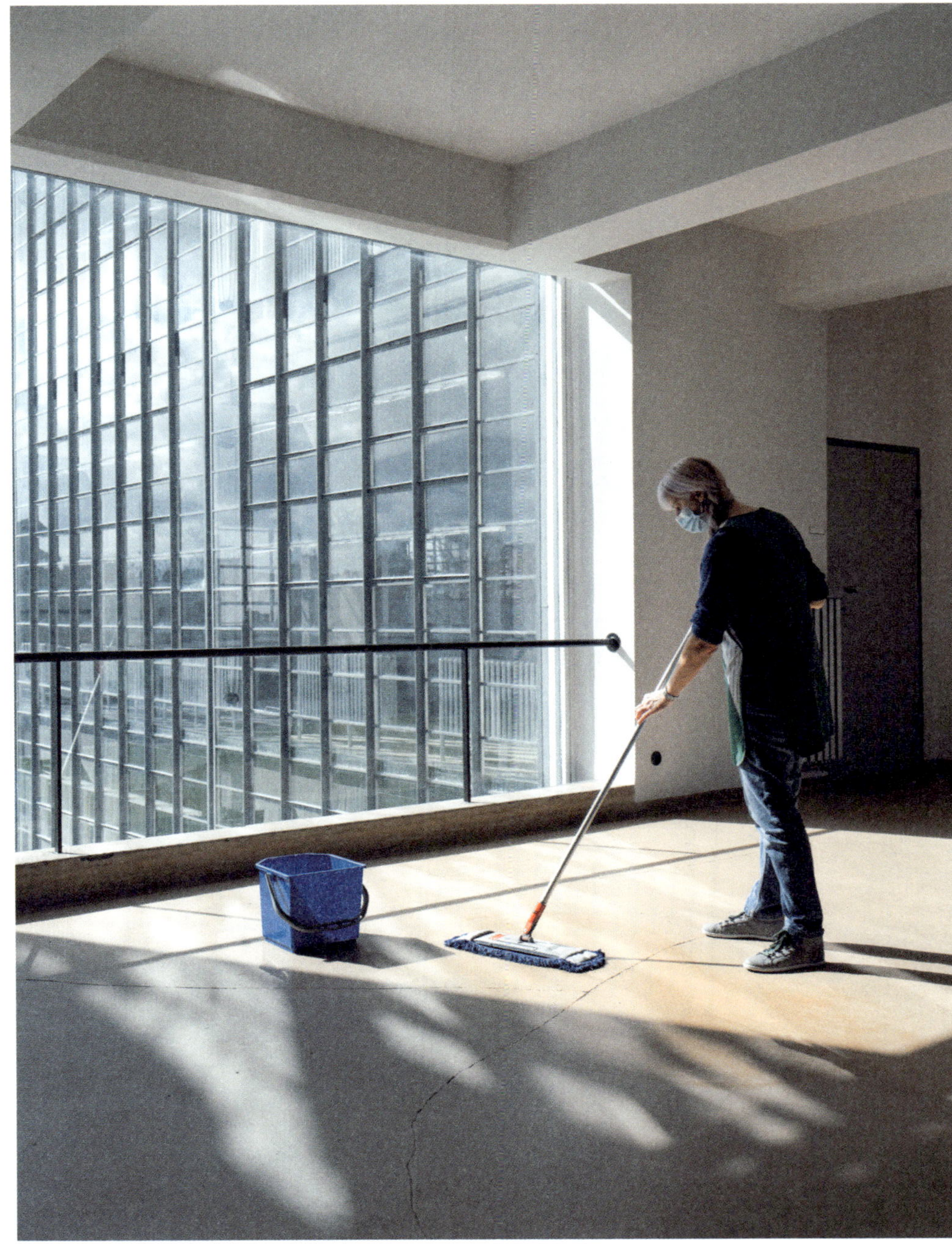

Bibliography

Anonymous 1934
'Überdachung des Bauhauses: Unterlassungssünden werden wieder gutgemacht', in *Anhaltische Abendzeitung,* 10 January 1934

Arge Bauhaus 1999
Arge Bauhaus, Brambach und Ebert, Halle/Saale, and Pfister Schiess Tropeano, Zurich: *Generalsanierung Bauhaus Dessau, Denkmalpflegerische Zielstellung,* Dessau 1999

bauhaus dessau (no year)
bauhaus dessau prospekt, Dessau (no year)

Bauhaus LAB 2016 (2017)
Bauhaus Dessau Foundation (ed.): *Bauhaus LAB 2016: Desk in Exile,* Leipzig 2017

Bauwelt Katalog 1929/1930
Bauwelt Katalog 1929/1930: Handbuch des gesamten Baubedarfs, Berlin 1929

BDA 2018
Bund Deutscher Architekten BDA: 'verdrängte substanz. zum denkmalwert häuslicher infrastrukturen', in *der architekt,* 3/2018

Benevolo 1964
Leonardo Benevolo: *Geschichte der Architektur des 19. und 20. Jahrhunderts*, vol. 2, Munich 1964

Berger 1976/I
Hans Berger: 'Bauhausbauten als Gegenstand der Denkmalpflege', in *Wissenschaftliche Zeitschrift,* vol. 23 (1976), 5/6, p. 556–59

Berger 1976/II
Hans Berger: 'Bauhausbauten als Gegenstand der Denkmalpflege', in *Architektur der DDR,* vol. XXV, Berlin 1976, p. 722–25

Blieske 2020
Jan Blieske: 'Die Instandsetzung der Lichtsituation', in Philipp Kurz for the Wüstenrot Stiftung: *Meisterhaus Kandinsky/Klee. Die Geschichte einer Instandsetzung,* Leipzig 2020, p. 148–57

Blomeier 1994
Oliver Blomeier: 'Kleine Chronik der Heizanlage im Bauhaus Dessau', in *Rekord. Die Spur der Kohlen* (booklet accompanying the exhibition in the Bauhaus Dessau), Dessau 1994

Blomeyer/Milzkott 1990
Gerald R. Blomeyer and Rainer Milzkott: 'Einleitung', in *Zentrum:Berlin, Klausurtagung am Bauhaus Dessau, Arbeitsmaterial für das Symposium Zentrum: Berlin veranstaltet vom Magistrat Berlin,* 1990, p. 6–7 (introduction)

Blunck 1927
Erich Blunck: 'Das Bauhaus in Dessau', in *Deutsche Bauzeitung,* no. 17, 26 February 1927, vol. 61, p. 153–60

Brenne 2011
Brenne Architekten: *Wertebilanz Energetische Sanierung,* Berlin 2011, unpublished document, Bauhaus Dessau Foundation

Brenne 2012
Winfried Brenne, Ulrich Nickmann, Mark Mathijssen, Bernhard Weller, Stefan Reich: 'Innovative Stahlfensterkonstruktion für das Weltkulturerbe Bauhaus Dessau', in Silke Tasche and Bernhard Weller (ed.): *Glasbau 2012,* Berlin 2012, p. 348–63

Danzl 2002
Thomas Danzl: 'Bauhaus in Dessau', in *restauro,* 2002, no. 6, p. 387–88

Danzl 2003
Thomas Danzl: 'Konservierung, Restaurierung und Rekonstruktion der Architekturoberflächen am Meisterhaus Muche/Schlemmer', in August Gebeßler (ed.): *Gropius Meisterhaus Muche/Schlemmer. Die Geschichte einer Instandsetzung,* Stuttgart 2003

Deutsche Linoleumwerke n. y.
Deutsche Linoleumwerke: *Linoleum, Unterböden, Legen, Behandlung,* Bietigheim bei Stuttgart, n. y., p. 22–23

Düchting 1996
Hajo Düchting: *Farbe am Bauhaus. Synthese und Synästhesie,* Berlin 1996

Ehrenburg (1927)
Ehrenburg, Ilja: 'Über das Bauhaus Dessau', in *Visum der Zeit,* Leipzig 1929. Quoted in Margaret Kentgens-Craig (ed.): *The Dessau Bauhaus Building 1926–1999.* Basel, Berlin, Boston 1998

Fischer-Leonhardt 2005
Dorothea Fischer-Leonhardt: *Die Gärten des Bauhauses,* Berlin 2005

Fischli 1968
Hans Fischli: *Malerei Plastik Architektur. Kunsthaus Zürich 1968,* exhibition catalogue

Göttke-Krogmann et al. 2018
Bettina Göttke-Krogmann, Franzi Kohlhoff, Ingrid Radewaldt, Monika Markgraf: *Dokumentation Nachwebung Aulastoffe Bauhaus Dessau,* Halle/Saale 2018, unpublished document, Bauhaus Dessau Foundation

Graf 2011
Franz Graf, Francesca Albani (ed.): *Glass in the 20th Century Architecture.* Mendrisio 2011

Gropius 1926/I
Walter Gropius: 'Das flache Dach. Internationale Umfrage über die technische Durchführbarkeit horizontal abgedeckter Dächer und Balkone', in *Bauwelt,* issues 9/1926, p. 223–27; 14/1926, p. 322–24; 16/1926, p. 361-62

Gropius 1926/II
Walter Gropius: 'glasbau', in *Die Bauzeitung 23,* issue 20, 1926, p. 159–62

Gropius 1965
Walter Gropius: *The New Architecture and the Bauhaus,* New York 1965

Gropius 2021
Walter Gropius: *bauhaus buildings dessau,* Zurich 2021 (English version of Walter Gropius. bauhaus bauten dessau, Munich 1930)

HORTEC GbR 1998
HORTEC GbR: *Bauforschung im Bereich der Außenanlagen des Bauhauses Dessau,* Rehsen 1998 (unpublished document, Bauhaus Dessau Foundation)

Huschenbeth 2019
Firma Huschenbeth, Denkmalpflege Mühlhausen, Dokumentation Bauhaus Dessau: *Fassadensanierung Ateliergebäude 2018/2019,* Mühlhausen 2019 (unpublished document, Bauhaus Dessau Foundation)

ICOMOS Australia 1999
ICOMOS Australia: Burra Charter. *The Australia ICOMOS Charter for Places of Cultural Significance (1999),* Burwood 2000 (https://australia.icomos.org/wp-content/uploads/BURRA_CHARTER.pdf; charter outlining practical approaches to the conservation of historical sites of cultural significance; accessed 4 June 2021)

ICOMOS International 1964
ICOMOS International: *Venice Charta. International Charter for the Conservation and Restoration of Monuments and Sites,* Venice 1964 (www.icomos.org/charters/venice_e.pdf; accessed 4 June 2021)

ICOMOS International 1996
ICOMOS International: *World Heritage List, Advisory Body Evaluation, 1996* (https://whc.unesco.org/en/list/729/documents; accessed 17 March 2021)

ICOMOS ISC20C 2011
ICOMOS International Scientific Committee on Twentieth Century Heritage (ISC20C): *Approaches for the Conservation of Twentieth-Century Architectural Heritage, Madrid Document 2011,* Madrid 2011 (http://www.icomos-isc20c.org/pdf/madriddocumentforpublication2012with-2011copyright.pdf; accessed 29 June 2021)

ICOMOS Preventive Monitoring 1999
ICOMOS: *Report of the ICOMOS Monitoring Group in charge of the World Heritage sites in Germany,* 8 May 1999 (Unpublished document, Bauhaus Dessau Foundation)

ICOMOS Preventive Monitoring 2010
ICOMOS: *World Heritage site Bauhaus Dessau, Preventive Monitoring report from 24 March 2010* (unpublished document, Bauhaus Dessau Foundation)

Kandinsky 1946
Wassily Kandinsky: *On the Spiritual in Art,* New York 1946

Kimmel 2011
Matthias Kimmel: 'Das Bauhaus in neuem Gewand', in *Garten + Landschaft,* 2, 2011, p. 18–21

Korn 1928 (1968)
Arthur Korn: *Glass in Modern Architecture,* New York 1968 (https://modernistarchitecture.wordpress.com/2010/11/03/arthur-korn's-"glass-in-modern-architecture"-1928/, accessed 4 June 2021)

Korrek/Wolf 2016
Norbert Korrek and Christiane Wolf: *Das Internationale Bauhaus-Kolloquium in Weimar 1976 bis 2016: Ein Beitrag zur Bauhaus-Rezeption. Dokumentation, Ausstellungsteil,* Prolog, Weimar 2016

Lattermann 2009
Günther Lattermann: 'Triolin—ein wenig bekannter Fußbodenbelag der 1920er Jahre', in *e-plastory. Zeitschrift für Kunststoffgeschichte,* no. 2, 2009

Lietz 2005
Bettina Lietz: 'Architekturoberflächen an Bauten der Moderne, Fußbodenbeläge in den Dessauer Bauhausbauten und ihre Wiederherstellung'. In *Denkmalpflege in Sachsen-Anhalt,* issue 1, 2005, p. 14–25

Lietz/Markgraf 2004
Bettina Lietz and Monika Markgraf/Bauhaus Dessau Foundation: *Architekturoberflächen. Bauhausbauten Dessau: Fußböden,* Dessau 2004

Linke 2020
Dietmar Linke: '100 Jahre Triolin—ein historisch bedeutsamer Fußbodenbelag aus Cellulosenitrat im Bauhaus Dessau', in Verband der Restauratoren: *Beiträge zur Erhaltung von Kunst- und Kulturgut,* issue 2, 2020, p. 96–104

Lipp 2006
Wilfried Lipp: 'Prävention beginnt im Kopf!', in Ursula Schädler-Saub (ed.): *Weltkulturerbe Deutschland. Präventive Konservierung und Erhaltungsperspektiven. Internationale Fachtagung des Deutschen Nationalkomitees von ICOMOS, der Hochschule für angewandte Wissenschaft und Kunst Hildesheim/Holzminden/Göttingen und der Diözese Hildesheim in Zusammenarbeit mit der Evangelisch-lutherischen Landeskirche Hannover.* Hildesheim 2006, p. 32–40

Loebermann 1998
Matthias Loebermann: 'Transparenz heute', in *Arch+, 144/145,* 1998, p. 100–02

Mader 1999
Günter Mader: *Gartenkunst des 20. Jahrhunderts,* Stuttgart 1999

Manzke/Thöner 1996
Dirk Manzke and Wolfgang Thöner: *das bauhaus zerstört 1945, 1947 das bauhaus stört,* Dessau 1996

Markgraf 2017/I
Monika Markgraf (ed.), *Bauhaus World Heritage Site,* Dessau 2017

Markgraf 2017/II
Monika Markgraf: 'The Architectural Surfaces of the Masters' Houses', in *The New Masters' Houses in Dessau,* 1925–2014, Leipzig 2017

Markgraf 2019
Monika Markgraf: 'The Building Research Archive', in Lutz Schöbe, Wolfgang Thöner and Claudia Perren for the Bauhaus Dessau Foundation (ed.): *Bauhaus Dessau. The Collection,* Bielefeld/Berlin 2019, p. 417–70

Markgraf/Weisbach 2011
Monika Markgraf and Rainer Weisbach: *Energetisches Gesamtkonzept. Bauhausgebäude und Bauhausbauten in Dessau,* Dessau 2011 (unpublished document, Bauhaus Dessau Foundation)

Mazzoni 2004
Mazzoni, Ira: 'Offene Denkmale', in Thomas Will (ed.). *Das öffentliche Denkmal. Denkmalpflege zwischen Fachdisziplin und gesellschaftlichen Erwartungen* (publication of the Arbeitskreis Theorie und Lehre der Denkmalpflege e. V., 15), Dresden 2004, p. 65–66

MFPA 1999
Materialforschungs- und Prüfanstalt für das Bauwesen Leipzig e. V. (MFPA): *Zustandsuntersuchungen der metallischen Ausbau- und Hüllelemente am Bauhaus Dessau,* Leipzig 1999 (unpublished document, Bauhaus Dessau Foundation)

Mörsch 1989
Georg Mörsch: *Aufgeklärter Widerstand,* Basel et al. 1989

Mörsch 2003
Georg Mörsch: 'Thesen zur Nachhaltigkeit denkmalpflegerischer Ziele und Maßnahmen', in Marion Wohlleben and Hans Rudolf Meier (ed.), *Nachhaltigkeit und Denkmalpflege,* Zurich 2003, p. 139–44

Moholy-Nagy 1928
László Moholy-Nagy: *The New Vision and Abstract of an Artist,* New York 1928, 4th edition, 1947

Müller 2004
Ulrich Müller: *Raum, Bewegung und Zeit im Werk von Walter Gropius und Ludwig Mies van der Rohe,* Berlin 2004

Münzer 1963
Ministerium für Kultur (ed., compiled by Georg Münzer): *Kulturrecht. Eine Sammlung kulturrechtlicher Bestimmungen für Kulturfunktionäre und Kulturschaffende,* Berlin 1963; including list of monuments of special national importance and international aristic value, 1962

Oswalt 2014
Philip Oswalt and Henri Cartier-Bresson: *Dessau 1945: Moderne zerstört,* Leipzig 2014

Paul 1978
Wolfgang Paul: 'Rekonstruktion Bauhaus Dessau 1976', in *Dessauer Kalender 1978,* p. 46–63

Petzet 2004
Michael Petzet: *Principles of Preservation* (www.icomos.org/venicecharter2004/petzet.pdf; accessed 4 June 2021)

Pollmeier 2005
Klaus Pollmeier: *Gutachten zur Rekonstruktion der Farbigkeit des Bauhaus-Vestibüls im Jahre 1927,* Mülheim 2005 (unpublished document, Bauhaus Dessau Foundation)

Pro Denkmal 2014
Pro Denkmal: *Fortschreibung der denkmalpflegerischen Zielstellung für das Bauhausgebäude 2014,* Berlin/Dessau 2014 (unpublished document, Bauhaus Dessau Foundation)

Rehm 2005
Robin Rehm: *Das Bauhausgebäude in Dessau. Die ästhetischen Kategorien Zweck Form Inhalt,* Berlin 2005

Ruskin 1849
John Ruskin: *Seven Lamps of Architecture,* London 1849 (https://www.gutenberg.org/files/35898/35898-h/35898-h.htm, accessed 2 June 2021)

Scheper 1930 (2012)
G. L. (Hinnerk and Lou) Scheper: 'Architektur und Farbe', in *Maljarnoe delo 1930,* issue 1–2, 1930. Cited after Johannes Cramer and Anke Zalivako (ed.): 'Das Narkomfin-Kommunehaus in Moskau (1928–2012)',

in *Berliner Beiträge zur Bauforschung und Denkmalpflege 11,* Petersberg 2012, p. 66–67

Schlesier/Püschel 1964
Rat der Stadt Dessau Stadtbauamt and Hochschule für Architektur und Bauwesen Weimar: *Bauhaus Dessau: Rekonstruktion Teil I und II, Leitung Karlheinz Schlesier und Konrad Püschel,* Dessau/Weimar 1964 (unpublished document, Bauhaus Dessau Foundation)

Schmidt 1998
Hartwig Schmidt: 'Der Umgang mit den Bauten der Moderne in Deutschland', in *Konservierung der Moderne? Tagung des deutschen Nationalkomitees von ICOMOS in Zusammenarbeit mit der „denkmal '96",* Munich 1998 (ICOMOS Hefte des Deutschen Nationalkomitees XXIV), p. 39–44

Schneck 1932
Adolf G. Schneck: *Fenster aus Holz und Metall, Konstruktion und Maueranschlag,* Stuttgart 1932

Schöne 2002
Peter Schöne: *Dessau Bauhausgebäude, PR (Ateliergebäude), Flure und Atelierräume. Restauratorische Auswertung zu den materialspezifischen Untersuchungen des bauzeitlichen Steinholzestrichfußbodens,* Halle/Saale 2002 (unpublished document, Bauhaus Dessau Foundation).

Schöne 2018
Peter Schöne: *Dessau Bauhausgebäude, Sanierung von Rissen im Steinholzestrich,* Halle/Saale 2018 (unpublished document, Bauhaus Dessau Foundation)

Schöne 2020
Peter Schöne: *Dessau Bauhausgebäude. Pflegekonzept Steinholzestrich.* Halle/Saale 2020 (unpublished document, Bauhaus Dessau Foundation)

Schwalacher 1927
Nelly Schwalacher: 'Das neue Bauhaus', in *Frankfurter Zeitung* (evening edition), 31 October 1927

Schwarting/Markgraf 2002
Andreas Schwarting and Monika Markgraf: *Bauforschungsarchiv Stiftung Bauhaus Dessau,* Dessau 2002
Staatliche Hochbauverwaltung 1987
Staatliche Hochbauverwaltung Baden-Württemberg (ed.): 'Weissenhof 1927–87; 1. Werkstattbericht während der Sanierung 1983; 2. Gesamtdokumentation der Sanierung 1987', in *info bau 87,* vol. 14, issue 2, 1987

Stein 1926
Georg Stein: 'Das Bauhaus in Dessau', in *Der Neubau, Halbmonatsschrift für Baukunst,* vol. 8, issue 24, Berlin, 24 December 1926, p. 277–82

Transsolar 2011
Transsolar Energietechnik GmbH in cooperation with June 14 Architects: *Energetisches Gesamtkonzept Bauhaus Dessau,* Stuttgart et al. 2011 (unpublished document, Bauhaus Dessau Foundation)

Van Doesburg 1928 (1984)
Theo van Doesburg: 'Farben in Raum und Zeit', in Hagen Bächler and Herbert Letsch: *De Stijl: Schriften und Manifeste,* Leipzig/Weimar 1984, p. 221

Völkers 1948
Otto Völkers: *Bauen mit Glas,* Stuttgart 1948

Weber 1992
Klaus Weber: *Die Metallwerkstatt am Bauhaus* (publication accompanying the exhibition *Bauhaus-Archiv, Museum für Gestaltung,* Berlin, 9 February to 20 April 1992), Berlin 1992

Werner 2014/I
Frank Werner: *Die Nutzung des Bauhaus-Gebäudes von 1932–1945,* Dessau 2014 (unpublished document, Bauhaus Dessau Foundation)

Werner 2014/II
Frank Werner: *Recherche zur historischen Rekonstruktion des Ateliergebäudes,* Dessau 2014 (unpublished document, Bauhaus Dessau Foundation)

Wüstenrot Stiftung 2011
Wüstenrot Stiftung (ed.; texts by Monika Markgraf, Simone Oelker, Andreas Schwarting and Norbert Huse): *Denkmalpflege der Moderne: Konzepte für ein junges Architekturerbe,* Stuttgart 2011

Wüstenrot Stiftung 2020
Wüstenrot Stiftung and Philip Kurz (ed.): *Meisterhaus Kandinsky Klee. Die Geschichte einer Instandsetzung,* Leipzig 2020

Zentrum für Umweltbewusstes Bauen 2010
Zentrum für Umweltbewusstes Bauen e. V. (ZUB): *Bewertung von Maßnahmen zur Minderung des Energieverbrauchs des Bauhauses in Dessau,* Kassel 2010 (unpublished document, Bauhaus Dessau Foundation)

Picture Credits

1
Photo: Thomas Meyer/OSTKREUZ, © Bauhaus Dessau Foundation

2
Photo: Klaus Hertig, © Bauhaus Dessau Foundation (Besitz Scan) (I 36041/1-2)/StephanConsemüller (Eigentum Original Vintage Print)

3
Drawing: Petra Natho, Martin Brück, © Bauhaus Dessau Foundation

4
Photo: unknown, © Bauhaus Dessau Foundation (I 11541 F)/Image by Google

5
© Bauhaus Dessau Foundation (I 911 F)/© (Walter Gropius) VG Bild-Kunst, Bonn 2021

6
Photo: Stella Steyn, © Bauhaus Dessau Foundation (I 18972 F)/Image by Google

7
Photo: Gertrud Arndt (née Hantschk), © Bauhaus Dessau Foundation (I 51529)/© Archiv Alfred u. Gertrud Arndt, Hugo Arndt/Image by Google

8
© Deutsches Museum, Munich, Archiv, CD68839

9
© Bauhaus Dessau Foundation

10
Photo: Christian Schädlich, © Bauhaus-Universität Weimar, Archiv der Moderne

11
Photo: Wilhelm Schulze, © Bauhaus Dessau Foundation/© (Walter Gropius) VG Bild-Kunst, Bonn 2021

12
© Bauhaus Dessau Foundation

13
Photo: Wilhelm Schulze, © Bauhaus Dessau Foundation / © (Walter Gropius) VG Bild-Kunst, Bonn 2021

14–20
Photos: Thomas Meyer / OSTKREUZ, © Bauhaus Dessau Foundation

21
Photo: Martin Brück, © Bauhaus Dessau Foundation / © (Walter Gropius) VG Bild-Kunst, Bonn 2021

22
Photo: FH Müller Leipzig, © Bauhaus Dessau Foundation / © (Walter Gropius) VG Bild-Kunst, Bonn 2021

23
© Bauhaus Dessau Foundation

24–26
Photos: Nikolaus Brade, © Bauhaus Dessau Foundation / © (Walter Gropius) VG Bild-Kunst, Bonn 2021

27
Photo: Yvonne Tenschert, cleaning: Limbach, Dessau, © Bauhaus Dessau Foundation / © (Walter Gropius) VG Bild-Kunst, Bonn 2021

28
Photo: Bettina Lietz, restoration: Keller und Linke Restaurierung, © Bauhaus Dessau Foundation

29
Photo: Emil Theis, © Bauhaus Dessau Foundation (I 2576/4 F) / © (Emil Theis) Andreas Elze

30
Photo: E. Metzke

31
Bauhaus-Archiv Berlin / © (Walter Gropius) VG Bild-Kunst, Bonn 2021 / Photo: unknown

32
Photo: Justus Herrenberger, © Bauhaus Dessau Foundation

33
Photo: William Falcett, © Bauhaus Dessau Foundation

34
Photo: Kelly Kellerhoff, © Bauhaus Dessau Foundation

35
Photo: Thomas Meyer / OSTKREUZ, © Bauhaus Dessau Foundation

36–69
© Bauhaus Dessau Foundation

70
Photo: Lucia Moholy (née Schulz), © Bauhaus Dessau Foundation (I 9394 F) / © (Lucia Moholy) VG Bild-Kunst, Bonn 2021

71
Photo: Lucia Moholy (née Schulz), © Bauhaus Dessau Foundation (I 21263) / © (Lucia Moholy) VG Bild-Kunst, Bonn 2021 / Image by Google

72–73
Photo: Thomas Meyer / OSTKREUZ, © Bauhaus Dessau Foundation / © (Walter Gropius) VG Bild-Kunst, Bonn 2021

74
Photo: unknown, © Bauhaus-Archiv Berlin / © (Walter Gropius) VG Bild-Kunst, Bonn 2021

75
Photo: unknown, © Bauhaus Dessau Foundation (I 14292 F) / © (Walter Gropius) VG Bild-Kunst, Bonn 2021 / Image by Google

76
Photo: William Fawcett, © Bauhaus Dessau Foundation

77
Drawing: Wilhelm Schulze, © Bauhaus Dessau Foundation

78
Photo: Manfred Sack, © Karola Sack

79
Photo: Thomas Meyer / OSTKREUZ, © Bauhaus Dessau Foundation / © (Walter Gropius) VG Bild-Kunst, Bonn 2021

80–81
Drawings: Petra Welhöner, © Bauhaus Dessau Foundation

82
Photo: Yvonne Tenschert, © Bauhaus Dessau Foundation

83
In: Adolf G. Schneck: *Fenster – aus Holz und Metall,* Julius Hoffmann Verlag, Stuttgart, 1932

84 a
Drawing: Brambach + Ebert Architekten, © Bauhaus Dessau Foundation

84 b + c
Drawing: Petra Welhöner, © Bauhaus Dessau Foundation

85
Photo: Roland Zschuppe, © Bauhaus Dessau Foundation

86
Zeichnung: Petra Welhöner, © Bauhaus Dessau Foundation

87
Photo: Martin Brück, © Bauhaus Dessau Foundation

88
Photo: Monika Markgraf, © Bauhaus Dessau Foundation

89
Drawing: Petra Natho, Fritz Becker, © Bauhaus Dessau Foundation

90
© Brenne Architekten

91–92
Photo: Thomas Meyer / OSTKREUZ, © Bauhaus Dessau Foundation

93
Dokumentation: Huschenbeth, © Bauhaus Dessau Foundation

94
Documentation: Schöne, © Bauhaus Dessau Foundation

95
Photo: unknown, © Bauhaus-Archiv Berlin / © (Walter Gropius) VG Bild-Kunst, Bonn 2021

96
Photo: Martin Brück, © Bauhaus Dessau Foundation / © (Walter Gropius) VG Bild-Kunst, Bonn 2021

97
Drawing: Bettina Lietz, © Bauhaus Dessau Foundation

98
© Unknown

99
Photo: Schütze-Rodemann, © Bauhaus Dessau Foundation / © (Walter Gropius) VG Bild-Kunst, Bonn 2021

100
Photo: Martin Brück, © Bauhaus Dessau Foundation / © (Walter Gropius) VG Bild-Kunst, Bonn 2021

101
© Bauhaus Dessau Foundation (I 14299 F) / © (Walter Gropius) VG Bild-Kunst, Bonn 2021 / Image by Google

102
Photo: Doreen Ritzau, © Bauhaus Dessau Foundation

103
Photo: Martin Brück,
© Bauhaus Dessau Foundation

104
Photo: Gunter Binsack,
© Bauhaus Dessau Foundation

105
Photo: Martin Brück,
© Bauhaus Dessau Foundation

106–107
In: Völkers 1948

108
Photo: Gunter Binsack,
© Bauhaus Dessau Foundation

109
© Walter Dexel

110
Photo: unknown, © Bauhaus Dessau Foundation (I 9369 F) / © (Walter Gropius) VG Bild-Kunst, Bonn 2021

111
Photo: Doreen Ritzau, © Bauhaus Dessau Foundation / © (Walter Gropius) VG Bild-Kunst, Bonn 2021

112
Photo: Doreen Ritzau,
© Bauhaus Dessau Foundation

113
Photo: Thomas Meyer / OSTKREUZ,
© Bauhaus Dessau Foundation

114
Drawing: Bettina Lietz,
© Bauhaus Dessau Foundation

115
Photo: Gunter Binsack,
© Bauhaus Dessau Foundation

116
© Bauhaus Dessau Foundation

117
Photo: Martin Brück,
© Bauhaus Dessau Foundation

118
Photo: Thomas Meyer / OSTKREUZ,
© Bauhaus Dessau Foundation

119
Photo: Jutta Stein, © Bauhaus Dessau Foundation / © (Walter Gropius) VG Bild-Kunst, Bonn 2021

120
Photo: Thomas Meyer / OSTKREUZ,
© Bauhaus Dessau Foundation /
© (Walter Gropius) VG Bild-Kunst, Bonn 2021

121–122
© Schöne

123
Photo: Yvonne Tenschert, © Bauhaus Dessau Foundation / © (Walter Gropius) VG Bild-Kunst, Bonn 2021

124–128
Photos: Thomas Meyer / OSTKREUZ,
© Bauhaus Dessau Foundation /
© (Walter Gropius) VG Bild-Kunst, Bonn 2021

129
Photo: Sebastian Gündel, © Bauhaus Dessau Foundation / © (Walter Gropius) VG Bild-Kunst, Bonn 2021

130
Photo: Thomas Meyer / OSTKREUZ,
© Bauhaus Dessau Foundation /
© (Walter Gropius) VG Bild-Kunst,
Bonn 2021

131
Photo: Martin Brück / OSTKREUZ,
© Bauhaus Dessau Foundation / © (Walter Gropius) VG Bild-Kunst, Bonn 2021

132
Photo: Thomas Meyer / OSTKREUZ,
© Bauhaus Dessau Foundation /
© (Walter Gropius) VG Bild-Kunst,
Bonn 2021

133
Photo: FH Müller, © Bauhaus Dessau Foundation / © (Walter Gropius) VG Bild-Kunst, Bonn 2021

134
Photo: Thomas Meyer / OSTKREUZ,
© Bauhaus Dessau Foundation /
© (Walter Gropius) VG Bild-Kunst, Bonn 2021

135
Photo: Tadash Okochi, © Bauhaus Dessau Foundation / © (Walter Gropius) VG Bild-Kunst, Bonn 2021 / ©Pen Magazine, 2010

136
Photo: Yvonne Tenschert, © Bauhaus Dessau Foundation / © (Walter Gropius) VG Bild-Kunst,Bonn 2021

137
In: Moholy-Nagy: *Von Material zu Architektur,* Munich 1929 / Photo: l.: *Technische Rundschau;* centre: Moholy-Nagy, r.: Consemüller

138
Photo: Fritz Schiff, © Bauhaus-Archiv Berlin /
© *The New York Times*

139
Photo: Thomas Meyer / OSTKREUZ,
© Bauhaus Dessau Foundation /
© (Walter Gropius) VG Bild-Kunst, Bonn 2021

140–141
Artist: Hinnerk Scheper,
© Bauhaus-Archiv Berlin

142
Drawing: Mandy Kulczynsky, Felix Noelke,
© Bauhaus Dessau Foundation

143
Artist: Hinnerk Scheper,
© Bauhaus-Archiv Berlin

144
Drawing: Mandy Kulczynsky, Felix Noelke,
© Bauhaus Dessau Foundation

145
Artist: Hinnerk Scheper,
© Bauhaus-Archiv Berlin

146
Zeichnung: Mandy Kulczynsky, Felix Noelke,
© Bauhaus Dessau Foundation

147
Analysis of findings of restoration research: Restaurierungsatelier Schöne 1999,
© Bauhaus Dessau Foundation

148–149
Evaluation of colour hues: Restaurierungsatelier Schöne 1999, © Bauhaus Dessau Foundation

150
Drawing: Johannes Bausch, Nicole Wahl,
© Bauhaus Dessau Foundation

151
Photo: FH Müller, © Bauhaus Dessau Foundation / © (Walter Gropius) VG Bild-Kunst, Bonn 2021

152–155
Photos: Thomas Meyer / OSTKREUZ,
© Bauhaus Dessau Foundation /
© (Walter Gropius) VG Bild-Kunst, Bonn 2021

156
Artist: Hinnerk Scheper,
© Bauhaus-Archiv Berlin

157
Zeichnung: Mandy Kulczynsky,
Felix Noelke,© Bauhaus Dessau Foundation

158
Photo: Martin Brück,
© Bauhaus Dessau Foundation

159
Photo: Doreen Ritzau,
© Bauhaus Dessau Foundation

160
Artist: Hinnerk Scheper,
© Bauhaus-Archiv Berlin

161
Photo: Nikolaus Brade, © Bauhaus Dessau Foundation / © (Walter Gropius) VG Bild-Kunst, Bonn 2021

162
© Brenne Architekten, Berlin 2014

163
© Bauhaus Archiv Berlin, © (Marianne Brandt) VG Bild-Kunst, Bonn 2021

164
Photo: Nikolaus Brade, production: Weberei PURPUR, © Bauhaus Dessau Foundation / © (Walter Gropius) VG Bild-Kunst, Bonn 2021 / © (Adelgunde Stadler-Stölzl (Gunta)) (design) VG Bild-Kunst, Bonn 2021

165
Photo: Erich Consemüller, © Bauhaus Dessau Foundation (SBD_I 46250/1-2)

166
Photo: Yvonne Tenschert, © Bauhaus Dessau Foundation / © (Walter Gropius) VG Bild-Kunst, Bonn 2021

167
Photo: Thomas Meyer / OSTKREUZ, © Bauhaus Dessau Foundation / © (Walter Gropius) VG Bild-Kunst, Bonn 2021

168
Kaloriferwerk Hugo Junkers GmbH Dessau In the archive of Bernd Junkers, © Archiv Bernd Junkers in the Saxony-Anhalt state archive, I 411, no. 71

169
Photo: Nikolaus Brade, © Bauhaus Dessau Foundation / © (Walter Gropius) VG Bild-Kunst, Bonn 2021

170
Photo: Gunter Binsack, © Bauhaus Dessau Foundation (I 7217/1-2 M) / © (Marianne Brandt [née Liebe]) VG Bild-Kunst, Bonn 2021

171
Photo: Thomas Meyer / OSTKREUZ, © Bauhaus Dessau Foundation / © (Marianne Brandt (née Liebe)) VG Bild-Kunst, Bonn 2021

172
Photo: Werner Zimmermann, © Bauhaus Archiv Berlin

173
Photo: Doreen Ritzau, © Bauhaus Dessau Foundation / © (Walter Gropius) VG Bild-Kunst, Bonn 2021

174
Photo: Gunter Binsack, © Bauhaus Dessau Foundation

175
Photo: unknown, © Bauhaus Dessau Foundation (I 44976)

176
Photo: Martin Brück, © Bauhaus Dessau Foundation / © (Walter Gropius) VG Bild-Kunst, Bonn 2021

177
Photo: Thomas Meyer / OSTKREUZ, © Bauhaus Dessau Foundation / © (Walter Gropius) VG Bild-Kunst, Bonn 2021

178
Photo: Nikolaus Brade, © Bauhaus Dessau Foundation / © (Walter Gropius) VG Bild-Kunst, Bonn 2021

179–181
Photos: Thomas Meyer / OSTKREUZ, © Bauhaus Dessau Foundation / © (Walter Gropius) VG Bild-Kunst, Bonn 2021

182
© Bauhaus-Archiv Berlin / © (Walter Gropius) VG Bild-Kunst, Bonn 2021

183
Photo: Jürgen Hohmuth © ZEITORT, © Bauhaus Dessau Foundation / © (Walter Gropius) VG Bild-Kunst, Bonn 2021

184
Photo: Ruth Hollos-Consemüller, © Bauhaus Dessau Foundation (owner of scan) (I 44765/1-2) / © (Ruth Hollos-Consemüller) Stephan Consemüller (owner of original vintage print)

185
Photo: unknown, © Bauhaus Dessau Foundation

186
© Unknown

187
Photo: unknown, © Bauhaus Dessau Foundation (I 17139 F)

188
Design drawing: Mann Landschaftsarchitekten 2004, © Bauhaus Dessau Foundation

189
Zeichnung: Pro Denkmal / © Bauhaus Dessau Foundation

190–192
Photo: Thomas Meyer / OSTKREUZ, © Bauhaus Dessau Foundation

193
Photo: unknown, © Bauhaus-Archiv Berlin

194
Photo: Nikolaus Brade, © Bauhaus Dessau Foundation / © (Walter Gropius) VG Bild-Kunst, Bonn 2021

195
Photo: Erich Consemüller, © Bauhaus Dessau Foundation (I 46172/1-2) / Klassik Stiftung Weimar, Bauhaus-Museum (on permanent loan, privately owned) / © (Erich Consemüller) Stephan Consemüller / © (Walter Gropius) VG Bild-Kunst, Bonn 2021

196
Photo: Marianne Brandt, © Bauhaus-Archiv Berlin / © (Marianne Brandt) VG Bild-Kunst, Bonn 2021

197
Photo: Thomas Meyer / OSTKREUZ, © Bauhaus Dessau Foundation / © (Walter Gropius) VG Bild-Kunst, Bonn 2021

198
Photo: Yvonne Tenschert, © Bauhaus Dessau Foundation / © (Walter Gropius) VG Bild-Kunst, Bonn 2021

199–200
Photos: Thomas Meyer / OSTKREUZ, © Bauhaus Dessau Foundation / © (Walter Gropius) VG Bild-Kunst, Bonn 2021

201
Photo: Yvonne Tenschert, © Bauhaus Dessau Foundation

202–205
© Bauhaus Dessau Foundation

206
Photo: Thomas Meyer / OSTKREUZ, © Bauhaus Dessau Foundation / © (Walter Gropius) VG Bild-Kunst, Bonn 2021

207
Photo: Martin Brück, © Bauhaus Dessau Foundation

208
Photo: Thomas Meyer / OSTKREUZ, © Bauhaus Dessau Foundation

209–228
© Bauhaus Dessau Foundation

229
Cleaning and photo: Glas Panzer, © Bauhaus Dessau Foundation

230
Photo: Martin Brück, © Bauhaus Dessau Foundation

231–232
Structure: Pro Denkmal, Software: Byron / BIS 2021,© Bauhaus Dessau Foundation

233
In: *Deutsche Linoleumwerke,* ca. 1958

234
Photo: Thomas Meyer / OSTKREUZ, © Bauhaus Dessau Foundation / © (Walter Gropius) VG Bild-Kunst, Bonn 2021

Imprint

Editor
Bauhaus Dessau Foundation
Director (ad. int.)
Prof. Dr. Regina Bittner
Gropiusallee 38
06846 Dessau-Roßlau
www.bauhaus-dessau.de

Concept and text
Monika Markgraf

Introduction
Prof. Dr. Jörg Haspel

Coordination and picture editing
Yvonne Tenschert

Graphic design
Andreas Dimmler, Tania Mourinho
after a design concept by Herburg Weiland

Copy editing, German
Dr. Ilka Backmeister-Collacott

Translation
Rebecca Williams

Copy editing, English
Petra Frese

Picture editors
Reproline mediateam GmbH & Co. KG

Printed in the European Union.

Archaeology of Modernism. Conservation of the Bauhaus Dessau is the revised and supplemented edition of the publication *Archaeology of Modernism. Renovation Bauhaus Dessau,* published by jovis in 2006 as vol. 23 in the series EDITION BAUHAUS and continued as vol. 58.

Bibliographic information published by the Deutsche Nationalbibliothek
The Deutsche Nationalbibliothek lists this publication in the Deutsche Nationalbibliografie; detailed bibliographic data are available on the Internet at http://dnb.d-nb.de

jovis Verlag GmbH
Lützowstraße 33
10785 Berlin

www.jovis.de

jovis books are available worldwide in select bookstores. Please contact your nearest bookseller or visit www.jovis.de for information concerning your local distribution.

ISBN 978-3-86859-684-7